WORKSHOPS IN COMPUTING
Series edited by C. J. van Rijsbergen

Also in this series

Persistent Object Systems
Proceedings of the Fifth International Workshop on
Persistent Object Systems, San Miniato (Pisa),
Italy, 1–4 September 1992
Antonio Albano and Ron Morrison (Eds.)

**Formal Methods in Databases and Software
Engineering,** Proceedings of the Workshop on
Formal Methods in Databases and Software
Engineering, Montreal, Canada, 15–16 May 1992
V.S. Alagar, Laks V.S. Lakshmanan and
F. Sadri (Eds.)

Modelling Database Dynamics
Selected Papers from the Fourth International
Workshop on Foundations of Models and
Languages for Data and Objects, Volkse, Germany,
19–22 October 1992
Udo W. Lipeck and Bernhard Thalheim (Eds.)

14th Information Retrieval Colloquium
Proceedings of the BCS 14th Information
Retrieval Colloquium, University of Lancaster,
13–14 April 1992
Tony McEnery and Chris Paice (Eds.)

Functional Programming, Glasgow 1992
Proceedings of the 1992 Glasgow Workshop on
Functional Programming, Ayr, Scotland,
6–8 July 1992
John Launchbury and Patrick Sansom (Eds.)

Z User Workshop, London 1992
Proceedings of the Seventh Annual Z User
Meeting, London, 14–15 December 1992
J.P. Bowen and J.E. Nicholls (Eds.)

Interfaces to Database Systems (IDS92)
Proceedings of the First International Workshop
on Interfaces to Database Systems,
Glasgow, 1–3 July 1992
Richard Cooper (Ed.)

AI and Cognitive Science '92
University of Limerick, 10–11 September 1992
Kevin Ryan and Richard F.E. Sutcliffe (Eds.)

Theory and Formal Methods 1993
Proceedings of the First Imperial College
Department of Computing Workshop on Theory
and Formal Methods, Isle of Thorns Conference
Centre, Chelwood Gate, Sussex, UK,
29–31 March 1993
Geoffrey Burn, Simon Gay and Mark Ryan (Eds.)

**Algebraic Methodology and Software
Technology (AMAST'93)**
Proceedings of the Third International Conference
on Algebraic Methodology and Software
Technology, University of Twente, Enschede,
The Netherlands, 21–25 June 1993
M. Nivat, C. Rattray, T. Rus and G. Scollo (Eds.)

Logic Program Synthesis and Transformation
Proceedings of LOPSTR 93, International
Workshop on Logic Program Synthesis and
Transformation, Louvain-la-Neuve, Belgium,
7–9 July 1993
Yves Deville (Ed.)

Database Programming Languages (DBPL-4)
Proceedings of the Fourth International
Workshop on Database Programming Languages
– Object Models and Languages, Manhattan, New
York City, USA, 30 August–1 September 1993
Catriel Beeri, Atsushi Ohori and
Dennis E. Shasha (Eds.)

**Music Education: An Artificial Intelligence
Approach**, Proceedings of a Workshop held as
part of AI-ED 93, World Conference on Artificial
Intelligence in Education, Edinburgh, Scotland,
25 August 1993
Matt Smith, Alan Smaill and
Geraint A. Wiggins (Eds.)

Rules in Database Systems
Proceedings of the 1st International Workshop on
Rules in Database Systems, Edinburgh, Scotland,
30 August–1 September 1993
Norman W. Paton and
M. Howard Williams (Eds.)

Semantics of Specification Languages (SoSL)
Proceedings of the International Workshop on
Semantics of Specification Languages, Utrecht,
The Netherlands, 25–27 October 1993
D.J. Andrews, J.F. Groote and C.A. Middelburg
(Eds.)

Security for Object-Oriented Systems
Proceedings of the OOPSLA-93 Conference
Workshop on Security for Object-Oriented
Systems, Washington DC, USA,
26 September 1993
B. Thuraisingham, R. Sandhu and
T.C. Ting (Eds.)

continued on back page...

John T. O'Donnell and Kevin Hammond (Eds.)

Functional Programming, Glasgow 1993

Proceedings of the 1993 Glasgow
Workshop on Functional Programming,
Ayr, Scotland, 5–7 July 1993

Published in collaboration with the
British Computer Society

Springer-Verlag
London Berlin Heidelberg New York
Paris Tokyo Hong Kong
Barcelona Budapest

John T. O'Donnell, PhD
Kevin Hammond, PhD

Department of Computing Science
The University, Glasgow G12 8QQ, Scotland

ISBN-13: 978-3-540-19879-6   e-ISBN-13: 978-1-4471-3236-3
DOI: 10.1007/978-1-4471-3236-3

British Library Cataloguing in Publication Data
Functional Programming, Glasgow 1993: Proceedings of the 1993 Glasgow
Workshop on Functional Programming, Ayr, Scotland, 5–7 July 1993.
– (Workshops in Computing Series)
   I.   O'Donnell, John T.   II.   Hammond, Kevin   III.   Series
   005.1

Library of Congress Cataloging-in-Publication Data
Glasgow Workshop on Functional Programming (1993 : Ayr, Scotland)
   Functional programming, Glasgow 1993 : proceedings of the 1993
Glasgow Workshop on Functional Programming, Ayr, Scotland, 5–7 July
1993 / John T. O'Donnell and Kevin Hammond, eds.
      p.   cm. – (Workshops in computing)
   "Published in collaboration with the British Computing Society."
   Includes bibliographical references.
   ISBN 0–387–19879–2
   1.   Functional programming (Computer science)–Congresses.
I.   O'Donnell, John T.   II.   Hammond, Kevin.   III.   Title.   IV.   Series.
QA76.62.G58 1993   94–15448
005.1'1–dc20   CIP

Typesetting: Camera ready by contributors
Printed by Athenæum Press Ltd., Newcastle upon Tyne
34/3830-543210 Printed on acid-free paper

Preface

The Functional Programming Group at the University of Glasgow was started in 1986 by John Hughes and Mary Sheeran. Since then it has grown in size and strength, becoming one of the largest computing science research groups at Glasgow and earning an international reputation.

The first Glasgow Functional Programming Workshop was organised in the summer of 1988. Its purpose was threefold: to provide a snapshot of all the research going on within the group, to share research ideas between Glaswegians and colleagues in the U.K. and abroad, and to introduce research students to the art of writing and presenting papers at a semi-formal (but still local and friendly) conference. The success of the first workshop has led to an annual series: Rothesay (1988), Fraserburgh (1989), Ullapool (1990), Portree (1991), Ayr (1992), and the workshop reported in these proceedings: Ayr (1993).

Most participants wrote a paper that appeared in the draft proceedings (distributed at the workshop), and each draft paper was presented by one of the authors. The papers were all refereed by several other participants at the workshop, both internal and external, and the programme committee selected papers for these proceedings. Most papers have been revised twice, based firstly on feedback at the workshop, and secondly using the referee reports.

The papers in this book cover the spectrum of functional programming, including implementation, performance, parallelism, algorithms and semantics. The trend noted in the preface to last year's workshop proceedings – more emphasis on practical issues – is continuing. One of the best features of the field of functional programming is its success in applying theoretical research to practical programming, and this book shows several examples.

We would like to thank the workshop organisers: John Launchbury was the general chair and arranged for industrial sponsorship, Simon Marlow handled finance, David King and Andy Gill made the local arrangements, and André Santos arranged transport. Thanks also to the other members of the programme committee, John Launchbury and Simon B. Jones, for their assistance in selecting papers. We are particularly grateful to our industrial sponsors, who supported the workshop by supplying both funding and active participants: British Telecom, Harlequin, I.C.L. and Software A.G. Finally, we would like to thank all the participants in the workshop for their efforts, both as authors and as referees.

Glasgow University   John O'Donnell
January 1994   Kevin Hammond

Contents

The Boom Hierarchy

Alexander Bunkenburg*

Computing Science Department, University of Glasgow,
Glasgow, Scotland

Abstract

The Boom Hierarchy is the family of data structures *tree, list, bag, set.*
By combining their properties in other ways, more data structures can
be made, like mobiles. The paper defines the data structures of this
extended Boom Hierarchy and shows how the functions *reduce, map, and
filter* are applied to them.

1   Introduction

The Boom Hierarchy is the family of data structures *tree, list, bag, set*, to be
used with the higher-order Squiggol functions *reduce, map, filter*.
Example
The term that filters the odd numbers from the list [1..10], and adds up their
squares is

$+/ \circ \mathsf{sqr}^* \circ \mathsf{odd} \triangleleft$. [1..10].

(Reduce $/$, map *, and filter $\triangleleft$ are defined further down.)
end of example
   In this paper the data structures are presented as free algebras. New data
structures in the family (e.g. mobiles) spring from algebras with new combinations of laws. The relations between the data structures are explained and
some sample data structures. No category theory required!

2   The Boom hierarchy

The hierarchy of data structures that [Mee86] attributes to H. J. Boom comprises four data structures: *tree, list, bag,* and *set*. It is a fitting coincidence that
Dutch "boom" means "tree", and *trees* are in the hierarchy. English "boom"
meaning "pole" reminds of *lists* in the same way.
   A data structure value is

- either [ ], the empty value containing no elements,

- or [a], the singleton containing one element,

- or $l \mathbin{+\!\!+} r$, the join of two values.

*Supported by a postgraduate research studentship from the Science and Engineering
Research Council

For nonempty data structures [ ] is excluded. *This notation is used for all data structures, not just lists.* Hopefully cutting away syntactic differences will expose the semantic similarities and differences between data structures more clearly.

Each data structure is the free algebra of its binary operation ++. The algebras (and therefore the data structures) differ in the laws they satisfy. More laws to an algebra mean less structural information in the data structure. The four laws of a binary operation that we'll consider are:

$$
\begin{array}{rcll}
a \otimes 1_\otimes = & a & = 1_\otimes \otimes a & \text{UNIT} \\
(a \otimes b) \otimes c & = & a \otimes (b \otimes c) & \text{ASSOC} \\
a \otimes b & = & b \otimes a & \text{COMM} \\
a \otimes a & = & a & \text{IDEM}
\end{array}
$$

Let's talk about these properties in shorthand. A binary operation has properties $a_1 a_2 a_3 a_4$ means that if a_i is 1 then it satisfies the i'th property, and if a_i is 0, then it doesn't. Addition for instance has properties 1110; it has a unit, is associative and commutative, but not idempotent. The join operations of the data structures *tree, list, bag, set* have properties 1000, 1100, 1110, and 1111.

Each set of properties specifies a variety of algebras. The properties 1100 are the variety monoid for example.

Adding a law to an algebra can be thought of as partitioning the carrier of the algebra into equivalence classes induced by that law, and regarding each class as one element. Partitioning all lists by commutativity puts the lists $[1, 2], [2, 1]$ into the same class, the class representing the bag $[1, 2]$. Each class will in general have many elements, therefore mapping an element to its class is a function, but mapping a class to one of its elements involves the choice of which element to take. Let's call data structure A *higher* than data structure B if A's laws are a subset of B's laws. The shorthand makes this relation obvious: The data structure with variety $a_1 a_2 a_3 a_4$ is higher than the one with variety $b_1 b_2 b_3 b_4$ if each $a_i \leq b_i$. Downward mappings (from lists to bags for instance) are easy, and can safely be implicit, but upward mappings (from sets to bags for instance) involve a choice, and therefore have to be written.

Figure 1 gives examples how different values of a higher data structure are translated downwards to the same value in a lower data structure. Two useful choices for upward translations are there too: *setToBag* takes a set to the bag that contains each element of the set once, and *sort* takes a a bag to the list with the same elements in order (*sort* obviously only makes sense if the type of the elements is ordered).

Figure 2 is a picture of the Boom hierarchy data structures. There's a free algebra (and therefore a data structure) for all 16 possible combinations of the above four laws. Each data structure is identified by the properties of its join-operation, and by name. The abbreviations "n." and "id." stand for "nonempty" and "idempotent". The original Boom hierarchy data structures plus *mobiles* are the diamond with tail on the left. Their nonempty versions form a diamond with tail in the middle. On the right the idempotent versions repeat the two diamonds. Their tails *idempotent bags* are just *sets*. The idempotent structures (1 in fourth position) exist; but *sets* seem the only useful ones. However guaranteed non-empty structures (0 in first position) are useful. If all edges of the *higher-than* relation are drawn, the picture becomes a 4d-cube.

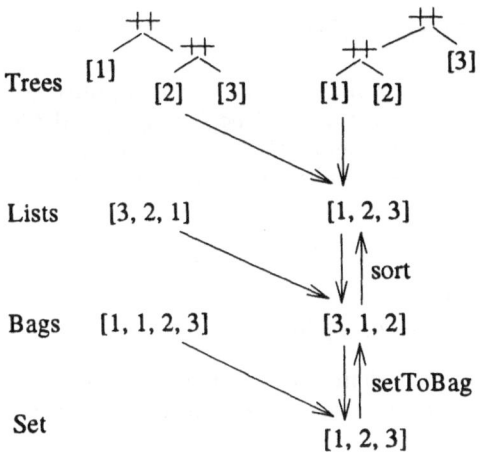

Figure 1: Some translations

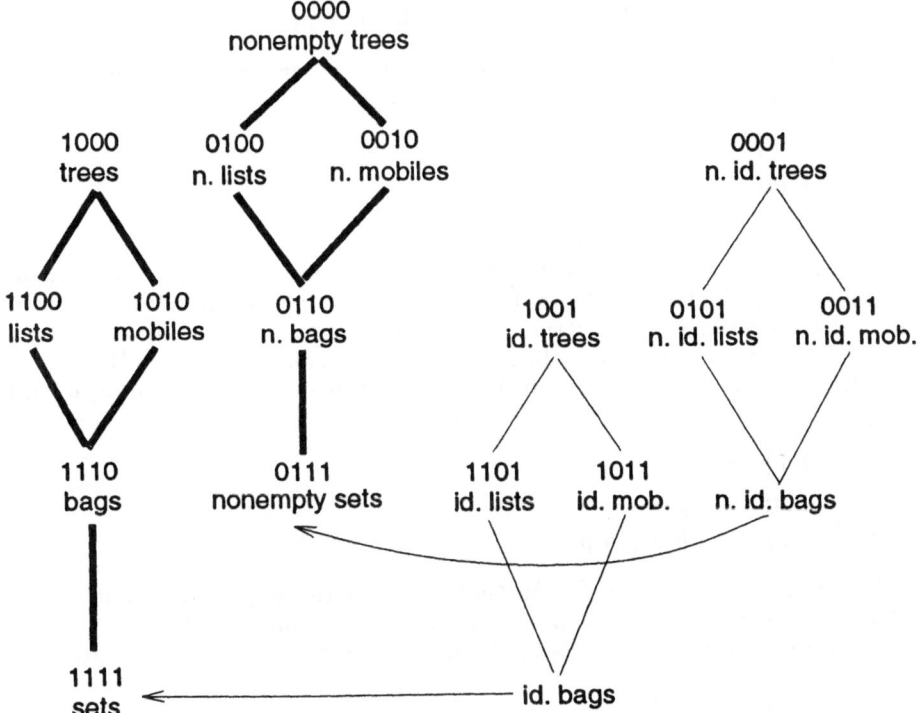

Figure 2: The Boom hierarchy

3   Reduce, map, filter

There are a couple of useful functions that can be applied to the Boom hierarchy data structures. The functions are *reduce* /, *map* *, and *filter* ⊲. Reduce is also called "fold". Filter removes elements from a structure, map applies a function to all elements of a structure, and reduce combines the elements in a structure.

The definition of reduce is:

$$
\begin{aligned}
\oplus/[\,] &= 1_\oplus \\
\oplus/[a] &= a \\
\oplus/(x \mathbin{+\!\!\!+} y) &= \oplus/x \ \oplus \ \oplus/y.
\end{aligned}
$$

The unit of operation $\otimes$ is denoted $1_\otimes$. The function $\oplus/$ is a homomorphism from $+\!\!\!+$ to $\oplus$ if $\oplus$ satisfies the laws of $+\!\!\!+$ and not well-defined otherwise. That is,

- if $+\!\!\!+$ has a unit, then $\oplus$ must have a unit,
- if $+\!\!\!+$ is associative, then $\oplus$ must be associative,
- if $+\!\!\!+$ is commutative, then $\oplus$ must be commutative,
- if $+\!\!\!+$ is idempotent, then $\oplus$ must be idempotent.

Let's abbreviate "homomorphism from $+\!\!\!+$ to $\oplus$" by "$+\!\!\!+ \to \oplus$ homomorphism". The definition of map is:

$$
\begin{aligned}
f^*[\,] &= [\,] \\
f^*[a] &= [f.a] \\
f^*(x \mathbin{+\!\!\!+} y) &= f^*x \mathbin{+\!\!\!+} f^*y.
\end{aligned}
$$

The function f^* is a $+\!\!\!+ \to +\!\!\!+$ homomorphism. Map and reduce are crucial in defining homomorphisms from data structures. Indeed any homomorphism from a free algebra (a data structure) can be defined as a composition of a map and a reduce. This is called the "homomorphism lemma" [Bir86], or the "Universal property of free algebras". A given $+\!\!\!+ \to \oplus$ homomorphism h satisfying:

$$
\begin{aligned}
h.[\,] &= 1_\oplus \\
h.[a] &= f.a \\
h.(x \mathbin{+\!\!\!+} y) &= h.x \oplus h.y
\end{aligned}
$$

can be written as $h = \oplus/ \circ f^*$. Reduce captures the way that $[\,]$ and $+\!\!\!+$ are replaced by $1_\oplus$ and $\oplus$, and map captures how h acts on singletons.

Filter ⊲ is defined on any possibly-empty data structures. Its definition is:

$$
\begin{aligned}
p \triangleleft [\,] &= [\,] \\
p \triangleleft [a] &= [a] \text{ if } p.a \text{ else } [\,] \\
p \triangleleft (x \mathbin{+\!\!\!+} y) &= p \triangleleft x \mathbin{+\!\!\!+} p \triangleleft y.
\end{aligned}
$$

The function $p\triangleleft$ is an $+\!\!\!+ \to +\!\!\!+$ homomorphism. Filter is convenient, but can be eliminated using map (see "trading" later).

4 Some data structures

Many useful functions from data structures are defined as homomorphisms from the join function of the data structure to another binary function. Therefore in the following most data structures are presented together with binary functions that have the same properties as the join of the data structure, and homomorphisms to them. We'll look at the four usual ones *tree, list, bags, set*, and at a couple of stranger ones.

4.1 1000 Trees

A tree is either the empty tree [ ] containing no elements, or a singleton tree [*a*] containing one element, or a join of two trees $r \mathbin{+\mkern-8mu+} l$. Tree-join has unit [ ], but it is not associative, not commutative, and not idempotent. These trees are binary trees with elements in their leaves.

4.2 1100 Lists

The organisational information that is lost in going from trees to lists is the shape of the tree. The law that is added to the algebra is associativity of $+\mkern-8mu+$.

Another operation with properties 1100 is square matrix multiplication of $n \times n$-matrices over complex numbers, where n is fixed. There is a square unit matrix I_n, and matrix multiplication is associative, but not commutative or idempotent. So Π defined over lists of matrices by:

$$\Pi.[\,] \;=\; I_n$$
$$\Pi.[A] \;=\; A$$
$$\Pi.(l \mathbin{+\mkern-8mu+} r) \;=\; \Pi.l \; mult \; \Pi.r$$

is a homomorphism from lists to matrix multiplication, but not from any lower data structure. Using map and reduce we can write $\Pi = mult/ \circ id^{\,*}$, which is just $mult/$. Composition of n-space transformations like translation, scaling, and rotation has properties 1100 too (and not surprisingly can be modelled by square matrix multiplication).

For lists of characters there is a more convenient notation: " " is the empty list, and "abc" is the list ['a','b','c'].

4.3 1110 Bags

Bags are like lists that have lost their order, and like mobiles that have lost their shape. Bag join is commutative, but not idempotent. A bag is not ordered, but can contain an element once, twice, or any natural number of times. The number of times an element is contained in a bag is called the element's *frequency* in the bag.

The classic function with properties 1110 is addition. It is used to define three important homomorphisms from bags, namely $size$, Σ, and $freq.x$. They return the number of elements in a bag, their sum, and the frequency of a given x in a bag. Their definitions are:

$$size \;=\; +/ \circ (1 \ll)^{*}$$

$$\Sigma = +/$$
$$freq.x = +/ \circ f^*,$$
$$\text{where } f.a = 1 \text{ if } a = x \text{ else } 0$$

Obviously Σ only applies to bags of numbers. The function $\ll$ is called "first" and defined by $a \ll b = a$, and $(1 \ll)$ above is the function $(\lambda x : 1 \ll x)$. The function "second" is written $\gg$.

4.4   1111 Sets

Sets are like bags, but they have lost the notion of containing an element a particular number of times (the element's frequency). The law that is added to the algebra in going from bags to sets is idempotency of join $+\!\!\!+$.

Binary operations with properties 1111 are logical disjunction and conjunction, and max, min (if they have units). Disjunction is used to define three homomorphisms from sets, namely existential quantification $\exists$, $nonEmpty$, and the element-function $x \in$ for a given x. Their definitions are:

$$\exists = \vee/$$
$$nonEmpty = \vee/ \circ (\text{true} \ll)^*$$
$$(x \in) = \vee/ \circ f^*,$$
$$\text{where } f.a = (x = a).$$

Universal quantification is defined similarly as a $+\!\!\!+ \rightarrow \wedge$ homomorphism.

4.5   0010 Nonempty mobiles

Another possible data structure is this: join $+\!\!\!+$ has no unit $[\ ]$, but it is not associative, and is not commutative or idempotent. One could think of these structures as mobiles[1]. They are like trees that can rotate. Any subtree can also rotate, independently of the rest of the tree. In going from trees to mobiles, the structures lose their sense of left and right.

This binary function of natural numbers has properties 0010:

$$n \oplus m = (n \max m) + 1.$$

It is not associative, but commutative. The function $depth$ is a homomorphism from nonempty mobiles to $\oplus$:

$$depth = \oplus/ \circ (1 \ll)^*$$

The function $depth$ is also a homomorphism from 0000 nonempty $trees$, because they are higher than 0010 nonempty mobiles, but not from possibly-empty mobiles, because $\oplus$ has no unit. However, its definition can be adjusted to have unit 0:

$$n \oplus m = (n \max m) \text{ if } (n \min m = 0) \text{ else } (n \max m) + 1,$$

and then $depth = \oplus/ \circ (1 \ll)^*$ is defined on possibly-empty mobiles too, with $depth.[\ ] = 0$.

---

[1]Mobiles were invented by the Alexander Calder (1989 - 1976) [Lip76]. They consist of objects suspended by threads from wires. Marcel Duchamp named them "mobiles" because the objects move in the wind. Calder called his *fixed* sculptures "stabiles".

4.6 0101 Nonempty idempotent lists

An idempotent list is like a normal list, but disregards equal adjacent sublists. So for idempotent lists we have:

"banana" = "bana" = "bbbabananana".

For lists $as +\!\!+ bs = cs$ has a unique solution for as, given bs and cs. That is not so for idempotent lists. The properties 0101 seem a strange combination, but there are functions that satisfy them: the pair projections $\ll$ and $\gg$. They have no (left *and* right) units, are associative, $a \ll (b \ll c) = (a \ll b) \ll c$, are not commutative, but they are idempotent, $a \ll a = a$. The well-known functions *head* and *last* are homomorphisms from nonempty idempotent lists to the pair-projections:

$$head = \ll/$$
$$last = \gg/.$$

Nonempty idempotent lists can be thought of as nonempty sets with two member-selecting functions. Since nonempty lists are higher than idempotent nonempty lists, *head* can be applied to them too.

5 Conclusion and related work

The Boom hierarchy comprises more than four data structures. In a Boom data structure any of the four properties UNIT, ASSOC, COMM, and IDEM can be present or absent, therefore there are 16 data structures (of varying practicality). Any data structure can be translated to one with a superset of properties, because it then loses structural information, but it can not be translated to one with a subset of properties, because it then would gain structural information, and there is a choice about what information should be added.

The Boom hierarchy and Squiggol are first presented in [Mee86] and [Bir86], and from then in many publications of the "Dutch School", mostly based on category theory. In [Bac89] they are compared to the Eindhoven quantifier expression notation. [Hoo92] presents the Boom hierarchy for relations, and [Jeu92] in a category context.

References

[Bac89] Roland Backhouse. An exploration of the Bird-Meertens Formalism. *International Summerschool on Constructive Algorithmics, Ameland 1989*, September 1989.

[Bir86] Richard S. Bird. An introduction to the theory of lists. In M. Broy, editor, *Logic of Programming and Calculi of Discrete Design*, volume F36 of *NATO ASI Series*. Springer Verlag, 1986.

[Hoo92] Paul F. Hoogendijk. *(Relational) Programming Laws in Boom Hierarchy of Types*, volume 669 of *Lecture Notes in Computing Science*. Springer, June/July 1992.

8

[Jeu92]   Johan Jeuring. Theories for algorithm calculation. *Lecture Notes of the STOP Summerschool on Constructive Algorithmics*, 1, September 1992.

[Lip76]   Jean Lipman. *Calder's Universe*. Harrison House, New York, 1976.

[Mee86]   Lambert Meertens. Algorithmics - towards programming as a mathematical activity. *Mathematics and Computer Science*, 1, 1986. CWI Monographs (J. W. de Bakker, M. Hazewinkel, J. K. Lenstra, eds.) North Holland, Puhl. Co.

FACTORING AN ADEQUACY PROOF (PRELIMINARY REPORT)

ROY L. CROLE AND ANDREW D. GORDON

Abstract

This paper contributes to the methodology of using metalogics for reasoning about programming languages. As a concrete example we consider a fragment of ML corresponding to call-by-value PCF and translate it into a metalogic which contains (amongst other types) computation types and a fixpoint type. The main result is a soundness property $(\star)$: if the denotations of two programs are provably equal in the metalogic, they have the same operationally observable behaviour. As usual, this follows from a computational adequacy result. In early notes, Plotkin showed how such proofs could be factored into two stages, the first non-trivial and the second (essentially) routine; our contribution is to rework his suggestion within a new framework. We define a metalogic, which incorporates computation and fixpoint types, and specify a modular translation of the ML fragment. Our proof of $(\star)$ factors into two parts. First, the term language of the metalogic is equipped with an operational semantics and a (generic) computational adequacy result obtained. Second, a simple syntactic argument establishes a correspondence between the operational behaviour of an object program and of its denotation. The first part is not routine but is proved once and for all. The second is a detailed but essentially trivial calculation that is easily adaptable to other object languages. Such a factored proof is important because it promises to scale up more easily than a monolithic one. We show that it may be adapted to an object language with call-by-name functions and one with a simple exception mechanism.

1. Motivation and Background

The motivation for this work is to contribute to the long term project of using denotational semantics to prove properties of programs written in realistic languages like Standard ML or Haskell.

Our contribution is to the methodology of expressing and reasoning about denotational semantics using what we term *metalogics*. By metalogic we mean a formal system (such as a type theory or logic) intended to express denotational semantics, that is implementable in a theorem-prover, and which is equipped with general proof principles, such as natural number induction or fixpoint induction. The intention is that the general proof infrastructure of the metalogic can be applied to a particular object language via a translation into the metalogic. We shall define a metalogic (called $\mathcal{M}$) which has a basic syntax of types and terms, and is equipped with both an equational and an operational semantics. $\mathcal{M}$ is closely allied to Crole and Pitts' FIX-logic [4, 3], a metalogic based on ideas from Moggi's *computational let-calculus* [10, 11] and a precursor of Pitts' *evaluation logic* [15]. An important principle underlying each of these metalogics is to distinguish simple data values from computations; more precisely, each uses *computation types*, of the form $T\sigma$, to represent computations that may return data values of type σ. Each of these metalogics is *monadic* in the sense that a computation type is modelled by a strong monad.

We consider the general problem of how to prove soundness of metalogical reasoning about an object language. The object language we use as a vehicle for this problem is $\mathcal{O}$, a small fragment of ML corresponding to call-by-value PCF. We give a translation into $\mathcal{M}$ and prove its soundness: if the denotations of two programs are provably equal in the metalogic, then the two are in fact observationally equivalent. Given that ML is defined operationally, the result justifies use of the metalogic to derive properties of the object language.

It is standard to derive such a soundness result from a proof that the denotational semantics respects evaluation in a sense known as computational adequacy [8]. Proofs of computational adequacy are, usually, directly linked to the denotational semantics of the object language in question. In his CSLI notes [17], Plotkin showed how such proofs can be factored in two, via an operational semantics for the metalogic. Our contribution is to rework (the idea of) such a factorisation in the setting of a metalogic endowed with computation and fixpoint types. First, we prove a (non-routine) adequacy result which relates the equational and operational semantics of $\mathcal{M}$. Second, we obtain soundness of metalogical reasoning for $\mathcal{O}$ via a simple but detailed proof of a correspondence between the operational behaviour of each $\mathcal{O}$ program and its denotation, which utilises the adequacy result for $\mathcal{M}$. The computational adequacy of $\mathcal{M}$ is *generic* in the sense that a computational adequacy result for a new programming language will only require a reworking of the second (and simpler) proof stage. We present two variants of $\mathcal{O}$ as evidence for this genericity: one with call-by-name functions and another with a simple exception mechanism. The use of computation types gives an elegant structure to the form of $\mathcal{O}$'s denotational semantics. This factored proof is important as it is likely to scale up more easily than a monolithic one, and the monadic presentation ought to be of use as monadic metalogics are mechanised and applied to more realistic object languages.

$$\frac{\Gamma \vdash M : \sigma}{\Gamma \vdash \mathsf{ValL}(M) : \sigma_\perp} \qquad \frac{\Gamma \vdash M : \sigma}{\Gamma \vdash \mathsf{EvalL}(M) : \sigma_\perp} \; (\sigma \text{ total}) \qquad \frac{\Gamma \vdash E : \sigma_\perp \qquad \Gamma, x{:}\sigma \vdash F : \tau_\perp}{\Gamma \vdash \mathsf{LetL}\, x \Leftarrow E \text{ in } F : \tau_\perp}$$

$$\frac{\Gamma, e{:}\sigma_\perp \vdash F : \sigma \qquad \Gamma \vdash N : \mathit{fix}}{\Gamma \vdash \mathsf{It}(e.\,F, N) : \sigma} \qquad \frac{}{\Gamma \vdash \omega : \mathit{fix}_\perp} \qquad \frac{\Gamma \vdash E : \mathit{fix}_\perp}{\Gamma \vdash \mathsf{Inc}(E) : \mathit{fix}}$$

TABLE 1. Type assignment for $\mathcal{M}$

2. An Equational Metalogic $\mathcal{M}$

We now present a Martin-Löf style (simple) type theory $\mathcal{M}$ which will be viewed as a programming metalogic. This is based on the term language of the FIX-logic [3, 4], though $\mathcal{M}$ has a few crucial differences. The term language of $\mathcal{M}$ is well known, except, perhaps, for the fragment associated with the fixpoint type and lifted types $\sigma_\perp$. Let us summarise the types and (raw) terms:

$$\sigma \quad ::= \quad \mathit{unit} \mid \mathit{nat} \mid \mathit{fix} \mid \sigma \times \sigma \mid \sigma + \sigma \mid \sigma \to \sigma \mid \sigma_\perp$$

$$M \quad ::= \quad x \mid \langle\rangle \mid \mathsf{Z} \mid \mathsf{S}(M) \mid (x.M)^M(M) \mid \omega \mid \mathsf{Inc}(M) \mid \mathsf{It}(x.\,M, M) \mid$$
$$\langle M, M \rangle \mid \mathsf{Split}(M, x.\,x.\,M) \mid \mathsf{Inl}(M) \mid \mathsf{Inr}(M) \mid \mathsf{Case}(M, x.\,M, x.\,M) \mid$$
$$\lambda x.\,M \mid M\,M \mid \mathsf{ValL}(M) \mid \mathsf{EvalL}(M) \mid \mathsf{LetL}\, x \Leftarrow M \text{ in } M$$

The types are given by a unit type, natural numbers, fixpoint type, (co)products, exponentials, and lifted types. In the cases of the unit type, natural numbers, products, coproducts and exponentials, the raw terms are the usual ones of Martin-Löf's (simple) type theory—for background see Nordström *et al* [12]. The raw terms of the fixpoint type are described elsewhere [3, 4].

The type $\sigma_\perp$ is thought of as the type of partial computations with values of type σ. If M is any term, then $\mathsf{ValL}(M)$ is a computation which evaluates immediately yielding result M. $\mathsf{EvalL}(M)$ is similar, but M is never a partial computation. If E and F are both partial computations, then $\mathsf{LetL}\, x \Leftarrow E \text{ in } F$ can be thought of as the computation $F[M/x]$ provided that the partial computation E is defined and evaluates with result M, and is undefined if E is undefined. Up to provable equality $\mathsf{EvalL}(M)$ is the same as $\mathsf{ValL}(M)$; the two will be distinguished by their operational semantics. Evaluation of the former forces evaluation of M but evaluation of the latter does not. EvalL will be vital later on in obtaining precise relationships between operational and denotational semantics.

We give a type assignment system for $\mathcal{M}$. This will consist of rules for deriving judgments of the form $\Gamma \vdash M : \sigma$ where the *environment* Γ is a finite list of (variable, type) pairs. We shall refer to σ as the type *assigned* to the raw term M in the environment Γ. Well formed judgments of the form $\Gamma \vdash M : \sigma$ are generated by the rules for simply typed lambda-calculus with unit, natural numbers, products and coproducts, plus the additional rules in Table 1. We write $\sigma \rightharpoonup \tau$ for $\sigma \to \tau_\perp$. We refer to a type σ, where $\sigma \not\equiv \tau_\perp$ for any τ, as a *total* type.

We can use the syntax of $\mathcal{M}$ as the basis for a pure equational type theory [4] in which theorems take the form $\Gamma \vdash M = M':\sigma$; in this abstract we omit the rules for proving such judgments.

We can give a categorical semantics to $\mathcal{M}$ in the usual way. We shall interpret $\mathcal{M}$ in the FIX-category [3, 4] $\omega\mathcal{CPO}$ of ωcpos and Scott continuous functions, equipped with the lifting monad, and topped vertical natural numbers with the successor structure map as FPO. We shall write $D_\perp \overset{\text{def}}{=} \{\perp\} \cup \{[d] \mid d \in D\}$ for (the underlying set of) the lift of the ωcpo D, with unit $\eta_D \overset{\text{def}}{=} \lambda d \in D.[d]:D \to D_\perp$. We denote the FPO by (N^∞, ∞, s) (using an obvious notation). If $f:C \times D_\perp \to D$ is a Scott continuous function, then the mediating morphism of the (indexed) FPO will be written $it(f):C \times N^\infty \to D$. We summarise the semantics of the less well known fragment of $\mathcal{M}$:

- $[\![\sigma_\perp]\!] \overset{\text{def}}{=} [\![\sigma]\!]_\perp$, $[\![fix]\!] \overset{\text{def}}{=} N^\infty$,
- $[\![\Gamma \vdash \mathsf{EvalL}(M):\sigma_\perp]\!] = [\![\Gamma \vdash \mathsf{ValL}(M):\sigma_\perp]\!] \overset{\text{def}}{=} \eta_{[\![\sigma]\!]} \circ [\![\Gamma \vdash M:\sigma]\!]$,
- $[\![\Gamma \vdash \mathsf{LetL}\, x \Leftarrow E \text{ in } F:\tau_\perp]\!] \overset{\text{def}}{=} [\![\Gamma, x:\sigma \vdash F:\sigma_\perp]\!]_\perp \circ \langle id_{[\![\Gamma]\!]}, [\![\Gamma \vdash E:\sigma_\perp]\!]\rangle$, where $f_\perp$ is the indexed Kliesli lifting of f in $\omega\mathcal{CPO}$,
- $[\![\Gamma \vdash \omega:fix_\perp]\!] \overset{\text{def}}{=} \infty \circ !$, where we have $[\![\Gamma]\!] \xrightarrow{!} 1 \xrightarrow{* \mapsto \infty} N^\infty_\perp$, 1 terminal in $\omega\mathcal{CPO}$,
- $[\![\Gamma \vdash \mathsf{Inc}(E):fix_\perp]\!] \overset{\text{def}}{=} s \circ [\![\Gamma \vdash E:fix_\perp]\!]$,
- $[\![\Gamma \vdash \mathsf{It}(e.F, N):\sigma]\!] \overset{\text{def}}{=} it([\![\Gamma, e:\sigma_\perp \vdash F:\sigma]\!]) \circ \langle id_{[\![\Gamma]\!]}, [\![\Gamma \vdash N:fix]\!]\rangle$.

3. Computation Types and the Let-Calculus

Moggi [10, 11] introduced a (simple) type theory which is now often referred to as the computational let-calculus. His calculus captures the following intuitions about (many) programming languages. First, it is sensible to separate out the notions of computations of values from values themselves; second that any value may be regarded as a "trivial" computation yielding itself as its value; and third, that computations may be composed sequentially. In fact this type theory corresponds with the notion of a category (with finite products) equipped with a strong monad. For these reasons an instance of the computational let-calculus is often referred to as a computational monad. More precisely, a computational monad is specified by a triple $(T, \mathsf{Val}, \mathsf{Let})$ where T is a type constructor and Val and Let are term constructors, that satisfy the following type assignment rules,

$$\frac{\Gamma \vdash M : \sigma}{\Gamma \vdash \mathsf{Val}(M) : T\sigma} \qquad \frac{\Gamma \vdash M : T\sigma \qquad \Gamma, x:\sigma \vdash N : T\sigma'}{\Gamma \vdash \mathsf{Let}\, x \Leftarrow M \text{ in } N : T\sigma'}$$

and the following rules for deducing equational theorems.

$$\frac{\Gamma \vdash M : \sigma \quad \Gamma, x{:}\sigma \vdash N : T\tau}{\Gamma \vdash \mathsf{Let}\, x \Leftarrow \mathsf{Val}(M)\, \mathsf{in}\, N = N[M/x] : T\sigma'} \qquad \frac{\Gamma \vdash M : T\sigma}{\Gamma \vdash \mathsf{Let}\, x \Leftarrow M\, \mathsf{in}\, \mathsf{Val}(x) = M : T\sigma}$$

$$\frac{\Gamma \vdash M : T\sigma \quad \Gamma, x{:}\sigma \vdash N : T\sigma' \quad \Gamma, y{:}\sigma' \vdash P : T\sigma''}{\Gamma \vdash \mathsf{Let}\, x \Leftarrow M\, \mathsf{in}\, (\mathsf{Let}\, y \Leftarrow N\, \mathsf{in}\, P) = \mathsf{Let}\, y \Leftarrow (\mathsf{Let}\, x \Leftarrow M\, \mathsf{in}\, N)\, \mathsf{in}\, P : T\sigma''}$$

As expected, the triple $((-)_\perp, \mathsf{ValL}, \mathsf{LetL})$ is a computational monad, usually known as the lifting monad. The equational logic of $\mathcal{M}$ must be omitted here for the sake of brevity, but (the appropriate instance of) the three (equational) rules above are indeed present in $\mathcal{M}$ [3, 4]. We include a small example at the end of the paper in Section 8 to illustrate the use of a monad other than the lifting monad.

4. An Operational Semantics for $\mathcal{M}$

Let us specify an operational semantics for (the term language of) $\mathcal{M}$, as done for a similar metalogic by Gordon [5]. We shall need a few auxiliary definitions. The *canonical* raw terms are given by the grammar

$$V ::= \langle\rangle \mid \mathsf{Z} \mid \mathsf{S}(V) \mid \langle M, M \rangle \mid \mathsf{Inl}(M) \mid \mathsf{Inr}(M) \mid \lambda x.M \mid \mathsf{ValL}(M) \mid \mathsf{Inc}(M).$$

We write $\mathcal{M}_\sigma$ for the set of $\mathcal{M}$-*programs*, that is, raw terms M for which $\vdash M{:}\sigma$ is provable, and $\mathcal{M}_\sigma^{can} \subseteq \mathcal{M}_\sigma$ for the subset of canonical terms. We specify an operational semantics in two equivalent ways: as a 'big step' *evaluation relation*, $M \Downarrow V$, and a 'small step' *reduction relation*, $M \to N$, where M, N and V are programs and V is canonical. The two relations are generated in the usual way, except for the syntax involving lifted types and the fixpoint type; the rules for the evaluation and reduction relations appear in Table 2. It is straightforward to prove that $M \Downarrow V$ if and only if $M \to^* V$ (where $\to^*$ means reflexive, transitive closure of $\to$). The semantics is deterministic and call-by-name. If $M \in \mathcal{M}_\sigma$ and $M \to N$ then $N \in \mathcal{M}_\sigma$ too. It is easy to prove the following result by rule induction.

Proposition 1. If $M \in \mathcal{M}_\sigma$ and also $M \Downarrow V$, then $V \in \mathcal{M}_\sigma^{can}$ and $\vdash M = V{:}\sigma$, where the latter judgment holds in the equational metalogic.

Our principal aim here is to prove the following (generic) adequacy theorem.

Theorem 2 (Generic Adequacy). The equational metalogic is computationally adequate for the operational semantics in the following sense. If $E \in \mathcal{M}_{\sigma_\perp}$ and $M \in \mathcal{M}_\sigma$ are such that $\vdash E = \mathsf{ValL}(M) : \sigma_\perp$ is provable, then there is $V \in \mathcal{M}_{\sigma_\perp}^{can}$ for which $E \Downarrow V$.

We also prove a normalisation result at total types.

$$\overline{V \Downarrow V}$$

$$\frac{M \Downarrow V}{\mathsf{S}(M) \Downarrow \mathsf{S}(V)} \qquad \frac{N \Downarrow \mathsf{Z} \quad M \Downarrow V}{(x.\,F)^N(M) \Downarrow V} \qquad \frac{N \Downarrow \mathsf{S}(U) \quad F[(x.\,F)^U(M)/x] \Downarrow V}{(x.\,F)^N(M) \Downarrow V}$$

$$\frac{P \Downarrow \langle M, N \rangle \quad F[M, N/x, y] \Downarrow V}{\mathsf{Split}(P, x.\,y.\,F) \Downarrow V}$$

$$\frac{C \Downarrow \mathsf{Inl}(M) \quad F[M/x] \Downarrow V}{\mathsf{Case}(C, x.\,F, x.\,G) \Downarrow V} \qquad \frac{C \Downarrow \mathsf{Inr}(M) \quad G[M/x] \Downarrow V}{\mathsf{Case}(C, x.\,F, x.\,G) \Downarrow V}$$

$$\frac{F \Downarrow \lambda x.\,N \quad N[M/x] \Downarrow V}{F\,M \Downarrow V}$$

$$\frac{M \Downarrow V}{\mathsf{EvalL}(M) \Downarrow \mathsf{ValL}(V)} \qquad \frac{E \Downarrow \mathsf{ValL}(M) \quad F[M/x] \Downarrow V}{\mathsf{LetL}\,x \Leftarrow E \,\mathsf{in}\, F \Downarrow V}$$

$$\frac{N \Downarrow \mathsf{Inc}(E) \quad M[\mathsf{LetL}\,y \Leftarrow E \,\mathsf{in}\, \mathsf{ValL}(\mathsf{It}(e.\,M, y))/e] \Downarrow V}{\mathsf{It}(e.\,M, N) \Downarrow V} \qquad \overline{\omega \Downarrow \mathsf{ValL}(\mathsf{Inc}(\omega))}$$

$$(x.F)^{\mathsf{Z}}(M) \to M$$

$$(x.F)^{\mathsf{S}(V)}(M) \to F[(x.F)^V(M)/x]$$

$$\mathsf{Split}(\langle M, N \rangle, x.\,y.\,F) \to F[M, N/x, y]$$

$$\mathsf{Case}(\mathsf{Inl}(M), x.\,F, x.\,G) \to F[M/x]$$

$$\mathsf{Case}(\mathsf{Inr}(M), x.\,F, x.\,G) \to G[M/x]$$

$$(\lambda x.\,N)M \to N[M/x]$$

$$\mathsf{LetL}\,x \Leftarrow \mathsf{ValL}(M) \,\mathsf{in}\, F \to F[M/x]$$

$$\mathsf{It}(e.\,M, \mathsf{Inc}(E)) \to M[\mathsf{LetL}\,y \Leftarrow E \,\mathsf{in}\, \mathsf{ValL}(\mathsf{It}(e.\,M, y))/e]$$

$$\omega \to \mathsf{ValL}(\mathsf{Inc}(\omega))$$

$$\mathsf{EvalL}(V) \to \mathsf{ValL}(V)$$

$$\frac{M \to N}{\mathcal{E}[M] \to \mathcal{E}[N]}$$

where $\mathcal{E}[-] ::= \mathsf{S}(-) \mid (x.F)^-(M) \mid \mathsf{Split}(-, x.\,y.\,F) \mid \mathsf{Case}(-, x.\,F, x.\,G) \mid (-\,M) \mid \mathsf{LetL}\,x \Leftarrow -\,\mathsf{in}\, E \mid \mathsf{It}(e.\,M, -) \mid \mathsf{EvalL}(-)$

TABLE 2. Operational semantics for $\mathcal{M}$

Theorem 3 (Normalisation). If $M \in \mathcal{M}_\sigma$ with σ total, then evaluation of M converges, that is, $\exists V.\ M \Downarrow V$.

To prove this we need some technical machinery. Let $[\![-]\!]:\mathcal{M} \to \omega\mathcal{CPO}$ refer to the semantics of $\mathcal{M}$ in the FIX-category $\omega\mathcal{CPO}$. We now define a logical relation which takes the form $\lhd_\sigma \subseteq [\![\sigma]\!] \times \mathcal{M}_\sigma$ for all types σ, and is defined through certain inductive clauses of which we give just a few examples:

- $e \lhd_{\sigma_\perp} E$ iff whenever $e = [d]$ for $d \in [\![\sigma]\!]$ then $\exists M.\ E \Downarrow \mathsf{ValL}(M)$ and $d \lhd_\sigma M$.
- $\infty \lhd_{fix} N$ iff $\forall n \in \mathbb{N}^\infty \setminus \{\infty\}$ we have $n \lhd_{fix} N$.
- $n + 1 \lhd_{fix} N$ iff $\exists E_n.\ N \Downarrow \mathsf{Inc}(E_n)$, $\exists N_n.\ E_n \Downarrow \mathsf{ValL}(N_n)$ and also for $1 \leq i \leq n$ we have $\exists E_{i-1}.\ N_i \Downarrow \mathsf{Inc}(E_{i-1})$, $\exists N_{i-1}.\ E_{i-1} \Downarrow \mathsf{ValL}(N_{i-1})$ and $\exists E.\ N_0 \Downarrow \mathsf{Inc}(E)$.
- $0 \lhd_{fix} N$ iff $\exists E.\ N \Downarrow \mathsf{Inc}(E)$.

We shall also need the following lemmas and proposition, for which we sketch the proof of the latter:

Lemma 4. Suppose that $d \lhd_\sigma M$ and also $M' \to^* M$; then $d \lhd_\sigma M'$.

Lemma 5. Let $(d_i \mid i \in \omega)$ be an ω-chain in $[\![\sigma]\!]$ for any σ. If $d_i \lhd_\sigma M$ for some M and each $i \in \omega$, then $\bigvee_{i \in \omega} d_i \lhd_\sigma M$.

Proposition 6. Let $x_1:\sigma_1, \ldots, x_n:\sigma_n \vdash M : \sigma$ be provable, let $M_i \in \mathcal{M}_{\sigma_i}$ for $1 \leq i \leq n$, and let $d_i \in [\![\sigma_i]\!]$ for $1 \leq i \leq n$ with $d_i \lhd_{\sigma_i} M_i$. Then it is the case that

$$[\![x_1:\sigma_1, \ldots, x_n:\sigma_n \vdash M : \sigma]\!](\vec{d}) \lhd_\sigma M[M_1, \ldots, M_n/x_1, \ldots, x_n]$$

where $\vec{d} \overset{\mathrm{def}}{=} (d_1, \ldots, d_n) \in \Pi_1^n [\![\sigma_i]\!]$.

Proof The proof proceeds by induction on the structure of M, and uses Lemma 4 and Lemma 5. We just give some example cases. We shall adopt the following convention: if (for example) $\Gamma \vdash M:\sigma$ is provable, we write $m:[\![\Gamma]\!] \to [\![\sigma]\!]$ for the morphism (here continuous function) $[\![\Gamma \vdash M:\sigma]\!]$. We shall also write (for example) $\tilde{M}$ for $M[M_1, \ldots, M_n/x_1, \ldots, x_n]$. We give two inductive cases:

(*Case M is* $\mathsf{It}(e.F, N)$): We need to prove that

$$[\![x_1:\sigma_1, \ldots, x_n:\sigma_n \vdash \mathsf{It}(e.F, N):\sigma]\!] = it(f)(\vec{d}, n(\vec{d})) \lhd_\sigma \mathsf{It}(e.\tilde{F}, \tilde{N}),$$

where $f:\Pi_1^n [\![\sigma_i]\!] \times [\![\sigma]\!]_\perp \to [\![\sigma]\!]$ and thus $it(f):\Pi_1^n [\![\sigma_i]\!] \times \mathbb{N}^\infty \to [\![\sigma]\!]$. By induction we know that $n(\vec{d}) \lhd_{fix} \tilde{N}$ (1) and

$$e \lhd_{\sigma_\perp} E \text{ implies } f(\vec{d}, e) \lhd_\sigma \tilde{F}[E/e]. \tag{2}$$

We consider the case when $n(\vec{d})$ is $\check{n} + 1 \in \mathbb{N}^\infty \setminus \{\infty\}$. We have $\check{n} + 1 \lhd_{fix} \tilde{N}$ from (1), and so $\tilde{N} \Downarrow \mathsf{Inc}(E_{\check{n}})$, $E_{\check{n}} \Downarrow \mathsf{ValL}(N_{\check{n}})$ and so on to $N_0 \Downarrow \mathsf{Inc}(E)$. It can be shown that

$$it(f)(\vec{d}, 0) \lhd_\sigma \mathsf{It}(e.\tilde{F}, N_0).$$

Now let $0 \leq r \leq \check{n}$. Write $N_{\check{n}+1} \stackrel{\text{def}}{=} \tilde{N}$; we prove that if

$$it(f)(\vec{d}, r) \lhd_\sigma \text{lt}(e.\tilde{F}, N_r) \tag{3}$$

then $it(f)(\vec{d}, r+1) \lhd_\sigma \text{lt}(e.\tilde{F}, N_{r+1})$. From (3) and that $E_r \Downarrow \text{ValL}(N_r)$ we may deduce

$$it(f)(\vec{d}, r+1) \lhd_\sigma \tilde{F}[\text{LetL } y \Leftarrow E_r \text{ in ValL}(\text{lt}(e.\tilde{F}, y))/e].$$

But $N_{r+1} \to^* \text{Inc}(E_r)$ and hence $\text{lt}(e.\tilde{F}, N_{r+1}) \to^* \tilde{F}[\text{LetL } E_r \text{ in ValL}(\text{lt}(e.\tilde{F}, y))/e]$, so we are done by appeal to Lemma 4.

(*Case M is* $\text{EvalL}(M)$): We wish to prove that

$$[\![x_1{:}\sigma_1, \ldots, x_n{:}\sigma_n \vdash \text{EvalL}(M){:}\sigma_\perp]\!](\vec{d}) = [m(\vec{d})] \lhd_{\sigma_\perp} \text{EvalL}(\tilde{M})$$

and so we need to show that there is $V \in \mathcal{M}_\sigma^{can}$ for which $\text{EvalL}(\tilde{M}) \Downarrow \text{ValL}(V)$ with $m(\vec{d}) \lhd_\sigma V$. By the induction hypothesis we have $m(\vec{d}) \lhd_\sigma \tilde{M}$, and by inspecting the clauses of the logical relation one can deduce that $\tilde{M} \Downarrow V$ for some V with $m(\vec{d}) \lhd_\sigma V$ and so we are done. ∎

Proof [*of Theorem* 2] Follows because the categorical semantics of $\mathcal{M}$ is sound, together with the application of Proposition 6 with $i = 1$ and $d_1 \equiv * \lhd_{unit} \langle\rangle \equiv M_1$. More precisely, we may deduce

$$[\![x{:}unit \vdash E{:}\sigma_\perp]\!](*) = [\![[x{:}unit \vdash M{:}\sigma]\!](*)] \lhd_{\sigma_\perp} E[\langle\rangle/x] \equiv E$$

and so $\exists V.E \Downarrow V$ by inspecting the clause defining the logical relation at lifted types. ∎

Proof [*of Theorem* 3] Just as in the last proof, apply Proposition 6 to deduce that the relation $[\![\vdash M{:}\sigma]\!](*) \lhd_\sigma M$. By inspection of the clauses defining relation $\lhd_\sigma$ it will follow that evaluation of M converges. ∎

5. The Object Language $\mathcal{O}$

The object language $\mathcal{O}$ is essentially a call-by-value form of PCF. Syntactically it is a tiny fragment of Standard ML. The $\mathcal{O}$-*types*, denoted by σ or τ, are generated from ground types bool of Booleans, int of numbers, by forming function types $\sigma \text{->} \tau$. Let metavariable ℓ range over a set, $\mathbb{N} \cup \{tt, f\!f\}$, of *literals*, and metavariable $\oplus$ over a set of *operators*, $\{+, -, \times, =, <\}$. The $\mathcal{O}$-*terms*, e, are generated by the following BNF grammar, which also defines *canonical* $\mathcal{O}$-terms, c.

$$
\begin{aligned}
e &::= \quad c \mid e \oplus e \mid \text{if } e \text{ then } e \text{ else } e \mid e\, e \\
c &::= \quad x \mid () \mid \ell \mid \text{fn } x => e \mid \text{let fun } f\, x = e \text{ in } f \text{ end}
\end{aligned}
$$

The last canonical term is a form of SML notation for a recursively defined function, named f and with argument x, which are both bound in e.

$$\frac{}{c \Downarrow c} \qquad \frac{e_1 \Downarrow \underline{\ell_1} \qquad e_2 \Downarrow \underline{\ell_2}}{e_1 \oplus e_2 \Downarrow \underline{\ell_1 \oplus \ell_2}} \qquad \frac{e_1 \Downarrow \underline{tt} \qquad e_2 \Downarrow c}{\text{if } e_1 \text{ then } e_2 \text{ else } e_3 \Downarrow c} \qquad \frac{e_1 \Downarrow \underline{f\!f} \qquad e_3 \Downarrow c}{\text{if } e_1 \text{ then } e_2 \text{ else } e_3 \Downarrow c}$$

$$\frac{e_1 \Downarrow \text{fn } x \Rightarrow e \qquad e_2 \Downarrow c_2 \qquad e[c_2/x] \Downarrow c}{e_1 \, e_2 \Downarrow c}$$

$$\frac{e_1 \Downarrow \text{let fun } f\, x = e \text{ in } f \text{ end} \qquad e_2 \Downarrow c_2 \qquad e[\text{let fun } f\, x = e \text{ in } f \text{ end}, c_2/f, x] \Downarrow c}{e_1 \, e_2 \Downarrow c}$$

TABLE 3. Operational semantics for $\mathcal{O}$

The type assignment system for $\mathcal{O}$ consists of a collection of rules for proving judgments of the form $\Gamma \vdash e : \sigma$ where Γ is a finite list of (variable, type) pairs; we shall write $x_1{:}\sigma_1, \dots, x_n{:}\sigma_n$ for Γ. The typing rules for $\mathcal{O}$ are a straightforward extension of those for simply typed lambda-calculus; we omit them all apart from the rule for recursively defined functions.

$$\frac{\Gamma, f{:}\sigma \rightarrow \tau, x{:}\sigma \vdash e : \tau}{\Gamma \vdash \text{let fun } f\, x = e \text{ in } f \text{ end} : \sigma \rightarrow \tau}$$

For each $\mathcal{O}$-type σ, let $\mathcal{O}_\sigma$ be the set of $\mathcal{O}$-terms e for which $\vdash e : \sigma$ is provable; such a term is known as a *program*. Let $\mathcal{O}_\sigma^{can}$ be the set of all programs from $\mathcal{O}_\sigma$ that are canonical.

The operational semantics of $\mathcal{O}$ is specified as an evaluation relation, consisting of 'big step' judgments of the form $e \Downarrow c$, where e and c are programs, the latter canonical. One should think of the canonical terms as values which are returned by (non-divergent) programs. The relation is given inductively by the rules in Table 3. One can deduce from the rules for forming such judgments that evaluation is deterministic and that if $e \in \mathcal{O}_\sigma$ and $e \Downarrow c$, then $c \in \mathcal{O}_\sigma^{can}$. If e is a program, write $e \Downarrow$ to mean $\exists c.\, e \Downarrow c$, in which case we say that program c *converges*.

The evaluation relation induces a Morris-style contextual equivalence between $\mathcal{O}$-terms: two terms are equivalent if each can replace the other in any program without changing its convergence behaviour. Informally, let a *context*, $C[-]$, be a term some of whose subterms have been replaced by a *hole*, $-$, and let $C[e]$ be the term obtained by filling each hole with the term e. Suppose that e_1 and e_2 are both members of one of the sets $\mathcal{O}_\sigma$. Write $e_1 \approx e_2$ to mean that $C[e_1] \Downarrow$ iff $C[e_2] \Downarrow$ whenever $C[e_1]$, $C[e_2]$ are both members of $\mathcal{O}_\tau$ for some type τ. In this case we say the two terms are *observationally equivalent*.

6. Translation of $\mathcal{O}$ into $\mathcal{M}$

In this section we give a denotational semantics for $\mathcal{O}$ using $\mathcal{M}$. The intention is that via this semantics, the metalogic can be applied to prove observational equivalences between $\mathcal{O}$-terms. This intention is vindicated by Theorem 12, the main result of the paper, which says that if the denotations of two $\mathcal{O}$-terms are provably equal in the metalogic, then in fact the two terms are observationally equivalent.

We adopt the usual inductive definition of numerals, $\lfloor 0 \rfloor \stackrel{\text{def}}{=} Z$ and $\lfloor n+1 \rfloor \stackrel{\text{def}}{=}$ $S(\lfloor n \rfloor)$. Booleans are represented by terms of type $unit + unit$; let $\lfloor tt \rfloor \stackrel{\text{def}}{=}$ $\mathsf{Inl}(\langle\rangle)$ and $\lfloor ff \rfloor \stackrel{\text{def}}{=} \mathsf{Inr}(\langle\rangle)$. For each arithmetic or relational operator, $\oplus \in \{+, -, \times, =, <\}$, we need an encoding $(M \lfloor + \rfloor N)$ in $\mathcal{M}$ such that suitably typed $(\lfloor \ell \rfloor \lfloor \oplus \rfloor \lfloor \ell' \rfloor)$ evaluates to $\lfloor \ell \oplus \ell' \rfloor$. Given the iteration on nat in $\mathcal{M}$, it is routine to do so; for instance, $(M \lfloor + \rfloor N)$ is $(x.S(x))^N(M)$.

Using iterations on the fix type we can define an operation $\mathsf{Fix}(-)$, that we will need for recursively defining partial functions of the form $\sigma \rightharpoonup \tau$.

Lemma 7. There is a term-former $\mathsf{Fix}(-)$ that satisfies the typing rule

$$\frac{\Gamma \vdash M : (\sigma \rightharpoonup \tau) \to (\sigma \rightharpoonup \tau)}{\Gamma \vdash \mathsf{Fix}(M) : \sigma \rightharpoonup \tau}$$

and for any M and N, $\mathsf{Fix}(M) \, N \to^* M \, (\mathsf{Fix}(M)) \, N$.

Proof   Let $\mathsf{Fix}'(M, N) \stackrel{\text{def}}{=} \mathsf{It}(e. \lambda x. \mathsf{LetL} \, y \Leftarrow e \text{ in } M \, y \, x, N)$ and then set $\mathsf{Fix}(M) \stackrel{\text{def}}{=} \mathsf{Fix}'(M, \mathsf{Inc}(\omega))$. It is straightforward to check that $\mathsf{Fix}(M)$ has the expected type. From the calculation,

$$
\begin{aligned}
\mathsf{Fix}(M) \, N \ &\equiv\ \mathsf{It}(e. \lambda x. \mathsf{LetL} \, y \Leftarrow e \text{ in } M \, y \, x, \mathsf{Inc}(\omega)) \, N \\
&\to\ (\lambda x. \mathsf{LetL} \, y \Leftarrow (\mathsf{LetL} \, z \Leftarrow \omega \text{ in } \mathsf{ValL}(\mathsf{Fix}'(M, z))) \text{ in } M \, y \, x) \, N \\
&\to\ \mathsf{LetL} \, y \Leftarrow (\mathsf{LetL} \, z \Leftarrow \omega \text{ in } \mathsf{ValL}(\mathsf{Fix}'(M, z))) \text{ in } M \, y \, N \\
&\to\ \mathsf{LetL} \, y \Leftarrow (\mathsf{LetL} \, z \Leftarrow \mathsf{ValL}(\mathsf{Inc}(\omega)) \text{ in } \mathsf{ValL}(\mathsf{Fix}'(M, z))) \text{ in } M \, y \, N \\
&\to\ \mathsf{LetL} \, y \Leftarrow \mathsf{ValL}(\mathsf{Fix}'(M, \mathsf{Inc}(\omega))) \text{ in } M \, y \, N \\
&\equiv\ \mathsf{LetL} \, y \Leftarrow \mathsf{ValL}(\mathsf{Fix}(M)) \text{ in } M \, y \, N \\
&\to\ M \, (\mathsf{Fix}(M)) \, N
\end{aligned}
$$

one sees that $\mathsf{Fix}(M)$ has the expected reduction behaviour too.   ∎

We give the translation of $\mathcal{O}$ into $\mathcal{M}$ in terms of an arbitrary computational monad $(T, \mathsf{Val}, \mathsf{Let})$. In this section and the next this computational monad will be an instance of the lifting monad, $((-)_{\perp}, \mathsf{ValL}, \mathsf{LetL})$. In Section 8 we will use a different monad to admit the possibility of an exception being raised.

The translation of $\mathcal{O}$ into $\mathcal{M}$ follows the pattern set by Pitts [15]. Map each $\mathcal{O}$-type σ to an $\mathcal{M}$-type $[\![\sigma]\!]$ inductively as follows: ground types $\mathtt{bool}$ and $\mathtt{int}$ are mapped to $unit + unit$ and nat respectively, while $\sigma \to \tau$ is mapped inductively to $[\![\sigma]\!] \to T[\![\tau]\!]$. Each $\mathcal{O}$-environment $\Gamma = x_1{:}\sigma_1, \dots, x_n{:}\sigma_n$ is mapped to $[\![\Gamma]\!] \stackrel{\text{def}}{=}$ $x_1{:}[\![\sigma_1]\!], \dots, x_n{:}[\![\sigma_n]\!]$. To begin the translation of $\mathcal{O}$ terms into $\mathcal{M}$, to each canonical $\mathcal{O}$-term c we assign a canonical $\mathcal{M}$-term $|c|$ as follows.

$$|x| \overset{\text{def}}{=} x$$
$$|\underline{\ell}| \overset{\text{def}}{=} \lfloor \ell \rfloor$$
$$|\mathtt{fn}\, x => e| \overset{\text{def}}{=} \lambda x.\, \llbracket e \rrbracket$$
$$|\mathtt{let\, fun}\, f\, x = e\, \mathtt{in}\, f\, \mathtt{end}| \overset{\text{def}}{=} \mathsf{Fix}(\lambda f.\, \lambda x.\, \llbracket e \rrbracket)$$

In keeping with the intuition that arbitrary $\mathcal{O}$-terms express computations rather than simple values, we assign to each $\mathcal{O}$-term e an $\mathcal{M}$-term $\llbracket e \rrbracket$ of computation type.

$$\llbracket c \rrbracket \overset{\text{def}}{=} \mathsf{Val}(|c|)$$
$$\llbracket e_1 \oplus e_2 \rrbracket \overset{\text{def}}{=} \mathsf{Let}\, x_1 \Leftarrow \llbracket e_1 \rrbracket \,\mathsf{in}\, (\mathsf{Let}\, x_2 \Leftarrow \llbracket e_2 \rrbracket \,\mathsf{in}\, \mathsf{EvalL}(x_1 \lfloor \oplus \rfloor x_2))$$
$$\llbracket \mathtt{if}\, e_1\, \mathtt{then}\, e_2\, \mathtt{else}\, e_3 \rrbracket \overset{\text{def}}{=} \mathsf{Let}\, b \Leftarrow \llbracket e_1 \rrbracket \,\mathsf{in}\, \mathsf{Case}(b, u.\, \llbracket e_1 \rrbracket, u.\, \llbracket e_1 \rrbracket)$$
$$\llbracket e_1\, e_2 \rrbracket \overset{\text{def}}{=} \mathsf{Let}\, f \Leftarrow \llbracket e_1 \rrbracket \,\mathsf{in}\, (\mathsf{Let}\, x \Leftarrow \llbracket e_2 \rrbracket \,\mathsf{in}\, f\, x)$$

The translation respects the type systems of $\mathcal{O}$ and $\mathcal{M}$ in the following sense, easily proved by structural induction.

Proposition 8 (Static Adequacy).

(1) Whenever $\Gamma \vdash e : \sigma$ is provable in $\mathcal{O}$, $\llbracket \Gamma \rrbracket \vdash \llbracket e \rrbracket : T\llbracket \sigma \rrbracket$ is provable in $\mathcal{M}$.
(2) Furthermore, if e is canonical, then $\llbracket e \rrbracket$ is canonical and $\llbracket \Gamma \rrbracket \vdash |e| : \llbracket \sigma \rrbracket$ is provable in $\mathcal{M}$.

Since the translation is compositional it is straightforward to prove the congruence and substitution parts of the following lemma by structural induction.

Lemma 9.

(1) If $\Gamma \vdash \llbracket e_1 \rrbracket = \llbracket e_2 \rrbracket : \sigma$, $\Gamma' \vdash \llbracket \mathcal{C}[e_1] \rrbracket : \tau$ and $\Gamma' \vdash \llbracket \mathcal{C}[e_2] \rrbracket : \tau$ are provable in $\mathcal{M}$, then $\Gamma' \vdash \llbracket \mathcal{C}[e_1] \rrbracket = \llbracket \mathcal{C}[e_2] \rrbracket : \tau$ is provable in $\mathcal{M}$ too.
(2) For any $\mathcal{O}$-term e and canonical $\mathcal{O}$-term c, $\llbracket e \rrbracket[|c|/x] \equiv \llbracket e[c/x] \rrbracket$.

We can establish the following exact correspondence between evaluation of any configuration and its translation by rule inductions and appeal to Lemmas 7 and 9.

Lemma 10. Suppose $e \in \mathcal{O}_\sigma$.

(1) Whenever $e \Downarrow c$ for some $c \in \mathcal{O}_\sigma^{can}$, then $\llbracket e \rrbracket \Downarrow \llbracket c \rrbracket$.
(2) Whenever $\llbracket e \rrbracket \Downarrow V$ for some $V \in \mathcal{M}_{T\llbracket \sigma \rrbracket}^{can}$, there is c with $e \Downarrow c$ and $V \equiv \llbracket c \rrbracket$.

Now we can prove adequacy for $\mathcal{O}$. This is the crux of the factorisation, where adequacy for $\mathcal{M}$—obtained from a domain-theoretic logical relations argument—is combined with the previous correspondence lemma—obtained by comparatively routine albeit detailed syntactic calculations.

Proposition 11 (Dynamic Adequacy). Suppose $e \in \mathcal{O}_\sigma$ and $c \in \mathcal{O}_\sigma^{can}$.

(1) Whenever $e \Downarrow c$ then $\vdash [\![e]\!] = [\![c]\!] : T[\![\sigma]\!]$ is provable.
(2) Whenever $\vdash [\![e]\!] = [\![c]\!] : T[\![\sigma]\!]$ is provable, then $e \Downarrow$.

Proof   (1) Suppose $e \Downarrow c$. By Lemma 10(1) we have $[\![e]\!] \Downarrow [\![c]\!]$. Hence we have $\vdash [\![e]\!] = [\![c]\!] : T[\![\sigma]\!]$ by Proposition 1. (2) Suppose $\vdash [\![e]\!] = [\![c]\!] : T[\![\sigma]\!]$. From Proposition 8(2) we know that $[\![c]\!]$ is canonical, so by Theorem 2, there is V such that $[\![e]\!] \Downarrow V$. Then by Lemma 10(2) there is c such that that $e \Downarrow c$ as required.   ∎

We now obtain soundness from adequacy as usual [8].

Theorem 12 (Soundness). If $e_1, e_2 \in \mathcal{O}_\sigma$ and $\vdash [\![e_1]\!] = [\![e_2]\!] : T[\![\sigma]\!]$ then $e_1 \approx e_2$.

Proof   Suppose $\vdash [\![e_1]\!] = [\![e_2]\!] : T[\![\sigma]\!]$. We are to show for all contexts $\mathcal{C}[-]$ such that $\mathcal{C}[e_1]$ and $\mathcal{C}[e_2]$ are both $\mathcal{O}$-programs of some type τ, that $\mathcal{C}[e_1] \Downarrow$ iff $\mathcal{C}[e_2] \Downarrow$. We show the forwards direction; the reverse follows by symmetry. Suppose then that each $\mathcal{C}[e_i] \in \mathcal{O}_\tau$, and that $\mathcal{C}[e_1] \Downarrow c$ for some canonical $c \in \mathcal{O}_\tau$. By Proposition 11(1), we have $\vdash [\![\mathcal{C}[e_1]]\!] = [\![c]\!] : T[\![\tau]\!]$. By Lemma 9(1) we have $\vdash [\![\mathcal{C}[e_1]]\!] = [\![\mathcal{C}[e_2]]\!] : T[\![\tau]\!]$. By transitivity and symmetry, $\vdash [\![\mathcal{C}[e_2]]\!] = [\![c]\!]$, and then since c is canonical $\mathcal{C}[e_2] \Downarrow$ by Proposition 11(2), as required.   ∎

7. Variant 1: call-by-name $\mathcal{O}$

In this and the following section we show how our modular proof of adequacy can easily be modified to apply to two variants of the object language $\mathcal{O}$.

The first of these is a form of $\mathcal{O}$ in which functions are applied using a call-by-name instead of a call-by-value strategy. The syntax and type system of $\mathcal{O}$ is unchanged except that variables are no longer included among the canonical $\mathcal{O}$-terms.

$$c ::= \ell \mid \mathtt{fn}\, x => e \mid \mathtt{let\ fun}\, f\, x = e \mathtt{\ in\ } f \mathtt{\ end}.$$

The evaluation relation, $e \Downarrow c$, is given inductively by the original rules from Table 3, except that the two rules for the two kinds of function application are replaced by call-by-name forms in Table 4. One can easily deduce that evaluation is deterministic and preserves types as before. We adopt the same notions of program convergence and observational equivalence as before.

We must also modify the translation of $\mathcal{O}$ into $\mathcal{M}$. As before, ground types bool and int are mapped to $unit + unit$ and nat respectively, but this time each (call-by-name) function type $\sigma \rightarrow \tau$ is mapped to $T[\![\sigma]\!] \rightarrow T[\![\tau]\!]$ (instead of $[\![\sigma]\!] \rightarrow T[\![\tau]\!]$ in the call-by-value case). A call-by-name strategy applies functions to computations rather than values. Each $\mathcal{O}$-environment $\Gamma = x_1{:}\sigma_1, \ldots, x_n{:}\sigma_n$ is mapped to $\mathcal{M}$-environment $[\![\Gamma]\!] \stackrel{def}{=} x_1{:}T[\![\sigma_1]\!], \ldots, x_n{:}T[\![\sigma_n]\!]$. The mapping of environments reflects a change in denotation of object variables—in the call-by-value setting they denoted values; here they denote computations. The

$$\frac{e_1 \Downarrow \text{fn } x \Rightarrow e \qquad e[e_2/x] \Downarrow c}{e_1\, e_2 \Downarrow c}$$

$$\frac{e_1 \Downarrow \text{let fun } f\, x = e \text{ in } f \text{ end} \qquad e[\text{let fun } f\, x = e \text{ in } f \text{ end}, e_2/f, x] \Downarrow c}{e_1\, e_2 \Downarrow c}$$

TABLE 4. Rules for call-by-name function application in $\mathcal{O}$

translations of terms are the same as before except for the following changes. The rules for recursive functions and applications are changed, the rule for canonical variables is dropped, and a new one for non-canonical variables is introduced.

$$|\text{let fun } f\, x = e \text{ in } f \text{ end}| \stackrel{\text{def}}{=} \text{Fix}(\lambda g.\, \lambda x.\, (\lambda f.\, [\![e]\!])(\text{Val}(g)))$$

$$[\![x]\!] \stackrel{\text{def}}{=} x$$

$$[\![e_1\, e_2]\!] \stackrel{\text{def}}{=} \text{Let } f \Leftarrow [\![e_1]\!] \text{ in } f\, [\![e_2]\!]$$

The third of these equations effects the call-by-name strategy, while the remaining two reflect the change in denotation of object variables—from values to computations.

Given the change in translation of environments, the following static adequacy result is easily proved.

Proposition 13 (Static Adequacy).

(1) Whenever $\Gamma \vdash e : \sigma$ is provable in $\mathcal{O}$, $[\![\Gamma]\!] \vdash [\![e]\!] : T[\![\sigma]\!]$ is provable in $\mathcal{M}$.

(2) Furthermore, if e is canonical, then $[\![e]\!]$ is canonical and $[\![\Gamma]\!] \vdash |e| : [\![\sigma]\!]$ is provable in $\mathcal{M}$.

The congruence lemma is stated and proved as before, but the substitution lemma this time concerns the substitution of arbitrary $\mathcal{O}$-terms, rather than simply canonical ones.

Lemma 14.

(1) If $\Gamma \vdash [\![e_1]\!] = [\![e_2]\!] : \sigma$, $\Gamma' \vdash [\![C[e_1]]\!] : \tau$ and $\Gamma' \vdash [\![C[e_2]]\!] : \tau$ are provable in $\mathcal{M}$, then $\Gamma' \vdash [\![C[e_1]]\!] = [\![C[e_2]]\!] : \tau$ is provable in $\mathcal{M}$ too.

(2) For any $\mathcal{O}$-terms e and e', $[\![e]\!][[\![e']\!]/x] \equiv [\![e[e'/x]]\!]$.

The correspondence between evaluation of an $\mathcal{O}$-program and its denotation is proved much as before, by a detailed but routine rule induction and appeal to the previous lemmas.

Lemma 15. Suppose $e \in \mathcal{O}_\sigma$.

(1) Whenever $e \Downarrow c$ for some $c \in \mathcal{O}_\sigma^{can}$, then $[\![e]\!] \Downarrow [\![c]\!]$.

(2) Whenever $[\![e]\!] \Downarrow V$ for some $V \in \mathcal{M}_{[\![\sigma]\!]}^{can}$, there is c with $e \Downarrow c$ and $V \equiv [\![c]\!]$.

$e_1 \Downarrow \mathbf{wrong}$	$e_1 \Downarrow \mathbf{wrong}$	$e_1 \Downarrow \mathbf{wrong}$
$e_1 \oplus e_2 \Downarrow \mathbf{wrong}$	$e_1\, e_2 \Downarrow \mathbf{wrong}$	if e_1 then e_2 else $e_3 \Downarrow \mathbf{wrong}$
$e_1 \Downarrow \ell \qquad e_2 \Downarrow \mathbf{wrong}$	$e_1 \Downarrow c \qquad c \not\equiv \mathbf{wrong} \qquad e_2 \Downarrow \mathbf{wrong}$	
$e_1 \oplus e_2 \Downarrow \mathbf{wrong}$	$e_1\, e_2 \Downarrow \mathbf{wrong}$	

TABLE 5. Rules for a single exception in $\mathcal{O}$

Once these detailed calculations are complete the soundness theorem follows exactly as before.

Theorem 16 (Soundness). If $e_1, e_2 \in \mathcal{O}_\sigma$ and $\vdash [\![e_1]\!] = [\![e_2]\!] : T[\![\sigma]\!]$ then $e_1 \approx e_2$.

Proof   From Lemma 15 by the same arguments that established Proposition 11 and Theorem 12 in the call-by-value case.   ∎

8. Variant 2: $\mathcal{O}$ plus an exception

Our second variant consists in adding a single exception, $\mathbf{wrong}$, to the original call-by-value $\mathcal{O}$. The point of this variant is that our methods work for computational monads other than the lifting monad.

We introduce a new canonical expression, $\mathbf{wrong}$, and extend the typing relation so that judgment $\Gamma \vdash \mathbf{wrong} : \sigma$ is provable for any type σ and (well-formed) environment Γ. The evaluation relation is generated from the original call-by-value rules in Table 3—amended with the side-condition on both rules for function application that $c_2 \not\equiv \mathbf{wrong}$—together with the new rules in Table 5. Convergence and observational equivalence are defined as before.

To give the translation of $\mathcal{O}$ into $\mathcal{M}$, we shall need a new computational monad $(T, \mathsf{Val}, \mathsf{Let})$. Intuitively, computations may either converge to a value, diverge, or go wrong, that is, converge to the exceptional value $\mathbf{wrong}$. To model such computations set $T\sigma \stackrel{\text{def}}{=} (\sigma + 1)_\perp$. A computation that goes wrong will be modelled by $\mathsf{Wrong} \stackrel{\text{def}}{=} \mathsf{ValL}(\mathsf{Inr}(\langle\rangle))$. The terms of the computational monad are defined by

$$\mathsf{Val}(M) \stackrel{\text{def}}{=} \mathsf{ValL}(\mathsf{Inl}(M))$$
$$\mathsf{Let}\, x \Leftarrow M \text{ in } N \stackrel{\text{def}}{=} \mathsf{LetL}\, y \Leftarrow M \text{ in } \mathsf{Case}(y, x.\, M, u.\, \mathsf{Wrong}).$$

Given the metalogic's coproduct rules [3, 4], it is routine to check that this is indeed a well defined computational monad in the sense given earlier.

Apart from the re-interpretation of the triple $(T, \mathsf{Val}, \mathsf{Let})$ there are two other changes needed to the translation of $\mathcal{O}$ into $\mathcal{M}$. First, we need to change the translation of canonical terms, $[\![c]\!]$, to the following.

$$[\![c]\!] \stackrel{\text{def}}{=} \begin{cases} \text{Wrong} & \text{if } c \equiv \texttt{wrong} \\ \text{Val}(|c|) & \text{otherwise} \end{cases}$$

Note that the interpretation of each canonical term $c \in \mathcal{O}_\sigma$ as a value $|c| \in \mathcal{O}_{[\![\sigma]\!]}$ does not need to be extended to **wrong**—and in fact would not make sense. Second, we need to change the translation of $[\![e_1 \oplus e_2]\!]$ to the following,

$$[\![e_1 \oplus e_2]\!] \stackrel{\text{def}}{=} \text{Let } x_1 \Leftarrow [\![e_1]\!] \text{ in } (\text{Let } x_2 \Leftarrow [\![e_2]\!] \text{ in Eval}(x_1 \oplus x_2))$$

where $\text{Eval}(M) \stackrel{\text{def}}{=} \text{LetL } y \Leftarrow \text{EvalL}(M) \text{ in Val}(y)$ for any M. There is no need to re-interpret the definition of recursive functions using Fix because although the definition of $T\sigma$ is different, the interpretation of an $\mathcal{O}$-function $\sigma \rightarrow \tau$ is still a partial function, this time $[\![\sigma]\!] \rightharpoonup [\![\tau]\!] + 1$.

Given these modifications to the denotational semantics, the soundness argument goes through much as before. Static adequacy (Proposition 8) holds as before, except that the judgment in part (2) holds only when $e \not\equiv \texttt{wrong}$. Compositionality, Lemma 9(1) holds as before, and so does the second part, substitution, except again for a side-condition that $c \not\equiv \texttt{wrong}$—but the side-condition on function applications ensures that **wrong** is never substituted for a variable in the operational semantics. The correspondence between the evaluation of each $\mathcal{O}$-program and its denotation, Lemma 10, holds as before. The proof requires the easily verified facts that

$$\begin{aligned} \text{Let } x \Leftarrow \text{Val}(M) \text{ in } N &\rightarrow^+ & N[M/x] \\ \text{Let } x \Leftarrow \text{Wrong in } M &\rightarrow^+ & \text{Wrong} \\ \text{Eval}(\lfloor \ell \rfloor \lfloor \oplus \rfloor \lfloor \ell' \rfloor) &\rightarrow^+ & \text{Val}(\lfloor \ell \oplus \ell \rfloor) \end{aligned}$$

for suitably-typed terms M, N and literals ℓ and ℓ' (where $\rightarrow^+$ is the transitive closure of $\rightarrow$). Given these lemmas, dynamic adequacy and soundness (Proposition 11 and Theorem 12) follow exactly as before.

9. Related and Future Work

This paper has shown how adequacy (and hence soundness) for a call-by-value object language $\mathcal{O}$ may be factored into two parts: a (non-routine) adequacy proof for a metalogic coupled with a comparatively routine proof of correspondence between the evaluation of each object program and its denotation in the metalogic. The factorisation is of interest because the second part can easily be adapted to other object languages without needing to repeat the first part. Variants of $\mathcal{O}$ with call-by-name functions and with a simple exception mechanism illustrated this genericity.

Apart from the unpublished notes [17, Chapter 3] that inspired this reworking, the only previous work to factor an adequacy proof via a metalogic is in Gordon's dissertation [5]. There the meaning of the metalogic was given using Abramsky's applicative bisimulation rather than domain theoretically. Others have equipped a metalogic with an operational semantics [1, 6, 7, 8, 9, 14, 21] but none has reworked Plotkin's original factorisation. Crole presents unfactored adequacy proofs for two PCF style languages mapped into the FIX-logic [2]. Apart from their application to denotational semantics, monads have been popularised by Wadler and others as a way to incorporate imperative features into lazy functional programming [13, 19, 20].

The key feature of this paper is the reworking of Plotkin's idea for factoring adequacy, but within a more structured and foundational framework; nonetheless the absence of recursive types from M prohibits modelling of many object language features. Hence in future work we intend to extend M with recursive types; Pitts' recent advances [16] will be highly relevant to extending Theorem 2. A further goal is to mechanise some form of M in a theorem-prover, and hence take advantage of this paper's soundness result to prove operational equivalences of O-programs mechanically. The operational semantics of M itself induces an observational equivalence on M-terms. It is of interest to consider the relationship between the direct observational equivalence on O-terms and the indirect equivalence induced by the translation into M and observational equivalence on M-terms; Riecke pursues a related investigation [18]. Although space has prevented its full exposition here, application of M to verification of functional programs was the specific motivation for the theory in this paper.

Acknowledgements. We wish to thank everyone at the Ayr workshop who discussed this work, and to the referees for their detailed comments. Roy Crole holds a SERC Research Fellowship at Imperial College. During this work Andrew Gordon was a member of the Programming Methodology Group at Chalmers University of Technology, Gothenburg. The work was begun while we were visitors at the University of Cambridge Computer Laboratory. We thank Andrew Pitts, our host, and everyone else at the Lab for their hospitality. Roy Crole thanks the SERC and the CEC CLICS project for providing funding to visit Cambridge and Gothenburg. Andrew Gordon thanks Mary Sheeran for arranging his visit to the PMG.

References

1. Peter Nicholas Benton. *Strictness Analysis of Lazy Functional Programs*. PhD thesis, University of Cambridge Computer Laboratory, August 1993. Available as Technical Report 309.
2. R. L. Crole. Computational adequacy for the FIX-Logic. *Theoretical Computer Science*. Accepted. (To appear in 1994.).
3. R. L. Crole and A. M. Pitts. New foundations for fixpoint computations: FIX hyperdoctrines and the FIX-logic. *Information and Control*, 98:171–210, 1992. Earlier version in LICS'90.
4. Roy L. Crole. *Programming Metalogics with a Fixpoint Type*. PhD thesis, University of Cambridge Computer Laboratory, February 1992. Available as Technical Report 247.

5. Andrew D. Gordon. *Functional Programming and Input/Output*. PhD thesis, University of Cambridge, August 1992. To appear in Cambridge University Press' series Distinguished Dissertations in Computer Science.
6. Carl A. Gunter. *Semantics of Programming Languages: Structures and Techniques*. MIT Press, Cambridge, Mass., 1992.
7. Claire Jones. *Probabilistic Non-determinism*. PhD thesis, University of Edinburgh, 1990. Available as Technical Report CST–63–90, Computer Science Department, University of Edinburgh.
8. Albert R. Meyer and Stavros S. Cosmadakis. Semantical paradigms: Notes for an invited lecture. In *Proceedings of the 3rd IEEE Symposium on Logic in Computer Science*, pages 236–253, July 1988.
9. Eugenio Moggi. *The Partial Lambda-Calculus*. PhD thesis, Department of Computer Science, University of Edinburgh, August 1988. Available as Technical report CST–53–88.
10. Eugenio Moggi. Computational lambda calculus and monads. In *Proceedings of the 4th IEEE Symposium on Logic in Computer Science*, June 1989.
11. Eugenio Moggi. Notions of computation and monads. *Theoretical Computer Science*, 93:55–92, 1989.
12. Bengt Nordström, Kent Petersson, and Jan M. Smith. *Programming in Martin-Löf's Type Theory*, volume 7 of *The International Series of Monographs in Computer Science*. Clarendon Press, Oxford, 1990.
13. Simon L. Peyton Jones and Philip Wadler. Imperative functional programming. In *Proceedings 20th ACM Symposium on Principles of Programming Languages, Charleston, South Carolina, January 1993*. ACM Press, 1993.
14. Andrew M. Pitts. Notes on the call-by-value and call-by-name translation of the simply typed lambda-calculus into the computational lambda-calculus. Manuscript, October 1990.
15. Andrew M. Pitts. Evaluation logic. In G. Birtwistle, editor, *IVth Higher Order Workshop, Banff 1990*, Workshops in Computing, pages 162–189. Springer-Verlag, 1991. Available as University of Cambridge Computer Laboratory Technical Report 198, August 1990.
16. Andrew M. Pitts. Computational adequacy via 'mixed' inductive definitions. In *MFPS IX, New Orleans*, 1993.
17. Gordon D. Plotkin. Denotational semantics with partial functions. Unpublished lecture notes, CSLI, Stanford University, July 1985.
18. Jon G. Riecke. Fully abstract translations between functional languages. To appear in *Mathematical Structures in Computer Science*, December 1992.
19. Philip Wadler. Comprehending monads. *Mathematical Structures in Computer Science*, 2:461–493, 1992.
20. Philip Wadler. The essence of functional programming. In *Proceedings of the Nineteenth ACM Symposium on Principles of Programming Languages*, 1992.
21. Glynn Winskel. *The Formal Semantics of Programming Languages*. MIT Press, Cambridge, Mass., 1993.

Address, Crole: IMPERIAL COLLEGE, DEPARTMENT OF COMPUTING, HUXLEY BUILDING, 180 QUEEN'S GATE, LONDON SW7 2BZ, UNITED KINGDOM.

E-mail address, Crole: rlc@doc.ic.ac.uk.

Address, Gordon: UNIVERSITY OF CAMBRIDGE COMPUTER LABORATORY, NEW MUSEUMS SITE, CAMBRIDGE CB2 3QG, UNITED KINGDOM.

E-mail address, Gordon: adg@cl.cam.ac.uk.

Projection-based Termination Analysis

Kei Davis

Department of Computing Science, University of Glasgow

Scotland, UK

Abstract

Termination analysis is genuinely useful for enabling optimisation in state-of-the-art compilers for lazy functional languages. Termination analysis techniques are typically restricted to determining termination in evaluation to weak head normal form; our projection-based technique gives much more detailed information, such as the fact that evaluation of an entire list or the entire spine of a list is certain to terminate, and hence gives the potential for much better compile-time optimisation.

1 Introduction

In the simplest case termination analysis seeks to determine whether evaluation of an expression to weak head normal form (WHNF) is certain to terminate. In a non-strict functional language, when the argument of a function is certain to terminate it is safe to pass the argument by value rather than by name (pass a value rather than a closure) with potential run-time savings in time and space. Termination analysis complements strictness analysis: if a function f is strict, that is $f \perp = \perp$, it is also safe to pass its argument by value.

Mycroft [Myc81] gives a termination analysis technique for a first-order monomorphic language, and describes how a compiler for the language might exploit the results of the analysis. More up-to-date, Young [You89] describes a technique for a higher-order untyped language and shows genuine optimisation in a compiler that exploits the results of the analysis; Hartel [Har91] uses a simple technique with similar results in a compiler for a higher-order polymorphic language. All three techniques are restricted to determining termination in evaluation only to WHNF. Our technique can give more detailed information regarding the termination of all or part of a data structure. This information may be of an absolute nature, such as the fact that the evaluation of the spine of a list is certain to terminate, or of a conditional nature, such as the fact that each element of a list terminates if its enclosing cons cell terminates.

There is a caveat in changing evaluation order based on termination analysis—just because it is safe to pass an argument by value does not mean it is optimal: if a function does not require its argument and the cost of evaluating and storing the argument exceeds the cost of building a closure for it, it would be disadvantageous to transform to call-by-value. For this reason Young also uses a simple operation-count analysis which gives an upper bound on the number of primitive operations required to evaluate an argument that is certain to terminate. For our analysis technique to be usefully exploited it might appear that a correspondingly more sophisticated operation count analysis would be required (and perhaps a space-usage analysis); we hypothesise that these would be straightforward and do not consider them further. However, as we will show, it seems to be in the nature of our analysis technique that termination is determined only when a small number of operations (and a correspondingly small amount of space) is required, obviating the need for time or space analysis.

Projection-based analysis techniques have been proposed for strictness analysis and binding-time analysis. For strictness analysis Wadler and Hughes [WH87] give an analysis technique for a first-order monomorphic language, Hughes and Launchbury [HL92] for a first-order polymorphic language, and Davis and Wadler [DW91] for a higher-order monomorphic language. The situation is similar for projection-based binding-time analysis: Launchbury [Lau91] gives techniques for first-order monomorphic and polymorphic languages, and Davis [Dav93] for a higher-order monomorphic language. In this paper we will give a termination analysis technique for a monomorphic language; because of space limitations the treatment is restricted to first-order. The generalisation to higher-order is analogous to that given in detail in [Dav93]; the generalisation to polymorphism should be straightforward in the manner of [Lau91] and [HL92]. For all three analyses the question of higher-order *and* polymorphic projection-based analysis remains open.

2 Projections for Termination Analysis

The value denoted by an expression characterises its termination properties, for example, if expression e denotes $(3, \perp)$ then its first component terminates with 3 and its second component does not terminate. (The correspondence between denoted values and operational behaviour will necessarily be informal since no operational semantics will be given.) Any set of values that includes the value of an expression is regarded as *safely*, if not precisely, encoding the termination properties of that expression; we think of this set as a set of *possible* values of the expression. In turn, a set of values is encoded by a projection.

A domain *projection* is a continuous idempotent function that approximates the identity. The projections on a given domain form a complete lattice with greatest element the identity ID and least element the constant bottom function BOT. For example, the functions $FST\ (x, y) = (x, \perp)$ and $SND\ (x, y) = (\perp, y)$ are projections on pairs. We take the set of values encoded by a projection γ to be its image $Im(\gamma)$, which is the same as its set of fixed points. The domain of projections on domain U will be denoted $|\,U\,|$, and α, β, γ, and δ will always denote projections.

Smaller projections have smaller images, that is, $\alpha \sqsubseteq \beta$ implies $Im(\alpha) \subseteq Im(\beta)$, so smaller projections are more informative since they admit fewer possible values. However, in general the exact termination properties of an expression cannot be encoded by a projection for two reasons: $\perp$ is a fixed point of every projection, and for infinite value v there is no projection that has (other than $\perp$) only v as a fixed point. Below we give the solution to the first problem; the second is discussed later.

To allow the possibility of $\perp \in U$ not being a fixed point, the domain U is embedded (by *lift*) in domain $U_{\perp}$, and sets of values from U are encoded by projections on $U_{\perp}$: the set of values encoded by $\gamma \in |\,U_{\perp}\,|$ includes $v \in U$ if *lift* v is a fixed point of γ. Thus if γ maps *lift* $\perp$ to $\perp$ then the possibility of non-termination is excluded. The operations $\cdot_{\perp}$ and $\underline{\cdot}_{\perp}$ on functions are defined as follows. For $f \in U \to V$,

$$
\begin{array}{llll}
f_\perp \in U_\perp & \stackrel{\mathrm{sr}}{\to} V_\perp \,, & \qquad f_{\underline{\perp}} \in U_\perp & \to V_\perp \,, \\
f_\perp \quad \perp & = \perp \,, & \qquad f_{\underline{\perp}} \quad \perp & = \perp \,, \\
f_\perp \quad (\mathit{lift}\ v) & = \mathit{lift}\ (f\ v)\,, & \qquad f_{\underline{\perp}} \quad (\mathit{lift}\ \perp) & = \perp\,, \\
& & \qquad f_{\underline{\perp}} \quad (\mathit{lift}\ v) & = \mathit{lift}\ (f\ v),\ \text{if}\ v \neq \perp \,.
\end{array}
$$

Then $\cdot_\perp$ is ordinary or *lazy* lifting and $\cdot_{\underline{\perp}}$ will be called *eager* lifting; here $\stackrel{\mathrm{sr}}{\to}$ constructs the domain of continuous, strict, bottom-reflecting functions. Every projection on a lifted domain is either of the form $\alpha_\perp$ or $\alpha_{\underline{\perp}}$. Projections of the form $\alpha_{\underline{\perp}}$ specify *definite* termination with some fixed point of α other than $\perp$, while those of the form $\alpha_\perp$ specify *possible* termination with one of the same set of values. Thus $BOT_{\underline{\perp}}$ specifies definite non-termination (since BOT has no fixed points other than $\perp$), and $ID_{\underline{\perp}} \in |U_\perp|$ specifies definite termination with any value in U. Given termination properties specified by α and β, the projection $\alpha \sqcup \beta$ safely characterises their disjunction since $Im(\alpha) \cup Im(\beta) \subseteq Im(\alpha \sqcup \beta)$, and $\alpha \sqcap \beta$ underestimates their conjunction since $Im(\alpha) \cap Im(\beta) \supseteq Im(\alpha \sqcap \beta)$. In general $\alpha_\perp = \alpha_{\underline{\perp}} \sqcup BOT_\perp$ and $\alpha_{\underline{\perp}} = \alpha_\perp \sqcap ID_{\underline{\perp}}$, so for example $ID_\perp = ID_{\underline{\perp}} \sqcup BOT_\perp$ specifies possible termination with any value and so provides no information, while $BOT_{\underline{\perp}} = ID_{\underline{\perp}} \sqcap BOT_\perp$ specifies termination with no value and therefore gives contradictory information. (Note that $BOT_{\underline{\perp}}$ and $ID_\perp$ are BOT and ID respectively by different names.)

If expression f denotes function f and projection δ encodes the termination properties of the argument of f, then any projection γ satisfying $\gamma \circ f \sqsupseteq f \circ \delta$ encodes the termination properties of the application of f to its argument. In the other direction, given constraints on the result specified by γ any δ satisfying the inequality specifies arguments guaranteeing the constraints to be met. Given δ there is always some γ that satisfies the inequality (namely ID), but given γ there may be no such δ (functions can't be forced to give an arbitrary result). We claim that the natural direction of termination analysis is forward: intuitively, we know the termination properties of primitive language constants and we seek to determine the termination properties of expressions built from them, so for our purposes solutions always exist. Hence the central problem of termination analysis is, given f and δ to determine γ such that $\gamma \circ f \sqsupseteq f \circ \delta$, or more generally, to determine a function τ from projections to projections—a *projection transformer*—such that $(\tau\,\delta) \circ f \sqsupseteq f \circ \delta$ for all δ. Such a τ will be called a *forward liveness abstraction* (FLA) of f, and the inequality the *safety condition* (for τ and f). By the previous discussion smaller τ is more informative and greater τ is always safe.

Some further observations will be useful in developing a program analysis technique. First, if termination properties of $f \in U \to V$ are to be determined then it is $f_\perp \in U_\perp \stackrel{\mathrm{sr}}{\to} V_\perp$ that should be analysed since we require projections on lifted domains. Note that $f_\perp$ contains no more information than f; indeed, $U \to V$ is isomorphic to $U_\perp \stackrel{\mathrm{sr}}{\to} V_\perp$ and $f_\perp$ is the image of f under the natural isomorphism. (In fact, it will not be $f_\perp$ that we analyse, but $f_{\perp'} \in U_{\perp'} \stackrel{\mathrm{sr}}{\to} V_{\perp'}$, where $U_{\perp'}$ and $V_{\perp'}$ are isomorphic to $U_\perp$ and $V_\perp$ respectively and $f_{\perp'}$ is the image of $f_\perp$ under the implied isomorphism between $U_\perp \stackrel{\mathrm{sr}}{\to} V_\perp$ and $U_{\perp'} \stackrel{\mathrm{sr}}{\to} V_{\perp'}$.) Second, every FLA of a lifted function is greater than some strict and bottom-reflecting FLA, so will restrict attention to strict and bottom-reflecting projection transformers. Third, if τ_1 and τ_2 are strict and bottom-reflecting

$$
\begin{array}{lll}
\text{T} ::= & \text{A} & [\text{Type Name}] \\
\mid & \text{Int} & [\text{Integer}] \\
\mid & (\text{T}_1, \ldots, \text{T}_n) & [\text{Product}] \\
\mid & c_1 \, \text{T}_1 + \ldots + c_n \, \text{T}_n & [\text{Sum}] \\
\text{D} ::= & \text{A}_1 = \text{T}_1; \; \ldots; \; \text{A}_n = \text{T}_n & [\text{Type Definitions}]
\end{array}
$$

Figure 1: Types and type definitions.

FLAs of f_1 and f_2 respectively then $\tau_1 \circ \tau_2$ is a strict and bottom-reflecting FLA of $f_1 \circ f_2$, so abstract composition is ordinary composition.

Given function definition f x = e the goal is to determine a FLA of $f_\perp$, where f denotes f. We proceed by the following steps. First we define a standard semantics $\mathcal{E}^S$ mapping expressions e and free-variable environments ρ to values $\mathcal{E}^S[\![\, e \,]\!] \, \rho$. Free-variable environments are modelled as tuples (so variable lookup is indexing), then the function f denoted by f is simply $\mathcal{E}^S[\![\, e \,]\!]$. Bearing in mind that it is a FLA of $f_\perp$ that is required we define a 'lifted' semantics $\mathcal{E}^{S_\perp}$ such that $\mathcal{E}^{S_\perp}[\![\, e \,]\!]$ is $(\mathcal{E}^S[\![\, e \,]\!])_\perp$ (up to isomorphism as just discussed). Next we define the termination semantics that for each e yields a FLA of $\mathcal{E}^{S_\perp}[\![\, e \,]\!]$. Finally we extend the analysis technique to first order to allow multiple function definitions and mutual recursion.

3 Language and Standard Semantics

The source language is a simple, strongly typed, monomorphic, non-strict functional language. The grammar for the language of types and type definitions is given in Figure 1.

Nullary product corresponds to the so-called *unit* type. A unary product (T) will always have the same semantics as T. Sums may be unary or multiary. Two types that will be used in examples are Bool, the booleans, and IntList, lists of integers, defined by

```
Bool = true () + false () ,
IntList = nil () + cons (Int, IntList) .
```

The grammar for expressions is given in Figure 2. Addition for integers is provided as typical of arithmetic operations in this setting. A unary tuple (e) will always have the same semantics as e. The (monomorphic) typing of expressions is entirely standard and is omitted.

```
e ::= x                                              [Variable]
    |  n                                              [Numeral]
    |  e₁ + e₂                                        [Integer addition]
    |  (e₁, ... ,eₙ)                                  [Tuple construction]
    |  let (x₁, ... ,xₙ) = e₀ in e₁                   [Tuple decomposition]
    |  cᵢ e                                           [Sum construction]
    |  case e₀ of c₁ x₁ -> e₁ ; ... ;cₙ xₙ -> eₙ     [Sum decomposition]
```

Figure 2: Expressions.

3.1 Expression semantics

Since three different expression semantics will be given, it is convenient to express all of the semantics by a *generic* semantics $\mathcal{E}$ that is parameterised by a set of *defining constants*. A particular instance of $\mathcal{E}$ will be indicated by a superscript, e.g. $\mathcal{E}^S$ for the standard semantics. The corresponding type semantics will have the same superscript, e.g. $\mathcal{T}^S$, as will the defining constants. It is useful to regard the free-variable environment of each expression as having some tuple type $(T_1, \ldots, T_n)$, and environment lookup as indexing (as in a categorical semantics, or De Bruijn indexing); variables are indexed implicitly or explicitly by their index in the free variable environment. Then for all versions of the semantics and expressions e of type T with environment of type $(T_1, \ldots, T_n)$,

$$\mathcal{E}[\![e]\!] \in \mathcal{T}[\![(T_1, \ldots, T_n)]\!] \to \mathcal{T}[\![T]\!].$$

The generic semantics is defined in Figure 3. Recalling that $\rho[\![x_i]\!]$ is short for $sel_i \rho$, environment update is defined by

$$\rho[x_i \mapsto v] = tuple (sel_1 \rho, \ldots, sel_{i-1} \rho, v, sel_{i+1} \rho, \ldots, sel_n \rho).$$

It is convenient to regard Int as being defined by the infinite sum

$$\text{Int} = \ldots + n_{-1} () + n_0 () + n_1 () + \ldots,$$

where in practice we write n_i as short for $n_i ()$, and $i \in \mathbf{Z} = \{\ldots, -1, 0, 1, \ldots\}$. Then the semantics of numerals is given by the semantics of constructors, and for each expression semantics we need only define the constants sel_i, *mkunit*, *plus*, *tuple*, *inc_i*, *outc_i*, and *choose*.

3.2 Standard semantics

The S type and expression semantics defined in Figure 4 are entirely standard. Then $\mathcal{T}^S[\![()]\!]$ is $\mathbf{1} = \{()\}$, the identity for $\times$. Note that products are unlifted;

$$\mathcal{E}[\![\mathbf{x}_i]\!] \ \rho \ = \ \rho[\![\mathbf{x}_i]\!] \ = \ sel_i \ \rho \ ,$$

$$\mathcal{E}[\![\ () \ ]\!] \ \rho \ = \ mkunit \ \rho \ ,$$

$$\mathcal{E}[\![\mathbf{e}_1 + \mathbf{e}_2]\!] \ \rho \ = \ plus \ (\mathcal{E}[\![\mathbf{e}_1]\!] \ \rho, \ \mathcal{E}[\![\mathbf{e}_2]\!] \ \rho) \ ,$$

$$\mathcal{E}[\![\ (\mathbf{e}_1, \ldots, \mathbf{e}_n) \ ]\!] \ \rho \ = \ tuple \ (\mathcal{E}[\![\mathbf{e}_1]\!] \ \rho, \ \ldots, \ \mathcal{E}[\![\mathbf{e}_n]\!] \ \rho) \quad [n \geq 1],$$

$$\mathcal{E}[\![\texttt{let} \ (\mathbf{x}_1, \ldots, \mathbf{x}_n) \ = \ \mathbf{e}_0 \ \texttt{in} \ \mathbf{e}_1]\!] \ \rho$$
$$= \ \mathcal{E}[\![\mathbf{e}_1]\!] \ \rho[\mathbf{x}_i \mapsto sel_i \ (\mathcal{E}[\![\mathbf{e}_0]\!] \ \rho) \ | \ 1 \leq i \leq n] \ ,$$

$$\mathcal{E}[\![\mathbf{c}_i \ \mathbf{e}]\!] \ \rho \ = \ inc_i \ (\mathcal{E}[\![\mathbf{e}]\!] \ \rho) \ ,$$

$$\mathcal{E}[\![\texttt{case} \ \mathbf{e}_0 \ \texttt{of} \ \mathbf{c}_1 \ \mathbf{x}_1 \ \texttt{->} \ \mathbf{e}_1 ; \ \ldots ; \mathbf{c}_n \ \mathbf{x}_n \ \texttt{->} \ \mathbf{e}_n]\!] \ \rho$$
$$= \ choose \ (\mathcal{E}[\![\mathbf{e}_0]\!] \ \rho,$$
$$\mathcal{E}[\![\mathbf{e}_1]\!] \ \rho[\mathbf{x}_1 \mapsto outc_1(\mathcal{E}[\![\mathbf{e}_0]\!] \ \rho)],$$
$$\vdots$$
$$\mathcal{E}[\![\mathbf{e}_n]\!] \ \rho[\mathbf{x}_n \mapsto outc_n(\mathcal{E}[\![\mathbf{e}_0]\!] \ \rho)]) \ ,$$

Figure 3: Generic semantics.

a unary sum-of-products gives a lifted product. Domain $\oplus$ is coalesced sum, so for binary sum

$$U_1 \oplus U_2 = \{\bot\} \cup \{(1, u) \mid u \in U_1, u \neq \bot\} \cup \{(2, u) \mid u \in U_2, u \neq \bot\} \ ,$$

and $in_i \ \bot = \bot$, $in_i \ u = (i, u)$ if $u \neq \bot$, $out_i \ \bot = \bot$, $out_i \ (j, u) = \bot$ for $i \neq j$, and $out_i \ (i, u) = u$. Recursive type definitions give rise to recursive domain specifications which have the usual least fixed point solutions. Here $mkunit^S$ makes no use of its argument; this is the exception rather than the rule.

4 Lifted Semantics

The lifted semantics is designated by $S_\bot$ and is defined in Figure 5. The type semantics is defined such that for all types T that $\mathcal{T}^{S_\bot}[\![\mathrm{T}]\!]$ is isomorphic to $(\mathcal{T}^S[\![\mathrm{T}]\!])_\bot$. Then $\mathcal{T}^{S_\bot}[\![\ () \ ]\!] = \mathbf{1}_\bot$, the identity for $\otimes$. Here the solutions of recursive type definitions are taken to be the least fixed points greater than $\mathbf{1}_\bot$. We define $\cdot_{\bot'}$ on domains and functions such that $\mathcal{T}^{S_\bot}[\![\mathrm{T}]\!] = (\mathcal{T}^S[\![\mathrm{T}]\!])_{\bot'}$, and for $f \in \mathcal{T}^S[\![\mathrm{T}_1]\!] \to \mathcal{T}^S[\![\mathrm{T}_2]\!]$ the function $f_{\bot'} \in \mathcal{T}^{S_\bot}[\![\mathrm{T}_1]\!] \overset{\mathrm{sr}}{\to} \mathcal{T}^{S_\bot}[\![\mathrm{T}_2]\!]$ is the image of $f_\bot$ under the implied isomorphism. The semantic function $\mathcal{E}^{S_\bot}$ is defined so that $\mathcal{E}^{S_\bot}[\![\mathbf{e}]\!] = (\mathcal{E}^S[\![\mathbf{e}]\!])_{\bot'}$ for all e. This is guaranteed if each defining constant $con^{S_\bot}$ is $(con^S)_{\bot'} \circ smash$ (where $smash$ on nullary and unary products

$$\mathcal{T}^S[\![\,\text{Int}\,]\!] \;=\; Int \;=\; \mathbf{Z}_\perp \,,$$

$$\mathcal{T}^S[\![\,(\mathbf{T}_1,\ldots,\mathbf{T}_n)\,]\!] \;=\; \mathcal{T}^S[\![\,\mathbf{T}_1\,]\!] \times \ldots \times \mathcal{T}^S[\![\,\mathbf{T}_n\,]\!]\,,$$

$$\mathcal{T}^S[\![\,\mathsf{c}_1\ \mathbf{T}_1 + \ldots + \mathsf{c}_n\ \mathbf{T}_n\,]\!] \;=\; (\mathcal{T}^S[\![\,\mathbf{T}_1\,]\!])_\perp \oplus \ldots \oplus (\mathcal{T}^S[\![\,\mathbf{T}_n\,]\!])_\perp \,,$$

$$mkunit^S\ \rho \;=\; ()\,,$$

$$plus^S\ (x,y) \;=\; x+y\,,$$

$$tuple^S\ (x_1,\ldots,x_n) \;=\; (x_1,\ldots,x_n)\,,$$

$$sel_i^S\ (x_1,\ldots,x_n) \;=\; x_i\,,$$

$$inc_i^S \;=\; in_i \circ lift\,,$$

$$outc_i^S\ x \;=\; drop \circ out_i\,,$$

$$choose^S\ (\perp,x_1,\ldots,x_n) \;=\; \perp\,,$$
$$choose^S\ ((i,v),x_1,\ldots,x_n) \;=\; x_i\,.$$

Figure 4: Standard type and expression semantics.

is the identity). In more detail, each constant is strict in each element of its argument tuple; Figure 5 defines the constants for non-bottom arguments. Here the environment argument of $mkunit^{S_\perp}$ and $mkint_n^{S_\perp}$ is essential to guarantee strictness of $\mathcal{E}^{S_\perp}$ (note the leaves of an expression are of the form (), n, or x).

Before defining the termination semantics we introduce the constructor notation for projections on the domains corresponding to the lifted semantics of types. Let $Proj_\mathbf{T}$ denote $|\mathcal{T}^{S_\perp}[\![\,\mathbf{T}\,]\!]\,|$. Given sum type $\mathsf{c}_1\ \mathbf{T}_1 + \ldots + \mathsf{c}_n\ \mathbf{T}_n$ with $T_i = \mathcal{T}^{S_\perp}[\![\,\mathbf{T}_i\,]\!]$, $1 \le i \le n$, define

$$C_i \in |(T_i)_\perp| \xrightarrow{\text{sr}} |((T_1)_\perp \oplus \ldots \oplus (T_n)_\perp)_\perp|\,,$$
$$C_i\ \alpha \;=\; (BOT_\perp \oplus \ldots \oplus BOT_\perp \oplus \alpha \oplus BOT_\perp \oplus \ldots \oplus BOT_\perp)_\perp\,.$$

Every eager projection in $Proj_{\mathsf{c}_1\ \mathbf{T}_1 + \ldots + \mathsf{c}_n\ \mathbf{T}_n}$ is of the form $\bigsqcup_{1 \le i \le n} (C_i\ \alpha_i)$. Let () denote $BOT_\perp$ in $Proj_{()}$. Then, for example, the eager projections in $Proj_{\text{Bool}}$ are $TRUE$ ()—the least projection that acts as the identity on $intrue^{S_\perp}$ ($lift$ ()) (the value of true () in the lifted semantics), $FALSE$ (), their lub $ID_\perp$, and their glb $BOT_\perp$. All of the eager projections in $Proj_{\text{Int}}$ are of the form $\bigsqcup_{i \in S} N_i$ for $S \subseteq \mathbf{Z}$, where N_i is shorthand for N_i (), the least projection that acts as the identity on $lift^2\ i$, the value of n_i in the lifted semantics.

$$\mathcal{T}^{S_\perp}[\![\,\mathtt{Int}\,]\!] = Int_\perp\ ,$$

$$\mathcal{T}^{S_\perp}[\![\,(\mathtt{T}_1,\dots,\mathtt{T}_n)\,]\!] = \mathcal{T}^{S_\perp}[\![\,\mathtt{T}_1\,]\!] \otimes \cdots \otimes \mathcal{T}^{S_\perp}[\![\,\mathtt{T}_n\,]\!]\ ,$$

$$\mathcal{T}^{S_\perp}[\![\,\mathtt{c}_1\,\mathtt{T}_1 + \dots + \mathtt{c}_n\,\mathtt{T}_n\,]\!] = (\mathcal{T}^{S_\perp}[\![\,\mathtt{T}_1\,]\!] \oplus \cdots \oplus \mathcal{T}^{S_\perp}[\![\,\mathtt{T}_n\,]\!])_\perp\ ,$$

$$mkunit^{S_\perp}\ \rho = lift^2\ ()\ ,$$

$$plus^{S_\perp}\ (x,y) = lift\ ((drop\ x) + (drop\ y))\ ,$$

$$tuple^{S_\perp}\ (x_1,\dots,x_n) = (x_1,\dots,x_n)\ ,$$

$$sel_i^{S_\perp}\ (x_1,\dots,x_n) = x_i\ ,$$

$$inc_i^{S_\perp} = lift \circ in_i\ ,$$

$$outc_i^{S_\perp}\ x = out_i \circ drop\ ,$$

$$choose^{S_\perp}\ (lift\ \perp,\ x_1,\ \dots,\ x_n) = lift\ \perp\ ,$$
$$choose^{S_\perp}\ (lift\ (i,v),\ x_1,\ \dots,\ x_n) = x_i\ .$$

Figure 5: Lifted type and expression semantics.

5 Termination Semantics

Recall the nominal goal of termination analysis is, given f, to determine as small τ as possible such that $(\tau\ \delta) \circ f_\perp \sqsupseteq f_\perp \circ \delta$ for all δ; in terms of expression semantics, given e, to determine τ such that $(\tau\ \delta) \circ \mathcal{E}^{S_\perp}[\![\,e\,]\!] \sqsupseteq \mathcal{E}^{S_\perp}[\![\,e\,]\!] \circ \delta$ for all δ. We define a termination semantics L satisfying the following correctness condition: if ρ^L is a FLA of g then $\mathcal{E}^L[\![\,e\,]\!]\ \rho^L$ is a FLA of $\mathcal{E}^{S_\perp}[\![\,e\,]\!] \circ g$; in particular, when g is the identity its least FLA is the identity $\lambda\alpha.\alpha$, and $\mathcal{E}^L[\![\,e\,]\!]\ (\lambda\alpha.\alpha)$ is a FLA of $\mathcal{E}^{S_\perp}[\![\,e\,]\!]$. We use the convention that for $e\!:\!\mathtt{T}$ and environments of type $\mathtt{E}$ that $g \in \mathcal{T}^{S_\perp}[\![\,\mathtt{E}_0\,]\!] \overset{\mathrm{sr}}{\to} \mathcal{T}^{S_\perp}[\![\,\mathtt{E}\,]\!]$ for some fixed $\mathtt{E}_0$. Then

$$\mathcal{T}^L[\![\,\mathtt{T}\,]\!] = Proj_{\mathtt{E}_0} \overset{\mathrm{sr}}{\to} Proj_{\mathtt{T}}\ .$$

For $e\!:\!\mathtt{T}$ with environment of type $\mathtt{E}$,

$$\mathcal{E}^L[\![\,e\,]\!] \in \mathcal{T}^L[\![\,\mathtt{E}\,]\!] \to \mathcal{T}^L[\![\,\mathtt{T}\,]\!] = (Proj_{\mathtt{E}_0} \overset{\mathrm{sr}}{\to} Proj_{\mathtt{E}}) \to (Proj_{\mathtt{E}_0} \overset{\mathrm{sr}}{\to} Proj_{\mathtt{T}}).$$

From the correctness condition we may derive correct definitions for the L constants. Let $\langle\!\langle f_1,\dots,f_n \rangle\!\rangle = smash \circ \lambda x.(f_1\ x,\dots,f_n\ x)$. Given τ_i a (least) FLA of f_i for $1 \le i \le n$, a (least) FLA of $\langle\!\langle f_1,\dots,f_n \rangle\!\rangle$ is $\lambda\alpha.(\tau_1\ \alpha \otimes \dots \otimes \tau_n\ \alpha)$. Given that τ_i is a FLA of f_i for $1 \le i \le n$ we need to define each L constant

con^L such that $con^L (\tau_1, \ldots, \tau_n)$ is a FLA of $(con^S)_{\perp'} \circ \langle\!\langle f_1, \ldots, f_n \rangle\!\rangle$, so each L constant is defined by

$$con^L (\tau_1, \ldots, \tau_n) \;=\; | (con^S)_{\perp'} | \circ \underline{\lambda}\alpha.(\tau_1 \; \alpha \otimes \ldots \otimes \tau_n \; \alpha) \;,$$

where $| f |$ denotes the least FLA of f (least FLAs exist for these functions). This is detailed following.

For $v \in V_\perp$, $v \neq \perp$, and v finite, define the *characteristic projection* γ_v to be the least projection that acts as the identity on v. The least FLA of the lifted constant function $\underline{\lambda}x.v \in U_\perp \overset{sr}{\to} V_\perp$ (where is $\underline{\lambda}$ defines strict functions) is $\underline{\lambda}\alpha.\gamma_v$—the projection transformer that maps projections other than $BOT_\perp$ to the projection γ_v that specifies termination with value v. Then the least $\overline{\text{FLA}}$ of $mkunit^{S\perp} = \underline{\lambda}\rho.lift\,()$ is $\underline{\lambda}\alpha.\gamma_{lift\,()} = \underline{\lambda}\alpha.BOT_\perp$, so

$$mkunit^L \; \rho^L = (\underline{\lambda}\alpha.BOT_\perp) \circ \rho^L = \underline{\lambda}\alpha.BOT_\perp \;.$$

Then $\mathcal{E}^L[\![\mathbf{n}_i]\!]\, \rho^L = \underline{\lambda}\alpha.N_i$.

For $tuple^L$ we have

$$tuple^L(\tau_1, \ldots, \tau_n) \;=\; \underline{\lambda}\alpha.(\tau_1 \; \alpha_1 \otimes \ldots \otimes \tau_n \; \alpha_n) \;.$$

Let SEL_i be the least FLA of $sel_i^{S\perp}$, defined by

$$SEL_i \;\in\; | (T_1)_\perp \otimes \ldots \otimes (T_n)_\perp | \overset{sr}{\to} | (T_i)_\perp | \;,$$
$$SEL_i \; \alpha \;=\; \sqcap\{\alpha_i \mid \alpha_1 \otimes \ldots \otimes \alpha_n \sqsupseteq \alpha\} \;.$$

In particular, $SEL_i (\alpha_1 \otimes \ldots \otimes \alpha_n) = \alpha_i$ when $\alpha_j \neq BOT_\perp$ for $1 \leq j \leq n$. Then

$$sel_i^L \; \tau = SEL_i \circ \tau \;.$$

For sums C_i is the least FLA of $inc_i^{S\perp}$, and the least FLA of $out_i^{S\perp}$ is $OUTC_i$, defined

$$OUTC_i \;\in\; | ((T_1)_\perp \oplus \ldots \oplus (T_n)_\perp)_\perp | \overset{sr}{\to} | (T_i)_\perp | \;,$$
$$OUTC_i \; (\alpha_1 \oplus \ldots \oplus \alpha_n)_\perp \;=\; \alpha_i \;.$$

Then

$$inc_i^L \; \tau \;=\; C_i \circ \tau \;,$$

$$outc_i^L \; \tau \;=\; OUTC_i \circ \tau \;.$$

The derivation of $choose^L$ is omitted; the result is

$$choose^L (\tau_0, \ldots, \tau_n) \; \alpha \;=\; \begin{array}{l} case \; (\tau_0 \; \alpha) \; of \\ \qquad \sqcup BOT_\perp \;\to\; BOT_\perp \\ \qquad \sqcup (C_i \; \beta_i) \;\to\; \tau_i \; \alpha \;. \end{array}$$

The value of this *case* function is the lub of all of the branches for which the selector matches the pattern; a selector matches a pattern if the selector is not $BOT_\perp$ (this guarantees strictness in the selector) and the pattern approximates the selector. Intuitively, in a `case` expression termination is determined by the branches corresponding to all patterns that can match, and if the selector may fail to terminate, so may the result.

The function $plus^L$ may be readily derived from $choose^L$ be regarding Int as a sum and + defined in terms of nested **case** expressions, the result is

$$plus^L \ (\tau_1, \tau_2) \ \alpha \ = \ case \ (\tau_1 \ \alpha) \ of$$
$$\sqcup BOT_\perp \ \rightarrow \ BOT_\perp$$
$$\sqcup N_i \quad \rightarrow \ case \ (\tau_2 \ \alpha) \ of$$
$$\sqcup BOT_\perp \ \rightarrow \ BOT_\perp$$
$$\sqcup N_j \quad \rightarrow \ N_{i+j} \ .$$

Example. Let b:Bool, x:Int, and y:Int be variables with corresponding type E of environments equal to (Bool,Int,Int). Let e stand for the expression

```
case b of
    true z -> x
    false z -> y .
```

Let ρ^L be the identity on $\lambda \alpha.\alpha \in Proj_{(Bool,Int,Int)}$. Then $\rho^L[\![b]\!] = SEL_1$, $\rho^L[\![x]\!] = SEL_2$, $\rho^L[\![y]\!] = SEL_3$, so for $\alpha_b \otimes \alpha_x \otimes \alpha_y \neq BOT_\perp$ we have for example $\rho^L[\![b]\!] \ (\alpha_b \otimes \alpha_x \otimes \alpha_y) = \alpha_b$. Then $\mathcal{E}^L[\![e]\!] \ \rho^L \ BOT_\perp = BOT_\perp$; for $\alpha_b \otimes \alpha_x \otimes \alpha_y \neq BOT_\perp$,

$$\mathcal{E}^L[\![e]\!] \ \rho^L \ (\alpha_b \otimes \alpha_x \otimes \alpha_y) \ = \ case \ \alpha_b \ of$$
$$\sqcup BOT_\perp \quad \rightarrow \ BOT_\perp$$
$$\sqcup TRUE \ () \ \rightarrow \ \alpha_x$$
$$\sqcup FALSE \ () \ \rightarrow \ \alpha_y \ .$$

This reveals, for example, that for x and y with termination properties α_x and α_y respectively, if b is certain to terminate with value *true* then the termination property of the whole expression is α_x; if b is certain to not terminate then the whole expression is certain not to terminate; and if b is certain terminate with some value then the termination property of the whole expression includes the possibilities for both x and y.

Example. Let x:Int be a variable and environments have type Int. The expression to be analysed is x + 1. Let ρ^L be the identity function $\lambda \alpha.\alpha$, the least FLA of the identity, so that $\rho^L[\![x]\!] = \lambda \alpha.\alpha$. Let the projection $OK_S \in |\mathcal{T}^{S_\perp}[\![Int]\!]|$ for $S \subseteq \mathbf{Z}$ be defined by $OK_S = \sqcup_{i \in S}(N_i \ ())$, so OK_S specifies termination with some value in S (lifted). Then $\mathcal{E}^L[\![x + 1]\!] \ \rho^L$ maps OK_S to $OK_{\{i+1 \ | \ i \in S\}}$; in particular it maps N_i to N_{i+1} for all $i \in \mathbf{Z}$, $BOT_\perp$ to $BOT_\perp$, $ID_\perp$ (which is $OK_\mathbf{Z}$) to $ID_\perp$, and $ID_\perp$ to $ID_\perp$.

Example. The expression to be analysed is cons (1, cons (2, nil ())). For environments of any type the L value of the expression maps $BOT_\perp$ to $BOT_\perp$ and all other projections to $CONS \ (N_1 \otimes CONS \ (N_2 \otimes NIL \ ()))$, giving perfect information.

6 First-order Analysis

The expression language is augmented with the expression form f e, where f is a first-order function symbol. The evaluation function takes a function-environment argument typically denoted by ϕ. The standard first-order semantics is

$$\mathcal{E}^S_\phi[\![\,\mathbf{f}\ \mathbf{e}\,]\!]\,\rho = \phi[\![\,\mathbf{f}\,]\!]\,(\mathcal{E}^S_\phi[\![\,\mathbf{e}\,]\!]\,\rho)\;.$$

The $S_\perp$ version is the same, with $S_\perp$ replacing S. The non-standard value of a function shall be a FLA of its value in the lifted semantics. Then the required relation between the $S_\perp$ and L semantics is as follows: for function environments $\phi^{S_\perp}$ and ϕ^L related, that is, $\phi^L[\![\,\mathbf{f}\,]\!]$ a FLA of $\phi^{S_\perp}[\![\,\mathbf{f}\,]\!]$ for each $\mathbf{f}$, the functions $\mathcal{E}^{S_\perp}_{\phi^{S_\perp}}[\![\,\mathbf{e}\,]\!]$ and $\mathcal{E}^L_{\phi^L}[\![\,\mathbf{e}\,]\!]$ must be related as before. This is satisfied when abstract function application is composition, that is,

$$\mathcal{E}^L_\phi[\![\,\mathbf{f}\ \mathbf{e}\,]\!]\,\rho = \phi[\![\,\mathbf{f}\,]\!]\circ(\mathcal{E}^L_\phi[\![\,\mathbf{e}\,]\!]\,\rho)\;.$$

Given expression $\mathbf{e}:\mathbf{T}$ with free variables (a subset of) $\mathbf{x}_i:\mathbf{E}_i$ for $1\le i\le n$, function definition $\mathbf{f}\ (\mathbf{x}_1,\ldots,\mathbf{x}_n) = \mathbf{e}$, and function environment ϕ^S we take $\mathbf{f}$ to denote the function $\mathcal{E}^S_{\phi^S}[\![\,\mathbf{e}\,]\!]$ from values in $\mathcal{T}^S[\![\,(\mathbf{E}_1,\ldots,\mathbf{E}_n)\,]\!]$ to values in $\mathcal{T}^S[\![\,\mathbf{T}\,]\!]$, and similarly for the $S_\perp$ semantics. In the L semantics, given ϕ^L, we take $\mathbf{f}$ to denote $\mathcal{E}^L_{\phi^L}[\![\,\mathbf{e}\,]\!]\,(\lambda\alpha.\alpha)$, a FLA of the value $\mathcal{E}^{S_\perp}_{\phi^{S_\perp}}[\![\,\mathbf{e}\,]\!]$ of $\mathbf{f}$ in the lifted semantics. (Another approach would be to take $\mathbf{f}$ to denote $\mathcal{E}^L_{\phi^L}[\![\,\mathbf{e}\,]\!]$, then abstract application would be ordinary application, and this value applied to $\lambda\alpha.\alpha$ would yield a FLA of the value of $\mathbf{f}$ in the lifted semantics. This is arguably the more natural approach, but the abstract values are more complex.)

Generalising, a set of mutually recursive first-order function definitions has the form

$$\mathbf{f}_i\ :\ (\mathbf{T}_{i,1},\ldots,\mathbf{T}_{i,a_i})\ \mathord{\text{->}}\ \mathbf{T}_i$$
$$\mathbf{f}_i\ (\mathbf{x}_{i,1},\ldots,\mathbf{x}_{i,a_i})\ =\ \mathbf{e}_i$$

for $1\le i\le n$ where each $\mathbf{e}_i$ is an expression with free variables (a subset of) $\{\mathbf{x}_{i,1},\ldots,\mathbf{x}_{i,a_i}\}$, where $\mathbf{x}_{i,j}:\mathbf{E}_{i,j}$. In each of the semantics such a set of definitions denotes a function environment. In the standard semantics it has the usual least fixed point semantics:

$$\mathit{fix}\,(\lambda\phi\,.\,[\mathbf{f}_i\mapsto\mathcal{E}^S[\![\,\mathbf{e}_i\,]\!]\,\phi\mid 1\le i\le n])\;.$$

The lifted version is the same, with $S_\perp$ replacing S. For a given set of function definitions, let $\phi^{S_\perp}_i$ be the ith approximation to the corresponding function environment in the lifted semantics. Now the least FLA of the least lifted function $\lambda x.\mathit{lift}\ x$ is $\lambda\alpha.BOT_\perp$, so let

$$F^L\ =\ \lambda\phi\,.\,[\mathbf{f}_i\mapsto\mathcal{E}^L_\phi[\![\,\mathbf{e}_i\,]\!](\lambda\alpha.\alpha)\mid 1\le i\le n])\;,$$

$$\phi^L_0\ =\ [\mathbf{f}_i\mapsto\lambda\alpha.BOT_\perp\mid 1\le i\le n]\;,$$

$$\phi^L_i\ =\ (F^L)^i\,\phi^L_0,\ i\ge 0\;.$$

By induction, $\phi^L_i[\![\,\mathbf{f}\,]\!]$ is a FLA of $\phi^{S_\perp}_i[\![\,\mathbf{f}\,]\!]$ for all i and $\mathbf{f}$. Further, the safety condition $(\tau\,\delta)\circ f\sqsupseteq f\circ\delta$ is inclusive (chain complete) in both τ and f. However, the sequence $\{\phi^L_0,\phi^L_1,\phi^L_2,\ldots\}$ is not generally increasing (or decreasing) and therefore does not have a limit. An example makes this clear.

First we introduce some shorthand for defining projections on lists. Let

$$FIN\ \alpha\ =\ \mu\gamma.NIL\ ()\sqcup CONS\ (\alpha\otimes\gamma)\ ,$$

$$INF\ \alpha\ =\ \mu\gamma.CONS\ (\alpha\otimes(BOT_\perp\sqcup\gamma))\ ,$$

$$FINF\ \alpha\ =\ \mu\gamma.NIL\ ()\sqcup CONS\ (\alpha\otimes(BOT_\perp\sqcup\gamma))\ .$$

Then $FIN\ BOT_\perp = INF\ BOT_\perp = BOT_\perp$, and $FINF\ BOT_\perp = NIL\ ()$ specifying termination with the value of nil (). For $\alpha \neq BOT_\perp$, projection $FIN\ \alpha$ specifies termination of the spine of a finite list with termination properties α for each list element. Projection $INF\ \alpha$ specifies termination with a cons node, that every tail diverges or terminates with a cons cell, and property α for every head. Those of the form $FINF\ \alpha$ specify termination in evaluation to WHNF, and property α for every head. Projection $FINF\ ID_\perp$ encodes head termination: it specifies that if evaluation of any tail terminates with a cons node then the head of the cons node terminates.

Let the function that returns the infinite list of ones be defined by

```
ones : () -> IntList
ones () = cons (1, ones ()) .
```

Let $ones_i^L$ denote the ith approximation of the value of ones in the L semantics. Then

$$ones_0^L\ =\ \lambda\alpha.BOT_\perp\ ,$$

$$ones_1^L\ =\ \lambda\alpha.CONS\ (N_1\otimes BOT_\perp)\ ,$$

$$ones_2^L\ =\ \lambda\alpha.CONS\ (N_1\otimes CONS\ (N_1\otimes BOT_\perp))\ ,$$

and generally, $ones_i^L = \lambda\alpha.(\lambda\beta.CONS\ (N_1\otimes\beta))^i\ BOT_\perp$ for $i \geq 0$. This sequence is neither increasing nor decreasing; every element is incomparable to every other.

Some observations motivate a solution. First, overestimation of FLAs is safe. Second, the projection transformers form a complete lattice, so lubs exist for every set. Last, when lubs exist any sequence $\{a_0, a_1, a_2, \ldots\}$ gives rise to an increasing sequence $\{\sqcup_{0\leq i\leq j}\ a_i\ |\ j \geq 0\}$ such that the limit of the second is the lub of the elements of the first. If we understand $\sqcup$ to denote this limit then taking $\phi^L = \sqcup_{i\geq 0}\ \phi_i^L$ is well defined and safe. We can overestimate this sequence by applying a *widening operator* [CC91] to the defining functional F^L. Define w by

$$w\ F\ x\ =\ x\sqcup(F\ x)\ .$$

Then for any function F we have that $w\ F\ x \sqsupseteq x$, so $\{(w\ F)^i\ x\ |\ i \geq 0\}$ is increasing, and therefore has limit, for all x. Since $w\ F \sqsupseteq F$ we may safely define the function environment ϕ^L to be $\sqcup_{i\geq 0}\ (w\ F^L)^i\ \phi_0^L$. Then

$$ones^L\ =\ \lambda\alpha.BOT_\perp \sqcup FINF\ N_1.$$

This tells us that the result of ones has the head-termination property, but not that any of the spine terminates. We can improve the result by *narrowing* [CC91]. Since ϕ^L is safe then so is $(F^L)^i\ \phi^L$ for all i. Since ϕ^L is a fixed point of $w\ F^L$ it must be that $\{(F^L)^i\ \phi^L\ |\ i \geq 0\}$ is decreasing. Now let $phi^L_{-i} = (F^L)^i\ \phi^L$ for all i. Then

$$ones^L_{-1}\ =\ \underline{\lambda}\alpha.FINF\ N_1\ ,$$
$$ones^L_{-2}\ =\ \underline{\lambda}\alpha.CONS\ (N_1 \otimes FINF\ N_1)\ ,$$
$$ones^L_{-3}\ =\ \underline{\lambda}\alpha.CONS\ (N_1 \otimes CONS\ (N_1 \otimes FINF\ N_1))\ ,$$

and so on. Hence we may determine that any prefix of `ones` () terminates. Note that the glb of this sequence is $\underline{\lambda}\alpha.BOT_\perp$ which is *not* a FLA of $ones^{S_\perp}$. Intuitively this is not unreasonable; it is not clear what it means to say that an infinite reduction terminates. However, when working in finite (abstract) domains of projections such descending sequences are guaranteed to reach a fixed point in a finite number of steps.

We consider one more example before abstraction to finite domains. Let

```
zero : Int -> Int
zero x = case (x = 0) of
              true z -> 0
              false z -> zero (x + 1) .
```

Skipping the details, the ith improved approximation $zero^L_{-i}$ shows that `zero` terminates with value 0 for arguments with values 0 through $-i$, may terminate with value 0 for arguments less than $-i$, and definitely fails to terminate for positive arguments, for $i \geq 0$. Thus it is possible to determine that `zero` terminates with any given non-positive argument, but not that it terminates for all non-positive arguments.

6.1   Finite abstraction

We now introduce a finite abstract projection domains $FProj_{Int}$ for `Int` and $FProj_{IntList}$ for `IntList`. For `Int` we choose to differentiate lifting but not particular summands, so $FProj_{Int}$ is $\{BOT_\perp, BOT_\perp, ID_\perp, ID_\perp\}$. We take $FProj_{IntList}$ to be projections of the form $FIN\ \alpha$, $INF\ \alpha$, and $FINF\ \alpha$ for α in $FProj_{Int}$, and their lazy counterparts. For every projection γ on $Proj_{Int}$ (and similarly for $Proj_{IntList}$) there is a least projection $\gamma^\#$ in $FProj_{Int}$ greater than γ, so $\gamma^\#$ is a safe abstraction of γ. Abstraction of projection transformers is induced pointwise, and this abstraction induces a safe abstraction of the termination semantics.

Repeating the last two examples in the abstract domains gives

$$ones^L\ =\ \underline{\lambda}\alpha.FINF\ STR\ ,$$

showing that `ones` () has the head-termination property and also that it terminates in evaluation to WHNF. For `zero` we have

$$zero^L\ BOT_\perp = BOT_\perp\ ,$$
$$zero^L\ ID_\perp\ \ = ID_\perp\ ,$$
$$zero^L\ ID_\perp\ \ = ID_\perp\ .$$

showing that `zero` fails to terminate if its argument fails to terminate, that is, that `zero` is strict.

Example. Define the identity on lists by

```
listid : IntList -> IntList
listid xs = case xs of
                nil u  -> nil ()
                cons p -> let (y,ys) = p in
                              cons (y, listid ys) .
```

Then

$$
\begin{aligned}
listid^F \alpha \ = \ case \ \alpha \ of \\
\sqcup BOT_\perp \ &\to\ BOT_\perp \\
\sqcup(FIN \ \alpha) \ &\to\ FINF \ \alpha \\
\sqcup(INF \ \alpha) \ &\to\ INF \ \alpha \ .
\end{aligned}
$$

Head termination information is preserved but spine termination is not.

Next we consider examples using numbers and lists where recursion is not involved. Let

```
duphead : (Int,IntList) -> IntList
duphead xs = case xs of
                 nil u -> nil ()
                 cons p -> let (y,ys) = p in
                               cons (y, cons (y, ys)) .
```

Then $duphead^L$ is the identity. Let

```
fa : () -> IntList
fa () = cons (1, fb ())

fb : () -> IntList
fb () = cons (1, fc ())

fc : () -> IntList
fc () = nil () .
```

Then all of the abstract functions are strict, fa^L and fb^L map $BOT_\perp$ to $FIN \ STR$, and fc maps $BOT_\perp$ to NIL (), all of which are optimal. In a similar vein, let

```
ga : Int -> Int
ga x = 1 + gb x

gb : Int -> Int
gb x = 2 + gc x

gc : Int -> Int
gc x = 3 .
```

The abstract functions ga^L and gb^L are the identity, and gc^L maps $BOT_\perp$ to $BOT_\perp$ and all other projections to STR.

6.2 Discussion

We make some informal observations. Working in the full projection domains, analysis will reveal termination of a function only when it occurs in a bounded number of steps (in addition to how much evaluation might be required to evaluate the arguments). Thus we can determine that the entire stucture of fa (), fb (), and fc () terminates, that any finite prefix of ones () terminates, that ga, gb, and gc terminate for terminating arguments, and that zero terminates for any given non-positive argument, but not that zero terminates for all non-positive arguments—the latter requires an inductive proof. In the finite projection domains this is, very roughly, further restricted to values that are not built up using recursion and do not depend on the particular values of integers. We believe that for an implementation this is exactly the information we would want to use: we do not want early evaluation of the entire spine of a list knowing only that it is finite, or to eagerly evaluate zero -10000000; the very limitations of the technique obviate the need for operation count analysis. It appears that the worst case number of operations required for any evaluation enabled by the analysis is exponential in the length of a program, for example if we define f_i x to be f_{i-1} x $+$ f_{i-1} x for $1 \leq i \leq n$, and f_0 x = 0 analysis will reveal that all of the functions terminate unconditionally, but this sort of program seems unlikely.

The method of finding fixed points in finite domains seems overly complex. We conjecture that $\{(F^L)^i \, \phi_0^L \mid i \geq 0\}$ always reaches a fixed point, that is, does not cycle. To see this suppose that for the purpose of comparing the results of successive iterations that the relative ordering of eager and lazy projections in the result domains of projection transformers is reversed, then the results of successive iterations will be increasing. Intuitively, better approximations of functions fail to terminate with a decreasing subset of the argument domain and have increasing subset of the result domain as possible results.

7 Conclusion

Projection-based termination analysis appears to yield potentially useful information for compile-time optimisation, for example, the head-termination property that cannot be captured in the BHA framework.

As mentioned, generalisation to higher-order is straightforward and generalisation to polymorphism should be straightforward. For essentially the same reasons as for projection-based binding-time and strictness analyses the question of effective projection-based analysis that is both higher-order *and* polymorphic remains open.

This abstract interpretation technique, like many others, suffers from two uncertainties: whether the rich information provided is genuinely exploitable, and whether the problem of finding fixed points (in the higher-order analysis) is tractable. Though the answer to the second question is currently negative, promising advances are begin made in this area, most notably using *frontiers* [Hun89] and *concrete data structures* [Fer92] to represent abstract functions only at the values at which they are actually required, and solving the recursive equations symbolically [Sew94].

References

[AH87]   S. Abramsky and C. Hankin. An introduction to abstract interpreta-
          tion. Chapter 1 of *Abstract Interpretation of Declarative Languages.*
          S. Abramsky and C. Hankin, eds. Ellis-Horwood, 1987.

[CC91]   P. Cousot and R. Cousot. Comparing the Galois connection and
          widening/narrowing approaches to abstract interpretation (prelim-
          inary draft). LIX, Ecole Polytechnique, 91128 Palaiseau Cedex,
          France, May 15, 1991.

[Dav93]   K. Davis. Higher-order Binding-time Analysis. *Proceedings of the
          1993 ACM on Partial Evaluation and Semantics-Based Program Ma-
          nipulation (PEPM '93).*

[DW91]   K. Davis and P. Wadler. Strictness analysis in 4D. *Functional Pro-
          gramming: Proceedings of the 1990 Glasgow Workshop, 13-15 August
          1990, Ullapool, Scotland.* Simon L. Peyton Jones *et al.*, eds. Springer
          Workshops in Computing. Springer-Verlag, 1991.

[DW90]   K. Davis and P. Wadler. Strictness analysis: Proved and improved.
          *Functional Programming: Proceedings of the 1989 Glasgow Work-
          shop, 21-23 August 1989, Fraserburgh, Scotland.* K. Davis and J.
          Hughes, eds. Springer Workshops in Computing. Springer-Verlag,
          1990.

[Fer92]   A. Ferguson. Concrete Data Structures. *Functional Programming:
          Proceedings of the 1992 Glasgow Workshop, 6-8 July 1992, Ayr,
          Scotland.* Springer Workshops in Computing, Springer-Verlag, 1992.

[Har91]   P.H. Hartel. On the benefits of different analyses in the compilation
          of lazy functional languages. *3rd Informal International Workshop on
          the Parallel Implementation of Functional Languages,* Southampton,
          1991.

[HL92]   R.J.M. Hughes and J. Launchbury. Projections for polymorphic first-
          order strictness analysis. *Math. Struct. in Comp. Science,* vol. 2, pp.
          301-326, CUP, 1992.

[Hun89]   S. Hunt. Frontiers and open sets in abstract interpretation. *Func-
          tional Programming and Computer Architecture.* (Imperial College,
          London, September 1989.) ACM, Addison-Wesley Publishing, Read-
          ing, MA, U.S.A. 1989.

[Lau91]   J. Launchbury. *Projection Factorisations in Partial Evaluation.*
          Ph.D. Thesis, Glasgow University, Nov 89. Distinguished Disserta-
          tion in Computer Science, Vol 1, CUP, 1991.

[Myc81]   A. Mycroft. *Abstract Interpretation and Optimising Transformations
          for Applicative Programs.* Ph.D. thesis, University of Edinburgh,
          1981.

[Sew94]   J. Seward. Solving recursive domain equations by term rewriting. *Functional Program-ming: Proceedings of the 1993 Glasgow Workshop, 5-7 July 1993, Ayr, Scotland.* Springer Workshops in Computing. Springer-Verlag, 1994 (this volume).

[WH87]   P. Wadler and J. Hughes. Projections for Strictness Analysis. *Proceedings of Functional Programming Languages and Computer Architecture.* LNCS 274. Springer-Verlag, 1987.

[You89]   J. Young. *The Theory and Practice of Semantic Program Analysis for Higher-Order Functional Programming Languages*, Ph.D. thesis, Research report YALEU/DCS/RR-669, Yale University, 1989.

A framework for optimising abstract data types *

Cordelia V. Hall

Computing Science Dept, Glasgow University

Glasgow, Scotland

Abstract

Hindley-Milner type inference and partial evaluation are all that is needed
to optimise lists, yielding considerable improvements in space and time
consumption for some interesting programs. This framework is applicable
to many abstract data types and their optimised representations, such as
lists and parallel implementations of bags, or arrays and quadtrees.

1 Introduction

Two trends have been developing in functional programming language research.
First, compilers are supporting optimisations of data types, such as unboxed
types [PJnLn91] and parallel bags [KuGl93]. Second, functional programmers
are increasingly writing code in a style that treats data types as if they were
abstract. They tend to create a library of higher order functions over a particular data type and then use them to access the type. Abstract data types
offer opportunities for optimisation because the representation of the type can
be optimised without affecting the program, allowing the programmer to use
operations on it and improve performance. At the same time, the original type
is often required by some part of the program, and the programmer is left to
figure out which to use where.

This paper presents a general framework in which good functional style automatically supports the efficient implementation of data types. It has been
implemented in the Glasgow Haskell [HdEtAl92] compiler specifically to introduce an optimised list representation, and this has been shown to cut execution
time in half on a Sun SPARCstation-1 for a substantial program. Recent tests
show that it improves performance by more than a factor of 4 on the GRIP
parallel processor [PJ86] for short tests, however more experiments will be necessary before we can assert that this speedup holds in general. Good results
have been reported elsewhere for a related list representation in ML on a Sun
SPARCstation-2 [ShReAp93].

Given the appropriate pragmas, this framework is applicable to many data
types and their optimised representations, such as lists and parallel implementations of bags [KuGl93], or arrays and quadtrees.

The framework provided accepts an abstract data type definition, including both unoptimised and optimised types, and operations on both types. It
automatically infers where optimised versions can be used in the program, first
using Hindley-Milner type inference and then partial evaluation.

---

*This work was supported by the GRASP Project.

1.1   Outline of paper

Much of the work given here is described in more detail elsewhere, including proofs of safety and termination [Ha94]. First, we give the main idea of the paper, and then a section in which we specify the abstract data type, followed by the type inference rules and partial evaluation algorithm.

2   The Idea

Compilers often perform an optimisation called 'loop unrolling', in which the loop body is substituted once for its call. This is applicable when a loop test is expensive and the body of the loop is small. It trades code size for the time and space needed to perform the loop test.

The same technique can apply in a functional language. Here is an unrolled version of map.

```
map' f (x1:x2:xs)
  = f x1 : f x2 : map' f xs
map' f (x1:xs)
  = f x1 : map' f xs
map' f []
  = []
```

So far, we have significantly reduced the number of recursive calls. Now, we'll compress the list type as follows:

```
data List2 a
  = Cons2 a a (List2 a)
  | Cons1 a
  | Nil
```

This new list type contains a "hydra" constructor Cons2, a cons-cell with more than one head. We can make map more efficient by using List2, building half the number of *cons* cells by coalescing two tails into one.

```
map2 :: (a -> b) -> List2 a -> List2 b
map2 f (Cons2 x1 x2 xs)
  = Cons2 (f x1) (f x2) (map2 f xs)
map2 f (Cons1 x1)
  = Cons1 (f x1)
map2 f Nil
  = Nil
```

Notice that a lazy language requires some strictness analysis to determine whether this transformation is valid.

This version is significantly more efficient than the original, but it isn't practical to expect the programmer to do it. Instead, we develop an analysis that allows it to be done at compile time.

We cannot use the compressed version of lists everywhere, as some functions may perform extra work. For example, the *append* function (++) cannot take an optimised list as its second argument. Suppose that its call was

```
(Cons2 1 2 (Cons1 3)) ++ (Cons2 4 5 Nil)
```

The result would be

```
(Cons2 1 2 (Cons2 3 4 (Cons1 5 Nil)))
```

which means that the second argument had to be recopied, requiring more work than was done by the unoptimised version. Restricting the second argument to be a simple list forces the result of ++ to be unoptimised as well. We can still have a choice over whether the first argument is an optimised list or not, as this list has to be traversed and rebuilt anyway.

This demonstrates that we have to be able to decide where we can use compressed lists and where we cannot. The goal is to select the most optimised version available, then settle for something worse when necessary. There is a reasonable degree of flexibility for, as we have seen, there are two possible versions of ++ we could choose between given the context. In the case of map, there are four versions; the types of these versions are given below.

```
append1 :: [a]      -> [a] -> [a]
append2 :: List2 a -> [a] -> [a]

map1 :: (a -> b) -> [a]      -> List2 b
map2 :: (a -> b) -> List2 a -> [b]
map3 :: (a -> b) -> List2 a -> List2 b
map4 :: (a -> b) -> [a]      -> [b]
```

Notice that we never have to coerce one type to another, which would be inefficient. The optimised and unoptimised types are completely separate.

How should we decide which version of lists to use in any particular situation? This is the problem posed and solved by the paper.

2.1 Using type inference to distinguish between forms of the type

Before the analysis, we *extend* data-type definitions to include a *selector field*. For example, the usual list type, defined as

```
data List a = Nil
            | Cons a (List a)
```

is extended as follows:

```
data List t a = Nil t
              | Cons t a (List t a)
```

The extra variable is only relevant to the analysis. The function map can take and produce any form of list, so we give it the type:

```
map :: (a->b) -> List t a -> List u b
```

where t and u are unconstrained selector fields. However, we give append the type:

```
append :: List t a -> List U a
              -> List U b
```

where U (unoptimised, or simple) is some predefined type known to the compiler. This indicates that the first argument to ++ may be either a simple list or a compressed list, but both its second argument and its result must be simple lists.

Now, unification will instantiate this selector field if either a producer or consumer of a given list requires it to be simple, otherwise it will remain polymorphic. If it remains polymorphic, then both producer and all consumers can handle compressed lists, so the compiler is at liberty to substitute optimised versions of the functions.

For example, suppose we have the expression

```
map f (xs ++ ys)
```

When this is typechecked, the argument type of map f will be unified with the type of (xs ++ ys). This type, and the type of ys, is constrained to be simple by our type for ++, and this in turn constrains the argument type of map. However, the type of xs is unconstrained, as is the *result* of map. Thus these may be either simple or optimised, depending upon the surrounding context of the entire expression.

This small example shows that constraints flow both forwards and backwards through the program, and this is exactly what unification is designed to handle. Propagation of global context information is described in more detail in [Ha94].

3   The abstract data type specification

The abstract data type implementation provides

- The optimised and unoptimised data type representations,

- Operations, including versions using the optimised type,

- A set of the unoptimised type's constructors, Σ_{adt},

- A type assignment, $\Delta_{adt} \in \texttt{Openv}$, mapping an operation name to the type of the 'best' operation version,

- A function $\Psi_{adt} \in \texttt{Adtf}$ mapping a version name and a list of monomorphic types to another, possibly different, version name.

The first two depend on the data type. For example, in the case of the list representation optimisation described in the previous section, the compiler writer determines the best possible version for each operation after deciding how to avoid unnecessary work.

The set of constructors will be used to handle the unoptimised type if it appears in the program. The other two are defined below.

3.1 Operation versions and their types

The transformation uses a special data type which does not appear in the source or target code. We'll call this the analysis type.

We can think of the analysis type as being a combination of both the unoptimised and optimised types, containing all of the constructors of each. It also contains an extra type argument, which we'll call the 'selector'. The type inference chooses the data type needed by instantiating the selector. If the selector is instantiated by the type U, then the type is unoptimised, otherwise it is optimised. For example, $T \ U \ a_1 \ldots a_n$ is the unoptimised data type, while $T \ t \ a_1 \ldots a_n$ is optimised.

In practice, the optimised type constructors will appear only in the operation definitions, so there is no need to include its constructors while analysing the program. However, the unoptimised type constructors may appear in the program itself, both in patterns and expressions. When this occurs, the type inference rules instantiate the constructor's type with U, forcing it to be unoptimised.

We write a data type declaration as

$$\texttt{data } T \ a_1 \ldots a_n \ = \ K_1 \ t_{11} \ldots t_{1k1} \mid \ldots \mid K_m \ t_{m1} \ldots t_{mkm}$$

where the type's name is T, its bound type variables are a_1 to a_n, and its constructors K_1 to K_m.

The new type is written as

$$\texttt{data } T \ \texttt{sel} \ a_1 \ldots a_n \ = \ K_1 \ \texttt{sel} \ t_{11} \ldots t_{1k1} \mid \ldots \mid K_m \ \texttt{sel} \ t_{m1} \ldots t_{mkm}$$

3.1.1 The lattice of version types

For each operation, the abstract data type must provide an 'optimal' version using the optimised data type wherever possible. Given the type of an optimal version, the abstract data type implementation must supply all versions with types below that type in the complete finite lattice induced by the Hindley Milner polymorphic type ordering on the selector argument of the analysis type. If it isn't possible to use the 'best' version because not all versions below it exist, then a poorer one must be given instead.

For example, the optimal version of **map** over lists has the type

```
map_O_O :: (a -> b) -> T o1 a -> T o2 b
```

The abstract data type for lists must also supply the functions

```
map_U_O :: (a -> b) -> T U a   -> T o2 b
map_O_U :: (a -> b) -> T o1 a  -> T U b
map_U_U :: (a -> b) -> T U a   -> T U b
```

The reason for this is that type inference may cause an instance of the optimal version for an operation to have a type that is instantiated in any one of these ways, in which case there must be a version available.

3.2 Selecting the operation versions

During partial evaluation, the appropriate versions of the abstract data type operations are selected. Each instance of the optimal version for an operation is labelled with the monomorphic types instantiating the version's polymorphic type.

For example, the type of the most optimised version of `map` is

```
(a -> b) -> T o1 a -> T o2 b
```

If an instance of `map` is labelled with `[Int, Bool, U, t]`, then the actual monomorphic type of this instance of `map` is

```
(Int -> Bool) -> T U Int -> T t Bool
```

Given the polymorphic type of the optimal version,

$$\forall \, \alpha_1 \ldots \alpha_n . \tau$$

and the label

$$\tau_1 \ldots \tau_n$$

we define a substitution

$$s \ = \ (\alpha_1, \tau_1), \ldots, (\alpha_n, \tau_n)$$

which will specialise the polymorphic type. However, the idea is to instantiate only those type variables corresponding to the selector arguments in the polymorphic type of the instance, since these are what determine the version required. So from s, we define another substitution that maps all type variables to themselves, unless the variable is instantiated by `U`.

$$s' \ = \ \{(\alpha, \alpha) \mid (\alpha, \tau) \in s, \tau \neq \text{U}\} \ \cup \ \{(\alpha, \text{U}) \mid (\alpha, \tau) \in s, \tau = \text{U}\}$$

To find the correct version for an operation, the function Ψ_{adt} applies s' to the type of the optimal version, then selects the version with this new type.

For example, suppose that `[Int, Bool, U, t]` is an instantiation for the operation `map`. The substitution created is `[(a,a),(b,b),(o1,U),(o2,o2)]`. When applied to `map`'s optimal version type, it produces the type

```
(a -> b) -> T U a -> T o2 b
```

and so the version selected is `map_U_O`.

3.2.1 Incorporating pragmas and the results of other analyses

It may be impossible to use the optimised data type in general because either the compiler has to perform an analysis, such as strictness analysis, to use it safely, or the programmer must provide some information with a pragma, such as the commutativity and associativity of a function passed to `foldr`. It is easy to extend this framework with a function f that maps an annotation paired

```
e   ::= v                                          variables
    |   con e₁ ...eₙ,              n ≥ 0           constructor applications
    |   e₁ e₂                                      application
    |   λ v e                                      lambda binding
    |   case e (p₁,e₁) ... (pₙ,eₙ),  n ≥ 1         case analysis
    |   let v e₁ e₂                                let binding



p   ::= v                                          variable patterns
    |   con p₁ ...pₙ,             n ≥ 0            constructor patterns
```

Figure 1: The core language

with an operation type to another operation type, by replacing Δ_{adt} with Δ'_{adt}, defined as

$$\Delta'_{adt} \ a \ t \ = \ f \ a \ (\Delta_{adt} \ t)$$

For example, if the program is written in a lazy functional language and an instance of **map** does not appear in a context that is at least tail strict, then f must take the optimal type for **map** and the annotation giving the context of that instance of **map**, and return the type

```
(a -> b) -> T U a -> T U b
```

4   The type inference rules

The analysis, which uses type inference, takes place after the program has been type checked, desugared, and after any other analysis, such as strictness analysis, that supports it.

4.1   Definitions of the translation source and target languages

The core language, which appears in Figure 1, is the source and target language of the translation. It is a standard intermediate language for functional compilers.

The type inference translates the program into a restricted form of the second order polymorphic lambda calculus, given by Figure 2. It contains two additional forms, one that applies an expression to types, and one that binds type variables.

$$
\begin{array}{llll}
\tau & ::= & \alpha & \text{type variables} \\
& | & \chi\ \tau_1 \ldots \tau_n, & n \geq 0 \quad \text{constructor types} \\
& | & \tau_1 \rightarrow \tau_2 & \text{function types} \\
\\
\sigma & ::= & \forall\ \alpha_1 \ldots \alpha_n.\tau, & n \geq 0 \quad \text{polymorphic types} \\
\end{array}
$$

$$
\begin{array}{llll}
e & ::= & v & \text{variables} \\
& | & \text{con}\ e_1 \ldots e_n & n \geq 0 \quad \text{constructor application} \\
& | & e_1\ e_2 & \text{application} \\
& | & e\ \tau_1 \ldots \tau_n, & n \geq 0 \quad \text{type application} \\
& | & \Lambda\ \alpha_1 \ldots \alpha_n.\ e, & n \geq 0 \quad \text{type lambda binding} \\
& | & \lambda\ v\ e & \text{lambda binding} \\
& | & \text{case}\ e\ (p_1, e_1) \ldots (p_n, e_n), & n \geq 1 \quad \text{case analysis} \\
& | & \text{let}\ v\ e_1\ e_2 & \text{let binding} \\
\end{array}
$$

$$
\begin{array}{llll}
p & ::= & v & \text{variable pattern} \\
& | & \text{con}\ p_1 \ldots p_n, & n \geq 0 \quad \text{constructor pattern} \\
\end{array}
$$

Figure 2: The second order polymorphic lambda calculus

4.2 The type environment and operations on it

The type environment Γ has three components; the type assignment Δ, the set of constructors from the unoptimised data type Σ_{adt} and the set of type variables free in the type assignment, Υ. These components are retrieved using the functions $\downarrow_\Delta$, $\downarrow_\Sigma$ and $\downarrow_\Upsilon$, and Γ is built using the function $MkTypeEnv$. We'll use $\bigoplus$ to define the extension of a variety of environments, letting the context make the meaning clear. In each case, the extended environment appears on the left.

The function **dom** returns the domain of an environment.

Extension of Δ is defined as

$$
\Delta_1 \bigoplus \Delta_2 = \lambda\ i.\ i \in \mathbf{dom}\ \Delta_2 \rightarrow \Delta_2\ i, \Delta_1\ i
$$

Extension of Δ within Γ is defined as

$$\Gamma \bigoplus \Delta = MkTypeEnv \ ((\Gamma \downarrow_\Delta) \bigoplus \Delta) \ (\Gamma \downarrow_\Sigma) \ (\Gamma \downarrow r)$$

The Σ component is never extended.
Extension of Υ within Γ is defined as

$$\Gamma \bigoplus \Upsilon = MkTypeEnv \ (\Gamma \downarrow_\Delta) \ (\Gamma \downarrow_\Sigma) \ (\Gamma \downarrow r \ \cup \ \Upsilon)$$

Extension of Γ is defined as

$$\Gamma_1 \bigoplus \Gamma_2 = MkTypeEnv \ ((\Gamma_1 \downarrow_\Delta) \bigoplus (\Gamma_2 \downarrow_\Delta)) \ (\Gamma_1 \downarrow_\Sigma) \ ((\Gamma_1 \downarrow r) \ \cup \ (\Gamma_2 \downarrow r))$$

4.3 Judgement forms

There are three judgement forms. The first, $\vdash^{polyexp}$, infers a polymorphic type for an expression, while the second, $\vdash$, infers a monomorphic type. The third, $\vdash^{pat}$, infers a type, and a type assignment for bound pattern variables.

4.4 Inference rules

The following rules are a slight variation on the usual rules for Hindley Milner type inference. Let Δ be an initial type assignment mapping primitive functions and constructors to types. The initial type environment is

$$MkTypeEnv \ (\Delta \bigoplus \Delta_{adt}) \ \Sigma_{adt} \ \emptyset$$

The rules are written in a style similar to that of the rules in [HaHaPJW]. The only significant difference is in the fact that there is an extra rule for constructor application and constructor patterns. These handle the unoptimised data type constructors.

5 Partial evaluation

This is the final step of the transformation. It takes a program in the second order polymorphic lambda calculus and converts it back into the core language, inserting the appropriate operation version names.

5.0.1 The code environment

The code environment maps **let** bound variables to their definitions.

$$\rho \in \text{Env} \ :: \ \text{Name} \ \rightarrow \ \text{Exp}$$

$$(\Gamma \downarrow_\Delta)\ \text{v} = \sigma$$

$$\frac{}{\Gamma \quad \vdash^{\text{polyexp}} \quad \text{v} : \sigma \ \leadsto \ \textbf{v}}$$

$$\frac{\Gamma \quad \vdash^{\text{polyexp}} \quad \text{v} : \forall \alpha_1 \ldots \alpha_n.\tau \qquad\qquad \leadsto \ \textbf{v}}{\Gamma \quad \vdash \quad \text{v} : \tau[\tau_1/\alpha_1 \ldots \tau_n/\alpha_n] \qquad \leadsto \ \textbf{v } \tau_1 \ldots \tau_n}$$

$$(\Gamma \downarrow_\Delta)\ \text{con} = \chi\ \tau_1 \ldots \tau_n$$
$$\chi\ \tau_1' \ldots \tau_m' = \text{con} \in (\Gamma \downarrow_\Sigma) \rightarrow$$
$$\chi \cup \tau_1 \ldots \tau_n,\ \chi\ \tau_1 \ldots \tau_n$$

$$\frac{\begin{array}{lll}\Gamma & \vdash & e_1 : \tau_1 \qquad\qquad\qquad\quad \leadsto\ \textbf{e}_1 \\ \ldots \\ \Gamma & \vdash & e_n : \tau_n \qquad\qquad\qquad\quad \leadsto\ \textbf{e}_n\end{array}}{\Gamma \quad \vdash \quad \text{con}\ e_1 \ldots e_n : \chi\ \tau_1' \ldots \tau_m' \quad \leadsto\ \textbf{con e}_1 \ldots \textbf{e}_n}$$

$$\frac{\begin{array}{llll}\Gamma & \vdash & e_1 : \tau_1 \rightarrow \tau_2 & \leadsto\ \textbf{e}_1 \\ \Gamma & \vdash & e_2 : \tau_1 & \leadsto\ \textbf{e}_2\end{array}}{\Gamma \quad \vdash \quad e_1\ e_2 : \tau_2 \quad \leadsto\ \textbf{e}_1\ \textbf{e}_2}$$

$$\frac{\Gamma \oplus \{\text{v} : \tau_1\} \quad \vdash \quad e : \tau_2 \qquad\qquad \leadsto\ \textbf{e}}{\Gamma \quad \vdash \quad (\lambda\ \text{v}\ e) : \tau_1 \rightarrow \tau_2 \quad \leadsto\ \lambda\ \textbf{v}\ \textbf{e}}$$

Figure 3: Inference rules

5.0.2 The version environment

We use a *version environment* to record the versions of function definitions. It maps a function name to a function mapping each version to its code. Versions are uniquely identified by the list of types that label their names, so we define labels as

$$\texttt{Label} \ :: \ [\texttt{Ty}]$$

and write a labelled variable as $\textbf{v}_{\bar{\tau}}$. During partial evaluation of a **let**, the versions for the local binding are retrieved by applying the version environment to the function name. The resulting function, φ, defined as

$$\varphi \in \texttt{Vfun} \ :: \ (\texttt{Name}, \texttt{Label}) \ \rightarrow \ \texttt{Exp}$$

replaces the local binding. We alter the grammar of the source language slightly, changing only the **let** form, which is redefined as

$$\text{let}\ \varphi\ e$$

and adding labels to variables.

The version environment itself has the type

$$
\begin{array}{llll}
\Gamma & \vdash & e : \tau_e & \leadsto e \\
\Gamma & \vdash^{pat} & p_1 : (\tau_e, \Gamma_1) & \leadsto \mathbf{p_1} \\
\Gamma \oplus \Gamma_1 & \vdash & e_1 : \tau & \leadsto \mathbf{e_1} \\
\cdots \\
\Gamma & \vdash^{pat} & p_n : (\tau_e, \Gamma_n) & \leadsto \mathbf{p_n} \\
\Gamma \oplus \Gamma_n & \vdash & e_n : \tau & \leadsto \mathbf{e_n} \\
\hline
\Gamma & \vdash & \text{case } e \ (p_1, e_1) \ldots (p_n, e_n) : \tau \\
& & \leadsto \mathbf{case\ e\ (p_1, e_1) \ldots (p_n, e_n)}
\end{array}
$$

$$
\begin{array}{llll}
\Gamma \oplus \{\alpha_1 \ldots \alpha_n\} & \vdash & e : \tau & \leadsto e \\
\hline
\Gamma & \vdash^{polyexp} & e : \forall \alpha_1 \ldots \alpha_n.\tau & \leadsto \Lambda \alpha_1 \ldots \alpha_n . e
\end{array}
$$

$$
\begin{array}{llll}
\Gamma & \vdash^{polyexp} & e_1 : \sigma & \leadsto \mathbf{e_1} \\
\Gamma \oplus \{v : \sigma\} & \vdash & e_2 : \tau & \leadsto \mathbf{e_2} \\
\hline
\Gamma & \vdash & (\text{let } v \ e_1 \ e_2) : \tau & \leadsto \mathbf{(let\ v\ e_1\ e_2)}
\end{array}
$$

$$
\begin{array}{llll}
(\Gamma \downarrow_\Delta) \ v & = & \tau \\
\hline
\Gamma & \vdash^{pat} & v : (\tau, \{v : \tau\}) & \leadsto \mathbf{v}
\end{array}
$$

$$
\begin{array}{llll}
(\Gamma \downarrow_\Delta) \ con & = & \chi \ \tau_1 \ldots \tau_n \\
\chi \ \tau'_1 \ldots \tau'_m & = & con \in (\Gamma \downarrow_\Sigma) \rightarrow \\
& & \chi \ \mathsf{U} \ \tau_1 \ldots \tau_n, \ \chi \ \tau_1 \ldots \tau_n \\
\Gamma & \vdash^{pat} & p_1 : (\tau_1, \Gamma^1) & \leadsto \mathbf{p_1} \\
\cdots \\
\Gamma & \vdash^{pat} & p_n : (\tau_n, \Gamma^n) & \leadsto \mathbf{p_n} \\
\hline
\Gamma & \vdash^{pat} & con \ p_1 \ldots p_n : (\chi \ \tau'_1 \ldots \tau'_m, \Gamma^1 \oplus \ldots \oplus \Gamma^n) \\
& & \leadsto \mathbf{con\ p_1 \ldots p_n}
\end{array}
$$

Figure 4: Inference rules

$$
\pi \in \mathbf{VEnv} \ :: \ \mathbf{Name} \ \rightarrow \ \mathbf{Vfun}
$$

The version environment is altered using **update**, defined as

$$
\mathbf{update} \ \pi \ v \ v_{\overline{\tau}} \ e \ = \ \pi[((\pi \ v)[e/v_{\overline{\tau}}])/v]
$$

5.0.3 Substitutions

The substitution **Subst** maps type variables to types.

$$
\sigma \in \mathbf{Subst} \ :: \ \mathbf{Tv} \ \rightarrow \ \mathbf{Ty}
$$

The function **aps** applies a substitution to a type.

$$\mathcal{T}\,[[\mathbf{v}]]\;\sigma\;\rho\;\pi\;\iota\quad=\quad([[\mathbf{v}_{[]}]],\pi)$$

$$\mathcal{T}\,[[\mathbf{con}\;\mathbf{e_1}\ldots\mathbf{e_n}]]\;\sigma\;\rho\;\pi\;\iota$$
$$=\quad\text{let}\quad(\mathbf{e_1'},\pi^1)\quad=\quad\mathcal{T}\;\mathbf{e_1}\;\sigma\;\rho\;\pi\;\iota$$
$$\ldots$$
$$(\mathbf{e_n'},\pi^n)\quad=\quad\mathcal{T}\;\mathbf{e_n}\;\sigma\;\rho\;\pi^{n-1}\;\iota$$
$$\text{in}$$
$$([[\mathbf{con}\;\mathbf{e_1'}\ldots\mathbf{e_n'}]],\pi^n)$$

$$\mathcal{T}\,[[\mathbf{e_1}\;\mathbf{e_2}]]\;\sigma\;\rho\;\pi\;\iota$$
$$=\quad\text{let}\quad(\mathbf{e_1'},\pi^1)\quad=\quad\mathcal{T}\;\mathbf{e_1}\;\sigma\;\rho\;\pi\;\iota$$
$$(\mathbf{e_2'},\pi^2)\quad=\quad\mathcal{T}\;\mathbf{e_2}\;\sigma\;\rho\;\pi^1\;\iota$$
$$\text{in}$$
$$([[\mathbf{e_1'}\;\mathbf{e_2'}]],\pi^2)$$

$$\mathcal{T}\,[[\mathbf{v}\;\tau_1\ldots\tau_n]]\;\sigma\;\rho\;\pi\;\iota@(\mathbf{\Delta_{adt}},\mathbf{\Psi_{adt}})$$
$$=\quad\text{let}\;\tau_1',\ldots,\tau_n'=\;\mathbf{aps}\;\sigma\;\tau_1,\ldots,\mathbf{aps}\;\sigma\;\tau_n$$
$$\overline{\tau}\quad=\;[\tau_1',\ldots,\tau_n']$$
$$\text{in}$$
$$\text{case}\;(\mathbf{v}\;\in\;\mathbf{dom}\;\mathbf{\Delta_{adt}})\;\text{of}$$
$$\text{True}\;\rightarrow\quad(\mathbf{\Psi}_{adt}\;\mathbf{v}\;\overline{\tau},\pi)$$
$$\text{False}\;\rightarrow\quad\text{let}\quad(\mathbf{\Lambda}\;\alpha_1\ldots\alpha_n.\;\mathbf{e})\;=\;\rho\;\mathbf{v}$$
$$(\mathbf{e'},\pi')\;=\;\mathcal{T}\;\mathbf{e}\;(\sigma[\tau_1'/\alpha_1]\ldots[\tau_n'/\alpha_n])\;\rho\;\pi\;\iota$$
$$\text{in}\;([[\mathbf{v}_{\overline{\tau}}]],\,\mathbf{update}\;\pi'\;\mathbf{v}\;\mathbf{v}_{\overline{\tau}}\;\mathbf{e'})$$

Figure 5: Partial evaluator

$$\mathcal{T} [[\text{case } e \ (p_1, e_1) \ldots (p_n, e_n)]] \ \sigma \ \rho \ \pi \ \iota$$

$$
\begin{aligned}
= \quad \text{let} \quad & (e', \pi') & = & \quad \mathcal{T} \ e \ \sigma \ \rho \ \pi \ \iota \\
& (e_1', \pi^1) & = & \quad \mathcal{T} \ e_1 \ \sigma \ \rho \ \pi' \ \iota \\
& \ldots \\
& (e_n', \pi^n) & = & \quad \mathcal{T} \ e_n \ \sigma \ \rho \ \pi^{n-1} \ \iota
\end{aligned}
$$

in

$$([[\text{case } e \ (p_1, e_1') \ldots (p_n, e_n')]], \pi^n)$$

$$\mathcal{T} [[\lambda \ v.e]] \ \sigma \ \rho \ \pi \ \iota$$

$$= \quad \text{let} \quad (e', \pi^1) \quad = \quad \mathcal{T} \ e \ \sigma \ \rho \ \pi \ \iota$$

in

$$([[\lambda \ v.e']], \pi^1)$$

$$\mathcal{T}[[\text{let } v \ e_1 \ e_2]] \ \sigma \ \rho \ \pi \ \iota$$

$$= \quad \text{let} \quad (e', \pi^1) \quad = \quad \mathcal{T} \ e_2 \ \sigma \ (\rho[e_1/v]) \ \pi \ \iota$$

in

$$([[\text{let } (\pi^1 \ v) \ e']], \ \pi^1[\bot/v])$$

Figure 6: Partial evaluator

5.0.4 The partial evaluator

The partial evaluator $\mathcal{T}$ takes an expression, a substitution, an environment, a version environment and a tuple containing the operation type assignment Δ_{adt} and the abstract data type function Ψ_{adt}. It returns an expression and the new version environment.

$$\mathcal{T} :: \text{Exp} \ \rightarrow \ \text{Subst} \ \rightarrow \ \text{Env} \ \rightarrow \ \text{VEnv} \ \rightarrow \ (\text{Openv}, \text{Adtf}) \ \rightarrow \ (\text{Exp}, \text{VEnv})$$

The interesting rules are those handling variables and let.

Variables that are not applied to a series of types are lambda bound, in which case the variable is given a label indicating that it is monomorphic and returned.

A variable applied to zero or more types is a let bound function that is either an abstract data type operation or is defined by the program. If it is an operation, it will be in the domain of the type assignment for operations, in which case the appropriate version is found by Ψ_{adt}. Otherwise, its definition is retrieved, the substitution is extended with a binding for each type variable bound by that definition, and it is partially evaluated. Finally, the version environment is updated with the new definition.

Versions of a `let` bound function are retrieved by applying the version environment to the function name.

6 Conclusion and further work

We have given a general framework for integrating operations over unoptimised data types with versions that use an optimised implementation. This has been successfully applied to operations on lists, and we expect it to apply to a number of other data types.

For example, a parallel implementation of bags [KuGl93] has been suggested as providing a new way to take advantage of implicit list parallelism in functional languages. Programmers import functions that handle bags, such as `map` and `foldr`, and then use them where sequential lists are not required by the program. The implementation of these functions, which is imperative, is hidden within the abstract data type. It should be possible to infer coercions between bags and lists using this framework if the programmer can supply pragmas identifying associative and commutative functions for `foldr`. The compiler would have to receive versions for list operations that have unoptimised types if the operation sequentially accesses a list. For example, the `nth` function, which retrieves the nth element of a list, would have a type that forces its argument to be unoptimised.

7 Acknowledgements

John Launchbury made several very useful suggestions that greatly improved the section on the basic idea.

References

[Gr83]   Gardner, M., Wheels, Life and Other Mathematical Amusements, W.H.Freeman and Company, New York, 1983.

[HlWs89]   Hall, C. V. and D. S. Wise, Generating function versions with rational strictness patterns, *Science of Computer Programming* 12 (1989) 39-74.

[HdEtAl92] Hudak, P., S. L. Peyton Jones, and P. Wadler, editors, Report on the Programming Language Haskell, version 1.2, *ACM Sigplan Notices*, 27(5), 1992.

[HaHaPJW] Hall, C. V., K. Hammond, S. L. Peyton Jones, P. Wadler, Type Classes in Haskell, to appear in *European Symposium on Programming*, 1994.

[Ha94]   Hall, C. V., Using Hindley-Milner Type Inference to Optimise List Representation, *Conf. on LISP and Functional Programming*, 1994.

[Jo93]   Jones, M. P., A system of constructor classes: overloading and implicit higher-order polymorphism, *Proc. Functional Languages and Computer Architecture*, Copenhagen, DK, Springer-Verlag, (1993).

[KuGl93]   Kuchen, H. and K. Gladitz, Parallel Implementation of Bags, *Proc. Functional Languages and Computer Architecture*, Copenhagen, DK, Springer-Verlag, (1993).

[Le92]   Leroy, X. Unboxed objects and polymorphic typing, in *Proc. Principles of Programming Languages*, New Mexico, USA, Springer-Verlag, (1992).

[MiHa88]   Mitchell, J.C. and R. Harper, The Essence of ML, *Proc. Principles of Programming Languages*, San Diego, California, Springer-Verlag, (1988).

[PJ86]   Peyton Jones, S. L. "Using Futurebus in a Fifth Generation Computer", *Microprocessors and Microsystems* 10(2), (March 1986), pp. 69-76.

[PJnLn91]   Peyton Jones, S. L. and J. Launchbury, Unboxed values as first class citizens, *Proc. Functional Languages and Computer Architecture*, Boston, Springer-Verlag, (1991).

[ShReAp93]   Shao, Z. J. H. Reppy and A. W. Appel, The efficient representation of lists in ML, to appear in Conf. on LISP and Functional Programming, 1994.

[Wa87]   Wadler, P. Views: A way for pattern matching to cohabit with data abstraction, *Proc. Principles of Programming Languages*, Munich, Germany, Springer-Verlag, (1987).

SPIKING YOUR CACHES

K. HAMMOND, G.L. BURN, AND D.B. HOWE

Abstract

Despite recent advances, predicting the performance of functional programs on real machines remains something of a black art. This paper reports on one particularly unexpected set of results where small variations in the dynamic heap settings occasionally gave rise to significant differences in CPU performance. These performance *spikes* can be traced to the direct-mapped cache of the machine being benchmarked, the widely-used Sun Sparcstation 1.

1. Introduction

In spite of the recent growth of interest in performance profiling[1, 2, 3, 4], we are still often surprised by the performance of functional programs on real machines. This paper reports on performance results obtained from a trivial functional program, whose performance we believed to be well understood, but which transpired to be rather subtle.

2. Benchmarking a Simple Program

Our benchmark program is a simple implementation of the classic Towers of Hanoi function in Haskell.

```
main resps = [AppendChan stdout (hanoi 15 'a' 'b' 'c')]

hanoi n a b c =
    if n == 0 then []
    else let nm1 = n-1; nm1 :: Int in
        append (hanoi nm1 a c b)
                (append (move a b) (hanoi nm1 c b a))

move a b = [a,' ','t','o',' ',b,'\n']

append x y = if x == [] then y else head x : append (tail x) y
```

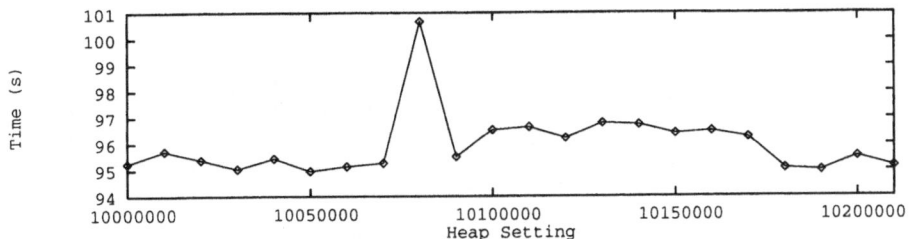

FIGURE 1. Execution Times on a Sun Sparc 1, 10000 Byte Increments

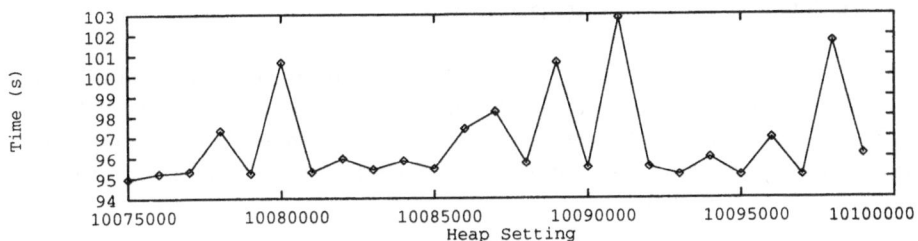

FIGURE 2. Execution Times on a Sun Sparc 1, 1000 Byte Increments

We used the Glasgow Haskell compiler[5], with explicit type signatures and our own definition of the **append** function. We originally benchmarked this program in order to explore the relationship between dynamic heap size and absolute run times for different garbage collectors. We expected to observe high run-times for low heap sizes, diminishing to a constant stable state at higher heap sizes, before rising sharply as paging-effects start to exact a penalty.

In fact, a rather curious effect was observed for the stable state. The program was run 50 times on a lightly-loaded 28MB Sun Sparcstation 1, with heap sizes varying by increments of 10000B from 10000000B to 10100000B. In order to reduce systematic error, times were averaged for 5 runs at each heap size. Figure 2 shows the result. We observe that the graph, which we expected to be perfectly level, in fact oscillates slightly. One of the values (at a heap setting of 10080000B) is a particularly bad fit to the straight line which we expected, being about 10% larger than its neighbours.

Taking a closer look at this area of the graph using a finer granularity for the heap size settings (Figure 2) confirms this *spike* in the graph. Worse still, other spikes have appeared, some larger than the original! In the worst case (not shown here), we have actually seen a different of 50% performance! These spikes are repeatable on the same workstation and even *different types of workstation* with the same program and heap settings, so are not an artefact of system load or other random factors. Clearly there is something about the Sparcstation architecture which is interacting badly with our program.

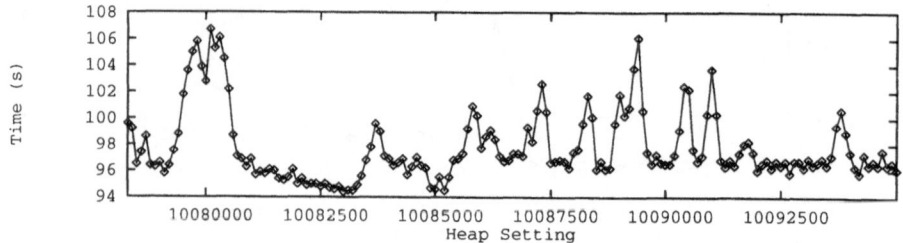

FIGURE 3. Execution Times on a Sun Sparc 1, 100 Byte Heap Increments

3. SPARC Cache Organisation

All Sun workstations before the Sparcstation 10 have a very simple cache organisation [6]. The cache is a 64K direct-mapped write-through cache, with 16B lines. The line used to store a value is chosen by simply ignoring the top bits of the address (the tag) and the bits which address a word within the cache line (the word address).

31 ... 16	15 ... 4	3 ... 0
tag	line	word

This organisation is simple and fast, but has the disadvantage of mapping addresses which are exactly the cache size apart (64K in this case) to the same cache line. If two or more such addresses prove to be accessed frequently, then cache performance will suffer. Because the cache is write-through, any changes written to the cache also have to be written back to the main memory immediately. This can also have a serious effect on performance, especially on a Sparcstation 1, where memory accesses are rather slow (14 cycles to read a line, or 6 cycles to write a word[7]).

We used two SPARC cache simulators: Gordon Irlam's SPA and Sun Microcomputer Inc.'s SPAT package. Each simulator has different strengths. SPA gives accurate performance figures for Sun Sparcstation 1 and 2 machines including a breakdown by instruction type, while SPAT allows the cache organisation to be specified, but has no timing model built-in. Since the Hanoi program runs for about 50 seconds, the trace is respectably long – approximately 1,000,000,000 instructions are traced.

The Hanoi program was run with two heap settings: one normal case **NoSpike**, and one which had been observed to cause a large spike, **Spike**. When these two traces were run through the SPA package they gave identical results, except for the number of cache cycles reported (load stalls and annulled delay slots account for the remaining 5% of execution time). The **Spike** case is 33% slower than the **NoSpike** case just because of poor cache performance!

Experiment	Category	Overall Cycles (%)	Raw Cycles (Millions)
NoSpike	Instructions	74.7	860
	Cache cycles	18.4	212
	Total	93.1	1072
Spike	Instructions	56.9	860
	Cache cycles	37.8	571
	Total	94.7	1431

The fact that we are using a direct-mapped cache is highly suspicious. Set-associative caches claim to give greater performance by grouping several lines into a set (the number of lines in a set defines the associativity of the cache)[8]. It is a reasonable question to ask whether increasing the associativity of the cache would solve our problem. It is also reasonable to ask whether the use of a unified cache for both instructions and data has any effect on the timings.

We compared several cache organisations: a 64K direct-mapped unified cache; 2-way and 4-way 64K unified set-associative caches; and a direct-mapped cache with separate 64K instruction and data caches. It proved impractical to simulate a fully associative cache, but results up to 64-way set associativity were identical to those for the 4-way case. For experimental purposes the total cache size was held constant for the set associative cases, thus allowing us to obtain the same pattern of cache access for each organisation. In reality, such a cache would have fewer lines than a direct-mapped one of the same hardware complexity. Because we wanted to determine the interaction between instructions and data in the unified cache, each separated cache is the same size as the unified cache. Halving the cache size would risk measuring spurious cache conflicts due to remapping instructions/data to the same cache lines.

Cache Organisation	Cache Misses (% Accesses)		
	Instr.	Data Read	Data Write
Direct-Mapped	0.52	4.30	7.34
	1.91	**8.19**	**12.42**
2-way Set-Associative	0.02	1.55	6.75
	0.14	**2.22**	**7.13**
4-way Set-Associative	0.01	1.51	6.74
	0.01	**1.52**	**6.74**
Separated Direct-Mapped	0.00	1.51	6.74
	0.00	**1.52**	**6.74**

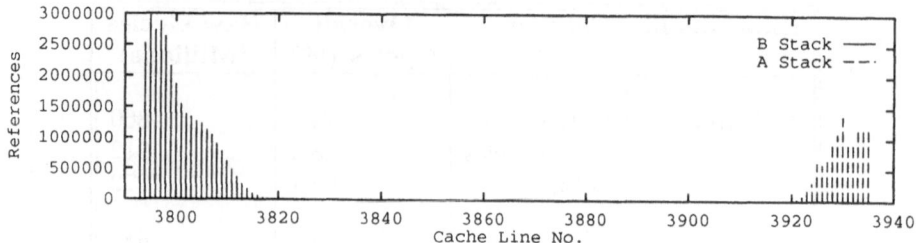

FIGURE 4. Stack Reference Pattern — No Spike

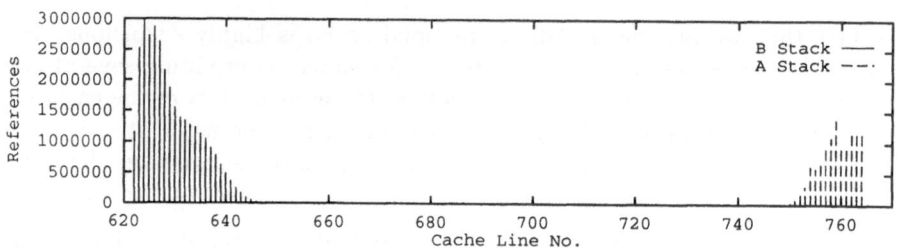

FIGURE 5. Stack Reference Pattern — Spike

The first row in each test is the non-spike case, the second (emboldened) row is the spike case. The cache miss rates are the percentage of the type of data access (instruction, read, write) which miss. It is interesting to observe in passing how high some of these cache miss rates are. Hammond [9] has performed more systematic experiments on a variety of programs, which suggests that such rates are not uncommon in practice.

Using a 4-way set-associative cache clearly would solve the spiking problem, but similar results can be obtained by separating the data and instruction accesses. This suggests that instruction and data accesses are hitting the same cache line(s) — the main advantage of using a set-associative cache is that it maps data and instruction accesses to different cache lines in the same set.

4. Inside the Cache

Clearly using a direct-mapped unified cache is a problem, but why? In order to improve the implementation, we would like to know which memory references are conflicting with the instruction set. We have constructed a detailed cache analyser, which allows us to trace which part of the memory space (stack, heap, instructions etc.) uses which cache line, and which also allows us to determine the conflicts between different parts of the memory space (for example we can determine whether cache misses on a particular line are due to heap addresses mapping onto stack addresses or vice-versa). For simplicity, we have assumed a virtually-addressed cache, but this should not affect our relative results.

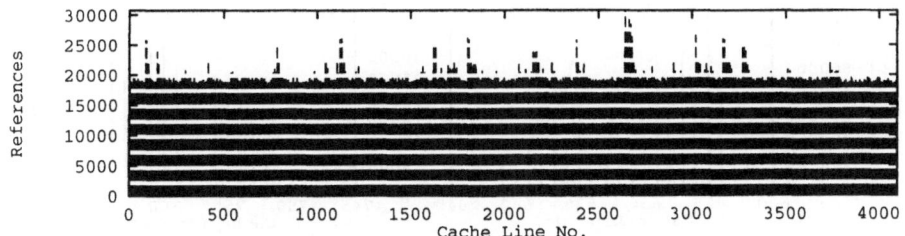

FIGURE 6. Heap Reference Pattern

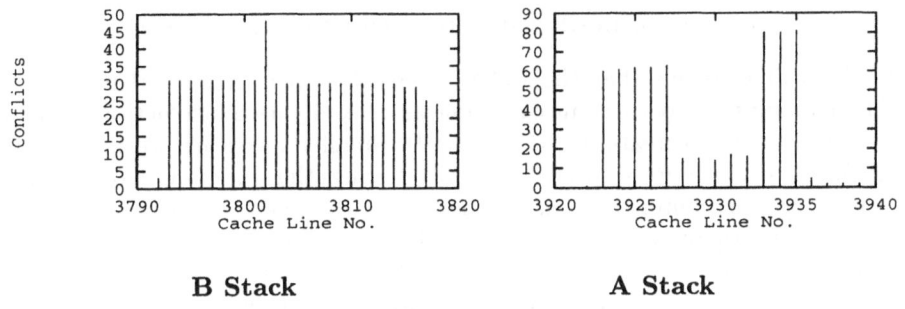

B Stack   **A Stack**

FIGURE 7. Stack and Instruction Conflicts — No Spike

Figures 4 and 5 show the patterns of stack reference for a spike and non-spike case respectively. These differ only in the cache lines which are accessed. Because our STG-machine implementation has two stacks, the A (Address) and B (Basic Value) stacks there are two sets of densely clustered stack references. We observe a similar pattern of stack reference locality for other programs – in fact this is one of the primary objectives in using a stack!

In contrast, the pattern of reference for the heap is relatively flat in either case. This is also expected — the dynamic heap allocator will allocate addresses sequentially from one end of the heap to the other, and most heap addresses are short-lived. The garbage collector used (a variant of Appel's generational collector described in [10]) does not significantly change the access pattern. Figure 6 shows this.

Comparing the same spike and non-spike examples used in Figures 4–5, and studying instruction↔data conflicts carefully, we observe that the patterns of reference and misses are identical for most cases. However, for instruction↔stack conflicts, there is a significant difference, which can be seen in Figures 7 and 8. There are many more instruction↔B Stack conflicts in the spike case than in the non-spike case (up to 700,000), but the instruction↔A Stack conflicts increase by a relatively small amount (to only 30,000).

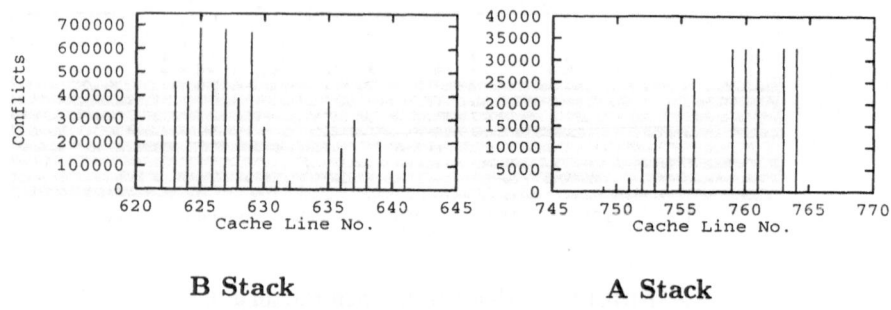

B Stack　　　　　　　　**A Stack**

FIGURE 8. Stack and Instruction Conflicts — Spike

This is clear evidence that the spike is caused by a heavily used part of the
B Stack mapping into the same cache line as a heavily used instruction sequence
(such as the code to create the `Nil` closure!). Smaller spikes are presumably due
to A Stack↔instruction or other conflicts. Because the stacks were located after
the heap by the compiler we used, changes in the heap size setting relocated
the stack, and therefore gave different cache behaviour. In a sense, this is quite
fortuitous – if the stack had been located before the heap we could have suffered
consistently bad performance for a given program without being aware of it.

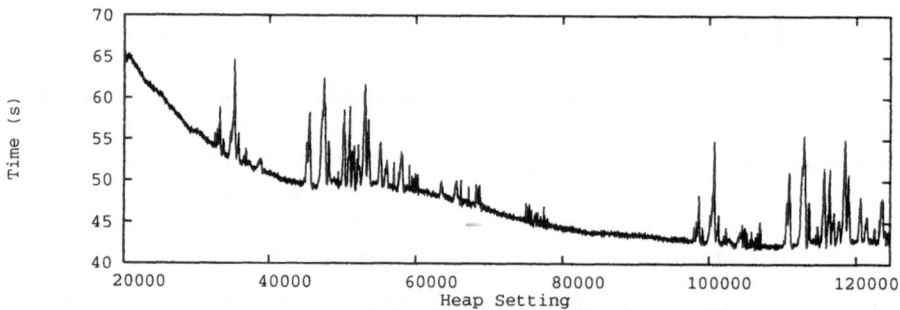

FIGURE 9. Spiking Over a Range of Stack Locations

5. Spike Frequency

It is reasonable to ask how frequently spikes occur. We ran our benchmark
program on a range of heap settings varying by 16 byte intervals (so moving
the stack by 16 bytes at each setting). The results are shown in Figure 9. To
save time, the benchmarks were run on a SparcStation ELC (with a processor
about 30% than a SparcStation 1 but the same general cache organisation).

We observe that spikes are not evenly distributed, but are concentrated over
parts of the graph. This suggests that in this case the spikes are due to relatively

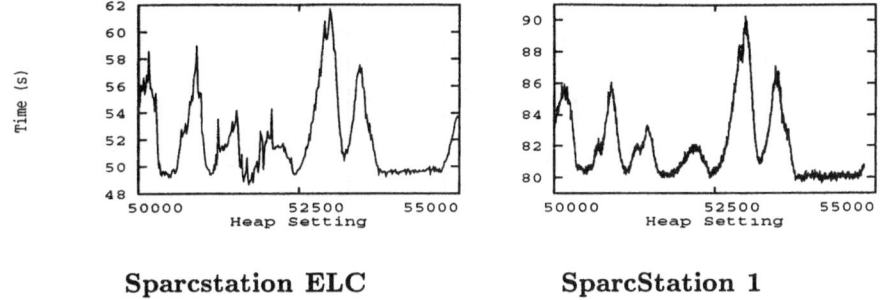

Sparcstation ELC   SparcStation 1

FIGURE 10. Relative Spiking – Sparcstations ELC and 1

localised stack/instruction conflicts. Approximately half the range of heap settings is prone to spiking. Interestingly, there are pronounced "bumps" in some of these areas, e.g. 45000B–80000B, perhaps due to smaller conflicts than those which cause the spikes. There is no evidence of negative spiking, i.e. extremely good cache behaviour, which might have been expected. This may be because the anticipated performance curve follows the line of minimal cache conflict due to the random distribution of heap accesses (shown in Figure 6).

For areas where spiking occurs, about half the timings are spikes, but only around 15% are significant (5% or greater variation in time over the expected baseline). If this pattern holds for other programs, we would expect significant spikes to occur for about 7.5% of all timings, and slight spikes around 25% of the time. For compilers that do not allow stacks to be relocated, there will be systematic errors > 5% for certain programs.

Comparison with the SparcStation 1 (Figure 10) shows that spikes occurred at the same points, and are the same *absolute* height. This shows that the memory system design is essentially identical for the two processors, and therefore that the overall plot for the ELC is indicative of that we would have obtained for the Sparcstation 1, given sufficient patience. The plot for the Sparcstation 1 is more detailed than that for the ELC in two respects: firstly 5 samples were taken at each point rather than 3; and secondly the heap settings were varied by 4 byte intervals rather than 16. The result is a much smoother graph, but with many tiny variations.

Given that spikes occur when addresses are mapped to the same cache line, it seems likely that the spiking pattern will repeat when the stack is mapped to a set of addresses exactly a cache size away. Figure 9 clearly shows this. The pattern of spikes which occurs around 30000B repeats exactly 64KB later at around 100000B, but superimposed on lower base timings. Figure 11 shows these two areas in more detail.

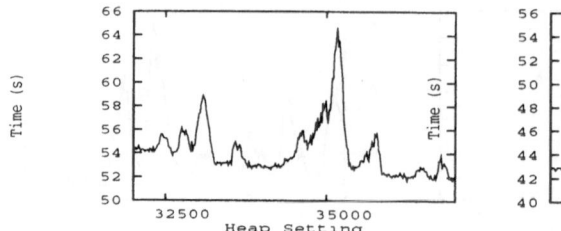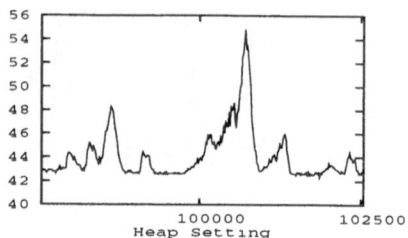

FIGURE 11. Repeated Spikes a Cache Width Apart

6. Avoiding Spikes

The crux of the problem is that two sets of locations which both display high locality of reference over a long period of time happen to map to the same cache lines. Given the popularity of Sun Sparcstation 1s, and other direct-mapped machines, the solution of simply using machines with set-associative caches seems impractical in the short term.

It also seems impractical to significantly change the addresses allocated to instructions, at least without detailed profiling information. For the Glasgow compiler, one possibility might be to destroy some of the stack address locality, by leaving randomly-sized "holes" between stack frames in the memory allocated to a stack. This would ensure that locations in successive stack frames would not map to the same physical address. Something similar is already done on GRIP for other reasons (the stacks are dynamically allocated from the normal heap) [11]. This is clearly not something that a user can influence (unless the compiler-writer provides the appropriate flags).

The principal disadvantage with this scheme is that it would introduce overhead, even when the cost was not justified (the majority of the time?). Its principal advantage (if it worked) would be to provide more predictable timings for a program through randomising stack cacheing patterns.

7. Conclusions

When we benchmarked our simple Towers-of-Hanoi program, we discovered significant performance variations when the location of the stack was changed by only a few hundred bytes. Increasing the level of detail showed that these *spikes* occurred irregularly, but frequently. The spikes proved to be repeatable, and were therefore not simply due to random factors such as the load of the benchmark machine. Simple cache simulations showed that the spikes were due to conflicts between instructions and data. More detailed simulations located the conflict as due to conflicts between heavily used basic value stack locations and instructions. These conflicts appear to be significant around 7.5% of the time for the program tested, and to appear in some form around 50% of the time. We have found similar results for other programs.

In other situations, conflicts are possible between individual heap locations, between heap and stack locations, or between instruction and stack locations, but these are likely to be less severe than stack/stack or stack/instruction conflicts because of reduced locality.

A major lesson for those benchmarking programs is that it is not adequate to simply compare performance without considering the cache organisation – it's possible (if reasonably unlikely) that a spike's been inadvertently discovered. Small performance variations in benchmarked programs are especially suspect, if the variation appears in only a few test cases. Systematic errors may even appear for some programs, if the instructions, stack and heap, always start at the same locations. To avoid this problem, the benchmarker would need to find the best settings for memory locations before performing benchmark tests, or ideally use a cache simulator such as ours to measure the frequency of conflicts between different memory locations.

It is, of course, unclear whether effects like these have silently affected published results, but Sansom's 1993 FPCA paper[10] contains one instance of a *virtual-memory* induced *spike*. It is possible that cache-induced spikes have been dismissed as "experimental errors" in the past or (legitimately) ignored as being irrelevant to the effect under examination.

A lesson for compiler writers is that ignoring cacheing effects can have serious performance consequences. A companion paper has explored the effects of cacheing for a variety of (large) programs compiled using 3 state-of-the-art functional compilers, using different garbage collectors [9]. For compilers such as ghc or hbc it is not unusual for cache misses to account for 30% or more of the total execution time. Thus apparently minor changes in the compiled program, such as reordering instructions or memory locations can have major implications for overall run-time performance. In the worst case (all commonly used locations mapped to the same cache line, for a program comprising repeated sequences of reads/writes), performance could degrade by around a factor of 10. Fortunately, this is infinitesimally improbable in practice.

Several questions remain unanswered:

- Do all functional compilers cause performance spikes, or is this just an artefact of the STG-machine implementation? Evidence collected so far suggests the former conclusion.
- Is this behaviour confined to machines with direct-mapped caches? At Imperial College we have detected spikes on Sun Sparcstation 10s with separate I/D caches, but it proved impossible to confirm this using similar machines at Glasgow — all spikes found were unrepeatable, and therefore presumably artefacts of using a busy machine, or else of physically tagged caches.
- Do similar problems occur with imperative programs? Presumably

68

they do, since the stack and instructions may well conflct, but the
effect is not noticable since the virtual location of stacks is often fixed
by the compiler. It is also relatively unusual to change the size of
dynamic memory allocated to an imperative program.

- Do the effects differ on non-Sparc machines? Our belief is that this will
  depend crucially on the cacheing scheme and relative memory costs.

Acknowledgements

We would like to thank Andy Gill, Simon Marlow and Patrick Sansom for
commenting on an earlier version of this paper. This work is partially supported
by a grant from the Royal Society of Edinburgh.

References

1. Sansom PM, "Time Profiling in a Lazy Functional Language", *This Proceedings*.
2. Hartel P, and Vree WG, "Benchmarking Lazy Functional Languages", *Proc. FPCA 93*, Copenhagen, Denmark, (June 1993).
3. Wakeling D and Runciman C, "Heap Profiling a Lazy Functional Compiler", *Proc. 1992 Glasgow Workshop on Functional Programming*, (1992), pp. 203–214.
4. Clayman S, Parrott D and Clack C, "A profiling technique for lazy higher-order functional programs", *Internal Report*, Department of Computing Science, University College London, (November 1991).
5. Peyton Jones SL, Hall CV, Hammond K, Partain WD, and Wadler PL, "The Glasgow Haskell compiler: a technical overview", *Proc. JFIT Conference*, Keele, UK, (March 1993).
6. Sun Microcomputers Inc., *Sun Performance Tuning Overview*, (December 1992).
7. Irlam G, "The Low Level Computational Performance of Sparcstations: a Guide for Compiler Writers", *Internal Report*, Dept. of Computing Science, Adelaide University.
8. Stone HS, *High-Performance Computer Architecture*, Addison-Wesley, Reading Mass., (1987).
9. Hammond K, "Functional Programming Languages and a Computer Architecture", *Internal Report*, Dept. of Comp. Sci., Glasgow University, (June 1993).
10. Sansom PM, "Generational Garbage Collection for Haskell", *Proc. FPCA 93*, Copenhagen, Denmark, (June 1993), pp. 106–116.
11. Hammond K, and Peyton Jones SL, "Profiling Scheduling Strategies on the GRIP Parallel Reducer", *Proc 4th Intl Workshop on Parallel Implementation of Functional Languages*, Kuchen H and Loogen R (Eds), RWTH, Aachen, (1992).

Address, Hammond: DEPARTMENT OF COMPUTING SCIENCE, GLASGOW UNIVERSITY,
17 LILYBANK GARDENS, GLASGOW, G12 8QQ, UK.

E-mail address: kh@dcs.glasgow.ac.uk

Address, Burn/Howe: COMPUTING DEPARTMENT, IMPERIAL COLLEGE, 180
QUEENSGATE, LONDON, SW7 2AZ, UK.

E-mail address: dbh@doc.ic.ac.uk

Experiments with destructive updates in a lazy functional language (extended abstract)

Pieter H. Hartel   Willem G. Vree

Department of Computer Systems, University of Amsterdam
Kruislaan 403, 1098 SJ Amsterdam, The Netherlands
Email: pieter@fwi.uva.nl

Abstract

The aggregate update problem has received considerable attention since pure functional programming languages were recognised as an interesting research topic. There is extensive literature in this area, which comprises over 100 papers. We have tried to apply some of the proposed solutions to our own applications to see how these solutions work in practice. We have been able to use destructive updates but are not convinced that this could have been achieved without application specific knowledge. In particular, no form of update analysis has been reported that is applicable to non-flat domains in polymorphic languages with higher order functions.

It is our belief that a refinement of the monolithic approach towards constructing arrays may be a good alternative to using the incremental approach with destructive updates.

1   Introduction

In a pure functional language it is difficult to implement an update on an aggregate data structure in an efficient way. The problem is that unless the aggregate is known to be single threaded [17], a copy must be made of the entire aggregate, which may then be destructively updated. Otherwise the vitally important referential transparency property is lost. For the sake of definiteness we will concentrate on the use of a particular aggregate data structure: the array. There are three basic operations to be implemented on arrays: create, subscript and update. An array can be implemented in many ways, but our preferred implementation is a *container* [14], which is just a contiguous block of memory. The container holds either the actual array elements, or pointers to the array elements. This depends on the implementation of the functional language. The use of a container of size N permits $O(1)$ subscript time, and $O(N)$ creation time. The problem is to also implement $O(1)$ update time.

There are two basically different ways of using arrays: incrementally or monolithically [20]. When the calculations involved in creating an array follow some kind of regular pattern, a monolithic operation should be appropriate: this creates an entire array in one single operation. When no sufficiently simple regularity can be discerned, an incremental approach is required: this repeatedly updates the current version of the array in one or more places to form the next version. Such updates are impossible with the monolithic approach. Monolithic array operations can be expressed in terms of incremental operations and vice versa, so the expressive power of both approaches is the same [1]. Depending on the implementation, there may be large differences in space and time complexity.

The incremental approach is of a lower level whereas the monolithic approach is of a higher level of abstraction. This favours the monolithic approach, and indeed some researchers have noted that programs using the monolithic approach are clearer [10]. The programming style that should be followed when writing functional programs using arrays should aim for using monolithic array operations. This is consistent with a commonly accepted preference for the use of higher order functions rather than explicit recursions [12].

Having said this, is the aggregate update problem still a major issue? Unfortunately, the answer is yes. Consider a monolithic array operation that transforms an old array into a new one, for instance by applying a certain function to all the array elements. This also presents the array update problem, for the result of the operation requires a container that has the same size as the container holding the input array. So the implementation should attempt to reuse that container [1].

There is a difference between the two manifestations of the aggregate update problem. Suppose that a certain algorithm requires an array of size N to be updated M times in its entirety. A naive incremental implementation, which copies the array upon each update, requires $O(N^2 \times M)$ space, whereas a naive monolithic implementation requires $O(N \times M)$ space. The naive incremental implementation is thus worse than the naive monolithic implementation. For some applications, even a naive monolithic implementation may be acceptable, if the work involved in calculating the $O(N \times M)$ array elements is sufficiently large.

In a non-strict functional language, both the monolithic and the incremental arrays have a further problem, because in such a language also the arrays are non-strict. This means that arrays may have undefined elements. Unless strictness analysis can prove otherwise, which is hard, array elements must be created as suspended computations and unfortunately suspensions are costly. Consider the creation of an array of N integers, as generated by N distinct function calls, say $(f\ 1) \ldots (f\ N)$. In a strict language this requires a container of size N integers. In a non-strict language, a container of the same size is required to store pointers to N suspensions. Each of these suspensions requires space capable of holding at least 2 pointers (one to point at the function and one to point at the argument) but often more. Let us assume that a pointer requires the same amount of space as an integer, then in total the non-strict array requires at least $3N$ space. The time required to manipulate a non-strict array is greater, not only because more space needs to be allocated but also because the storage occupied by $N + 1$ logically separate objects (1 container + N suspensions) must be collected. The time complexity of allocating and recovering a strict array is thus $O(1)$, and the time complexity for handling a non-strict array is $O(N)$.

The destructive update problem in lazy functional languages has a wide range of aspects, including strictness analysis, boxing analysis and subscript analysis [1], as well as the question of whether to use incremental or monolithic array primitives. The difficulty in implementing destructive updates lies not so much in developing the right kind of analysis for it, but more in the problems raised by combining the many different analyses, which all have to work together in harmony to achieve good results.

The destructive update problem can be avoided in a number of ways. The two most promising approaches are based on monads [15] or on unique types [18]. Both approaches ultimately use the type system to guarantee that a data structure is single threaded, and that destructive updates are therefore safe. These approaches are interesting because no clever analysis is required to detect single threadedness. It is annotated (but in very different ways) by the programmer and the annotations are verified by the system. These two alternative approaches thus represent a safe way to express imperative programming concepts in a functional context. We shall not consider these alternatives here, because our main interest is in contrasting the imperative and functional style. The former is represented by the incremental approach to array handling and the latter by the monolithic approach. In our view the monadic approach, the unique typing approach, and the analysis approach such as we have used, have the same net effect on the handling of arrays.

Also, because our main interest is in contrasting the imperative and functional style, we do not consider programs that cannot be implemented efficiently in a monolithic style. An example of such a program is in updating a large data base.

We are well aware of the fact that for many algorithms efficient functional implementations exists that work on lists, as opposed to arrays. In our earlier paper [8] we have investigated a number of different versions of the fast Fourier transform. We found that list based implementations can be efficient, but they are beyond the scope of our present focus on arrays. Such list based implementations will not be considered here.

In the full version of this paper [9] we discuss some of the related work, emphasising the pragmatic aspects of the proposals. In Section 2, two example problems are taken from the literature and another example problem is discussed in some detail. We have tried to apply the solutions proposed in the literature to these problems to see how they work in practice. Sometimes an appropriate analysis is able to discover the safety of the essential destructive updates, and sometimes this cannot be achieved without the help of the programmer. Each example is programmed in the monolithic and in the incremental style. Measurements are reported in Section 3 using an implementation that supports both strict and non-strict arrays. The last section presents our conclusions.

2 Example problems

The three examples are the ubiquitous quick sort program (qs), the fast Fourier transform (fft) and a tidal prediction program (wv), which simulates the be-

72

haviour of an estuary of the North Sea over a number of time steps. The monolithic version of qs is taken from Wadler's paper [21], the incremental version originates from Hudak's paper [11]. The fft program will be described briefly in the next section. A complete description of the fft and wv programs may be found in the full version of this paper [9]. The array primitives being used are borrowed from Haskell [13].

2.1 The discrete Fourier transform

Figure 1 shows two implementations of the discrete fast Fourier transform. An N-point transform makes $\log_2 N$ calls to the function *fft*. Each invocation of *fft* calls an auxiliary function *level*, of which there are two implementations: $level_i$ and $level_m$. These two functions have the same semantics but differ in the way the array is handled.

The function $level_i$ is based on the incremental approach towards array construction. At each invocation of $level_i$, elements at positions j and k of the input array x are replaced by two new values v_j and v_k, which are destined for the same positions j and k. The way in which the replacement is effectuated (i.e. destructively or non-destructively) will be considered later.

The monolithic approach towards array construction is embodied in the function $level_m$, which replaces the entire array by a new one rather than piecemeal as in the incremental approach. The contents of the new array are produced by the list comprehension under the keyword *where* as the list l. This list is actually a list of two-element lists, which must therefore be flattened by the function *concat*. The association pairs thus produced will appear in some particular order that is not the index order of the array. This explains why the function *array* has been used, which builds an array out of a list of index value pairs. The index computations are based on the regularity inherent in the fft algorithm. Without such a regularity, it would not have been possible to use the monolithic approach at all.

The monolithic implementation creates a considerable amount of intermediate list structure, which a good compiler should be able to avoid completely [1, 4]. Unfortunately, the compiler that we have been using (FAST [6]) does not have this capability.

The definition of the function *reorder* has been omitted from the program of Figure 1 as it does not play a role in the discussion on updating. The interested reader is referred to our paper [8] for a complete description of the program.

2.2 Can destructive update be made safe?

Depending on the choice made in the function *fft* in Figure 1, either the monolithic $level_m$ or the incremental $level_i$ is used. The time complexity of the destructively updating (incremental) and the monolithic implementations are the same: $O(N \times \log N)$. The non-destructively updating implementation can be ruled out, because it has a time complexity of $O(N^2 \times \log N)$. A selection can thus be based purely on the space behaviour of the two implementations.

The monolithic implementation of the fft makes $\log_2 N$ calls to *array* and therefore allocates $O(N \times \log N)$ space. The destructively updating implementation uses only $O(N)$ space. So the incremental approach is best, but only if

```
main  ::  array of complex
main              = fft (N ÷ 2) (reorder N input)

fft  ::  int → array of complex → array of complex
fft 0 x           = x
fft n x           = fft (n ÷ 2) y
                    where
                    m = log₂ (N ÷ (n × 2))
                    y = level 0 m n x        || Choose either levelₘ or levelᵢ

levelᵢ, levelₘ  ::  int → int → int → array of complex → array of complex
levelᵢ j m n x    = x,  if j = N
                    = levelᵢ (j + 1) m n z,  if bit j m = 0
                    = levelᵢ (j + 1) m n x,  otherwise
                    where
                    y = update x j vⱼ
                    z = update y k vₖ
                    [(j', vⱼ), (k, vₖ)] = bflylist j m n x

levelₘ j m n x  = array (bounds x) (concat l)
                    where
                    l = [bflylist j m n x | j ← [0 . . . N − 1];  bit j m = 0]

bflylist  ::  int → int → int → array of complex → list of (int × complex)
bflylist j m n x  = [(j, vⱼ), (k, vₖ)]
                    where
                    k = j + 2ᵐ
                    (vⱼ, vₖ) = bfly (n × j) (subscript x j) (subscript x k)

bfly  ::  int → complex → complex → (complex × complex)
bfly j xⱼ xₖ      = (xⱼ + z, xⱼ − z)
                    where
                    z = xₖ × wʲ
```

Figure 1: Two implementations of the `fft`: levelₘ follows the monolithic approach and levelᵢ follows the incremental approach towards array construction.

the updates can be performed destructively. If this cannot be guaranteed, the implementation will require $O(N^2 \times \log N)$ space.

The question is: can this guarantee be given? Unfortunately, the answer is no, unless some precautionary measures are taken. Let us first investigate why the required guarantee is difficult to give, and then come back to the measures that have been proposed in the literature.

Without special measures, a compiler for a lazy functional language may generate code similar to that shown on the left of Figure 2 as the function $level_i$. The generated code has been expressed as a C program; functions are thus called by value. Only the essential parts of the C code have been shown, which include the array manipulations.

As one would expect in a lazy language, we have assumed that *update* is strict in its first two arguments (the array and the index) and non-strict in its third argument (the new value). The strictness analysis of the compiler is then able to discover the following fact: since the *update* function is strict in its first two arguments (the array and the index), both j and k are needed and will therefore represent integers, rather than pointers to suspensions in the heap. Similarly, the variables x, y, and z represent proper arrays rather than suspensions, which only produce arrays as soon as they are evaluated. The two *update* functions are therefore called rather than embedded in suspensions. On the other hand, the variables v_j and v_k are not needed and therefore point at suspensions in the heap, because of the non-strictness of the third argument (the value) of *update*. The functions *fst* and *snd* select the first, respectively the second component of the tuple returned by *bfly*. The variables x_j and x_k cannot be proved to be needed, so suspensions should be made of the *subscript* functions, as shown in the body of $level_i$. These two suspensions make it impossible to use destructive updates, because pointers emanating from these suspensions will refer to the array x. This problem has been described by Stoye [19] and some others. We will present a solution that works for the `fft` program, but unfortunately this solution does not always apply.

2.3 Possible solutions to the suspended subscript problem

The update function as used by Bloss [3] is strict in all three arguments, rather than in just the first two as is the case here. Depending on the sophistication of the strictness analyser, this may or may not avoid the problem we are presently facing. Should the strictness analysis be capable of reasoning about structured data, such as the tuple returned by the *bfly* function, the values of v_j and v_k will be known to be needed and so will the values of x_j and x_k. It is possible to build a sufficiently sophisticated strictness analyser to prove the neededness of x_j and x_k, but the FAST compiler does not offer this.

An alternative approach has been implemented in the FAST compiler [7]. Even with a fairly simple strictness analyser, and when using a version of *update* that is non-strict in its third argument, it is still possible to use a destructive update. To achieve this, an optimisation called *cheap eagerness* is used: instead of building a suspension for a selector function and using the pointer to the suspension, cheap eagerness selects the required item and uses a pointer to that item. These two approaches are schematically shown in Figure 3. Here a

```
1.  level_i(j, m, n, x)                          level'_i(j, m, n, x)
2.  {                                            {
3.      if (j = N) {                                 if (j = N) {
4.          return x;                                    return x;
5.      } else if (bit(j, m) = 0) {                  } else if (bit(j, m) = 0) {
6.          k   = j + 2^m;                               k   = j + 2^m;
7.          x_j = suspend(subscript, x, j);              x_j = subscript'(x, j);
8.          x_k = suspend(subscript, x, k);              x_k = subscript'(x, k);
9.          v_jk = suspend(bfly, n × j, x_j, x_k);       v_jk = suspend(bfly, n × j, x_j, x_k);
10.         v_j = suspend(fst, v_jk);                    v_j = suspend(fst, v_jk);
11.         v_k = suspend(snd, v_jk);                    v_k = suspend(snd, v_jk);
12.         y   = update(x, j, v_j);                     y   = update(x, j, v_j);
13.         z   = update(y, k, v_k);                     z   = update(y, k, v_k);
14.         return level_i(j + 1, m, n, z);              return level'_i(j + 1, m, n, z);
15.     } else {                                     } else {
16.         return level_i(j + 1, m, n, x);              return level'_i(j + 1, m, n, x);
17.     }                                            }
18. }                                            }
```

Figure 2: The $level_i$ procedure taken from the C-code generated for the incremental version of the fft, showing on the left the code before and on the right the code after the cheap eagerness optimisation.

points at the suspension of the *subscript* function and b points at the item to be selected. The arguments of *subscript* are an array x and an index i. The cheap eagerness optimisation is also used in the LML compiler [2].

Assume that both the array and the index are head normal forms, that is, the index is an integer and the array is a block of memory containing pointers to the actual elements. Whether the array elements themselves are (head) normal forms or not is irrelevant. It is now possible to use the pointer b instead of the pointer a and thus avoid building the suspension of *subscript*. This amounts to selecting a certain element from a container while is is not known whether the resulting value will ever be needed. This is thus non-lazy. However, in the present case the amount of work involved in selecting the element, is less than the amount of work required to build the suspension for *subscript*. So even though the optimised code is not lazy, it is arguably more efficient and therefore desirable to have. It should be noted that the optimisation does not evaluate the selected item (in the dashed box), as that may involve an unlimited amount of computation, which would defeat the whole objective.

The cheap eagerness optimisation can only be applied if the compiler is able to prove that a limited form of eager evaluation requires less work than lazy evaluation. In the example of Figure 3, the compiler must thus know that both the index and the container of the array (but not necessarily the actual array elements) have indeed been evaluated sufficiently by the time the subscript operations at lines 7 and 8 in Figure 2 are executed. The cheap eagerness optimisation can be applied to all selector functions and most arithmetic functions.

Returning to the C-code of Figure 2 it becomes apparent that the cheap eagerness optimisation can be applied to the two subscriptions $x_j = \ldots$ and

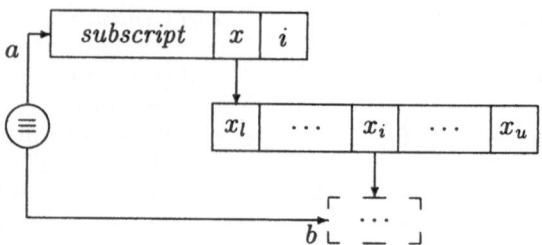

Figure 3: Applying the cheap eagerness optimisation to array subscription. The boxes represent heap cells.

$x_k = \ldots.$ During strictness analysis, the compiler has proved that both the array x and the two indices j and k are indeed evaluated by the time the suspensions of *subscript* are made (see lines 7 and 8 in Figure 2). The optimisation thus enables the two statements that build the suspensions of *subscript* to be repaced by calls to a special function *subscript'*. The latter differs from the regular *subscript* in that it does not guarantee to return a head normal form; *subscript'* merely returns (a pointer to) the selected item as found. The optimised version $level'_i$ is shown on the right of Figure 2.

After applying the cheap eagerness optimisation to the `fft` program, destructive updates are safe, because the array of complex numbers is now single threaded. We have thus achieved our goal, without having to modify the incremental version of the `fft` program. However, this particular version had been prepared with the capabilities of the compiler in mind. This gave the function $level_i$ its present form and helped the strictness analyser to discover that $level_i$ is strict in its first and its last argument, which happens to be just the information needed to make the cheap eagerness optimisation work. Cheap eagerness is a general optimisation, which applies many primitive as well as user defined functions. However, because it is an optimisation, cheap eagerness cannot be guaranteed to solve the problem of the suspended subscripts in other cases. As many researchers have observed, a small change to either the program or the compiler and the single threadedness is lost again, so that the performance of an incremental program deteriorates considerably because destructive updates are no longer safe.

The monolithic version of the `fft` can also be made to destructively update the array. This requires the call to *array* in $level_m$ to be replaced by a call to *accum*, so that access to the old array x is granted, yielding:

$$level'_m \; j \; m \; n \; x = accum \; (\lambda xy.y) \; x \; (concat \; l)$$
$$\text{where}$$
$$l = [bflylist \; j \; m \; n \; x \mid j \leftarrow [0 \ldots N-1]; \; bit \; j \; m = 0]$$

For the new function $level'_m$ to indeed reuse the container of the array x, the elements of the array must be read out two at a time. The two values must then be run through the *bfly* function to deliver the two new elements, which are then written in place of the old elements. The subscript analysis described by Anderson and Hudak [1] should be capable of achieving this. However, this requires a very powerful compiler and a programmer who knows exactly how to express a problem such that it can be recognised. These are both hard to achieve.

We should like to point out that the FAST compiler is not capable of verifying the safety of destructive updates. It is entirely up to the programmer to work this out. We do not propose to present arbitrary destructive updates as a tool to the casual programmer, but instead use such unsafe facilities as an object of study.

3   Measurements

Considerations similar to those made above for the fft program can also be made for the qs and wv programs to also obtain incremental and monolithic versions of these programs [9]. The three programs qs, fft and wv have been compiled by the FAST compiler [6] and executed on a SUN SPARC 4/690. Various statistics are collected by the runtime system, of which Table 1 presents the most important ones, as shown in the first column.

The three programs have been implemented using incremental arrays (see the columns marked *Incr*) as well as monolithic arrays (see the columns marked *Mono*). All incremental versions have been executed using a destructive implementation of the array update (columns marked *destr*). The wv program has also been executed using the naive copying implementation of the array update (column marked *copy*). With a naive copying implementation of the array update, the asymptotic complexity of the other programs is so bad that there is no point in presenting precise measurements. That this is not the case for the wv program can be explained as follows. Unlike the other two programs, wv uses $N \times N$ matrices, which are implemented as arrays of arrays. When naively updating a point in the matrix, only an array of size N has to be copied, not an entire matrix of size $N \times N$. Because of this implementation choice, even the incremental copying version of this program has an acceptable performance.

Two different array implementations have been used. The first implementation uses strict arrays, which means that every array primitive evaluates all array elements to head normal form when creating or updating an array. This implementation does therefore not allow arrays with undefined elements to be created. The array elements are always boxed. The measurements pertaining to this implementation may be found in the first section of the table (under the heading *Strict arrays*). The second implementation is based on non-strict arrays, for which the measurements may be found in the second section of the table (under the heading *Non-strict arrays*). These latter measurements are shown as a percentage of the corresponding statistic for the strict array implementation. A positive percentage corresponds to an increase, i.e. a worse performance. A negative percentage represents a decrease, i.e. a better performance.

The third section of the table presents a break down of the number of heap cells claimed with respect to the different ways in which the heap cells are used. The break down applies to the implementation of strict arrays only, non-strict arrays are not too different in this respect.

The row marked *input* for qs gives the length of the list to be sorted. For fft, the input parameter is the number of points transformed and for wv the input parameter gives the number of simulated time steps.

program	qs		fft		wv		Mono
version	Incr destr	Mono	Incr destr	Mono	Incr copy	destr	
input	32767	32767	8192	8192	10	10	10
Strict arrays							
calls	4155K	8009K	2645K	4038K	5262K	5262K	7201K
cells	360K	1657K	977K	2386K	2171K	2046K	2261K
reduce	5429K	9305K	2446K	6730K	8965K	8965K	12010K
seconds	7	15	6	20	24	15	19
Non-strict arrays							
calls			+10%				
cells			+36%	+1%	+7%	+7%	+10%
reduce	+23%		+48%		+13%	+13%	+15%
seconds	+4%	+2%	+88%	+3%	+10%	+14%	+28%
Strict arrays, break down of cell claims							
<SUSP>	36%	47%	3%	37%	17%	18%	18%
<CONS>	9%	40%	1%	11%			
<ARR>				5%	6%		
<NUMB>	27%	6%	61%	32%	12%	13%	15%
DBL			16%	7%	63%	66%	60%

Table 1: Function calls, cell claims, reducer activity and execution time for the different versions of each program. The blank entries in the second and third sections of the table indicate "no change for this entry".

The row marked *calls* in the first section presents the total number of function calls, including all primitive and user defined functions. Even a simple addition is counted as a function call, to give an impression of the amount of work involved in each of the computations. The row marked *calls* in the second section gives the increase/decrease in the number of function calls due to the use of non-strict instead of strict arrays. The total number of function calls for the incremental version of the fft program is 10% higher when using non-strict arrays. The two other programs are not affected by the choice of (non)-strict array primitives with respect to this statistic.

The row *cells* gives the number of heap cell claims required during the execution. Heap cells are an expensive resource so the larger this number, the larger the expected execution time. The number of cell claims is worse affected by the choice of strict/non-strict arrays than the number of function calls.

The row *reduce* gives a measure of the costs involved in implementing lazy evaluation. The statistic is incremented each time the reducer is called, and also when certain subfunctions of the reducer are called (for example a step during the unwind of the spine). Most versions show a significant increase, up to 48% with respect to this statistic when moving to non-strict arrays.

The row *seconds* gives the execution time of the different versions of the programs. The incremental versions, implemented with destructive updates are always the fastest. There is a relatively large error, of perhaps 50% in time measurements on a complex architecture, such as the SUN SPARC processor with caches [5]. Such large errors arise because small variations in heap size or code size may cause large variations in the effectiveness of the cache and thus in the execution time. Therefore it is safe only to conclude that the destructively updating incremental implementation of fft is significantly faster with strict than with non-strict arrays.

In the third section, a breakdown is presented of the number of cell claims as a percentage of the statistic *cell* in the first section. The measurements in the first as well as the third section apply to the implementations based on strict arrays. The following categories of cells appear in the table: $<SUSP>$ represents suspended function applications $<CONS>$ represents boxed list constructor cells, $<ARR>$ represents boxed array containers and $<NUMB>$ represents boxed numbers. The category DBL represents unboxed double precision numbers. There are other cell categories, such as array descriptor pairs, but they do not occur frequently and have therefore been omitted. This is also the reason that the percentages in each column of the third section do not add up to 100%.

For the wv program, the statistic DBL accounts for over 66% of the cell claims. This is entirely due to a problem in the implementation that we have used, which is not able to store unboxed double precision numbers directly in a stack frame. Instead, for each unboxed double, a heap cell is allocated, and a pointer to that heap cell is stored in a stack frame. There are implementation techniques to solve this problem but we have not implemented those. The fft program also suffers from this deficiency but to a much lesser extent, because at most 16% of its cell claims are unboxed doubles. The list structure being built by the fft can be avoided almost entirely, if better methods for compiling array comprehensions are used [1, 4].

The number of cells claimed by even the fastest version of each program is large when compared to the problem size. In particular, it should be possible to run the destructively updating versions of each program using a fixed number of cells, related to the size of the problem being solved. For qs and fft, the required number of cells is equal to the value of the input parameter. For wv, the number of cells does not depend on the input parameter, but only on the size of the three matrices involved. The destructively updating version of fft uses $977K/8192 \approx 119$ times more cells than we would like. It should come as no surprise that an implementation in C [16] is about 100 times faster than our best implementation. To solve this problem, it will be necessary to treat unboxed data, such as complex numbers, as first class citizens. This means that an array of complex numbers should be represented not as an array of pointers to cells but exactly as in C, by an array of structs that contain the real and imaginary parts. To achieve such a result requires both powerful boxing analysis as well as new techniques for supporting unboxed values at runtime, and in particular during garbage collection.

4 Conclusions

Using destructive updates in a lazy language is hard, even though the programs that we have studied are relatively small. The programmer requires intimate knowledge of the implementation and even worse, a slight change in the program may make it impossible for the compiler to prove the uniqueness of a pointer to an array. As we have seen in section 2.2, this has a disastrous effect on the performance of the program and therefore relying on destructive updates is unsatisfactory.

Although the safety of programs using monads or unique types is guaranteed, still the programmer is required to have the same intimate knowledge of the underlying implementation. Otherwise the program cannot be written in such a way that it will be accepted by the static checks of the compiler.

In the programs that we have used, destructive updates were found to be safe except in one case, where an annotation by the programmer proved essential. This annotation (in the wv program, see the full version of the paper [9]) turned out to be required also to curtail the space consumption of the program.

The three programs that have been studied admit solutions based on the use of monolithic arrays, which do not have the problem that a small change may influence the performance dramatically. The performance of these monolithic versions is at most a factor of 2 worse than that of the incremental versions. This performance difference may however change as soon as we correct the two shortcomings of our implementation described earlier (the use of heap cells to store unboxed double precision numbers and the generation of redundant intermediate list structure for array comprehensions).

The monolithic programs are neater than the incremental programs, and they have the advantage that even a simple implementation will give a reasonable performance. A sophisticated implementation should give a performance comparable to that of incremental implementations.

The monolithic array operations that we have used are relatively primitive. It would be worthwhile to extend the primitives to support operations over certain index patterns or index ranges. This would improve programs such as wv that reshape matrices. Such an extension would improve the appearance of programs using arrays and it would also offer the compiler more scope for optimisations. This route looks more promising than to try to build several complex analyses into the compiler that must operate in perfect harmony to achieve good results.

Acknowledgements

We thank Marcel Beemster, Bob Hiromoto, David King, Simon Marlow and John O'Donnell for their comments on a draft version of the paper. Kevin Hammond has helped to produce the camera ready copy of the paper.

References

[1] S. Anderson and P. Hudak. Compilation of Haskell array comprehensions for scientific computing. In *Programming language design and implementation*, pages 137–149, White Plains, New York, Jun 1990. ACM SIGPLAN notices,25(6).

[2] L. Augustsson and T. Johnsson. The Chalmers Lazy-ML compiler. *The computer journal*, 32(2):127–141, Apr 1989.

[3] A. Bloss. Update analysis and the efficient implementation of functional aggregates. In J. Stoy, editor, *4th Functional programming languages and computer architecture*, pages 26–38, London, England, Sep 1989. ACM.

81

[4] A. Gill, J. Launchbury, and S. L. Peyton Jones. A short cut to deforestation. In *6th Functional programming languages and computer architecture*, pages 223–232, Copenhagen, Denmark, Jun 1993. ACM.

[5] K. Hammond, G. L. Burn, and D. B. Howe. Spiking your caches. In K. Hammond and J. T. O'Donnell, editors, *Functional programming*, pages V.1–V.8, Ayr, Scotland, Jul 1993. Dept. of Comp. Sci, Univ. of Glasgow, Scotland.

[6] P. H. Hartel, H. W. Glaser, and J. M. Wild. Compilation of functional languages using flow graph analysis. Technical report CSTR 91-03, Dept. of Electr. and Comp. Sci, Univ. of Southampton, England, Jan 1991.

[7] P. H. Hartel, H. W. Glaser, and J. M. Wild. On the benefits of different analyses in the compilation of functional languages. In H. W. Glaser and P. H. Hartel, editors, *3rd Implementation of functional languages on parallel architectures*, pages 123–145, Southampton, England, Jun 1991. CSTR 91-07, Dept. of Electr. and Comp. Sci, Univ. of Southampton, England.

[8] P. H. Hartel and W. G. Vree. Arrays in a lazy functional language – a case study: the fast Fourier transform. In G. Hains and L. M. R. Mullin, editors, *2nd Arrays, functional languages, and parallel systems (ATABLE)*, pages 52–66. Publication 841, Dept. d'informatique et de recherche opérationelle, Univ. de Montréal, Canada, Jun 1992.

[9] P. H. Hartel and W. G. Vree. Experiments with destructive updates in a lazy functional language. Technical report CS-93-05, Dept. of Comp. Sys, Univ. of Amsterdam, Jun 1993.

[10] P. Hudak. Arrays, non-determinism, side-effects, and parallelism: A functional perspective. In J. F. Fasel and R. M. Keller, editors, *Graph reduction, LNCS 279*, pages 312–327, Santa Fé, New Mexico, Sep 1986. Springer-Verlag, Berlin.

[11] P. Hudak. A semantic model of reference counting and its abstraction. In *Lisp and functional programming*, pages 351–363, Cambridge, Massachusetts, Aug 1986. ACM.

[12] P. Hudak. Conception, evolution, and application of functional programming languages. *ACM Computing Surveys*, 21(3):359–411, Sep 1989.

[13] P. Hudak, S. L. Peyton Jones, and P. L. Wadler (editors). Report on the programming language Haskell – a non-strict purely functional language, version 1.2. *ACM SIGPLAN notices*, 27(5):1–162, May 1992.

[14] C. McCrosky, K. Roy, and K. Sailor. Falafel: Arrays in a functional language. In L. M. R. Mullin, M. Jenkins, G. Hains, R. Bernecky, and G. Gao, editors, *1st Arrays, functional languages, and parallel systems (ATABLE)*, pages 107–123, Boston, Massachusetts, Jun 1990. Kluwer Academic Publishers.

[15] S. L. Peyton Jones and P. L. Wadler. Imperative functional programming. In *20th Principles of programming languages*, pages 71–84, Charleston, South Carolina, Jan 1993. ACM.

[16] W. H. Press, B. P. Flannery, S. A. Tekolsky, and W. T. Vetterling. *Numerical recipes – The art of scientific computing.* Cambridge Univ. Press, Cambridge, England, 1986.

[17] D. A. Schmidt. Detecting global variables in denotational specifications. *ACM transactions on programming languages and systems*, 7(2):299–310, Apr 1985.

[18] S. Smetsers, E. Barendsen, M. C. J. D. van Eekelen, and M. J. Plasmeijer. Guaranteeing safe destructive updates through a type system with uniqueness information for graphs. Technical report 93-04, Dept. of Comp. Sci, Univ. of Nijmegen, The Netherlands, 1993.

[19] W. R. Stoye. *The implementation of functional programming languages using custom hardware.* PhD thesis, Univ. of Cambridge, England, Dec 1985. Technical report 81.

[20] P. L. Wadler. A new array operation. In J. F. Fasel and R. M. Keller, editors, *Graph reduction, LNCS 279*, pages 328–333, Santa Fé, New Mexico, Sep 1986. Springer-Verlag, Berlin.

[21] P. L. Wadler. The concatenate vanishes. Internal report, Dept. of Comp. Sci, Univ. of Glasgow, Scotland, Dec 1987.

The *aim* is laziness in a data-parallel language

Jonathan M.D. Hill*

Queen Mary and Westfield College

University of London

Abstract

Although many data-parallel functional languages exist, *Lisp [22], NESL [2], Paralation Lisp [20], FX [23] and Parallel EuLisp [14], few researchers have investigated incorporating data-parallelism with a lazy language. This paper describes data-parallel extensions which have been incorporated into the lazy functional language Haskell. We describe PODs, parallel data structures that share many of the characteristics of Haskell arrays—their distinguishing feature however is they are unbounded. We present POD comprehensions, a framework within which communication and parallel operations on PODs can be expressed. The semantics of these extensions is given in terms of translation rules into a core set of primitive parallel operations. Particular attention is given to the non-strict nature of these extensions. Development of the higher order parallel map, fold, and scan is presented, a trio of functions that is widely accepted as being fundamental to a data-parallel paradigm [21]. Ladner [12] classifies a problem as being susceptible to parallel scanning if it is of a fixed size and can be solved by a finite state transducer. We show that by utilising lazy evaluation, Ladner's requirements can be relaxed such that the lazy version of scan presented here has the potential to scan an infinite POD.

1 Data-parallelism vs. Lazy evaluation

The essence of data-parallelism is a $\mathcal{O}(1)$ map function. A data-parallel interpretation of map is the application of a function to every element of a parallel data structure at the *same time*. This model is at odds with a version of map on lists. Although list map can be interpreted as applying a function to every element of a list, in a non-strict language the function applications only occur to those elements required by a subsequent computation. To highlight this dichotomy we investigate the potential for data-parallelism on lazy lists and monolithic arrays.

The mapping of the increment function (+1) in exList of figure 1 could be applied in a data-parallel manner to each element of the list xs, because the surrounding sum consumes all of the resulting list. As a general rule, if a map expression is enclosed by a function that is both head and tail strict [25], then the data-parallel evaluation of the map is *probably* feasible. If we aim to implement this model on a massively parallel SIMD machine, parallelism can

---

*This work has been supported through a SERC case award in association with Cambridge Parallel Processing.

```
>map f []    = []            >amap f a= array b [i:=f (a!i)| i<-range b]
>map f (x:xs)= f x:map f xs   >         where b = bounds a
>                             >
>exList xs                    >exArray arr
>   = sum (map (+1) xs)       >   = sum (take 8 (elems (amap (1/) arr)))
```

Figure 1: List & Array Map

only be achieved on data-structures that span contiguous memory locations---
this is at odds with the conventional run-time representation of lists.

Although lists seem unsuitable for data-parallel evaluation, monolithic arrays [13, 9] provide a more practical framework. Figure 1 defines the Haskell
array mapping function. The function **array** creates a monolithic array. The
first argument defines the bounds of the array, and the second defines a list of
associations of the form '*index*:=*value*' where the contents of the array at *index*
are defined to be *value*. The **array** function is strict in both the bounds and
the indices of the association list. Yet as was seen to be the case with lists, the
non-strictness associated with the values of array elements interacts awkwardly
with data-parallel evaluation. For example, because of the non-strictness associated with **take** and **amap**, the mapping of the reciprocal function (1/) is
only applied to the first eight elements of **arr**. We can see from the definition
of **exArray** that it is possible to determine at *compile-time* that only the first
eight elements of **arr** are required; does this form a general rule?

Jouret [11] neatly side steps these issues whilst using a set of data-parallel
extensions similar to Haskell's array operations. He overcomes the difficulties of
laziness by ensuring that array creation, and the parallel map-like application
of functions to array elements, is strict on the entire array (akin to head and
tail strictness of a list). In Jouret's model, if any of the elements of **arr** in the
function **exArray** contain zero, then the result of evaluation will always be ⊥,
regardless of whether the array element that contained zero was required. We
find this extra strictness uncomfortable in a non-strict language.

We propose an evaluation mechanism that combines the desirable features
of the lazy and strict evaluation of map. Whenever a map-like computation
is forced, multiple elements of the parallel object being mapped evaluate their
results in synchrony. However, the mechanism retains non-strict semantics. So
far, non-strictness and data-parallelism have been mixed if it is possible to determine that the entirety (or portion) of the object resulting from a map-like
computation is known to be required at *compile-time*. The model we propose
delays this choice to *run-time* when we know exactly what needs to be evaluated. By maintaining a run-time data structure (called the *aim*) of those
elements that are required to be evaluated, whenever a map-like computation
is forced, the function applications of the map are evaluated in parallel *at those
elements defined by the aim*. At the cost of introducing a new data-parallel
non-strict evaluation mechanism, map can be implemented with a $\mathcal{O}(1)$ whilst
retaining all the benefits of non-strict evaluation.

Pragmatically the technique is a generalisation of conventional implementations of non-strict languages. The G-machine [17] has a single aim represented
by a pointer from the top of the spine stack to the redex under evaluation;
the STG machine's [18] aim is to evaluate the closure pointed to by the node
register.

The presentation of the material in the rest of the paper falls into four parts. First we give an informal definition of the parallel objects that form the basis of our language. This acts as an introduction to the parallel notation we propose—POD comprehensions. We informally present the syntax and semantics of this notation by contrasting it with list comprehensions present in languages such as Haskell and Miranda[1]. Next we give the formal semantics of POD comprehensions by giving translation rules into a set of primitive parallel operations. Unfortunately these operations are similar to the POD comprehensions given earlier—we have not presented anything new yet! We remedy this by developing a parallel implementation of higher order scan. We pay particular attention to the use of laziness in its implementation. Finally we describe how *aims* are used to utilise the operational characteristics of scan in the implementation of a parallel fold—although the *aim* is an implementation technique, it is all pervasive in data-parallel programs.

2 PODS and POD comprehensions

All parallelism in Data Parallel Haskell (DPHaskell) is achieved by operations on parallel data structures called PODs. A POD represents a collection of index/value pairs, where each index uniquely identifies a single element of a POD[2]. As PODs are an abstraction of the processing elements of a data-parallel machine, we choose to collect the index value pairs into a data type we call a 'processor'. For example, $(|42;"DON'T\ PANIC"|)$ represents a single processor of a one-dimensional POD (a vector). It determines that the value of the POD at a position identified by 42 is "DON'T PANIC". Higher dimensional PODs are characterised by having multiple indices to identify a single element of a POD. The general form of a processor is $(|e_1,\ldots,e_k;e|)$; where $k \geq 1$. The sequence of expressions e_1 to e_k uniquely identifies an element in a k-dimensional parallel object; e describes the data in that element.

In many ways monolithic arrays are a simple abstraction of conventional imperative arrays. Peyton-Jones and Wadler [19] outline a method of implementing monolithic arrays on top of imperative C-style arrays. PODs are different however. Because our non-strict evaluation mechanism only initialises and manipulates those elements of a POD that are required to be evaluated, PODs have the potential to be infinite[3]. For example, the expression $<<\ ..2..\ >>$ represents a POD in which every processor from $-\infty$ to $+\infty$ contains the number 2. In contrast, the expression $<<\ (|1;2|)\ ,\ (|3;4|)\ >>$ defines a POD in which two processors are defined. If a POD is evaluated at an index where no processor is defined, then the result of evaluation is $\perp$ (we describe the motivation behind this in section 3.5).

Parallel algorithms are expressed in DPHaskell by using a syntax analogous to list comprehensions (also known as Zermelo-Fraenkel expressions) introduced

---

[1] Miranda is a trademark of Research Software Ltd.

[2] Types that are instances of the class Pid (processor identifier) are assumed to be isomorphic to a subset of the integers, and may be used as the indices of a POD.

[3] In an implementation, a dense finite object is created, with a size equal to the difference between the smallest and largest indices defined by the aim. If PODs are re-evaluated with a different aim, then the representation of a POD grows accordingly—they have an extensible feature similar to O'Donnell's ESF arrays [15].

(a) List comprehension	`negateL xs= [-x | x <- xs]`	
(b) POD comprehension	`negateV vec= <<(|y;-x|) | (|y;x|) <<- vec >>`	
(c) Redefinition of (b) using higher order vector map	`vectorMap f vec= <<(|y;f x|) | (|y;x|) <<- vec >>` `negateV= vectorMap (\x -> -x)`	

Figure 2: From lists to vectors—mapping negate in parallel

by Burstall and Darlington in the language NPL [4], and Turner in the languages SASL, KRC and Miranda [24]. Figure 2(a) defines a function that negates each element of a list using a Haskell list comprehension. This syntax provides a good starting point for a parallel notation because it decomposes a problem into the transformations that occur at each element of a list. Figure 2(b) defines a corresponding POD comprehension. The desired reading of the function is "For each defined processor in **vec** identified by **y**, that contains data **x**, create a one-dimensional POD such that each processor at **y** contains the data **-x**". Examining the definition, we see that only '-' is specific to the **negateV** function. This means that the computation of the vector negate can be modularised by gluing together a general POD comprehension and a function that is applied to each defined element of a POD. By parameterising the definition of **negateV** we derive **vectorMap** defined in figure 2(c). As the motivation behind the aim evaluation mechanism was the efficient parallel implementation of a non-strict map, it is not surprising that **vectorMap** has a $\mathcal{O}(1)$ in relation to the size of the vector being mapped.

Whenever multiple generators are used in a list comprehension, all possible combinations of values are produced as a result. For example the expression
```
[ (x,y) | x <- [1..10], y <- [1..10] ]
```
generates the cartesian product of two lists. More surprisingly
```
[ x | x <- [1..10], y <- [1..10] ]
```
generates a list with 100 elements—the computational interpretation of generators is very much tied to iteration. Since we believe that effective use of a parallel machine with thousands of processing elements can only be attained with PODs containing thousands of elements, a strategy that relies upon a combinatorial explosion of values must somehow be avoided—the physical constraints of a machines memory will soon be exhausted if PODs contained millions of elements. The solution we adopt to this problem is two fold: (1) we ensure that for each element drawn from a generator, only one element will be drawn from subsequent generators—'zip like' drawing; (2) the drawing of elements from the generators of a POD comprehension is performed lazily such that values are drawn only as required.

Addressing the first of these issues, we exploit the fact that the index of a POD element is unique. If we draw an element $(|i;v|)$ from a POD, we can be sure that we will not be able to draw any other element with index i. We may however wish to draw an element $(|i;w|)$ with the same index i, from some other POD in a different generator. We therefore propose two versions of the generator: $(|p;p_d|)$ **<<-POD** is read as *drawn-from* and names in the patterns p and p_d are bound by the generator; $(|e;p_i|)$ **<<=POD** is read *indexed-from* and the value represented by the expression e determines which processor's contents should be matched against the pattern p_i. Drawn-

(a) `addV vecA vecB = << (|x;a+b|) | (|x;a|) <<- vecA, (|x;b|) <<= vecB >>`

(b) `shiftAnd vec = << (|x;a&&b|) | (|x;a|) <<- vec, (|x-1;b|) <<= vec >>`

(c) `negateV' vec = << (|x;-y|) | (|x;y|) <<- vec, (|x;z|) <<= ⊥ >>`

Figure 3: The lazy semantics of POD comprehensions

from generators provide a point of interest[4] for subsequent generators in a comprehension. Therefore the expression x in the index generator of figure 3(a) is bound by the pattern x in the preceding drawn-from generator. The intended semantics are that the constraint of the generators ensures zip-like drawing. The comprehension therefore defines a vector addition expression. Comprehensions are not just restricted to simple zip-like drawing. The index-generator in figure 3(b) defines a constraint x-1 which results in communication between elements of the PODs—we return to communication a little later.

The second issue, crucial to the semantics of generators, is lazy drawing. Using `<<-` draws elements from processors in a strict manner—the processors have to be defined for a result to be defined; however `<<=` draws processors and their contents from a POD lazily depending upon the strictness characteristics of their subsequent use. An analogy can be made between this model and refutable and irrefutable (strict and lazy) pattern matching in Haskell. The definition of **negateV'** shown in figure 3(c) has the same semantics as the earlier definition of **negateV** in figure 2(b), since the variable z is not used in the comprehension. In contrast a similar list comprehension below tries to draw elements from ⊥, resulting in the comprehension evaluating to ⊥.

$$[-x \mid x \gets [1..10], y \gets \perp]$$

Figure 3(b) shows a more subtle example in which processors and their contents only have to be defined depending upon the strictness of **&&**. Given a processor identified by x that contains **False**, due to the laziness of **&&**, neither the processor nor its contents at a position identified by x-1 need to be defined. We clarify such semantics in section 4.

The constraint used in the function **shiftAnd** of figure 3(b) causes communication between elements of the vector **vec**. We generalise such communication into two models: fetching data from a remote processor to a local processor, and sending data from a local processor to a remote one. The first expression shown in figure 4 uses the sending model of communication. Data stored in a processor identified by x is sent to a processor at location x+2. The effect is to shift every defined processors contents two places to their right. In contrast, the expression on the right of figure 4 uses the fetching model of data communication. The value x bound by the drawn-from generator (`<-`) represents the processor in which data will be placed. The data is fetched from the contents of a processor determined by the constraint on the index-generator (`<=`). By drawing elements from the infinite POD in the drawn-from generator (every processor and *index* is defined), a binding occurrence for x is provided for subsequent generators[5]. In these examples, as the lambda expression that represents the fetch is the inverse of that used in the send, the two expressions

---

[4]Comprehensions contain at most one drawn-from generator as multiple points of interest make little sense.

[5]Although the use of **inf** looks clumsy, rarely is such trickery required in a fetch computation. For example, the fetch used in the definition of parallel scan in section 5.2.

```
let f = \z -> z + 2                let f' = \z -> z - 2
in << (|f x;y|) | (|x;y|) <<- vec>>    inf = << .. 42 .. >>
                                   in << (|x;y|) | (|x;_|)    <<- inf,
                                        (|f' x;y|) <<= vec >>
```

Figure 4: The duality of send and fetch

are equivalent. This equivalence between sending and fetching expressions does not always hold as the inverse to a function used in data communication may not exist. For example, with the sending expression

<< (|f a; v|) | (|a;v|) <<- vec >>

vec may contain (|x;vx|) and (|y;vy|) where f x ≡ f y. In this case, either (| f x; vx|) or (| f y; vy|) might appear in the solution, though not both since an index must identify a unique value. An implementation may choose either solution (see section 3.5).

Constraints of a different nature can also be applied to POD comprehensions in the form of boolean guards. These guards act as filters that select those processors for which the guard is **True** from a more general stream created by the generators. For example the expression

<< (|x;x|) | (|x;42|) <<- vec , even x >>

defines a POD in which each processor contains the same number as its processor identifier as long as that processor originally contained the number 42, and its processor identifier is even.

3   The semantics of POD comprehensions: primitive operations

Note: On the first reading it may be advisable to go straight to section 5.

The formal semantics of PODs and POD comprehensions is given in terms of translation rules that produce Haskell enriched with the primitive parallel operations $\overline{MAP_n}$, $\overline{INDICES}$, $\overline{FETCH}$ and $\overline{SEND}$. The rules provide an insight into the implementation of the data-parallel extensions by using a 'concrete' representation of parallel objects, and all communication is performed by primitive data-rearrangement operations. The semantics of these parallel primitives can be found in [8]; here we give an informal description of the primitives, backed-up by some equations (figure 6) which we hope are not completely circular.

3.1   Bottom and the representation of PODs

Before describing the primitive parallel operations, we set the scene by highlighting various problems and peculiarities associated with bottom ($\perp$) in data-parallel programs.

Figure 5(a) defines an expression with a value equivalent to $\perp$. Evaluation at an undefined processor of a POD results in $\perp$; the expression in figure 5(b) is therefore interpreted as only defining values for processors one and three. The semantics of (b) differs from the POD shown in figure 5(c), although indexing (b) and (c) at any index produces the same values. The difference between the two expressions is highlighted by mapping (\x -> 42) over each POD. Indexing the resulting PODs at processors two results in $\perp$ and 42 for (b) and

```
(a) let bot = bot in bot          (d) let f 0 = bot
(b) << (|1;2|),(|3;4|) >>                  f n = n
(c) << (|1,2|),(|2;bot|),(|3;4|) >>   in << (|f x;y|) | (|x;y|) <<- vec >>
```

Figure 5: A selection of bottoms

(c) respectively. Figure 5(d) shows a peculiar case of bottom; if the expression in the index position of a processor on the left-hand side of comprehension results in bottom (such as processor zero in (d)), the effect is to erase that processor's contents from the resulting POD representation—a POD can never be indexed at processor $\perp$.

Keeping such characteristics of PODs in mind, we present a representation of a POD suitable for implementation on a SIMD machine. A conventional non-strict evaluation mechanism enables expressions such as (a) to be manipulated. An extended evaluator based upon the *aim* mechanism allows expressions such as (c) and (d) because only those processors defined by the aim are ever evaluated. Unfortunately, (b) poses problems. PODs are implemented as extensible, dense, array-like structures—if processors $x-1$ and $x+1$ exist, then processor x exists. Such an 'implementation' POD has no representation for the semantics required in figure 5(b). The implementation POD requires a representation of "not here" for any undefined processors. A solution to this problem is to represent PODs by the product type:

```
data << (|Int;a|) >> = MkPod <<< Bool >>> <<< a >>>
```

where `<<< a >>>` represents an implementation POD of type a. Wherever the value of an entry in the boolean mask defined in the first part of the product type is **True**, the corresponding element in the second POD has a defined processor—"I'm here". Although it seems that a lot of trouble has been expended on fulfilling the desired semantics of figure 5(b), they ensure an important invariant that is required in the implementation of $\overline{MAP}_n$ (see [8] for details).

3.2 map

The primitive function $\overline{MAP}_n$ is analogous to the family of list functions, map, zipWith, zipWith$_3$, ..., zipWith$_n$. For $n > 1$, the drawing of elements occurs as required in a zip-like manner by index. All the function applications of the map occur synchronously and in parallel at those processors defined by the aim of evaluation. However, there seems to be a flaw with this approach. How can a potentially infinite number of application closures be initialised in an infinite POD all at the same time? The solution is to use a special kind of closure that can represent head normal forms and function closures at the same time. Evaluation of a POD with a *finite* aim, results in a finite data-structure which details the evaluated parts of the POD, and includes a closure which represents the rest. If a subsequent evaluation of this POD occurs, and all the head normal forms are detailed for the current aim, then no computation arises—the implementation is lazy. Otherwise the closure is evaluated and the detail is updated. There are many subtle problems associated with such a strategy: updating of algebraic data types; multiple function-valued closures; potential space leaks because of the retention of both the result and the original

$$\overline{\text{INDICES}}\ mask \quad = \quad \ll (|x;x|) \mid (|x;\text{True}|)\texttt{<<-}mask \gg$$

$$\overline{\text{FETCH}}\ ipod\ data \quad = \quad \ll (|x;d|) \mid (|x;i|)\texttt{<<-}ipod,\ (|i;d|)\texttt{<<=}data \gg$$

$$\overline{\text{SEND}}\ ipod\ data \quad = \quad \ll (|i;d|) \mid (|x;i|)\texttt{<<-}ipod,\ (|x;d|)\texttt{<<=}data \gg$$

Figure 6: The semantics of the primitive parallel operations

closure application. For a detailed description of the implementation of $\overline{\text{MAP}}_n$ in relationship to a modified Spineless Tagless G-machine, see [8].

3.3 indices

A POD comprehension manipulates the indices of a POD as integers. Like arrays, the indices of a POD are an abstraction of the contiguous nature of a machines memory. Given the index of the first array element, the nth array element can be calculated accordingly. As the indices are an implicit part of the POD representation, the primitive function $\overline{\text{INDICES}}$ 'recreates' the processor number by converting a POD of booleans into a POD in which each processor contains an integer that represents the processor number. The semantics of $\overline{\text{INDICES}}$ is encapsulated by the pseudo-POD comprehension shown in figure 6.

3.4 fetching

Evaluation of the primitive "$\overline{\text{FETCH}}$ ipod data" initially evaluates the index POD of integers ipod. Each processor of ipod ($|x;i|$) brings the contents of a processor identified by i from data into itself. The novel feature of fetching communication is that it is inherently lazy. In the implementation, if a fetching primitive is evaluated with an aim α, then only those processors of ipod defined by α are evaluated. Once evaluated, this POD is used to construct a new aim β which is used in the evaluation of data. Once data is evaluated, communication occurs that transfers the contents of each of the evaluated processors into a destination specified by the original index POD ipod. This technique of implementing fetch ensures that where possible, data-valued closures are communicated *and not functions*.

3.5 sending

Two problems need to be addressed with the sending primitive: (1) sending does not fit into the 'aim' model of evaluation—a search of a potentially infinite POD is required; (2) multiple processors may send their contents to the same processor—it is not clear how this should be resolved.

The first of these problems is a result of incorporating laziness into a data-parallel language. Aims are a technique of ensuring that map can be implemented in a synchronous manner on a data-parallel machine. In the implementation, a data-parallel evaluation mechanism threads the aim throughout a program, continually calculating which set of processors needs to be evaluated. The sending primitive throws a spanner into the works of the aim mechanism.

$aexp \rightarrow$ << $(\|exp;exp\|)$ | $pqual_1,\dots,pqual_n$ >>	(POD comprehension)
$pqual \rightarrow exp$	(filter)
| $(\|var;var\|)$ <<- exp	(drawn-from)
| $(\|exp;var\|)$ <<= exp	(index-from)

Figure 7: Simplified syntax of POD comprehensions

If the primitive "$\overline{\text{SEND}}$ *ipod data*" is evaluated with an aim α (where $i \in \alpha$), then the index pod *ipod* is searched to find a corresponding processor ($\|x;i\|$) to create a new index pod *ipod'*:

$$ipod' = \{\ (\|i;x\|)\ |\ \forall i \in \alpha\ \wedge\ (\|x;i\|) \in ipod\}$$

Once *ipod'* is evaluated, the primitive "$\overline{\text{FETCH}}$ *ipod' data*" is performed; the essence of send is the run-time calculation of what processors are needed to convert the send into a fetch. Unfortunately an arbitrary amount of the potentially infinite index pod *ipod* has to be generated to determine which elements send their data to all the processors defined by the aim. If no processor sends its data to a processor identified by the aim, then evaluation of the index vector may continue for a *very* long time. This is the motivation behind the 'bottom' semantics for undefined processors—the search of the index pod may not terminate (ouch!).

The second problem associated with sending has been addressed many times elsewhere [20, 22]. The common technique used to resolve collisions in a send is to apply an associative binary operator to all colliding data. Jouret [11] generalises this technique by accumulating the results of a send as a list in each processor. Unfortunately, these techniques are not generally applicable in an environment that allows infinite parallel objects. Using Jouret's model, the results of a send will be accumulated as a list within each defined processor. However, each list will not be nil (i.e []) terminated—the tail of the list will always contain bottom as we cannot determine when a potentially infinite set of processors have stopped sending data. This means strict functions such as + cannot be used to resolve collisions. The solution we adopt is to choose a single value from the colliding data. Although this implies a non-deterministic semantics, an implementation on a SIMD machine will always be deterministic.

In the implementation of DPHaskell, the unsatisfactory nature of send has led to ad-hoc techniques that try and resolve the problems of send. As send is only trying to convert itself into a fetch at runtime, one solution is to convert sending-type communications into fetches at compile-time. For a description of some remedies for send, and general techniques for optimizing communication operations into simpler communications that utilise a specific machines capabilities (such as shifting communication), see [8].

4 The semantics of POD comprehensions: desugaring

The semantics of a syntactically restricted subset of the POD comprehension notation is presented in-terms of a series of translation rules that 'desugar' comprehensions into the primitive parallel operations presented in the previous section (figure 7). The motivation behind this desugaring is the conversion of the 'microscopic' view of transformations applied to the elements of a

POD, into a 'macroscopic' view of applying monolithic operations to the POD as a whole. This translation provides the foundations for the vectorization of functional programs described in [8]. The translation scheme TPOD performs the conversion of 'views'. The initial state of the translation scheme is TPOD [[*pod*]] [] <<<..True..>>>. To eliminate scoping problems the patterns of the generators are assumed to be unique variables. The following information is required for book-keeping purposes:

1. a mapping from bindings in a source language comprehension that represent elements of a parallel object, to bindings in the translated language that represent entire parallel objects. For example, given the expression '$x + 2$' where x represents an element of a parallel object, the translation produces expressions of the form '$\overline{MAP}_1$ (\ x ->$x + 2$) **x**' in which **x** represents the entire parallel object that x is an element of—the mapping $x \mapsto$ **x** is recorded during translation.

2. a mask which defines the valid processors in the POD resulting from the comprehension.

4.1 Drawn-from

Drawn-from generators provide a mechanism of anchoring a point of interest for subsequent generators in a comprehension. Those processors defined in the POD being drawn-from are used to define the processors in the POD that results from the comprehension. Translation rule 1 below encapsulates such semantics. Case analysis is first performed on the POD on the right-hand side of the generator to expose its implementation structure. The exposed **mask** that represents the defined processors of *vec* is then threaded through successive calls to the translation scheme, eventually re-emerging in rule 4 to define the valid processors of the POD that results from the comprehension. Notice how the **x** and **y** in the translated code represent all the indices and contents of *vec*, whereas x and y in the original comprehension represented a single index and element of the POD *vec*. The implementation structure of PODs is reinforced by this rule, as a vector of integers that represents *vec*'s indices is created by the $\overline{\text{INDICES}}$ primitive.

```
TPOD [ << e | (| x ; y |) <<- vec , q >> ] binds mask_junked
  = case vec of
      MkPod mask y ->   let x = INDICES mask                      Rule 1
                        in TPOD [ << e | q >> ] (binds; x ↦ x; y ↦ y) mask
```

4.2 Indexed-from

Indexed-from generators provide a mechanism of expressing communication in DPHaskell. They have non-strict semantics because elements are drawn from the POD on the right-hand side of the generator as required. We achieve this in translation rule 2 by using the non-strict properties of let expressions and irrefutable pattern matching (contrast the case expressions in rules 1 and 2). Elements are 'logically' drawn from *vec* only when y is evaluated in an inner scope of the comprehension. Unlike rule 1, the defined processors of *vec* are not used to define the processors of the resulting comprehension. In other data-parallel languages a zip-like computation results in a parallel object whose extent is defined by the intersection of the argument objects. In DPHaskell, the resulting POD will have processors defined wherever they are defined in the drawn-from generator. Any further restrictions caused by the index generators depend upon the strictness characteristics of the functions that force the index generator's vector. This is achieved in rule 2 by suspending the 'processor exists' check within the let expression identified by **y**. When **y** is forced, a fetch communication occurs that evaluates the index vector represented by the expression e_f. This vector is then used to create the aim for evaluation of **data'**. Only at this point in the whole computation is the processor exists check performed, and **data'** evaluated.

$$\begin{aligned}
&\textsf{TPOD}\ [\![\ <<\ e\ |\ (|\ e_f\ ;\ y\ |)\ <<=\ vec\ ,\ q\ >>\ ]\!]\ (b_1 \mapsto b_1; \ldots; b_n \mapsto b_n)\ mask \\
&=\ \textsf{case}\ vec\ \textsf{of} \\
&\quad \tilde{}(\textsf{MkPod mask' data'})\ \text{->} \\
&\qquad \textsf{let y} = \overline{\textsf{FETCH}}\ (\overline{\textsf{MAP}}_n\ (\backslash b_1 \ldots b_n\ \text{->}\ e_f)\ b_1 \ldots b_n) \\
&\qquad\qquad\qquad\qquad (\overline{\textsf{MAP}}_2\ (\backslash \textsf{m d}\ \text{->}\ \textsf{if m then d else}\ \bot\ )\ \textsf{mask' data'}) \\
&\qquad \textsf{in TPOD}\ [\![\ <<\ e\ |\ q\ >>\ ]\!]\ (y \mapsto \textsf{y}; b_1 \mapsto b_1; \ldots; b_n \mapsto b_n)\ mask
\end{aligned}$$

Rule 2

4.3 Filtering

Translation rule 3 for filtering expressions is relatively straightforward. As a filter restricts those processors of the POD resulting from the comprehension, we apply the logical 'and' of the mask that represents the defined processors and the filtering expression.

$$\begin{aligned}
&\textsf{TPOD}\ [\![\ <<e|\ e_f\ ,\ q\ >>\ ]\!]\ (b_1 \mapsto b_1; \ldots; b_n \mapsto b_n)\ mask \\
&=\ \textsf{TPOD}\ [\![\ <<e|\ q\ >>\ ]\!]\ (b_1 \mapsto b_1; \ldots; b_n \mapsto b_n) \\
&\qquad\qquad (\overline{\textsf{MAP}}_{n+1}\ (\backslash m\ b_1 \ldots b_n \text{->}\ m\ \&\&\ e_f)\ mask\ b_1 \cdots b_n)
\end{aligned}$$

Rule 3

4.4 Left-hand side

The base case for the translation scheme is shown in rule 4. An expression such an e_1 in the index position of a processor represents a sending type communication. We apply such communication to the mask that represents the defined processors, and the expression e_2 that represents the contents of those processors. This new mask and parallel object is finally used to recreate the user representation of a POD that encapsulates the meaning of the original POD comprehension.

$$\begin{aligned}
&\textsf{TPOD}\ [\![\ <<\ (|\ e_1\ ;\ e_2\ |)\ |\ >>\ ]\!]\ (b_1 \mapsto b_1; \ldots; b_n \mapsto b_n)\ \textsf{mask} \\
&=\ \textsf{let svec} = \overline{\textsf{MAP}}_n\ (\backslash b_1 \ldots b_n\ \text{->}\ e_1\ )\ b_1 \ldots b_n \\
&\quad \textsf{in MkPod}\ (\overline{\textsf{SEND}}\ \textsf{svec mask}) \\
&\qquad\qquad (\overline{\textsf{SEND}}\ \textsf{svec}\ (\overline{\textsf{MAP}}_n\ (\backslash b_1 \ldots b_n\ \text{->}\ e_2\ )\ b_1 \ldots b_n\ ))
\end{aligned}$$

Rule 4

Section 2 hinted at the possibility of simplifying communications expressed in terms of send into semantically equivalent communications using fetch. Rule 4 of **TPOD** always introduces a sending communication which, with a little effort, can be eliminated from the translated code. For example, in the translation below, the index vector **svec** used in both $\overline{\textsf{SEND}}$ operations is the vector created by the $\overline{\textsf{INDICES}}$ function. As the send communicates each processor's contents to itself, the send primitive can be removed from the translated program.

```
TPOD [ << (|x;a&&b|) | (|x;a|)<<- vec, (|x-1;b|)<<= vec,f x >> ] [] <<<..True..>>>
⇒ case vec of
    MkPod mask a ->
       let x = INDICES mask
       in case vec of
           ˜(MkPod mask' data') ->
               let y = FETCH (MAP₂(\x a -> x -1) x a)
                             (MAP₂(\m d -> if m then d else ⊥) mask' data'
               in let svec = MAP₃(\b x a -> x) b x a)
                   in MkPod (SEND svec (MAP₄(\m b x a -> m && f x) mask b x a))
                           (SEND svec (MAP₃(\b x a -> a && b ) b x a))
```

5   Deriving a parallel scan function

Scan is widely accepted as a fundamental technique of a data-parallel paradigm. Its uses have been as diverse as sorting, line drawing [1], normal order reduction of the λ-calculus [16], lexical analysis [22, 7], word searching [6], implementing iterative constructs such as **for** and **while** loops [3], and LL(1) parsing [6, 7] to name but a few. A step-by-step guide to the parallel implementation of scan is presented. By concentrating on the associated problem of evaluating the partial sums of a series $\{x_0, \ldots, x_n\}$, defined by equation (1), the relationship between parallelism and non-strictness is explored. Unlike existing implementations of scan, a non-strict version presented here, has the potential to scan an infinite POD—Ladner's [12] requirement of a fixed length input for a parallel scan no longer applies.

$$f(\{x_0, x_1, \ldots, x_n\}) = \{x_0, \sum_{i=0}^{1} x_i, \sum_{i=0}^{2} x_i, \ldots, \sum_{i=0}^{n} x_i\} \tag{1}$$

5.1   Sequential: the partial sums of a list

Since the partial sums function computes a series of numbers, it is natural to represent this series as a list. By reading equation (1) denotationally, we can inductively define the partial sums function over a non-empty list as: the partial sums of the singleton list is the singleton list; the kth partial sum of the list $[x_0, \ldots, x_k, \ldots, x_n]$ is equal to the kth element added to the sum of the preceding $k - 1$ elements, i.e.

```
> partialSums :: Num a => [a] -> [a]
> partialSums []     = error "partialSums: [] list"
> partialSums (x:xs) = psums x xs
>    where psums acc []     = [acc]
>          psums acc (x:xs) = acc :psums (acc+x) xs
```

The accumulating parameter of the auxiliary function **psums** is used to represent the partial sum of the preceding $k - 1$ elements of the list. The function's complexity is $\mathcal{O}(N)$ for a list of length N.

5.2   Parallel: a first attempt

Using a parallel implementation of graph reduction such as that offered by the GRIP [5] machine, there are opportunities for parallelism in an application of

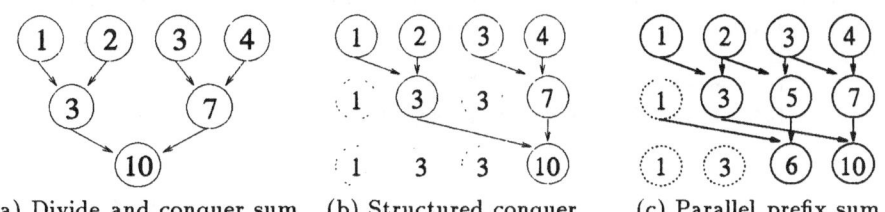

(a) Divide and conquer sum   (b) Structured conquer   (c) Parallel prefix sum

Figure 8: The path to a parallel scan

`partialSums`. Yet if the entire list of results are needed from such an application, the complexity of the `partialSums` function can be no better than $\mathcal{O}(N)$. One reason for this bound on complexity is the sequential ordering of solutions caused by the kth element of the solution depending on all preceding elements. The first step towards a truly parallel implementation is attained by breaking this dependence.

A similar problem to that of generating the partial sums is shown in figure 8(a), where the sum of a one-dimensional POD of numbers (the circles represent processors) is achieved by a divide and conquer technique. The dependence between consecutive elements of the POD has been broken by utilising the associativity of addition. If we were implementing this divide and conquer algorithm on a data-parallel machine, we would impose a structure on the combination of processors such that all the combinations at each level of the evaluation tree shown in figure 8(a) occur synchronously, and in parallel.

Such a structure is enforced in the divide and conquer algorithm shown in figure 8(b). As would be expected, the last element of the vector contains the sum of the vector, yet the first two processors also contain their partials sums. The key to producing a parallel partial sums function is to utilise all of the processors during each iteration of the divide and conquer algorithm.

Figure 8(c) shows such an algorithm which uses the parallel prefix technique [12, 1, 22]. We can generalise from this figure that during the kth iteration of the algorithm (where $k \geq 1$) a subset of the processing elements combine with a processor 2^{k-1} places to their left. If `vec` is the state of the vector during the start of each iteration, then we can express such a combination by the POD comprehension:

```
<< (|x;b+a|) | (|x;a|)              <<- vec,
            (|x - 2^(k-1); b|) <<= vec >>
```

Next, if `lo` is the processor identifier of the first element of the vector, then the processors in the range $-\infty$ to $\mathrm{lo}+2^{k-1}-1$ do not combine with any processors. This range of processors can be represented by the boolean vector:

```
<< (|x;x < lo+2^(k-1)|) | (|x;_|) <<- vec >>
```

Finally, we define the parallel partial sums function by merging the above expressions to form a single POD comprehension that represents the parallel combining process, and iterate this process a logarithmic number of times. The algorithms complexity is $\mathcal{O}(Log\ N)$ for an input of size N.

```
>parPartialSums::(Pid a,Ord a,Num a,Num b)=>a ->a -> <<(|a;b|)>> -> <<(|a;b|)>>
>parPartialSums lo hi vector = eachIter 1 vector
> where eachIter k vec
>          |2^k>hi-lo =vec
>          |otherwise =eachIter (k+1) << (|x;if x < lo+2^(k-1)
>                                            then a else b+a
>                                   |) | (|x;a|)              <<- vec,
>                                        (|x-2^(k-1);b|) <<= vec>>
```

5.3 Parallel: a lazier attempt

Having produced a parallel implementation of the partial sums function, we
aim to make the function lazier. One striking feature of figure 8(c) is the wave
of evaluation such that during the kth iteration of the algorithm, the processors
in the range lo to $lo+2^{k-1}-1$ contain their result. In a non-strict language, it
would be expected that if we evaluated the partial sums of processors 1 to n in
parallel, then only $Log_2(n)$ iterations of the parallel prefix technique would be
required before those processors contain their results. The definition of partial
sums above fails to do this because it doesn't utilise the non-strictness available
in DPHaskell. By analogy with fold in Haskell, we propose to convert the 'foldl'
nature of the partial sums definition, in which the resulting data structure is
not available until all the iterations of the partial sums function are complete
(because the definition is tail recursive), into a 'foldr' type definition in which
the results are available as soon as possible.

```
>parPartialSums'::(Pid a,Ord a,Num a,Num b)=> a -> <<(|a;b|)>> -> <<(|a;b|)>>
>parPartialSums' lo vector = eachIter' 1 vector
> where eachIter' k vec =let vec'= << (|x;b+a
>                                   |) | (|x;a|)              <<- vec,
>                                        (|x - 2^(k-1); b|) <<= vec>>
>                        in << (|x;if x < lo+2^(k-1) then a else b
>                                   |) | (|x;a|) <<- vec,
>                                        (|x;b|) <<= eachIter' (k+1) vec' >>
```

Notice how the lazy version of **parPartialSums'** above has no upper bound
(i.e no **hi** as an argument). The computation potentially continues indefinitely,
summing from a fixed point within a POD (represented by **lo**) up to ∞. Because
of the non-strict nature of DPHaskell's evaluation mechanism, *and* the non-
strictness associated with index-generators, a recurrence relation such as that
shown in the lower POD comprehension can be expressed. If we want to evaluate
the processors between 1 and n, then only $Log_2(n)$ iterations of **eachIter'** need
to be evaluated before the processors in the range 1 and n satisfy the condition
in the **if** expression. No more evaluation is required because the results are in
a normal form and the wave of evaluation has passed over them.

5.4 Higher order glue and fold

By examining the definition of the sequential and parallel partial sums function, we see that only the '+' is specific to the computation. We can therefore
parameterise both functions producing **scan11** as defined in the Haskell report
[9] and **vectorScan**.

```
>vectorScan::(Ord a,Num a,Pid a)=>(b->b->b) -> a -> <<(|a;b|)>> -> <<(|a;b|)>>
>vectorScan fn lo vector = eachIter 1 vector
> where eachIter k vec =let vec'=<< (|x;fn b a
>                                 |) | (|x;a|)                    <<- vec,
>                                    (|x - 2^(k-1); b|) <<= vec >>
>                    in << (|x;if x < lo+2^(k-1) then a else b
>                                 |) | (|x;a|) <<- vec,
>                                    (|x;b|) <<= eachIter (k+1) vec' >>
```

As opposed to the $\mathcal{O}(N)$ complexity of **scanl1**, **vectorScan** has a $\mathcal{O}(Log\ N)$ complexity. Unlike other implementations of scan in a data-parallel programming language, the definition here has the potential to scan an infinite POD—this is more general than the definition of parallel scan proposed by Ladner[12].

Having presented a scan algorithm, we re-use its definition in an implementation of fold. To calculate the result of a parallel fold between two indices of a POD *lo* and *hi*, we apply a parallel scan starting from *lo*, then index the resulting POD at index **hi**. We are applying a similar technique to **foldl f i xs** $\equiv$ **last (scanl f i xs)**. It would be expected that $Log_2(hi - lo)$ iterations of the parallel prefix technique would be forced, producing a logarithmic complexity fold. Unfortunately this doesn't work! Operationally the indexing of the POD will: (1) set the aim of evaluation to be the processor at the position we want to index; (2) evaluate the scan with this single aim; (3) extract the contents of the processor at the index in question. As there is only a singleton aim, the data-parallel evaluation mechanism is reduced to a sequential non-strict evaluation mechanism. Effective data-parallel evaluation relies upon a large aim such that sufficient elements of a parallel object evaluate their results synchronously.

It looks as though we have made a monumental mistake—yet all we have done is ignored the essence of DPHaskell. PODs and POD comprehensions allow the operational characteristics of data-parallelism to be expressed in a non-strict language. The fundamental characteristic of scan is that a collection of processors apply an associative binary operator in a synchronous manner. All we need to do is ensure that fold makes scan do this. We achieve this by forcing evaluation of all the processors between the indices we want to fold between, at the *same time*. The programmer controls such an operational behaviour by using **vectorStrict**. This function sets the aim of evaluation to all those processors between *lo* and *hi*, then evaluates the scan in parallel.

```
>vectorFold::(Ord a,Num a,Pid a)=> (b -> b -> b) -> a -> a -> <<(|a;b|)>> -> b
>vectorFold fn lo hi vec
>  = vectorIndex (vectorStrict lo hi (vectorScan fn lo vec)) hi
```

6 Conclusions

POD comprehensions provide a mechanism of expressing data-parallel computations. Using an evaluation strategy that maintains a record of the elements of a parallel object that need evaluating, data-parallelism and non-strictness can be incorporated in the same language. The features of DPHaskell that distinguish it from other data-parallel languages is its non-strict evaluation mechanism and higher order functions—the rationale behind the language is the same as Hughes's [10]. Higher order functions promote software re-use, however the

data-parallel versions of higher order **map**, **fold** and **scan** presented here, all
have better complexities than their sequential counterparts. Central to this
work is the ability to express computations on infinite PODs. As described in
Hughes [10], lazy data-structures provide a powerful mechanism of modularis-
ing programs because functions that compute over infinite data-structures can
be simply composed, or 'glued' together. In practical terms this means we
can ignore problems that arise from composing functions that perform computations over differing sized parallel data structures. By using infinite PODs
with functions such as **vectorScan**, finite computations can be performed on
the resulting 'glued' functions. Unlike existing data-parallel languages, POD
comprehensions provide a single framework within which communication and
parallelism can be expressed. We believe these extensions fit into the 'style'
of Haskell, their simplicity allows the programmer to express much 'bigger
thoughts' concisely [24].

7 Acknowledgements

I would like to thank Richard Bornat, Keith Clarke, Peter Flanders and Heather
Liddell for their help and guidance. Thanks also to Andy Ben-Dyke and all
those who reviewed this paper (particularly Simon Peyton Jones), for their
numerous constructive comments.

References

[1] G. E. Blelloch. Scans as primitive parallel operations. *IEEE Transactions on computers*, 38(11):1526–1538, Nov. 1989.

[2] G. E. Blelloch. NESL: A nested data-parallel language. Technical Report CMU-CS-93-129, Carnegie Mellon University, Apr. 1993.

[3] K. Clarke and J. M. D. Hill. Parallel Haskell: The not-so parallel features in parallel. Technical Report 658, QMW CS, Dec. 1993. Available by FTP from ftp.dcs.qmw.ac.uk in /pub/cpc/jon_hill/pHiterative.ps.

[4] J. Darlington. Program transformation and synthesis: present capabilities. Technical Report 77/43, Dept of Computing and Control, Imperial College, London, Sept. 1977.

[5] K. Hammond and S. L. Peyton Jones. Profiling scheduling strategies on the GRIP parallel reducer. Technical report, Glasgow University, 1991.

[6] J. M. D. Hill. Data Parallel Haskell: Mixing old and new glue. Technical Report 611, QMW CS, Dec. 1992. Available by FTP from ftp.dcs.qmw.ac.uk in /pub/cpc/jon_hill/dpGlue.ps.

[7] J. M. D. Hill. Parallel lexical analysis and parsing on the AMT Distributed Array Processor. *Parallel Computing*, 18(6):699–714, July 1992.

[8] J. M. D. Hill. Vectorizing a non-strict functional language for a data-parallel "Spineless (not so) Tagless G-Machine". In *Proc. of the 5th international workshop on the implementation of functional languages*, Nijmegen, Holland, Sept. 1993. Available by FTP from ftp.dcs.qmw.ac.uk in /pub/cpc/jon_hill/vectorizeNonStrict.ps.

[9] P. Hudak, S. L. Peyton Jones, and P. Wadler (editors). Report on the Programming Language Haskell, A Non-strict Purely Functional Language (Version 1.2). *ACM SIGPLAN Notices*, Mar. 1992.

[10] J. Hughes. Why functional programming matters. *The Computer Journal*, 32(2):98–107, 1989.

[11] G. K. Jouret. Compiling functional languages for SIMD architectures. In *Third IEEE Symposium on parallel and distributed processing*, pages 79–86, 1991.

[12] R. E. Ladner and M. J. Fischer. Parallel prefix computation. *JACM*, 27(4):831–838, Oct. 1980.

[13] P. J. Landin. A correspondence between ALGOL 60 and Church's lambda notation. *Communications of the ACM*, 8(2):89–101, Feb. 1965. Part 2 in CACM Vol 8(2) 1965, pages 158–165.

[14] S. Merall and J. Padget. Collections and garbage collection. In *International Workshop Memory Management, St.Malo*, pages 473–489. Springer-Verlag, 1992.

[15] J. T. O'Donnell. Data parallel implementation of extensible sparse functional arrays. In *PARLE*, 1993.

[16] W. D. Partain. Normal order reduction using scan primitives. In S. L. Peyton Jones, G. Hutton, and C. Holst, editors, *Functional Programming, Glasgow*. Springer Verlag, Aug. 1990.

[17] S. L. Peyton Jones. *The Implementation of Functional Programming Languages*. Prentice-Hall International, 1987.

[18] S. L. Peyton Jones. Implementing lazy functional languages on stock hardware: the Spineless Tagless G-machine. *Journal of Functional Programming*, 1992.

[19] S. L. Peyton Jones and P. Wadler. Imperative functional programming. In *POPL*, 1993.

[20] G. Sabot. *The Parallation Model : Architecture Independent SIMD Programming*. MIT Press, 1988.

[21] D. B. Skillicorn. The Bird-Meertens formalism as a parallel model. In *Software for Parallel Computation*, June 1992.

[22] G. L. Steele Jr. and W. D. Hillis. Connection machine Lisp : Fine-grained parallel symbolic processing. In *ACM Conference on Lisp and Functional Programming*, pages 279–297, 1986.

[23] J.-P. Talpin and P. Jouvelot. Compiling FX on the CM-2. In *Workshop on static analysis*, number 724 in LNCS, 1993.

[24] D. Turner. The semantic elegance of applicative languages. In *FPCA*, 1981.

[25] P. Wadler and R. J. M. Hughes. Projections for strictness analysis. In *FPCA*, 1987.

Address: Jon Hill, Department of Computer Science, Queen Mary and Westfield College, University of London, Mile End Road, E1 4NS.

E-mail: Jon.Hill@dcs.qmw.ac.uk

On the Comparative Evaluation of Parallel Languages and Systems: A Functional Note

Robert E. Hiromoto

The University of Texas at San Antonio

Division of Mathematics, Computer Science and Statistics
6900 North Loop 1604 West
San Antonio, Texas 78249-0664.
Email: hiromoto@ringer.cs.utsa.edu

Abstract

We propose a comparative approach to the incremental evaluation of parallel functional languages and their systems. The approach relies on the rich source of literature found in numerical software libraries though not restricted solely to them. The approach should extend itself to the analysis of imperative systems as well. This proposal will describe the advantages of such an approach using specific examples.

1   Introduction

Currently benchmarking practices for high-performance computing relies typically on Megaflop/s rates as a standard "class 1" metric of performance. The importance of compiler optimization (or lack of such optimizations) has also been discussed in the literature but little or no indepth compiler analysis is provided in many benchmarking reports. In general these approachs provide little insight into the complexity of the system or their capabilities. Instead the analysis rambles on about scalability and introduces a proliferation of averaging techniques designed to embellish the apparence of superiority for one system over another.

The language issues are muddled by array syntax, parallel extentions, message passing protocols, and parallel software libraries for portability. Where the design of algorithms for imperative systems concentrated on optimal computational (*time*) complexity, functional languages and their systems must cope with the additional burden of resource (*space*) and its management. Even though the *space-time* pair characterizing algorithms and systems is an important component in the imperative programming world, the *space* complexity is mitigated by relaxing the single assignment restriction; so fundamental to the pure functional programming discipline. This disparity between the algorithmic complexities of *imperative* versus *functional* algorithms and their implementations, coupled with the regretable state of performance evaluations in general puts the functional community at a clear disadvantage. With the maturity of functional languages and associated hardware platforms, a better approach is required: a systematic and rational approach to performance evaluation requires examination. The only prevailing agreement between state-of-the-art benchmarking practitioners appears to be: benchmarking is an art rather than a science. Unfortunately each has their own personal notion of beauty.

In this paper, we describe an approach and provide examples from the functional language Id to illustrate our considerations.

2   An Algorithmic Approach

The evaluation of a computer systems has proved to be a murky subject. Choosing a useful set of benchmarks appears not to be a straight forward task. Even now benchmarks such as those from Los Alamos and Livermore National Laboratories, NASA Ames, the Perfect Club, and the LINPACK community provide little practice insight into the potential capabilities of new systems other than for those specific kernels that make up the benchmark set.

In the above survey of benchmark sets, the NASA Ames benchmarks represent an intelligent collection of benchmark routines. Though these routines represent kernel of their production codes, the size and complexity of these routines emphasize the spirit of our approach. We advocate the philosophy that benchmarking computer systems requires *algorithmic probes* that can characterize the interaction of the language-compiler-machine triple. Though this is not a new ideal, a systematic approach has not been clearly defined. To address this deficiancy, the selection of algorithms is an essential first step. As the requirements of understanding the performance in detail is a triple of nested-layers, the algorithms must be characterized by *extensive development* for optimal execution; *well documented*; *well tested and analysed*; and *conceptually easy to understand*. What is particularly important is their ability to exhibit complex computational and data structures with local and global data motion, and dynamically varying granularities. The interaction of such a collection of routines with the language-compiler-machine is envisioned to provide a incremental, cyclic, and comparative evaluation procedure that characterizes the strengths and weakness between each stage of the coupled triad.

The NASA Ames benchmarks reflect this approach. To expand on this collection, we look to high-performance software libraries where numerical algorithms have been optimized for extensive and general applications. These routine are well documented and in many cases are only a few hundred lines of code. The full spectrum of data motion will also require the incorporation of sorting and database search and retrival routines as well.

2.1   Evaluation Tools

The evaluation of functional system will require the following tools:

- Idealized (abstracted) machine emulator;

  - All operations execute in one unit of time,
  - Infinite to fixed number of processors,
  - Latency variable parameters.

- Profilers and graphic interface to monitor abstracted execution.

- Algebraic (symbolic) manipulation tools (Mathematica, Macsyma, or Maple) to assist in the development of a parameterized execution model

  - (provides an comparative performance model where the behavior of hardware features may be introduced and analysed).

2.2 Algorithm and Performance analysis

- A space-time *Abstracted Complexity* of the algorithm;

- Abstracted machine performance vs. algorithmic complexity

  - Experimental approach:
    * Use of language constructs to investigate implementation issues;
      · Insight into language and compiler capabilities.
    * Modify data dependences of the algorithm;
      · Language and compiler capabilities,
      · Effects of algorithm and system organization,
      · Development of new algorithms.
    * Machine performance vs. abstracted machine performance;
      · Run-time statistics
      · Hardware dependent parametrization of execution model.
    * Theoretical approach;
      · Develop new compiler technology,
      · Compiler Optimization,
      · Develop new hardware or hardware organization.

3 A Functional Example

A very elegant approach in controlling and analysing the behavior of hardware under different computational loads can be found in [2]. Here a detailed understanding of the algorithmic behavior is the key ingredience to the analysis performed. Likewise as an example of our approach, we study the functional implementation of the Fast Fourier Transform written in Id and targeted for execution on Motorola's dataflow machine Monsoon. Apart from the use of I-structures, we rely only on the functional features of the MIT language Id [3].

The FFT application is of interest because of its computational parallelism, its requirement for global communications, and its array element data dependences. We use the parallel profiling simulator Id-world to study the dataflow performance of various implementations. Our approach is *incremental, cyclic,* and *comparative.* We studied two approaches [5] but only report on the recursive formulation of the algorithm here. A variety of implementations were studied. We contend that only through such comparative evaluations can significant insight be gained in the computational and structural details of functional algorithms. Interestingly a comparative analysis has also been reported on by [1] on a lazy functional formulation of various FFT algorithms.

3.1 Parallel Complexity Measures

Initial evaluation of a dataflow program is performed using the *Id World* simulator, which collects statistics while it executes the code [4]. Simulation proceeds in discrete *time steps* during which all instructions, for which all data is available, are executed. It is assumed that every instruction executes and sends its resulting data to its successor instructions in exactly one time step: Id-world simulates the behavior of the "Tagged Token Dataflow Architecture" [8]. Two time related measurements are recorded: the *total work per time step* S_1 is the total number of instructions executed per time step; and the *critical path length* S_∞ is the total number of time steps required. The parallelism of the program is displayed in an *(ideal) parallelism profile* by plotting the number of executed instructions at each time step. A related measure $\pi = \lfloor S_1/S_\infty \rfloor$ gives the average parallelism. Other measures are space related and are also recorded per time step, *TSO*: the *total storage occupancy* storage required, and *ISO*: the *I-store occupancy* amount of data structure storage required. Important machine level phenomena such as the effect that global communication time may have on the computation are not addressed when executing programs on the simulator. In this example we will study the time complexity measures S_1, S_∞ and the space complexity *ISO* and *TSO*.

3.2 A Recursive FFT Algorithm

Figure 1 shows a first version of a recursive formulation of the FFT written in Id, straight from the mathematical definition.

```
def fft v =
 { (_,SizeV) = bounds V
  in
  if (SizeV == 1) then V
  else
  {(OddV,EvenV) = shuffle V ;
   fftO    = fft OddV ; fftE = fft EvenV ;
   Mid     = SizeV / 2 ; X    = TwoPi / SizeV ;
   Coeff   = {array (1, Mid)
   | [i]   = Cmplx  (cos(X*(i-1))) (-sin (X*(i-1)))
   || i  <- 1 to Mid };
   Prod    = {array (1, Mid)
   | [i]   = Cmplx_Mul Coeff[i] fftE[i] || i <- 1 to Mid } }
  in
    {array (1, SizeV)
    | [i] = Cmplx_Add fftO[i] Prod[i] || i <- 1 to Mid
    | [Mid+i] = Cmplx_Sub fftO[i] Prod[i] || i <- 1 to Mid };};
def shuffle V =
 {(_, SizeV)  = bounds V ; Mid = SizeV / 2
  in
    ({array (1, Mid) | [i] = V[(i*2)-1] || i <- 1 to Mid };
     {array (1, Mid) | [i] = V[(i*2)]   || i <- 1 to Mid }) }
```

Fig. 1. Recursive FFT.

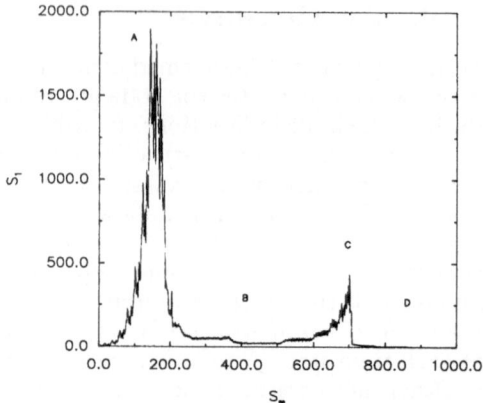

Fig. 2. Ideal parallelism profile for unoptimized recursive
FFT, SizeV = 128.

Note that in *fft* recursive invocations are applied to the odd and even elements of V until the size of V is one. The data dependencies occurring in the recombination of smaller results into larger ones form "butterfly" patterns. In Fig. 1, the definitions of the arrays *Coeff*, *Prod*, and the result of *fft* implement this recombination.

3.3 FFT Complexity

In the recursive FFT, $O(SizeV)$ arrays are allocated, 2 of size $SizeV$, 4 of size $SizeV/2$, 8 of size $SizeV/4$, etc. Because there are $O(log(SizeV))$ stages each allocating k arrays of size $SizeV/k$, the total size of the allocated arrays is $O(SizeV(log(SizeV)))$. For each array element that is allocated, there is a constant amount of work to calculate its value, so there is $O(SizeV(log(SizeV)))$ total work. This suggests a critical path length of $O(log(SizeV))$ and no sequential stretches.

The above measures provide an *Abstracted Complexity* of the algorithm, free from the issues concerning language implementations, computational models, and the architecture. We will use the abstracted complexity as a yard stick for the actual complexity measures obtained from running the program. This is useful in incrementally evaluating the path from algorithm, via language and computational model, to machine architecture. The parallelism profile seen in Fig. 2 is the the result of running the program in Fig. 1 ($SizeV = 128$) on the Id world simulator.

3.4 Performance for TTDA

The execution profile seen in Fig. 2 is far from what is expected from the abstracted complexity measures defined above. Observe that first there is explosive divide and conquer parallelism (A) peaking at 1900, followed by (B) a stretch of low parallelism of about 20. A second less significant burst of parallelism (C) follows which dies down to an almost sequential tail (D). For larger problems the two sequential stretches (B and D) are observed to dominate more and more. This parallelism profile is disappointing since the computational parallelism is known to be very large. We know from the abstracted complexity of the FFT program takes $O(log(SizeV))$ parallel steps to unfold all *fft* and *shuffle* functions, which accounts for the first burst (A) of the divide and conquer parallelism. Once the functions have been unfolded, the loops in the array comprehensions dictate the parallelism and consequently the speed of the computation.

The dynamics of loops and double recursion is now studied using the following kernels and their performance is summarized in Table 1:

```
def w n     = {s=0 In {while s<n do next s=s+1; finally s}};

def ww m n  = {s=0;r=0 In {while s<m do next s=s+1;
                                next r=r+w n; finally r}};

def a n     = {R=1D_I_array (1,n) In {for i <- 1 to n
                                do R[i] = i; finally R}};

def d n     = {if n == 1 then 1 else d (div n 2) + d (div n 2)};
```

The function w increments a number s in a while loop with loop carried data dependence, ww increments a number r and applies w in a nested loop, a creates an array with elements 1 to n using a simple loop, and d sums n 1-s together in a double recursive style.

S_1 and S_∞ for these programs are listed in table 1. These results brings us to the following observation. In the mapping from Id to Tagged Token Dataflow Code, it takes 5 steps along the critical path to spawn a loop, no matter whether it is an inner loop, an outer loop, or a loop in an array comprehension. We call the number of steps along the critical path to spawn a loop the *loop rate*. The loop rate plays an important role in the parallelism of a program. A high loop rate decreases the parallelism of a program. In a nested loop, for example, the number of inner loops that run in parallel is $S_\infty(innerloop)/looprate$. Note that this is independent of the total number of inner loops. Therefore, the amount of parallelism that is actually exploited in a program with loops can differ from our abstract complexity measure. The behavior of ww on the TTDA is an example of how the loop rate influences the parallelism of a program. The inner loop is almost sequential and its critical path length can be varied by varying n. The outer loop spawns inner-loops every *loop rate* time steps, so the inner loops are skewed on top of each other. The critical path length of the ww program is therefore $O(m + n)$.

Divide and conquer programs do not suffer from this skewing effect, as exemplified by the function d, where S_1 grows linearly, S_∞ grows logarithmically with n and the parallelism is $O(n)$.

We are now in a position to explain the parallelism profile in Fig. 2. While the dynamic call tree unrolls along the lines of Fig. 1 in $O(log(SizeV))$ time (phase A), the *shuffles* in the first *fft* produce one element every *loop rate* time steps. This results in a producer/consumer mismatch. That is, the array elements are not all available at the moment the dynamic call tree is ready to manipulate them. The elements are put in place during the $O(log(SizeV))$ shuffle stages without data dependence problems. In the $O(log(SizeV))$ butterfly stages, the elements must wait to combined with their corresponding elements that are not yet available. Phase B starts after the call tree is unrolled, and the program behaves very much like the *ww* function with an inner loop of length $O(log(SizeV))$. In this case the "inner loop" is spread over a number of butterfly stages. The parallelism in phase B is therefore $O(log(SizeV))$ instead of the expected $O(SizeV)$. Phase B ends when the last array element has been shuffled into place. The remaining stages in the butterfly can now be done in divide and conquer fashion (phase C). The sequential tail (phase D) is caused by the array comprehension in *fft* that generates the final array. The solution to this problem is to spawn loops fast enough so that they don't cause unnecessary delay. Neither the tagged token dataflow machine nor the Monsoon machine [7] have this type of instructions. Still the loop delay problem can be address by optimizing compilation, such as loop unrolling. Therefore, it is still possible, although at a higher cost in terms of instruction counts, to create array elements at a higher rate. As stated, this should and can best be done by an optimizing compiler. However, as this optimization is not available in the current Id compiler, we resort to a rather inelegant programming trick very similar to *strip-mining* [9] in a vector context.

Strip-mining, also called *chunking*, makes a loop parallel and efficient by turning it into a nested loop, where the outer loop provides the parallelism and the inner loop the efficiency. As an example, compare the function a to a strip-mined version ab both in Table 1 where the depth of the loop unrolling is defined by $chunk = 16$.

```
def ab n chunk  = {R=1D_I_array (1,n)  In
                    {for j <- 1 to n by chunk do
                    {for i <- j to j+chunk-1 do R[i] = i };
                    finally R} };
```

Where in the procedure a defined above the array elements are created at the loop rate, in ab *chunk* array elements are created per *loop rate*. Because we have strip-mined by hand, this comes at the cost of a higher S_1 value. A compiler could do a much better job at strip-mining. When we apply strip-mining to all loops in the fft and shuffle functions program, the parallelism profile, as shown in Fig. 2, is satisfactory. The critical path length is now logarithmic, and the two sequential stretches B and D have disappeared.

Although the array comprehensions in fft and shuffle (Fig. 1) make for an elegant and functional programming style, they lack expressive power: it is impossible to derive two or more values in the expression part of the comprehension and assign these to two or more targets in the array. This is exactly what we would like to do in the butterfly part of the *fft* function. In order to avoid recomputation of the operands of the butterfly combine operation, we are forced to put intermediate results in array *Prod*. We can avoid doing this extra work by rewriting the butterfly part of *fft* using a loop instead of an array comprehension.

3.5   Comparative Performance for Monsoon

The comparative study that follows requires the use of the Mint emulator of the Monsoon machine. For this reason differences in the simulated performance of the FFT

function	m	n	TTDA		Monsoon	
			S_1	S_∞	S_1	S_∞
w		1	27	16	23	13
		2	34	21	25	14
		3	41	26	27	15
ww	1	10	140	80	111	51
	2	10	251	85	185	84
	3	10	362	90	259	117
	1	20	210	130	131	61
	2	20	391	135	225	104
	3	20	572	140	319	147
a		16	223	101	316	159
		32	399	181	572	287
		64	751	342	1084	543
ab		16	277	118	623	158
c=8		32	504	123	1166	176
		64	958	133	2250	210
abe2		16			385	103
		32			641	166
		64			1153	292
d		1	13	7	26	10
		2	56	19	113	30
		4	142	31	287	50
		8	314	43	635	70
		16	658	55	1331	90

Table 1: Behavior of loops and recursion on TTDA and Monsoon

under TTDA are noted. Realizing the important effects simple loops and double recursive functions have on the parallel performance of the FFT, we begin a comparison of TTDA with Monsoon by evaluating Mint on the previous functions w, ww, a, d, a modified ab with explicit control over loop bounds, and the additional loop $abe2$ that creates an array applying two independent loops. The comparison between TTDA and the Monsoon is listed in in Table 1.

```
def ab n chunk  = {R=1D_I_array (1,n)  In
                  {for j <- 1 to n by chunk bound (div n chunk) do
                  {for i <- j to j+chunk-1 do R[i] = i };
                   finally R}};

def abe2   n    = {R = 1D_I_array (1, n);  h =  div n 2;
                  {for i <- 1 to h do  R[i]  = i };
                  {for i <- h+1 to n do R[i] = i }
                   in R } ;
```

As we noted above, on the TTDA it takes 5 time steps along the critical path to spawn a loop body, whether it is an inner loop, an outer loop or an array comprehension.

As with TTDA the divide and conquer programs on Monsoon do not suffer from the skewing effect, as demonstrated by the function d, where S_1 grows linearly, S_∞ grows logarithmically with n and the parallelism is $O(n)$.

Machine	Chunk	Bound	S_1	S_∞
TTDA	16	16	109716	330
MONSOON	16	16	178471	4260
MONSOON	4	L/4	235318	860
MONSOON	4	4	230632	1660

Table 2: S_1 and S_∞ of recursive FFT algorithms with SizeV $= 128$

The S_1 numbers for Monsoon and TTDA differ for a number of reasons. First, where the TTDA is an idealized architecture with a complex instruction set, the Monsoon is a real machine, built upon the reduced instruction set principles. Second, the Id compilers for TTDA and Monsoon differ. The combined effect on machine behaviour cannot always be precisely predicted. This is why we need to measure these phenomena. On the Monsoon the loop rate varies from 1 for w to 8 for a (Table 1). Because of its simplicity the w function gets highly optimized by the new Id to Monsoon compiler. On Monsoon the default bound for loops is 1. The *bound* of a loop determines the number of loop bodies that will execute in parallel. With a loop bound of 1, even nested loops run almost sequentially ($\pi = 2$ for ww).

Creating more parallelism by increasing the loop bound turns out to be very costly on Monsoon, especially in S_1. This is because the implementation of a k-bounded loop involves setting up a circular buffer of activation frames, and assessing the termination of individual loop bodies. This is exemplified by the numbers for ab, which is a strip-mined [9] parallel version of a. Note that the bound in ab is declared explicitly, overriding the default bound of 1 for loops on Monsoon. Where on the TTDA ab performs much better than a in terms of S_∞ at a small cost in S_1, the S_1 of ab doubles that of a on Monsoon. When it is possible to break a loop in two completely independent sub-loops (which involves breaking a data dependence most of the time), this pays off especially in terms of S_1. We can see this by comparing the numbers for ab to those of $abe2$ on Monsoon.

For both the TTDA and the Monsoon it is essential to get the loop rate down so that the parallelism inherent in the algorithm is exposed. As we have seen, we can do this either by strip-mining or by explicitly breaking a loop into a number of data independent sub-loops. In the FFT codes, the technique of explicitly breaking a loop in two or four independent sub-loops can be applied to the Iterative Shuffle and the Roots of Unity computation as discussed in [5].

Referring back to Table 1, the S_1 and S_∞ measures for the Monsoon increase rapidly for larger bounds. For *chunk* $= 16$ and *bound* $= 16$, which are time optimal for the recursive FFT on the TTDA, the performance on Monsoon shows a degradation in S_∞. In Table 2 comparisons between the TTDA and the Monsoon can be seen for the optimized recursive versions of the algorithm. In the table, L is the length of the corresponding *while-loop* or *for-loop*. Where several chunk or bound values are listed, the respective implementations use these values within different segments of the code. On Monsoon there is a winner: the recursive algorithm with *chunk* $= 4$ and *bound* $= L/4$.

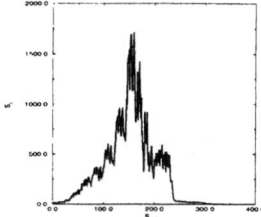 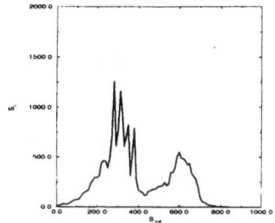

Fig. 3. Ideal parallelism profiles for TTDA (left) and MONSOON (right), SizeV = 128.

The results in Table 2 indicate the importance of choosing both the chunk and bound sizes for the Monsoon machine. The strategy of picking the optimal chunk and bound sizes is unfortunately not straight forward. Look, for example, at the bounds set at $L/4$. Here L varies for each invocation of the loop, and consequently the loop bound varies as well. By fixing the loop bounds, as in the last line of Table 2, we find that S_1 decreases but S_∞ increases by factors between 2 and 5. Fig. 3 depicts the time optimal parallelism profiles of the recursive FFT algorithm for TTDA and Monsoon. The chunk and bound sizes for these profiles are chunk = 16 and bound = 16 for the TTDA, and chunk = 4 and bound = $L/4$ for the Monsoon.

The differences in S_1 and S_∞ should not lead one to the conclusion that the TTDA design is superior over the Monsoon machine, rather that the Monsoon machine has a more realistic instruction set design. Moreover, the resource requirements of our the FFT algorithms still have to be explicitly managed and to be taken into account in our comparative evaluation.

3.6   Resource Issues on Monsoon

The Id compiler does not generate code for garbage collection. However, the compiler supported by Mint does allow us to manage resources explicitly. On the Monsoon the explicit release of memory involves the use of deallocation constructs combined with a barrier construct ---
In a block:

```
{ x = e1;  y = e2;  z = f(x,y);
  ---
  @deallocate x; @deallocate y
  in z }
```

the barrier ensures that the three assignments are terminated, and consequently the use of the intermediate values x and y has been completed, before the deallocations occur. There are two distinct forms of deallocation. This has to do with the representation of composite data structures, such as arrays. An array of scalar values is represented by (a pointer to) an I-structure containing the scalar values. In order to deallocate such a structure, the release pragma is used, as in:

```
def f n j = {
R = 1D_I_array (1,n);  res = R[j];
```

Versions	S_1	S_∞	π	ISO_{max}	TSO_{max}
R_CH_NR	235318	860	254	6780	61710
R_CH_RM	186071	2800	66	3452	33103

Table 3: Monsoon Time, Parallelism and Space measures for FFT algorithms with SizeV = 128.

```
{ R[1] = 1; for i <- 2 to n do  R[i] = h R[i-1] finally R };
---
@release R
in res }
```

An array of composite structures, such as tuples, is represented by (a pointer to) an I-structure of pointers to I-structures containing the tuple elements. It turns out that release deallocates the array of pointers only. Deallocating the whole structure, including the components, requires a more elaborate construct, that first deallocates all components and then the array of pointers to these components. In the case of a 1D_I_array this is performed by a library function called $free\_1d\_I\_array\_and\_components$. Complex numbers are tuples, hence composite objects. When a composite array element gets a value assigned, there are two options.

1. A new composite object is created and a pointer to this object is stored in the array. This occurs for instance in the butterfly part of function fft:

   ```
   R[i] = add_c fft_left[i] prod;
   ```

2. The element is an existing element e.g., of another array. In this case a pointer to the already existing composite object is created. This occurs in the shuffle function:

   ```
   { for i <- 1 to m do L[i] = v[(i*2)-1];
                        R[i] = v[i*2] finally (L,R) }
   ```

The programmer needs to know whether to deallocate the array of pointers only, or the whole structure. This depends on whether other data-structures share components with the one to be deallocated. In the case of the fft codes, most of the time an array is created solely out of new objects (butterfly), or solely out of old objects (shuffle). When deallocating a shuffle array result, the complex numbers need to be kept, i.e., only the array of pointers needs to be deallocated, hence a release is used. When deallocating a intermediate butterfly array result, there is no sharing, hence the whole structure including the complex components, can be deallocated using $free\_1d\_I\_array\_and\_components$.

We refer the interested reader to [6] for the details of our implementation. We merely note here the importance of measuring the I-structure and total storage requirements.

In Table 3 is a list of the FFT algorithms studied using the MINT simulator. We adopt the following naming convention: R is Recursive, CH is Chunked,

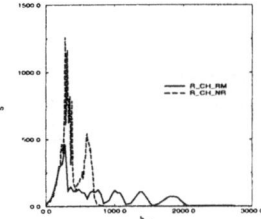 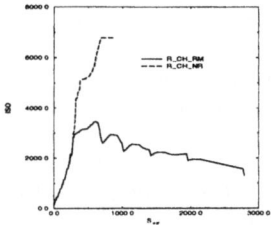

Fig. 4. Ideal parallel (left) and I-storage (right) profiles
for the Recursive FFTs, SizeV = 128.

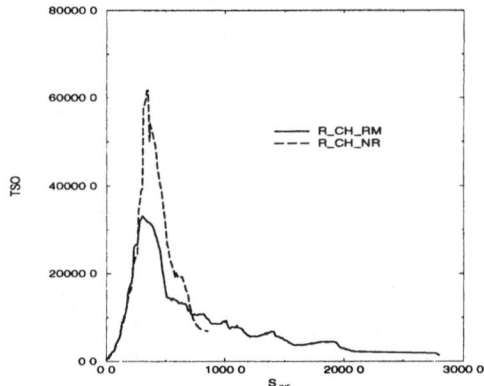

Fig. 5. Total storage profiles for the Recursive FFTs
SizeV = 128.

NR is Not Resource managed and RM is Resource Managed. The I-storage
and parallelism profiles for the recursive FFTs are seen in Fig. 3. R_CH_NR
is the program developed for the TTDA. Its TTDA and Monsoon measures
are shown in Table 3. R_CH_RM stops recursion at $size == 4$, which yields a
considerable improvement in S_1.

Resource management saves about half of the maximal I-storage use in the
recursive algorithms. This is because deallocation can start after the innermost
fft terminates, which is halfway though the computation. The parallelism profile in Fig. 4. reveals the price that must be paid in S_∞ to achieve resource
management.

The Total Storage Occupancy TSO, takes into account both the I-store
occupancy and the frame store occupancy. The frame store contains the activation record tree of the enabled parallel execution streams. We see in Fig. 5
that the total space requirements are closely related to the available parallelism
in the corresponding FFTs as seen in Fig. 4. Note that when the parallelism
is unconstrained, an enormous amount of space is used. However as barriers
and lower loop bounds are restricting the available parallelism, a drastic space
savings can be obtained. No doubt the decision to default loop bounds to 1 for
the Monsoon machine is strongly related to the results shown in Fig. 4. The
price paid for asynchronous parallelism is not only in extra instructions, but
also in excessive storage use.

The analysis of the iterative FFT and related implementations can be found
in [6].

4 Conclusions

The paper argues for an *incremental, cyclic and comparative* approach in the evaluation of languages, compilers and machine architectures. The interactions of this triple requires a detailed understanding of the algorithmic complexities beginning with its abstracted form (free of language, compiler and machine issues) to their behaviorial form on the various levels of evaluation.

The contributions of this paper are:

- We have described an approach in selecting, analysing, and evaluating numerical algorithms for pure functional languages;

- Made use of the expressive power of functional programming, annotations, and algorithmic parallelism;

- Shown that the implementation of such algorithms are still challenging, requiring a complexity of both *space* and *time*.

References

[1] P.H. Hartel and W.G. Vree, Arrays in a Lazy Functional Language - a Case Study: the Fast Fourier Transform, Department of Computer Systems, Faculty of Mathematics and Computer Science, University of Amsterdam, Tech. Rep. CS-92-02.

[2] Profiling Scheduling Strategies on the GRIP parallel reducer Department of Computing Science, University of Glasgow, 17 Lilybank Gardens, Glasgow, Scotland.

[3] R.S. Nikhil, Id (version 90.0) Reference Manual, *TR CSG Memo 284-1*, MIT LCS 1990.

[4] D. R. Morais, ID World: An Environment for the Development of Data flow Programs Written in ID, MIT LCS TR-365, may 1986.

[5] A.P.W. Böhm and R.E. Hiromoto, The Dataflow Time Complexity of FFT, *The Second Workshop on Data-flow: The 19th International Symposium on Computer Architecture*, Hamilton Island, Australia, May 25-26, 1992.

[6] A.P.W. Böhm and R.E. Hiromoto, The Dataflow Time and Space Complexity of FFT, *The Journal of Parallel and Distributed Computing*, Vol. 18, pp. 301-313 (1993).

[7] K. R. Traub, G. M. Papadopoulos, M. J. Beckerle, J.E. Hicks and J. Young, Overview of the Monsoon Project, ICCD91, IEEE, Oct 1991, pp 150-155.

[8] Arvind, R.A. Ianucci, Instruction Set Definition for a Tagged Token Dataflow Machine, LCS, MIT, 1983

[9] M. Wolfe, Optimizing Supercompilers for Supercomputers, MIT Press, 1989.

Deterministic Concurrency

Ian Holyer
David Carter
Department of Computer Science, University of Bristol
Bristol, England

Abstract

Existing functional languages appear not to be suitable for implementing systems which are inherently concurrent, such as operating system environments or reactive systems. Adaptations to functional languages developed to support such applications have in the past always involved the introduction of non-determinism. This paper proposes an adaptation of a functional language which provides concurrency without the introduction of non-determinism or timing information, and indeed without any alteration to the usual semantics, thus retaining the purely declarative nature of functional programming.

The expressiveness of this deterministic form of concurrency is explored by presenting and discussing outlines of designs for a file manager, a window system and a process communication mechanism. Taken together, these demonstrate the feasibility of a deterministic design for a complete single-user concurrent working environment.

1   Introduction

Functional languages provide for the simple and semantically clean treatment of complex sequential systems. However, when systems are themselves inherently concurrent, as with operating system environments or reactive systems, existing functional languages appear not to have enough expressive power to implement such systems directly. Previous approaches to the adaptation of functional languages to support such concurrent programming have always involved the introduction of non-determinism in some guise, that is the behaviour of a program is allowed to depend on the accidental timings of events in the system rather than just on the values of its inputs. Various schemes have been devised to limit the potentially damaging effects of non-determinism. However, the aim of this paper is to show that a purely deterministic, and purely declarative, form of concurrency can be implemented. The concurrency model is discussed in Section 3.

The purely deterministic nature of this form of concurrency appears restrictive at first sight, since many traditional designs of concurrent systems are inherently non-deterministic. However, this non-determinism is often unnecessary, and in Section 4, several examples are given of the way in which such systems can be redesigned to make them purely deterministic, and thus implementable using a concurrent functional language. The examples discussed are a file manager, a window system and a communication mechanism.

Many of the problems with functional language interfaces stem from their guest status within procedural operating systems, and concurrency opens up the possibility of reversing this situation. The examples already mentioned can be extended into a complete functional operating system environment, at least for a single user, as discussed in Section 5.

2 Concurrency

It is useful to make an explicit distinction here between parallelism and concurrency. Parallelism is taken to mean the use of multiple agents or processes in the internal implementation of a program, but in a way which does not affect the semantics of the program or its externally visible behaviour, except in terms of efficiency. Although many activities may be carried out at the same time, they are coordinated in such a way that the results are the same as if the program were executed sequentially. Thus parallelism alone does not increase the expressive power of languages beyond sequential execution.

On the other hand, concurrency is taken to be a property of the externally visible behaviour of a program; a program is concurrent if it is able to do several things at once in an unsynchronised way. Of course, a concurrent program requires some measure of parallelism, or at least pseudo-parallelism, in its implementation.

In procedural programming, it has often been recognised that concurrency does not necessarily involve non-determinism, but concurrency primitives are in practice always potentially non-deterministic. Previous work on concurrent programming in functional languages has also always involved non-determinism in one form or another. In fact, the two are often treated as being synonymous. Various schemes have been proposed to limit the damaging effects of non-determinism or to find declarative ways of dealing with it.

Perhaps the simplest additional feature which has been proposed for functional languages to provide concurrency is the non-deterministic merge of two streams, as described by Henderson [8], in which items are interleaved into a single result stream in an 'arbitrary' order, depending on the relative times at which they get evaluated or read in. In this way, a program can have two separate input streams, and can respond to events on either stream as they occur, so that the program appears to be doing two things at once. However, this destroys the declarative nature of the language, reducing the clarity of programs and making them difficult to reason about. This is mostly due to the loss of referential transparency; an expression does not necessarily have the same value each time it is evaluated, and so equational reasoning cannot be used, as explained by Clinger [3].

One way to reduce the effects of this is to use the sorting office model of Stoye [11], also used by Turner [12], where functional processes send messages to each other via a central delivery service called a sorting office. Each process is purely functional, and the non-determinism is confined to the sorting office and communication channels.

A different approach by Burton [1] is to record choices; every time a non-deterministic choice is made in evaluating an expression, the choice is recorded so that if the same expression is evaluated again, the same value is obtained. Alternatively, timing information can be introduced explicitly, eg in the form of timestamps on input events, as described by Harrison [6]. Both of these approaches restore referential transparency, but at the cost of extra complexity for the programmer. This problem can be partially solved by an implicit treatment of time, as in Harrison & Jones [7], or by explaining non-determinism in terms of programming with sets, as in Hughes & O'Donnell [9].

The main result in this paper is that a purely deterministic form of concurrency can be implemented with only a minimal effect on functional languages or on programming techniques.

3 Concurrent Functional Programming

In this section, concurrency is examined from a functional point of view, a simple model of concurrency is proposed, and its implementation and semantics are discussed.

A concurrent program is one which carries out several tasks at the same time, each continuing at its own rate. The conventional point of view is a data-driven one in which the tasks which the program is carrying out are seen as being driven by independent input streams to a program. This leads to the conclusion that the program must respond to whichever event arrives first on any of the streams – effectively requiring a timed merge.

Laziness challenges the data-driven point of view, introducing the ability to produce output at the same time as reading input, and thus providing a mechanism for implementing interactive programs in purely functional languages. In a lazy implementation, expressions are not forced to be evaluated until their values are known to be required. In particular, items are not read from input streams until required. This leads to a demand-driven point of view in which program execution is seen as being driven by the need to produce results on the output stream.

This demand-driven view of execution can be extended to a simple model of concurrency. The essence of concurrency can be captured by introducing multiple output streams, driven by independent demands. If a purely functional program carries out several tasks at once, it is only possible to see the progress being made by looking at the outputs produced. The outputs from distinct tasks are independent, and it is natural to separate them into distinct streams. We propose a mechanism for introducing extra output streams, and thus tasks, into programs. It is remarkable that this extension alone provides concurrency in a completely deterministic way, without any change to the underlying syntax or semantics of functional languages; non-determinism is restricted to the operational and I/O aspects of programs.

3.1 The Concurrency Model

The proposed model of concurrency is very simple, but has some subtle consequences. A program may have many output streams rather than just one, each being driven by demand and representing a separate task. In the implementation, each output stream is associated with a separate thread of execution. If a task requires an input item, its thread is suspended until that item arrives, but this does not affect the execution of other threads. Although tasks are executed independently, there may be data dependencies between them in the usual way.

This proposed model will be illustrated here with a simple extension to Haskell [4], using the dialogue model of I/O. The ideas can be adapted to other languages and other I/O models, such as the monadic style of I/O.

A sequential Haskell program produces as output a single stream of I/O requests of type **Request**, and accepts as input a single stream of corresponding responses of type **Response**. We will only consider the channel requests here:

```
data Request = ReadChan Name | AppendChan Name Stream | ...

data Response = Str Stream | Success | ...
```

Laziness is crucial in the dialogue model, as each request must be output before its response is read in. Multiple input channels, ie streams of characters, can be opened up with requests of the form **ReadChan chan**, where **chan** is a channel name. Such a request produces the response **Str cs** where **cs** is a new, lazy input stream.

However, multiple independent output channels cannot be created. The only output request for channels is **AppendChan chan cs**, where **chan** is a channel name and **cs** is a string which is fully evaluated and dispatched on the given channel before the next request is obeyed. Thus separate output channels have to be interleaved explicitly by the program.

The extension proposed here is to add a single new request, **WriteChan**, for opening a new output channel:

```
data Request = ... | WriteChan Name Stream | ...
```

In a request **WriteChan chan cs**, the string **cs** represents the entire stream of characters to be sent along the channel (so there is only one **WriteChan** request per channel).

Moreover, the execution mechanism does not evaluate **cs**, but rather starts up a new thread of execution to evaluate it independently before moving on to the next request. There is now a new independent output stream connecting the program to the outside world, in addition to the usual request stream. The outside world is regarded as responsible for demanding items on these two streams at will; the program must respond to whatever pattern of demand occurs:

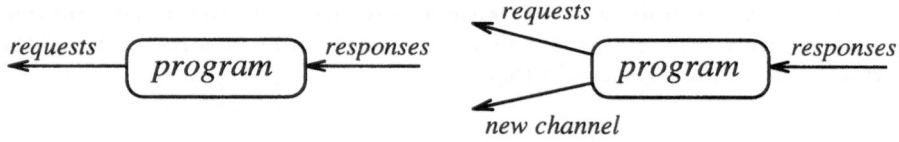

before WriteChan   after WriteChan

The initial thread of execution evaluates and obeys all the requests. When it reaches the end of the list of requests, the thread terminates. The program itself does not terminate, as a sequential Haskell program would, since other threads may still be running. Instead, the program terminates when all its threads have terminated.

It is not specified here where new output channels should go to; the intention is that they should go to independent devices or services. We will see in the next section that likely destinations are windows on a workstation screen, any number of which can be created.

If two channels go (eventually) to the same service, say a file manager, which is implemented procedurally and is capable of non-deterministic merging, then the program could produce non-deterministic effects. However, the program itself has no internal non-determinism, and we will see in Section 4.3 that if channels are connected to other concurrent functional services rather than to procedural services, non-deterministic effects cannot arise.

Input streams cannot be merged non-deterministically. However, it is still possible for a program to respond to whichever event arrives first on any of several input streams. This happens if several tasks are currently blocked, each waiting for an input item from one of the streams. The first item to arrive causes the relevant task to be woken up and to produce some more output. Thus the timing of the arrival of input items affects the timing of the production of output items (as with a sequential program), but cannot affect the values produced.

The `WriteChan` proposal is a simple illustrative one. A more complicated possibility, including the ability to introduce new request and response streams, is described in Section 4.2.

3.2   Implementation

The deterministic concurrency model requires some measure of parallelism in its implementation, using the parallel implementation techniques which have already been developed for functional languages. In particular, pseudo-parallel execution on a single processor can be introduced with only minor changes to the usual graph reduction model, and adds only a very small overhead to ordinary sequential execution [5].

Parallel execution can be introduced by implementing separate lightweight threads of execution to evaluate subexpressions, with simple interlocks to prevent multiple evaluation of the same subexpression. The threads share a single heap, but each has its own stack.

If several threads are suspended, each waiting for an input item on a different input stream, the underlying implementation must be able to respond to whichever item arrives first by waking up the corresponding thread. Such time-dependent behaviour is not, however, directly available in the high-level functional language. Thus pure concurrency can be seen as a way of delivering some of the extra expressive power of existing concurrent operating system primitives in a completely safe and deterministic way.

Suspension while waiting for input, and wakeup when input items arrive, are common causes of thread-switching. However, an implementation on a sequential computer also requires time-slicing to ensure fairness; if one thread carries out a long computation without requiring input, perhaps even getting stuck in an infinite loop, it must be possible to interrupt it and switch threads, so that all runnable threads make definite progress.

3.3   Semantics

In the proposed model, concurrency permeates the whole language, so that it applies to all functions and not just to I/O, as with laziness. Thus the semantics

118

must describe arbitrary functions in the context of concurrent execution. A full operational semantics would involve non-determinism, eg it must explain the ability to respond to whichever of several inputs arrives first. However, the denotational semantics is just the usual lazy semantics for functional languages; it is simply the fact that functions are evaluated in the context of multiple demands which increases their expressive power. The operational and denotational points of view agree; non-determinism is used in the implementation in a restricted way which provides a purely deterministic increase in expressive power. Rather than attempting to prove this agreement, we content ourselves here with a few comments.

The fact that the denotational semantics is unchanged has powerful consequences. It means that traditional declarative methods can be used to determine program properties. For example, a true deadlock, ie one caused by the accidental timings of events or communications, is impossible. If output on a particular stream is suspended indefinitely, it can only be because the remainder of the stream has value $\bot$, which means that the effect is repeatable and can be investigated easily.

As a concrete illustration of the relationship between the operational and denotational points of view, consider a function `copy` which takes a single stream as input and returns two copies of that stream as outputs:

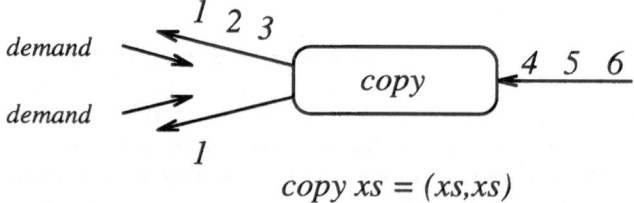

$$copy\ xs = (xs,xs)$$

The denotational semantics of this is very simple; for every possible value which `xs` can take, including partial values, the result must consist of two copies of that value. If the two output streams are evaluated independently by separate tasks, the results seen by those two tasks must be completely determined by the value of `xs`. If `xs` has the value [1,2,3,...], the first task demands three items from the first output stream, and the second task demands one item from the second output stream, then the situation will be as shown above. Each task sees the items it has demanded, and the values 2 and 3 are 'buffered' until demanded by the second task.

A function such as `copy` is not very useful in writing application programs, partly because of the buffering effect if the speed of one output thread outstrips the other. However, it can be used to explain the operational behaviour of a complete program (with a fixed number of output streams). If you make separate versions of a program, one defining each of its output streams, use `copy` to distribute the input streams to each version, and then execute each version sequentially, the effect will be the same as running the original program concurrently. Of course, this is likely to be very inefficient and is not intended as a practical programming technique.

Although the denotational semantics described is particularly clean, and the model is simple and self-consistent from a functional point of view, a deeper investigation of the semantic aspects of deterministic concurrency would be desirable. As well as studying the relationship with the operational semantics, there is a need to compare and contrast the approach with other models of concurrency such as CSP or CCS, and ask whether it couldn't be used as an alternative to them in some contexts. Several observations can be made immediately. The most obvious is that the inherent non-determinism of existing models is not reflected in the functional model. Another is that the existing models are very low level; even describing the I/O behaviour of a simple function like copy in a traditional model is quite complex. Also, the functional model has a simple and unproblematic equivalent of 'hiding' operators, and has fairness properties which are not easily described at all in the existing models.

4 Concurrent Design

Programmers regularly use explicit non-determinism in the design of concurrent systems. However, this may often be simply because existing operating system libraries and concurrent languages provide non-deterministic primitives. This in turn encourages system programmers to develop non-deterministic solutions to problems. Moreover, such observable non-determinism is often undesirable in practice. It makes systems more complicated and difficult to program and debug, and more confusing for users, because of unexpected and unrepeatable behaviour.

In this section we provide very brief sketches of work in progress to redesign some familiar systems to make them deterministic, and thus implementable with deterministic concurrency. They illustrate the fact that deterministic concurrency genuinely increases the expressive power of functional languages, and that purely declarative versions of concurrent systems can be designed.

4.1 A Design for a File Manager

Suppose we want to provide an environment which allows a user to run processes and manage files. For simplicity, suppose that a window system is available in which simple independent text windows, each with its own input and output stream, can be created. The system as a whole will be regarded here as a monolithic functional program with a single shared heap, rather than regarding each process as having its own heap as in conventional operating systems.

To show how separate processes can be run, here is a concurrent Haskell program which runs two separate processes, each in its own window.

```
main rs =
    [WriteChan windowA outA, ReadChan windowA,
     WriteChan windowB outB, ReadChan windowB]
    where
        [Success, Str inA, Success, Str inB] = rs
        outA = processA inA
        outB = processB inB

processA cs = ...

processB cs = ...
```

For simplicity, we assume that the only extension to Haskell is the extra `WriteChan` réquest described earlier, and that each `WriteChan` request creates a new named window. Each process is described as a function from the input channel to the output channel of one of the windows. The program issues requests to open channels to and from the two windows, and then reads in their responses and attaches the channels to the two process functions.

The design of the file manager is not very different from conventional ones, but care has to be taken to avoid contention problems. We have to avoid the need to merge file access requests from different processes, to merge separate character streams into a single output stream to a window, or to merge control requests such as interrupts with the normal input to a process. We also have to ensure that the file manager is reliable, ie that it continues to run even if user processes fail. One way to do this is to use the following design features:

- The file manager is a process which is separate from user processes, whether it is presented as a text-based command interpreter (shell) or as a graphics-based tool. It provides built-in commands to examine and manipulate file names and directories.

- The manager supports commands to run user processes. A user process is always run in its own window; it never sends output directly to the manager window.

- The manager alone has access to file names and directories; user processes do not. On the other hand, user processes alone display or alter file contents; the manager does not.

- User processes are functions which are given file contents and window input as arguments, and which return new file contents and window output as results. They do not **request** access to files dynamically, except as described below.

- The manager keeps old versions of files, and provides built-in commands to restore them, thus allowing file updates caused by user processes to be undone.

The way in which such a system would work, and particularly how it would differ from a conventional file manager, can be illustrated informally by describing its behaviour in several circumstances where non-determinism is common in traditional designs.

How is contention for files resolved, eg what happens if two user processes attempt to update the same file? When the command is given to start up the first process, the file manager replaces the file contents with an unevaluated expression representing the new contents which will eventually be returned by the process. When the second process is started up, it is passed this unevaluated expression as argument, and has to wait until it becomes evaluated, ie until the first process has finished updating it, before it can continue. Thus the two processes, instead of running independently as usual, must run one after the other because of the data dependency between the two. A process can display a message to the effect that it is waiting for a file, provided that it always does so (it will appear for an invisibly short time if the file is instantly available).

How is the question of contention for output resolved? The problem of two processes sending their output to the same window does not arise, as each process has its own window. However, a process may wish to send both the echoing of its input and its normal output to its own window. It is desirable to be able to encapsulate echoing in a single functional component which sits between a process and a window:

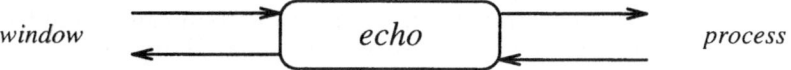

window   *echo*   *process*

This has the advantage that other features such as line-editing, a history mechanism and so on can be added to the component and made available to any process which requires them. However, such a component needs information with which to determine how to merge the input from the window with the output from the process in a deterministic way. This is possible if the process includes in its output stream a marker of some sort at each position in the output at which it expects to read in a line of input – normally just after each prompt.

How is an unwanted process interrupted? In traditional systems, this is a particularly dirty business. Typing some special character causes a signal to be sent to the process. If the process is allowed to trap the signal, then faulty processes which ignore it cannot be interrupted; if the process is not allowed to trap it, then correct processes can be stopped in the middle of important updates, leaving an inconsistent filestore or environment behind.

In our setting, it is not possible to regard an interrupt as a signal to the process, because this would have to be merged in a time-dependent way with its other inputs. Instead, the ability of the manager to undo the effects of processes is used. The files which the process is updating are made to revert to their previous contents, thus removing all references to the results of the process. If the process window is also destroyed, indicating that there will never be any more demand for window output, all the threads associated with the process terminate, and the memory taken up by the process can be reclaimed. In cases where programs expect to be interrupted, they can start up subprocesses and the interruption can be treated as normal input to the parent process. For a program to be able to save work done up to the point of interruption, a synchronisation feature can be added to the window interface; at each possible commit point, the program sends a request on the output to the window which causes a response in the input from the window, synchronised with the user's input, so that the program can tell if an interruption request has been received up to that point.

How can dynamic access to files be provided? To provide, say, an editor in which new files can be loaded at will, the editor process would have a list of files as one of its inputs. A command would be given to the file manager to add the contents of a new file to the list, and a command would be given to the program to read the new file contents from the list. These two commands could be incorporated into a single 'drag and drop' activity.

How are files committed to permanent storage? In the system described so far, it seems that the contents of a file need never be produced or stored until they are next used. This can be overcome using a primitive function **par**, say, for introducing speculative parallelism. The call **par x y** is semantically equivalent to **y**, but creates a new speculative thread of execution to evaluate **x** before returning **y**. Such a primitive is easy to add in a system which already has a parallel underlying implementation.

4.2 A Design for a Window System

It has already been demonstrated that a window system can be implemented in a sequential functional language, as in Carlsson & Hallgren [2]. However, there are two ways in which concurrency can improve on such a design. First, of course, it allows concurrent window applications to be written. Second, as Carlsson & Hallgren point out, it allows the design of sequential applications and of the window system itself to be simplified (though they propose the introduction of non-deterministic concurrency in the style of Burton [1]).

Problems arise in the sequential design of window systems because logically independent streams must be merged in order to 'multiplex' them on a single output stream. To do this deterministically, high level information must be used to determine a suitable interleaving. In many cases, as with echoing, it is necessary to design stream processing functions in such a way that they include markers of some kind in their output streams to indicate the points at which they create demands for items on their input streams. Such problems can make programming very awkward and unnatural.

We follow the lead of Carlsson & Hallgren [2] in assuming that a sophisticated but low level window server such as the X Window System [10] (at the Protocol or Xlib level) is available which can be regarded as a device driver, and show how a high level window system might be built on top of it. Such a window server supports a complex hierarchical arrangement of windows on a workstation screen. These windows have a high degree of independence from each other; graphics drawn into a window do not affect any other window, they move with the window, and they are exposed or hidden with the window.

This independence of windows makes it reasonable to associate a separate output stream of graphics commands with each window. As windows can be created at will, this provides a rich source of concurrency. To increase the concurrency still further, and avoid any merging of logically independent streams, the management of subwindows is associated directly with each parent – the subwindows of one window are independent of the subwindows of an unrelated window. This leads to a design in which each window is associated with a 'widget' in a program.

A widget is a function with two pairs of input and output streams; event and graphics command streams for data transfer, and request and response streams providing a dialogue service for handling subwindows. The types involved might look like:

```
data Event = Key ... | Mouse ...
data Command = Paint ... | Draw ... | Write ...

data Request = Open [Command] [Request] | ...
data Response = Window [Event] [Response] | ...

type Widget = ([Event],[Response]) -> ([Command],[Request])
```

Low-level events which a program may be interested in, such as those concerned with the resizing of windows, can be included with user input in event streams in a correctly synchronised way since they are the direct result of user actions. Low-level events which are better hidden from programs, such as requests for redrawing (in most cases), can be built into the implementation. Also, the inputs associated with subwindows can optionally be associated with the parent window instead, so that interleaving information is not lost. The mechanisms for handling such details are not described here.

These basic facilities can then be used to build up a library of widgets and combinators. If we ignore the issue of integrating this scheme with the normal I/O conventions, the result of a complete program is a single top level widget.

Simple widgets to display a string, and to display a given widget as a subwindow inside a plain frame window, might be programmed roughly as follows (ignoring many details):

```
string s (es,rs) = ([Write s], [])

frame w (es,rs) = ([], [Open cs qs]) where
   [Window es1 rs1] = rs
   (cs,qs) = w (es1,rs1)
```

A minimal prototype of a window system of this kind has been implemented. It is hoped that experience with a fully implemented system will show that it provides considerable freedom and natural expressive power.

4.3   A Design for a Communications Mechanism

The model presented so far has been described in terms of a single shared heap supporting all the concurrent threads in the system. This is feasible on a single sequential computer or on a sufficiently closely coupled parallel computer.

However, it may be desirable to split the system up into separate processes, each with its own heap, eg to distribute the system across a number of processors or to allow functional programs to cooperate with procedural programs or services. These component processes can cooperate via conventional communication channels. However, the challenge here is to restrict the use of these channels and arrange the protocols they use so that the entire collection of processes still fits within the deterministic concurrency model. Communication channels can be regarded simply as a more restricted way of sharing data than using a single global heap.

An arbitrary network of processes connected by communication channels must be completely equivalent to a single deterministically concurrent program. The channels which connect the network as a whole to the 'outside world' become the input and output channels of the combined program. The only difference between the network and the equivalent program in a single heap should be that the network has more internal parallelism, which doesn't affect the semantics. (In an actual transformation of the network into a single program, the channels would have to be replaced by stream processing functions which precisely simulate the properties of the channel such as strictness and buffering.)

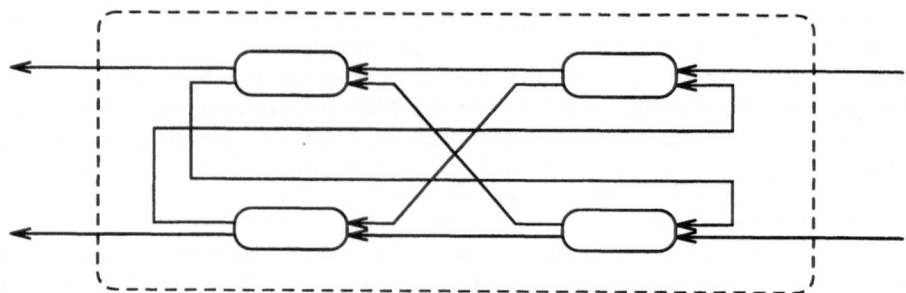

Each process is a concurrent functional program, or at least a procedural program or service which is protected by a functional 'wrapper' which prevents it from being misused. These processes are connected via their input and output channels which carry either simple data streams, or request and response streams. Simple data streams are equivalent to passing data values from one process to another (usually in a hyperstrict manner). An item such as a `WriteChan` request or `Str` response sent along a channel can be interpreted as an instruction to set up a new channel connection; this is equivalent to passing a lazy list value from one process to the other.

The creation of a new process can be thought of as the evaluation of a function which takes streams as arguments and passes streams back as results. With the ability to create new processes as well as channels, the process and communication network becomes completely dynamic. Such dynamic networks need some complex supporting mechanisms for efficiency. For example, process creation often leads to a situation where a process passes on an input stream unchanged as an output stream. A facility for 'replugging' the streams so that the other two processes communicate directly is clearly highly desirable. One way to achieve this automatically, without programmer support, is to detect the situation during garbage collection of the middle process and for the run-time execution mechanism to negotiate the replugging with the other two processes.

Conventional operating system communication channels can be adapted for these purposes, but care is needed to ensure that they cannot be used to create observable non-determinism, and that they are sufficiently lazy. The simplest unbuffered channel protocol which is semantically sound can be described as follows. When the consumer process reaches a point where a value is required from the channel, it creates a 'demand' for the next item from the producer and is suspended. The producer is woken, evaluates the item, sends it, and is suspended again. The arrival of the item allows the consumer to continue. Buffering is traditionally used to reduce the number of process switches. A buffered protocol can be regarded as one in which a number of items are demanded before they are needed, so that the producer process evaluates them speculatively. Conventional buffered channels can be used, but care must be taken to ensure, for example, that the consumer process is never suspended indefinitely when the buffer is non-empty.

5 Future Work

The concurrency model presented in this paper shows that concurrency can be supported in functional programs, while confining non-determinism to the implementation and I/O. The language itself remains purely deterministic and declarative. The communication mechanism of Section 4.3 shows that non-determinism can also be eliminated from a collection of communicating programs. Thus non-determinism can be banished to the outer edges of a system, ie to real physical I/O with the 'outside world'.

This suggests the possibility of building a complete single-user operating system environment out of functional components. Such an environment would provides all the features which users expect, but avoid all the pitfalls for the unwary which non-determinism produces. A functional environment can be built on top of an existing procedural operating system, but the operating system features would be regarded as providing implementation support for an extended functional language, rather than as facilities which programmers can access directly. With a few extra features, the functional language itself is powerful enough to express the high level structure of such an environment, including the programming of components such as a file manager and window system, as described in Sections 4.1 and 4.2.

Extra features of a functional language which would be required for program development in such an environment, and which have not already been discussed, are dynamic loading and dynamic types. If the functional environment is viewed as a single persistent program, then compiling and running a new module is equivalent to creating new functions and data types dynamically and then loading them up dynamically into the already running program.

In such a functional environment, procedural programs would have guest status, reversing the current situation. A procedural program would have to be adapted or else run within some kind of restrictive 'wrapper' to turn it into a safe functional component.

It would also be interesting to investigate the extent to which deterministic concurrency can be used in the design of multi-user systems, in which non-determinism problems occur when users want to share resources. The main aim would be to keep each user's environment as deterministic as possible. For example, if users can read each other's files, then in any one login session, one user should see a static view of the files of a second user, as they were at the second user's most recent logout. This could be achieved, for example, by adding timing information to login and logout requests. Closer cooperation such as the use of shared updatable databases would, of course, require some similar treatment at the level of individual transaction requests.

The advantages of a functional environment would be that I/O and interfacing problems would be reduced for functional programmers, that programs would become components which can be combined and reused more easily, and that a functional language could be used for combining programs in place of such things as shell scripts. In addition, the environment would support concurrent programming, eg of reactive systems, in a purely declarative setting.

Acknowledgements

Many thanks are due to Neil Davies and Chris Dornan who shared in the development of many of the ideas in this paper, and to the referees who have help in refining the presentation.

References

[1] F.W. Burton, "Nondeterminism with referential transparency in functional programming", Proc. 1st international Lisp conference, 1980.

[2] M. Carlsson & T. Hallgren, "Fudgets: a graphical user interface in a lazy functional language", submitted to FPCA, 1993.

[3] W. Clinger, "Nondeterministic call by need is neither lazy nor by name", Proc. Symposium on LISP and Functional Programming, 1982.

[4] P. Hudak et. al., "Report on the programming language Haskell", ACM SIGPLAN Notices Volume 27 Number 5, 1992

[5] S.L. Peyton Jones & C. Clack & J. Salkild, "High-performance parallel graph reduction", Proc. Parallel Architectures and Languages Europe, Lecture Notes in Computer Science 365, Springer Verlag, 1989

[6] D. Harrison, "RUTH: a functional language for real-time programming", Proc. Parallel Architectures and Languages Europe, Lecture Notes in Computer Science 259, Springer-Verlag, 1987

[7] D. Harrison & S.B. Jones, "The Semantics of Implicit Time Determinate Choice", in W. Joosen & E. Milgrom (editors), Parallel Computing: From Theory to Sound Practice, IOS Press, 1992

[8] P. Henderson, "Purely functional operating systems", in J. Darlington, P. Henderson, D.A. Turner (editors) "Functional Programming and its Applications", Cambridge University Press, 1982.

[9] J. Hughes & J. O'Donnell, "Nondeterministic Functional Programming with Sets", Proceedings of the 1990 Banf Conference on Higher Order Reasoning, 1990.

[10] The MIT X Window System Manual Set (Volumes 1 and 2), IXI Ltd.

[11] W. Stoye, "A new scheme for writing functional operating systems", Technical report 56, Cambridge University Computer Laboratory, 1984.

[12] D. Turner, "Functional programming and communicating processes" LNCS 259, 1987.

Using Strictness in the STG Machine

Denis B Howe   Geoffrey L Burn

Computing Department, Imperial College

London, UK

e-mail: dbh@doc.ic.ac.uk

Abstract

To implement lazy evaluation, closures representing unevaluated expressions must be built in the heap and garbage collected and may need to be updated. Functions must include extra code to ensure that their needed arguments are evaluated. It is more efficient to pass arguments using call-by-value wherever this will give the same result as lazy evaluation.

We examine Spineless Tagless G-Machine code for different argument passing conventions: lazy, call-by-value and unboxed. We also consider the costs of updates and give performance results for some program fragments.

1   Introduction: using strictness analysis

Strictness analysis tells us when we can evaluate the arguments of a function application in advance (call-by-value) without changing the termination properties of the program from those implied by lazy evaluation (call-by-need). For primitive types, represented by flat domains, it will just tell us whether we can evaluate an argument in advance or not. For constructed types such as tuples or lists, evaluation transformer analysis [Bur91] can also tell us how much of the argument's structure we can evaluate in advance given the amount of evaluation allowed for the application. We can use this to compile different versions of a function corresponding to different degrees of evaluation of its result.

If a function is strict in an argument then evaluating that argument in advance is safe, meaning that it cannot introduce any new non-terminating reduction sequence. This knowledge is useful for two reasons. Firstly, though the referential transparency of purely functional programs suggests that we should be able to evaluate the arguments in a function application in any order, including in parallel, lazy evaluation requires that nothing is evaluated until it is found to be the argument of a strict built-in function. Thus lazy evaluation is normally completely sequential. However, if we know that an argument's value will be needed then it can be evaluated in parallel with the evaluation of the rest of the application without the risk of creating any new non-terminating tasks.

The second potential benefit, and the subject of this paper, is faster sequential execution. Lazy evaluation is slower than call-by-value because closures representing unevaluated expressions must be built in the heap and garbage

*Research funded by SERC grant GR/H 17381 ("Using the evaluation transformer model to make lazy functional languages more efficient")

collected and may need to be updated. Furthermore, functions cannot assume their arguments are evaluated so they must include extra code to test each needed argument.

We describe several ways of transforming lazy evaluation into call-by-value and their effect on the performance of some simple functions. We also summarise the effects of these transformations on memory space requirements.

2 Experiments

We have transformed some test programs by hand to force the compiler to evaluate certain argument expressions in advance rather than building thunks for them. We have based our experiments on GHC (version 0.10), the compiler produced by the GRASP project at Glasgow University. This compiles Haskell into an intermediate "Core" language and thence, via STG abstract machine code to C. See [Pey92] for a description of STG machine code and how to compile it into C.

As in [Pey92] we use the term "closure" both for unevaluated function applications ("thunks") and also for data values.

3 Example 1

We will take as our first example the function:

```
f x = g (h x)
```

This function is simple enough that we can follow its evaluation under different strategies in detail. It would normally be compiled into the following lazy STG code:

```
f x = let v = h x in
      g v
```

A let in STG code always implies the construction of a closure. This is what the STG machine does when f is called (and the approximate number of SPARC instructions required):

1. f builds a thunk in the heap for the expression (h x) (6),

2. copies x to the thunk as a free variable (1),

3. tail-calls g with the thunk's address as an argument (2).

4. g eventually demands its argument, triggering evaluation of the thunk.

5. The thunk's code pushes an update frame so that it will be overwritten with its value when it returns (6),

6. loads its free variable x as an argument to h (1) and

7. tail-calls h (1).

8. h eventually returns to g (5).

9. The thunk (h x) is updated (7).

10. g uses its argument and

11. eventually returns to f's caller (5).

3.1 Call-by-value STG code

If we can determine that g is strict, either because it is a primitive or by using strictness analysis, then f can safely evaluate (h x) in-line and pass the result to g. The transformed STG code looks like this:

```
f x = case h x of v -> g v
```

A case in STG code implies evaluation so (h x) is evaluated and variable v is bound to the value returned. (Note that if the above was written in Haskell the compiler would be obliged to transform the case into a lazy STG let because matching against a single variable pattern (an "irrefutable" pattern) cannot fail and so does not imply evaluation in Haskell).

When this version of f is called the following happens:

1. f pushes a continuation (3) and

2. tail-calls h with argument x (1).

3. h eventually returns to f's continuation (5).

4. f's continuation binds v to h's result (6) and

5. tail-calls g with argument v (1).

6. g demands its (already evaluated) argument,

7. uses its argument and

8. eventually returns to f's caller (5).

3.2 It's faster

The good news is that this version of f takes 27% less time than the lazy version. Table 1 shows the times for the lazy and call-by-value versions. We performed 4 000 000 evaluations of (f 1). The "Rel" column gives each value as a fraction of the figure for the lazy version with updates. The other functions involved were g x = x and h x = x. All types were Int. Using more expensive g or h would simply add the same time to both results.

The main savings are from not building, entering and updating the thunk for (h x). One problem with the call-by-value code is that the value of (h x) is now returned twice whereas under lazy evaluation it would not be returned until it was demanded by g. It is now also returned when first evaluated by f. This extra return is inevitable since we are only allowed to evaluate (h x) in advance because we know g will demand it. In the lazy version, g enters the thunk which then enters h with a tail call so there is only one return corresponding to these two enters. In the transformed version, f's call to h and g's entry of v are separate calls with separate returns.

Version	Example 1		Example 2		Example 3		Section
	Time	Rel	Time	Rel	Time	Rel	
Lazy (update)	28.1	1.00	95.9	1.00	12.6	1.00	3
Call-by-value	20.4	0.73	33.7	0.35	9.7	0.77	3
Lazy (no update)	21.3	0.76	78.1	0.81	9.2	0.73	5
Unboxed argument	11.8	0.42	19.5	0.20	6.8	0.54	7

Table 1:
Versions are explained in the section indicated.

4 Example 2: data structures

Our second example appears rather similar to the first:

```
f x = let (v1,v2) = h x in
      g (v1,v2)
```

Now h returns a pair of values, a copy of which is passed to g. The following lazy STG code is produced:

```
f x = let p = h x in
      let v1 = (case p of
                   (v1',v2') -> v1') in
      let v2 = (case p of
                   (v1',v2') -> v2') in
      let p' = (v1,v2) in
      g p'
```

All these lets (closures) look rather redundant but they are necessary if f is to be lazy — p is not evaluated unless g demands one of the components of its argument. If g is strict then we can transform the above into the following rather good STG code:

```
f x = case h x of (v1,v2) ->
      let p' = (v1,v2) in
      g p'
```

(This case *would* imply evaluation, even in Haskell, since the pattern (v1,v2) is not a single variable).

Table 1 shows the time to evaluate (f 1) 4 000 000 times with g (x,y) = x+y and h x = (x,x). All types are Int. This transformation reduces execution time for Example 2 by 65%. As in Example 1, the savings are from not building, entering and updating closures (p, v1 and v2 in this example). Also as before, there is an extra return (of p' to f) in the transformed version in addition to the return demanded by g.

It looks as though the call-by-value STG code for Example 2 has to take apart the pair returned by h and build a copy of it but the STG Machine usually returns values *unboxed*. Thus h will return v1 and v2 in registers and f then has to *box* them by building them into the pair p' in the heap. Under lazy evaluation, this boxing would be done by an update but now it is done in-line.

4.1 Other types

The boxing of any data type can be in-lined. If the intermediate result is of type T:

```
data T = C t1 t2 ... tN
```

where C is a constructor name and t1 ⋯ tN are types, then we can transform let v = E in B where v is a variable and E and B are expressions, into:

```
case E of
C a1 a2 ... aN -> let v = C a1 a2 ... aN in B
```

where a1 ⋯ aN are new variables. GHC's Int type is also a constructed data type [PL91]:

```
data Int = MkInt Int#
```

MkInt is the constructor with which integers are boxed and Int# is the type of unboxed machine integers. We can use this to rewrite Example 1 with the boxing made explicit:

```
f x = case h x of
      MkInt v# -> let v = MkInt v# in
                  g v
```

We can only evaluate *data* types in advance because we need to know their top level constructors in order to know how the results will be returned. This means that we cannot always evaluate polymorphic expressions in advance, even when evaluation transformers indicate that it would be safe to do so. For example, we cannot produce a version of map which will return a list with every element evaluated unless we know the type of those elements. This requirement also prevents us from evaluating function-typed expressions in advance (which would also invalidate transformations based on eta conversion).

5   Omitting updates

The most important benefit of using call-by-value in our examples is avoiding updates. We can show this by building closures as before but not updating them. We have done this by hand-editing the C code produced by the compiler to remove the pushing of update frames from closures. Omitting updates in Examples 1 – 3 reduces execution time by about 20% as shown in Table 1. This is similar to the speed-up obtained with call-by-value for Examples 1 and 3.

In Example 2 the pair p = h x is shared so some of the time saved by not updating it is wasted in recomputing it. This explains why the non-updating version did not show as big a speed-up as the call-by-value version.

Peyton Jones and Partain's experiments [PP93] indicate that some programs need both strictness analysis and update analysis to minimise the number of updates performed.

6 Evaluating lists

Example 3 is a function which returns a list of n zeros.

```
zeros :: Int -> [Int]
zeros n = case n of
          0 -> []
          _ -> let nm1 = n - 1 in
               let tl = zeros nm1 in
               0 : tl
```

If we want a version of zeros which evaluates the spine of its result then evaluation transformers tell us that it is safe to evaluate tl and nm1 in advance. Since tl is a list, we need a transformation which can handle types with multiple constructors. We transform let v = E in B where E is of type T:

```
data T = C1 t11 t12 ... t1N1
       | C2 t21 t22 ... t2N2

       ...
       | CM tM1 tM2 ... tMNM
```

   into

```
case E of
C1 t11 t12 ... t1N1 ->
        let v = C1 t11 t12 ... t1N1 in B
C2 t21 t22 ... t2N2 ->
        let v = C2 t21 t22 ... t2N2 in B
...
CM tM1 tM2 ... tMNM ->
        let v = CM tM1 tM2 ... tMNM in B
```

Note that we have duplicated the code B. We can avoid this by introducing a new function:

```
let fB v = B in
case E of
C1 ... -> let v = C1 ... in fB v
...
```

This gives a smaller increase in code size but introduces an extra function call (which will compile to a jump). The difference in code size is negligible for our function zeros so we apply the original transformation to give:

```
zeros n
 = case n of
   0 -> []
   MkInt n# ->
     case (MkInt n#) - 1 of
     MkInt nm1# ->
       let nm1 = MkInt nm1# in
       case zeros nm1 of
       []    -> let tl = []    in z : tl
       x:xs -> let tl = x:xs in z : tl
```

Both `nm1` and `tl` are evaluated in advance and boxed in-line. The result is a 23% reduction in execution time compared to the lazy version.

Most of the speed-up is due to evaluating `zeros`'s argument `nm1` in advance. Ordinary strictness analysis would allow this as long as the evaluation was done inside the closure for `tl`. This is highly beneficial because it does not require a function call and is compiled to in-line code. A single machine instruction is needed to perform the subtraction and a few more to box the result. This is much more efficient than building and updating a closure for this expression, as is done by the lazy code.

In fact, it is well known that we don't need *any* strictness analysis to tell us that we can evaluate n - 1. It is guaranteed to terminate since n is already evaluated so it is always better to evaluate it than to build a closure (assuming subtraction cannot terminate with an overflow exception). This is what Hartel refers to as "cheap eagerness" [Har91].

7 Unboxed arguments

So far we have considered various different ways of boxing an intermediate result to pass it to a strict function. A strict function will eventually enter its argument in order to obtain the desired unboxed value so it would be better to pass the unboxed value to the function and save the work of boxing and unboxing it.

Using GHC's notation for unboxed integers we can apply this to Example 1. Here is the original version where g's argument is boxed and unevaluated:

```
f,g,h :: Int -> Int
f x = g (h x)

g x = x
```

And here is a version where g takes an unboxed argument:

```
f,h :: Int -> Int
f x = case h x of
        MkInt v# -> g# v#

g# :: Int# -> Int
g# x# = MkInt x#
```

Function g had to enter its boxed argument in order to evaluate and unbox it but g# will receive the unboxed value in a register.

Incidentally, it looks like g# boxes its argument with a MkInt constructor before returning it but since results are normally returned unboxed, no boxing code is generated.

Similar transformations can be applied to our other example functions. Table 1 shows that we get reductions in execution time of 58%, 80% and 46% from this transformation for Examples 1 – 3. This looks very promising but there are a number of complications:

- Separate compilation modules

Call-by-value relies on a global analysis to determine which expressions may be evaluated in advance but the transformation may be applied locally and optionally so that transformed and untransformed code may be freely mixed in the same program. This is obviously not true when passing unboxed values since we have altered the type of the strict function. This becomes a problem when using separate compilation modules. We must either ensure that both f and g are compiled with the same assumption about the type of g or we must provide both g and g# and link in whichever versions are required.

- Higher-order functions

  The identity of the function being applied (and thus its argument passing convention) might not be known until run-time if it has been passed as an argument to a higher-order function. [Bur91] suggests giving each function an extra "prelude" entry point with code to ensure the correct degree of evaluation of each argument. [Har91] has code preludes which also include unboxing. When the function is known at compile time, strict arguments can be passed unboxed but when the function is entered because it was an argument to some other function then we assume all its arguments will be boxed and enter its prelude to evaluate and unbox them as necessary.

- Algebraic types

  The argument's type might have more than one constructor. If we still want to pass it unboxed we would need a different version of the function for each constructor. For example, a function which was strict in a list argument could be split into two functions, one to handle empty lists and another to handle non-empty lists. Many functions start by performing a case on one argument. The different versions would then correspond to the alternatives of that initial case.

  To do this for more than one unboxed algebraic-type argument would involve duplication of code in the caller and multiplication of versions of the called function and is probably not practical. Even for a single argument, the gain in performance is unlikely to justify the increase in code size.

Rather than pass g's argument unboxed, the compiler could produce code for g which assumed that its argument was evaluated (but still boxed). This would allow it to access the value more efficiently than is possible using the general lazy mechanism which must handle either evaluated or unevaluated arguments. This optimisation has been implemented in Johnsson and Augustsson's LML compiler [Aug87] and in the FAST project compiler [Har91].

8 Memory space requirements

What effect do these transformations have on the amount of heap used? This question becomes important when dealing with lists or other recursive types. Under lazy evaluation, each cell of a list is built as a thunk which is subsequently evaluated by its first consumer and eventually garbage collected when its last consumer has finished with it. It is usually possible to arrange for the generation and consumption of a list to be interleaved so that only one cell of the list is alive in the heap at any instant. If the list is shared then this will not be possible; the first consumer may force the evaluation and updating of the whole list before the last consumer can start processing and freeing it. Such a "space leak" can dramatically increase the heap size required and the time spent in garbage collection.

Evaluating the structure of the list in advance has the same effect as sharing — the whole list is built in the heap before any of it is consumed. The total number of heap words allocated will be of the same order for either lazy or advance evaluation — either a thunk or a cons cell is allocated for each element — but the maximum heap size required can be greatly increased. Evaluating each element of the list in advance as well as the structure may increase or decrease the amount of heap required depending on the relative sizes of the evaluated and unevaluated elements but the whole list will still be resident at once.

One possible solution would be to evaluate the list in "chunks", say five cons cells at a time [Hal92]. This would allow a compromise between time and space efficiency but would also complicate the evaluation mechanism.

The maximum size of stack required is also affected by changing evaluation order. It is often possible to execute recursive functions in constant stack space by forcing the early evaluation of arguments which would otherwise remain unevaluated until the function returned. This kind of space leak is well known ([BW88]) and is typified by functions like `foldl` which, if written naïvely and evaluated lazily, build and return a large graph which is then immediately reduced to a single value. Strictness analysis can be used to ensure that the result is never built as graph but is instead passed evaluated.

9 Related work

Burn and Finne [FB93] describe some similar experiments to ours but based on the Spineless G-Machine rather than the Spineless Tagless G-Machine. They consider both compile-time choice of versions and run-time choice of versions. We have considered only compile-time choice of versions in this paper. They show that the additional information provided by evaluation transformer analysis, compared with simple strictness analysis, is useful for some programs.

After the Spineless G-Machine evaluates an expression the value is always returned boxed and on the top of the stack. This makes it easy to generate code to evaluate an argument expression in advance when compiling a function application. In contrast, the STG Machine returns values unboxed and in different places depending on the type of the expression evaluated. This makes lazy evaluation very efficient but if we want to evaluate expressions in advance we must either provide extra code to box the results or transform the function to expect its strict arguments unboxed. The latter approach is the one adopted in [PP93].

Hartel [Har91] describes how strictness and boxing analyses are used in the FAST compiler. This compiler generates C code, but unlike the STG Machine, uses the C argument passing and return mechanisms directly. Thus, like the Spineless G-Machine, it has a conventional flow of control and a uniform mechanism for returning values. Strictness and boxing information can be incorporated in the generated code in the form of C functions which force the evaluation and boxing or unboxing of argument expressions as required. Different versions of each function can be generated to cope with arguments and result evaluated and boxed to different degrees.

The Clean compiler has a phase where it determines some strictness information using *abstract reduction* [SNvGP91, Noc93]. This information is used to allow expressions of base type and elements of tuples to be evaluated early and passed unboxed, and to allow the unboxed return of values. Each function has two entry points: one for when its strict arguments have been evaluated and one to force their evaluation to the required form before falling through to the other entry point.

10 Conclusions

Using strictness to change evaluation order is important for good performance. Some method is required to reconcile the STG machine's unboxed returns with the fact that functions usually expect their arguments to be boxed. We can avoid updates for lazy arguments by sharing analysis and for strict arguments by providing our own in-line boxing code. We can provide such code for any data type, including integers. If the result has a multi-constructor type we need different boxing code for each constructor, as does an update.

Rather than try to make the boxing more efficient, it is quicker to pass intermediate results as unboxed values and compile functions to expect their strict arguments unboxed. In some cases this eliminates the need for any heap allocation but it requires a global program transformation and is difficult to do for types with more than one constructor. An easier alternative would be just to guarantee that strict arguments were evaluated but still boxed.

References

[Aug87] L. Augustsson. *Compiling Lazy Functional Languages, Part II.* PhD thesis, Chalmers Tekniska Högskola, Göteborg, Sweden, 1987.

[Bur91] G.L. Burn. *Lazy Functional Languages: Abstract Interpretation and Compilation.* Research Monographs in Parallel and Distributed Computing. Pitman in association with MIT Press, 1991. 238pp.

[BW88] R. Bird and P. Wadler. *Introduction to Functional Programming.* Prentice Hall, 1988.

[FB93] S.O. Finne and G.L. Burn. Assessing the evaluation transformer model of reduction on the Spineless G-Machine. In *Proceedings of the Conference on Functional Programming and Computer Architecture.* ACM, June 1993.

[Hal92] C.V. Hall. An optimist's view of life: Transforming list expressions. Technical report, Department of Computer Science, University of Glasgow, 1992.

[Har91] P.H. Hartel. On the benefits of different analyses in the compilation of lazy functional languages. In *3rd Informal International Workshop on the Parallel Implementation of Functional Languages*, pages 123–145, Southampton, 1991.

[Noc93] E. Nocker. Strictness analysis using abstract reduction. In *Proceedings of the Conference on Functional Programming and Computer Architecture*. ACM, June 1993.

[Pey92] S.L. Peyton Jones. Implementing lazy functional languages on stock hardware: the Spineless Tagless G-machine. Technical Report 2, Department of Computing Science, University of Glasgow G12 8QQ., April 1992. FTP: ftp.dcs.glasgow.ac.uk in /pub/glasgow-fp/papers/spineless-tagless-gmachine.dvi.

[PL91] S.L. Peyton Jones and J. Launchbury. Unboxed values as first class citizens in a non-strict functional language. In J. Hughes, editor, *Proceedings of the Conference on Functional Programming and Computer Architecture*, pages 636–666, Cambridge, Massachussets, USA, 26–28 August 1991. Springer-Verlag LNCS523.

[PP93] S.L. Peyton Jones and W. Partain. Measuring the effectiveness of a simple strictness analyser. In J.T. O'Donnell, editor, *Glasgow Workshop on Functional Programming 1993*, Lecture Notes in Computer Science. Springer-Verlag, 5–7 July 1993.

[SNvGP91] S. Smetsers, E. Nöcker, J. van Groningen, and R. Plasmeijer. Generating efficient code for lazy functional languages. In J. Hughes, editor, *Proceedings of the Conference on Functional Programming and Computer Architecture*, number 523 in Lecture Notes in Computer Science, pages 592–617, Cambridge, Massachussets, USA, 26–28 August 1991. Springer-Verlag.

The Implementer's Dilemma: A Mathematical Model of Compile Time Garbage Collection

Simon B Jones

Department of Computing Science and Mathematics, University of Stirling
Stirling, Scotland

Andrew S Tyas

Department of Computing Science and Mathematics, University of Stirling
Stirling, Scotland

Abstract

Optimization by compile time garbage collection is one possible weapon in the functional language implementer's armoury for combatting the excessive memory allocation usually exhibited by functional programs. It is an interesting idea, but the practical question of whether it yields benefits in practice has still not been answered convincingly one way or the other.

In this short paper we present a mathematical model of the performance of straightforward versions of mark-scan and copying garbage collectors with programs optimized for *explicit deallocation*. A mark-scan heap manager has a free list, whereas a copying heap manager does not — herein lies the dilemma, since a copying garbage collector is usually considered to be faster than a mark-scan, but it cannot take advantage of this important optimization.

For tractability we consider only heaps with fixed cells.

The results reported show that the garbage collection scheme of choice depends quite strongly on the *heap occupancy ratio*: the proportion of the total heap occupied by accessible data structures averaged over the execution of the program. We do not know what typical heap occupancy ratios are, and so are unable to make specific recommendations, but the results may be of use in tailoring applications and heap management schemes, or in controlling schemes where the heap size varies dynamically.

An important result arising from the work reported here is that when optimizing for explicit deallocation, a very large proportion of cell releases must be optimized before very much performance benefit is obtained.

1 Compile time garbage collection: A reminder

Compile time garbage collection is an optimization technique in which a compile time analysis is applied to a program to determine whether special purpose storage management operations can be placed in the compiled code. The aim is to place them where the expense of run time decision making about the recycling of storage cells can be avoided: run time garbage collection is replaced by "compile time garbage collection" (for one approach to this see [3]). There are two possible optimizations:

- Deallocation: when, at a particular point in a program where a cell reference is discarded, *every* time that the discard occurs it fully dereferences the cell, then the cell can be explicitly returned to the pool of free cells.

- Direct re-use (or destructive allocation): when a cell can be explicitly deallocated, and a fresh cell is required immediately afterwards, then the dereferenced cell can be re-used directly without the expense of passing it via the free list. (This is easy in the case of fixed size cells, but of more limited scope if cells are variable sized.)

We consider the case of a simple first order functional language with pattern matching of function arguments, and strict, left to right evaluation.

Example: Deallocation Consider the following function definition:

```
sum [] = 0
sum (x:xs) = x + sum xs
```

and the reduction sequence for a "main program" consisting of the expression
sum (1:2:3:[]):

```
    sum (1:2:3:[])
=> 1 + sum (2:3:[])
=> 1 + (2 + sum (3:[]))
=> 1 + (2 + (3 + sum []))
=> etc...
```

In each of the three reduction steps shown, the second equation for sum has been used, and the head cons cell that appears in the pattern matched argument is not referred to in the result of the reduction. Thus the second equation of sum is optimizable: code could be inserted which returns the head cons cell to the free list as soon as x and xs have been extracted from it.
[Note that sum may not be optimizable in all contexts: if the argument list is not an unshared storage reference, then sum cannot be optimized. Here is an example of this problem: suppose that sum is called in the context:

```
f xs = sum xs + sum xs
```

with a call of f as the main program expression. In the left hand sum xs, the xs does not have a unique reference, so it would be disastrous if sum were to deallocate the cons cells of xs.]

Example: Direct re-use Consider the following function definition:

```
append [] ys = ys
append (x:xs) ys = x : append xs ys
```

and the reduction sequence for a "main program" consisting of the expression
append (1:2:[]) (3:[]):

```
    append (1:2:[]) (3:[])
=> 1 : append (2:[]) (3:[])
=> 1 : 2 : append [] (3:[])
=> etc...
```

140

In each of the two reduction steps shown, the second equation for **append** has been used, and the head cons cell that appears in the pattern matched argument is not referred to in the result of the reduction, but a fresh cons cell has been allocated for the result. Thus the second equation of **append** is optimizable: code could be inserted which re-uses the head cons cell of the argument to construct the result.

Again, this optimization depends on the context of the call of **append**.

These simple examples show the possibilities, and illustrate that the optimization requires a *global analysis* of the program. Schemes have been proposed for carrying out this analysis, for example [3]. In this paper it is not our concern to discuss the analysis techniques themselves, but to consider the interaction between optimization options and heap management schemes.

2 Which heap management scheme? A dilemma for optimization

The implementer who wishes to choose a heap management scheme and an optimization technique faces a dilemma. Simplifying the choice of heap management schemes, we have:

- "Mark-scan": Here the time per gc is proportional to the size of the heap; thus, for programs which do not occupy much memory relative to the heap size, it is an expensive option. However, since the scheme involves a free list, *both* deallocation *and* re-use optimizations are possible. It is not widely used at present.

- "n-space copying": Here time per gc is proportional to the number of accessible cells; thus, for programs which do not occupy much memory relative to the heap size, it is a fast option. Most copying schemes do not employ a free list, and so *only* re-use optimization is possible; thus we would expect that less optimization could be carried out than with a mark-scan scheme. Currently, this gc scheme is widely used.

We now see the implementer's dilemma: "slow gc/high optimization" *vs* "fast gc/low optimization". It is pertinent to ask the question:

How does the performance of
mark-scan + deallocation optimization
compare with
copying (with no optimization) ?

Note: The referees suggested that, since there exist mark-scan gcs *without* free lists (e.g. [4]), and also copying gcs *with* free lists, the question could be more generally phrased as:

How does the performance of
a gc with free list + deallocation optimization
compare with
a gc without free list (with no optimization) ?

This paper then addresses the question in one particular context.

3   An analytical assessment of deallocation optimization

In [5] Tyas presents an analytical model for predicting the total time involved recycling storage cells — that is in returning cells which have no references to the free list. The analysis is performed for mark-scan with an adjustable percentage of the released cells returned to the free list via explicit deallocation, and for copying with no deallocation optimization (because it is not possible).

The models assume that the cells are of a uniform, fixed size (so that the model does not need to deal with fragmentation), and that the active heap size, that is the actual number of accessible cells, is at a steady state. The copying heap scheme comprises two semi-spaces; therefore, since the total available memory in both cases is assumed to be the same, each semi-space is half the size of the mark-scan heap (the formulae are easily adjusted to handle the case of them being the same size).

The models are expressed in terms of the following parameters,:

H The total number of heap cells available (maximum memory size).

R The mean number of cells in use (accessible in the hypothetical steady state).

N The total number of cell allocations that occur in a given program.

P The percentage of released cells that are explicitly deallocatable.

and the following time constants are required:

C_1	Time to copy a cell.	(Estimate: $48\mu s$)
C_2	Time to add a cell to the free list.	(Estimate: $5\mu s$)
C_3	Time to mark & unmark a cell.	(Estimate: $16\mu s$)
C_4	Time to determine the mark on a cell.	(Estimate: $2\mu s$)

The values estimated for the time constants were obtained on an HP9000/375 (details are given in [5]). They agree in their magnitudes with those given in [1], which reports a similar, but simpler analysis comparing copying collection with stack allocation. (These values must be accepted in a qualified way, since there may be cache effects involved.)

[5] derives the following formulae for the total time taken in recycling cells with mark-scan gc, T_{ms}, and copying gc, T_{cp}:

$$T_{ms} = (C_2(H-R) + C_3R + C_4H) \left\lfloor \frac{\frac{100-P}{100}(N-R)}{H-R} \right\rfloor + C_2\frac{P}{100}(N-R)$$

$$T_{cp} = C_1R \left\lfloor \frac{N-R}{H/2-R} \right\rfloor$$

Here are some hints for interpreting these formulae:

- $N - R$ The total number of cells released by the program (since R is the steady state occupancy, we assume that this many cells remain allocated at the end of the execution).

- In mark-scan $\frac{P}{100}(N - R)$ cells are explicitly deallocated, and $\frac{100-P}{100}(N - R)$ are collected by ordinary garbage collection.

- $H - R$ The number of cells that must be recycled at each mark-scan gc. ($H/2 - R$ for copying.)

- $\left\lfloor \frac{\text{\# of released cells}}{H-R} \right\rfloor$ The number of mark-scan gcs. ($H/2$ instead of H for copying.

- $C_2(H - R) + C_3R + C_4H$ Time for a single mark-scan gc: C_3R: mark and unmark accessible cells; C_4H: check mark on *all* cells in the heap; $C_2(H - R)$: add all released cells to the free list.

The figure (next page) graphs the formulae for (i) mark-scan with no optimization, i.e. T_{ms} with $P = 0\%$ (the MarkScan line), (ii) mark-scan with *all* cells recycled explicitly, i.e. T_{ms} with $P = 100\%$ (the Explicit line), (iii) copying, T_{cp} (the Copying line). In each case the total number of allocations, N, is 10^6 cells, and the steady state occupancy, R, is 10^4 cells. Practical experiments (reported in [5]) confirm the validity of the curves, but it is hard to reproduce them precisely. For intermediate values of P, in the case of mark-scan, the general trend of the curves is intermediate between the $P = 0\%$ and $P = 100\%$ cases shown (but their saw-tooth nature causes them to cross and re-cross as the heap size grows). Further, P must be substantially greater than 50% before the curve drops significantly below the $P = 0\%$ curve.

The most interesting and relevant part of this graph is for heap sizes between 0 and $0.5 * 10^6$ cells — this is where the executing program performs many gcs. We can observe the following:

- Unoptimized mark-scan is faster than copying if $H/R < 12$

- Copying is faster than fully optimized mark-scan if $H/R > 20$

- Therefore, if the available heap is at least "15 or so" times the size of the average occupancy, then we ought to be using a copying collection scheme rather than a mark-scan scheme optimized for deallocation.

We can compare the results above with the conclusion of [1]. Appel analyses the cost per collected cell of gc for a copying collector and compares this with the cost of popping a cell from a stack. Re-casting in the notation of this paper, Appel's cost per cell in a copying gc, g, is:

$$ g \;=\; \frac{C_1 R}{N - R} \left\lfloor \frac{N - R}{H/2 - R} \right\rfloor \;=\; \frac{T_{cp}}{N - R} $$

This is consistent with Tyas' formula above. Hence, with his time constants, Appel deduces that copying is cheaper than explicit deallocation, and hence fully optimized mark-scan, if

$$ g < C_2 \quad \Longleftrightarrow \quad H/R > 14 $$

This heap occupancy ratio is consistent with Tyas' predictions.

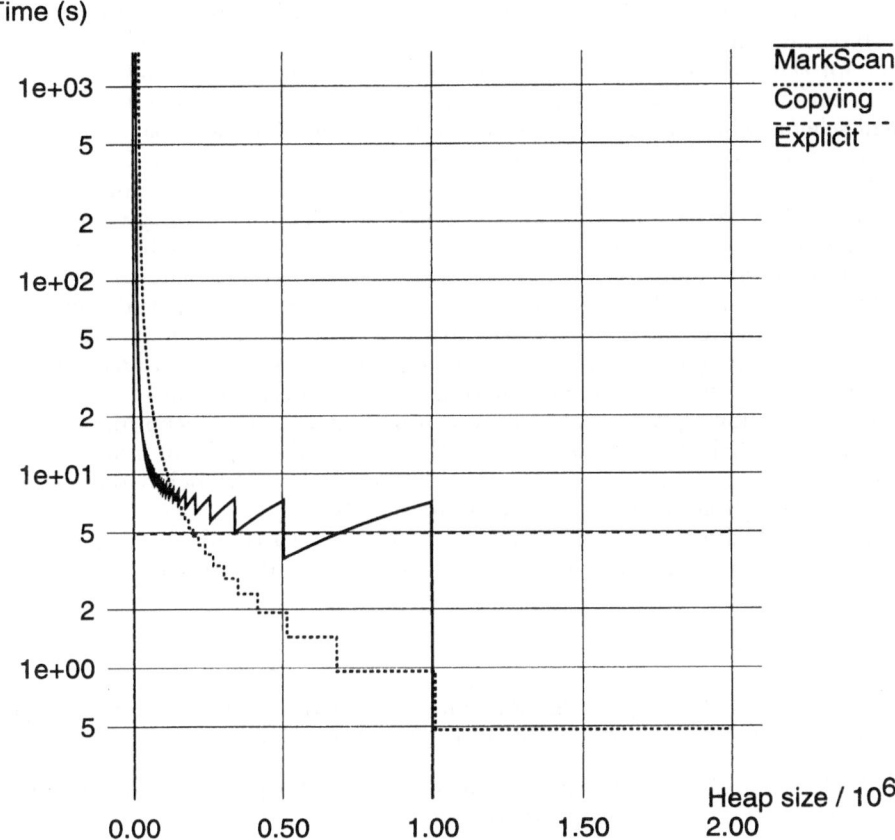

The variation of total recycling time with heap size. $N = 10^6, R = 10^4$.
Unopt mark-scan (MarkScan), fully opt mark-scan (Explicit), and Copying.
Note: at heap size $1 * 10^6$ mark-scan time drops to zero,
and at heapsize $2 * 10^6$ the copying time drops to zero.
(*Reproduced from [5]*)

4   Conclusions

The results of the previous section are quite interesting: they predict that, if
our programs will be running with a relatively small heap (less than roughly 15
times the average occupancy of the program), then we would be better with a
mark-scan heap management scheme (whether optimized or not); otherwise a
copying scheme will behave better. An important new result obtained from the
analysis presented here is that, if the heap is small and we are using optimized
mark-scan, then we need a *very high proportion* of optimized deallocations
before the performance benefit is appreciable (well over 50%).

144

The threshold occupancy ratio observed above is probably too high. The analysis here does not take into account the full heap management costs: the time for the *allocation* of cells has been omitted (since it is not altered by the deallocation optimization). Heyman [2] has a more complex memory management scheme which incorporates allocation costs, but does not take into account deallocation optimization; his results place the crossover point at 2.8.

So, the choice of scheme depends on the expected heap occupancy ratio. Unfortunately we have no available data on typical heap occupancy ratios, so we are unable to make specific recommendations. It is hard to predict how large-scale functional application programs and large-scale functional programming systems are going to develop, and so it is hard to know what typical occupancy ratios are realistic. In the conventional software arena, programs have grown to fit the ever larger memories available, and there is no reason to assume that the same won't be true in the functional arena. Perhaps the results in this paper, and follow-up work on re-use optimization and other heap management schemes, may help to establish rules of thumb for tailoring heap managers and heap sizes to application programs, or for controlling the behaviour of heap managers which adapt the heap size dynamically.

Acknowledgements: The authors would like to thank the two referees, Pieter Hartel and Patrick Sansom, for their very useful comments.

References

[1] A.W. Appel. Garbage collection can be faster than stack allocation. *Information Processing Letters*, 25(4):275–279, June 1987.

[2] J. Heyman. A comprehensive analytical model for garbage collection algorithms. *ACM SIGPLAN Notices*, 26(8), August 1991.

[3] S.B. Jones and D. Le Métayer. Compile-time garbage collection by sharing analysis. In *Proceedings of the Fourth International Conference on Functional Programming Languages and Computer Architecture*, pages 54–74, 1989.

[4] P. Sansom. Combining copying and compacting garbage collection. In R. Heldal, C.K. Holst, and P. Wadler, editors, *1991 Glasgow Workshop on Functional Programming*. Springer-Verlag, Workshops in Computing, August 1991.

[5] A.S. Tyas. An investigation into the optimization of garbage collection within functional languages. Final Year Dissertation, Department of Computing Science and Mathematics, University of Stirling, April 1993.

Functional Graph Algorithms with Depth-First Search (Preliminary Summary)

David J. King   John Launchbury

University of Glasgow*

Abstract

Performing a depth-first search of a graph is one of the fundamental approaches for solving a variety of graph algorithms. Implementing depth-first search efficiently in a pure functional language has only become possible with the advent of imperative functional programming. In this paper we mix the techniques of pure functional programming in the same cauldron as depth-first search to yield a more lucid approach to viewing a variety of graph algorithms. This claim will be illustrated with several examples.

1   Introduction

Graph algorithms have long been a challenge to functional programmers. It has not been at all clear how to express such algorithms without using side effects to achieve efficiency. For example, many texts provide implementations of search algorithms which are quadratic in the size of the graph (see [7, 3, 2], for instance), compared with the standard linear implementations given for imperative languages (see [1], for instance). In this paper we implement a variety of algorithms based on *depth-first search* (DFS), obtaining linear time efficiency for them all.

The importance of depth-first search for graph algorithms was established by Tarjan and Hopcroft [10, 4]. They demonstrated how depth-first search could be used as a skeleton on which to build efficient graph algorithms. The particular code-fragments relevant to a particular algorithm are embedded into the DFS procedure in order to compute relevant information while the search proceeds. While this is quite elegant it has a number of drawbacks. Firstly, the DFS code becomes intertwined with the code for the particular algorithm, resulting in opaque programs. Secondly, reasoning about such algorithms is *dynamic*—it is a process under discussion rather than a value—and such reasoning is complex. In response to this, DFS algorithms are commonly introduced with respect to the *DFS-tree* (or forest in general), providing a *static* intermediate value for reasoning.

We build on this latter idea. If having an explicit DFS tree is good for reasoning then, so long as the overheads are not unacceptable, it is good for

---

*Authors' address: Department of Computing Science, University of Glasgow, Glasgow G12 8QQ, Scotland, United Kingdom. Electronic mail: {gnik, jl}@dcs.glasgow.ac.uk.

programming. In particular, we present a variety of DFS algorithms as combinations of standard components, passing explicit intermediate values from one to the other. In doing so we gain a far greater degree of modularity than is usually found in implementations of these algorithms, while still retaining the standard complexity measure.

There is one place where we do need to use destructive update in order to gain the same complexity (within a constant factor) of imperative graph algorithms. The Glasgow Haskell compiler provides extensions to the non-strict, pure functional language Haskell [5] including updatable arrays, and also allows us to encapsulate these state-based actions so they return pure functional values. Consequently we obtain linear algorithms and yet retain the ability to perform purely functional reasoning on all but one reusable component.

2   Representing graphs

There are many ways to represent (directed) graphs. For our purposes, we use an array of adjacency lists. The array is indexed by vertices, and each component of the array is a list of those vertices reachable along a single edge. This adjacency structure is linear in the size of the graph, that is, the sum of the number of vertices and the number of edges. We use a standard Haskell immutable array which gives constant time lookup (but not update—these arrays may be shared arbitrarily).

We can use the same mechanism to represent *undirected* graphs as well, simply by ensuring that we have edges in both directions.

```
type Graph = Array Vertex [Vertex]
type Edge  = Assoc Vertex Vertex

out :: Graph -> Vertex -> [Vertex]
out g v = g ! v

vertices :: Graph -> [Vertex]
vertices = indices

mapG :: (Vertex -> [Vertex] -> a) -> Graph -> Array Vertex a
mapG f g = array (bounds g)
                 [ v := f v (out g v) | v <- vertices g]

edges :: Graph -> [Edge]
edges g = [ v := w | v <- vertices g, w <- out g v ]

buildG :: (Vertex,Vertex) -> [Edge] -> Graph
buildG b es = accumArray (flip (:)) [] b es
```

Figure 1: Graph abstract data type

In the abstract data type presented in Figure 1, `Vertex` can be any type belonging to the Haskell index class `Ix`, which includes `Int` and `Char` as well as many other types. Haskell arrays come with indexing (`!`) and the functions `indices` (returning a list of the indices) and `bounds` (returning a pair of the least and greatest indices). We provide graph versions of `bounds` and (`!`) namely `vertices` and `out`. The function `mapG` applies a function to every graph vertex, building a table (an array indexed by the vertices) of the result. For example, we might define,

```
outdegree :: Graph -> Array Vertex Int
outdegree g = mapG numEdges g
  where  numEdges v ws = length ws
```

to build a table of the number of edges leaving each vertex.

Haskell provides an easy and general method for building an array from an association list (essentially a list of pairs using the infix `:=` constructor). This operation takes linear time with respect to the length of the adjacency list. So in linear time, we can define a graph in terms of edges, and then convert to a graph using the function `buildG`. For example,

```
graph = buildG ('a','j')
          ['a':='b', 'a':='f', 'b':='c', 'b':='e',
           'c':='a', 'c':='d', 'e':='d', 'g':='h',
           'g':='j', 'h':='f', 'h':='i', 'h':='j']
```

will produce the array representation for the graph in Figure 2.

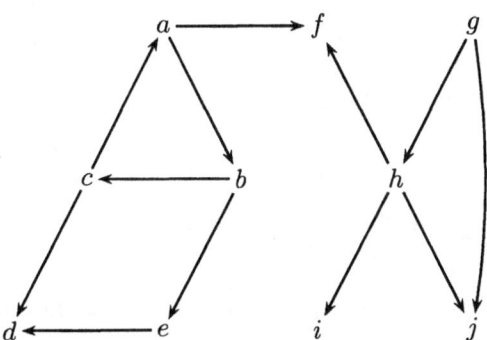

Figure 2: A directed graph

Then, to find the immediate successors to `'h'`, say, we compute:

```
out graph 'h'
```

which returns `['f', 'i', 'j']`.

The function `edges` lets us go in the other direction, extracting an edge list from the array representation, again in linear time. This immediately gives us a way to create the *transpose* of a graph:

```
transposeG :: Graph -> Graph
transposeG g = buildG (bounds g) (map reverseE (edges g))
  where  reverseE (v:=w) = w:=v
```

We extract the edges from the original graph, reverse their direction, and rebuild a graph with the new edges. Then, for example,

```
out (transposeG graph) 'h'
```

will return ['g'].

3 Depth-first search

Depth-first search may be loosely described as follows. Initially, all the vertices of the graph are deemed "unvisited", so we choose one and explore an edge leading to a new vertex. Now we start at this vertex and explore an edge leading to another new vertex. We continue in this fashion until we reach a vertex which has no edges leading to unvisited vertices. At this point we backtrack, and continue from the latest vertex which does lead to new unvisited vertices.

Eventually we will reach a point where every vertex reachable from the initial vertex has been visited. If there are any unvisited vertices left, we choose one and begin the search again, until finally every vertex has been visited once, and every edge has been examined.

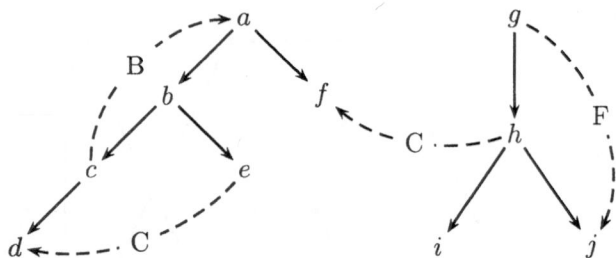

Figure 3: A depth-first forest of the graph

It is common to identify the *spanning forest* defined by a depth-first traversal of a graph. This forest (a list of trees) is depicted in Figure 3 for the graph in Figure 2. The (solid) tree edges are those graph edges which lead to unvisited vertices. The remaining graph edges are also shown, but in dashed lines. These edges are classified according to their relationship with the tree, namely, *forward edges* (connect ancestors in the tree to descendants), *back edges* (the reverse), and *cross edges* (connect nodes across the forest, but always from right to left). This standard classification is useful for thinking about a number of algorithms. In particular, we will take it as read that no graph contains left-right cross edges with respect to a depth-first spanning forest. If a forest did contain left-right cross edges it could not have been created by a depth-first traversal.

149

4 Implementing depth-first search

The approach to DFS algorithms which we advocate in this paper is to manipulate the DFS forest *explicitly*. The first step, therefore, is to construct the depth-first spanning forest from a graph. For this we still need two things: the first is an appropriate definition of trees and forests (Section 4.1), and the second is a method for marking vertices so that we can determine when a vertex has been visited (Section 4.2).

Once we have seen how to build DFS forests (Section 4.3), we will see how to use them in a variety of algorithms (Section 5).

4.1 Representing trees and forests

In Figure 4 we provide an implementation for trees and forests. A forest is a list of trees, and a tree is a node containing some value, together with a forest of sub-trees. Both trees and forests are polymorphic in the type of data they may contain.

```
data Tree a   = Node a (Forest a)
type Forest a = [Tree a]

preorder :: Tree a -> [a]
preorder (Node a ts) = [a] ++ preorderF ts

postorder :: Tree a -> [a]
postorder (Node a ts) = postorderF ts ++ [a]

preorderF :: Forest a -> [a]
preorderF ts = concat (map preorder ts)

postorderF :: Forest a -> [a]
postorderF ts = concat (map postorder ts)
```

Figure 4: Tree and forest flattening functions

The functions `preorder` and `postorder` are standard flattening functions, `preorder` placing ancestors before descendants, and `postorder` doing the reverse. Both place the components of subtrees in left-to-right order[1].

4.2 Marking vertices

The purpose of marking vertices during a search is to determine whether a vertex has been previously visited or not. One way of viewing this is to think of maintaining a set of those vertices which have been visited. The operations we

---

[1]Because of repeated appends (++) caused by `concat` these operations incur an extra logarithmic factor. Removing this is easy, but the definitions become a little less clear.

150

require on the set are to add new members, and to test for membership. In imperative language implementations of graph algorithms, marking is performed by destructive update, giving constant time for both operations. Indeed, within the standard von Neumann architecture there seems to be no way to obtain constant time for both operations unless destructive update is used. This means that to implement the construction of the DFS forest, we will need to make use of explicit state within Haskell.

Imperative features were initially introduced into the Glasgow Haskell compiler to perform input and output [8]. The approach is based on monads [11], and can easily be extended to achieve *in-situ* array updates. Launchbury showed how the original model could be extended to allow the imperative actions to be delayed until their results are required [6]. This is the model we use.

The type constructor of the monad is called `Seq` (because it sequences actions) and is an instance of the standard state transformer monad. So elements of type `Seq Int`, say, are functions which, when applied to the state, return a pair of an integer together with a new state. As usual we have the unit `return` and the sequencing combinator `bind`:

```
return :: a -> Seq a
return a s = (a,s)

bind :: Seq a -> (a -> Seq b) -> Seq b
(m 'bind' k) s = k a t  where  (a,t) = m s
```

but we will hide this behind some syntactic sugar. We extend Haskell expressions with an expression of the form {Q} which is expanded as follows[2]:

```
Q ::= E | E;Q | x<-E;Q

{E}        = E
{E;Q}      = E 'bind' \_ -> ({Q})
{x<-E;Q}   = E 'bind' \x -> ({Q})
```

The `Seq` monad provides three basic array operations:

```
newArr   :: Ix a => (a,a) -> b -> Seq (ArrRef a b)
readArr  :: Ix a => ArrRef a b -> a -> Seq b
writeArr :: Ix a => ArrRef a b -> a -> b -> Seq ()
```

The first, `newArr`, takes a pair of index bounds (the type a must lie in the index class `Ix`) together with an initial value, and returns a reference to an initialised array. The time this operation takes is linear with respect to the number of elements in the array. The other two provide for reading and writing an element of the array, and both take constant time.

Finally, the `Seq` monad comes equipped with a function `newSeq`.

```
newSeq :: Seq a -> a
```

This takes a state-transformer function, applies it to an initial state, extracts the final value and discards the final state.

---

[2]In Haskell the symbols {, }, and ; are sometimes used as layout markers, but we will only use them for monad syntax.

4.3   Performing depth-first search

The algorithm for DFS is given in Figure 5. The function dfs takes a graph g
and a list of vertices vs, and returns the depth-first spanning forest of g. The
list of vertices vs gives an initial ordering for searching the vertices, which is
used to resume the search whenever one is completed. Clearly the head of vs
will be the root of the very first tree.

```
dfs :: Graph -> [Vertex] -> Forest Vertex
dfs g vs = newSeq {marks <- newArr (bounds g) False;
                   search marks vs}

where search :: ArrRef Vertex Bool -> [Vertex]
                   -> Seq (Forest Vertex)
      search marks    []   = return []
      search marks (v:vs) = {visited <- readArr marks v;
                             if visited then
                               search marks vs
                             else
                               {writeArr marks v True;
                                ts <- search marks (out g v);
                                us <- search marks vs;
                                return ((Node v ts): us)}}
```

Figure 5: Lazy depth-first search

The dfs function begins by introducing a fresh state thread, allocating an
array of marks initialised to False, and then calling the locally defined function
search. The result is a value/state pair. The state is discarded, and the value
returned as the result of dfs.

When searching a list of vertices, the mark associated with the first vertex is
examined, and if True the vertex is discarded and the rest are searched. If however the mark is False indicating that the vertex has not been examined previously, then it is marked True, and two recursive calls of search are performed,
each of which returns a forest. The first call, namely, search (out g v), is
given the edges leading from v, and it produces a forest ts which is built into
a tree with v at the root—all these nodes are reachable from v. The second recursive call (search vs) produces a forest of those vertices not reachable from
v and not previously visited. The tree rooted at v is added to the front of this
forest giving the complete depth-first forest.

At this point one may wonder whether any benefit has been gained by using
a functional language. After all, the code looks fairly imperative. To some
extent such a comment would be justified, but two things deserve mention.
The first is that the code above makes free use of data structures such as lists
and trees, and in doing so makes explicit how to restart the search once one
part has finished. It is rare for presentation based on traditional languages to
be so explicit. Secondly, this is the *only* place in the algorithms that follow that

152

state operations have to be used. It will become clear that we have managed to encapsulate the one place where imperative actions are necessary, and allow the full power of functional specification to be used on the rest of the algorithms.

5 Depth-first search algorithms

We now come to the payoff for our work. We will examine a variety of algorithms and express them in terms of what we have already done.

Algorithm 1. Depth-first search numbering

The first algorithm is straightforward. We wish to assign to each vertex a number which indicates where that vertex came in the search. A number of algorithms make use of this *depth-first search number*.

We can express DFS numbering of a graph g most simply by flattening the DFS forest in *preorder*:

```
dfsNum :: Graph -> [Vertex]
dfsNum g = preorderF (dfs g (vertices g))
```

Algorithm 2. Topological sorting

The problem of topological sorting is to arrange the vertices of a directed acyclic graph into a linear sequence $v_1, \ldots, v_n$ such that there are no edges from v_j to v_i where $i < j$. This problem arises quite frequently, where a set of tasks need to be scheduled, such that every task can only be performed after the tasks it depends on are performed.

Given a directed acyclic graph a topological sort may be defined by the following:

```
topSort :: Graph -> [Vertex]
topSort g = reverse (postOrd g)
```

where we define the *postordering* of graph vertices by:

```
postOrd :: Graph -> [Vertex]
postOrd g = postorderF (dfs g (vertices g))
```

To see that this is correct recall the definition of `postorderF`. Tree edges, forward edges, and right-left cross edges all end up pointing from right to left in the postordered list. Only back edges point left-to-right, but if the graph is acyclic then there are no back edges. Then the topological sort is simply the reverse of this postordering.

Algorithm 3. Connected components

Two vertices in an undirected graph are *connected* if there is a path from the one to the other. In a directed graph, two vertices are connected if they would be connected in the graph made by viewing each edge as undirected. Finally, with an undirected graph, each tree in the depth-first spanning forest will contain exactly those vertices which constitute a single component.

We can translate this directly into a program. The function `components` takes a graph and produces a forest, where each tree represents a connected component.

```
components :: Graph -> Forest Vertex
components g = dfs (buildG (bounds g) (es++map reverseE es))
                  (vertices g)
  where   es = edges g
          reverseE (v:=w) = w:=v
```

The undirected graph we actually search may have duplicate edges, but this has no effect on the structure of the components.

Algorithm 4. Strongly connected components

Two distinct vertices in a directed graph are said to be *strongly connected* if each is reachable from the other. A strongly connected component is a maximal subgraph, where all the vertices are strongly connected with each other. This problem is well known to compiler writers as the dependency analysis problem—separating procedures/functions into mutually recursive groups. We implement the double depth-first search algorithm of Kosaraju (unpublished), and Sharir [9].

```
scc :: Graph -> Forest Vertex
scc g = dfs (transposeG g) (reverse (postOrd g))
```

We order the vertices of a graph using the postordering of vertices. The reverse of this ordering is used to perform a depth-first traversal on the transpose of the graph. The result will be a forest, where each tree constitutes a single strongly connected component.

Intuition as to why the algorithm works comes from recalling the nature of the order of vertices produced by `postOrd`. We have already recognised that the only left-right edges in this order are back edges. If we reverse this list and perform a DFS on the transposed graph, then the only way to move forward in the list of vertices is by following what was a back edge in the original search, which is therefore bound to be in a cycle (follow the tree edges back to get to the original node).

A minor variation on this algorithm is to reverse the roles of the original and transposed graphs:

```
scc' :: Graph -> Forest Vertex
scc' g = dfs g (reverse (postOrd (transposeG g)))
```

The advantage now is that not only does the result express the strongly connected components, but it is also a valid DFS forest for the original graph (rather than for the transposed graph).

Algorithm 5. Finding reachable vertices

Finding all the vertices that are reachable from a single vertex v is a simple application of DFS. Commencing a search at v will construct a tree containing all of v's reachable vertices. We then flatten with preorder to give a list of all the reachable vertices from v.

```
reachable :: Graph -> Vertex -> [Vertex]
reachable g v = preorderF (dfs g [v])
```

One application of this algorithm is to determine if there is a path between two vertices:

```
path :: Graph -> Vertex -> Vertex -> Bool
path g v w = w 'elem' (reachable g v)
```

The `elem` test is lazy: it returns `True` the instant a match is found. Hence, the result of `reachable` is demanded lazily, so only produced lazily. As soon as the required vertex is discovered the generation of the DFS forest ceases. Thus `dfs` implements a true *search* and not merely a complete *traversal*.

6 Evidence that we achieve a linear complexity for DFS

The depth-first search algorithm presented should run in $O(V + E)$ time (for a graph with V vertices and E edges). To provide experimental evidence we took measurements on the strongly connected components algorithm, which uses two depth-first searches and should run in $O(V + E)$ time. The results of our experiment are in Figure 6. Timings were taken on randomly generated graphs (with differing numbers of vertices and edges) and are accurate to approximately 1%. The result is that the plotted points clearly all lie on a plane, indicating the linearity of the algorithm.

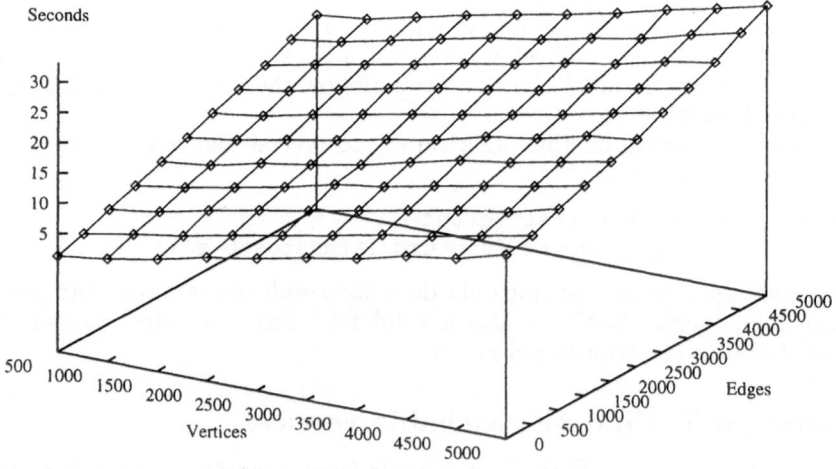

Figure 6: Measurements taken on the strongly connected components algorithm

References

[1] Thomas H. Corman, Charles E. Leiserson, and Ronald L. Rivest. *Introduction to Algorithms*. The MIT Press, Cambridge, Massachusetts, 1990.

[2] Rachel Harrison. *Abstract data types in Standard ML*. John Wiley and Sons, 1993.

[3] Ian Holyer. *Functional programming with Miranda*. Pitman, London, 1991.

[4] John E. Hopcroft and Robert E. Tarjan. Algorithm 447: Efficient algorithms for graph manipulation. *Communications of the ACM*, 16(6):372–378, June 1973.

[5] Paul Hudak, Simon L. Peyton Jones, Philip Wadler, Arvind, Brian Boutel, Jon Fairbairn, Joseph Fasel, María M. Guzmán, Kevin Hammond, John Hughes, Thomas Johnsson, Richard Kieburtz, Rishiyur S. Nikhil, Will Partain, and John Peterson. Report on the functional programming language Haskell, Version 1.2. *ACM SIGPLAN Notices*, 27(5), May 1992.

[6] John Launchbury. Lazy imperative programming. In *Workshop on State in Programming Languages*, ACM SIGPLAN, pages 46–56, Copenhagen, Denmark, June 1993.

[7] L. C. Paulson. *ML for the working programmer*. Cambridge University Press, Cambridge, 1991.

[8] Simon L. Peyton Jones and Philip Wadler. Imperative functional programming. In *20'th Symposium on Principles of Programming Languages*, ACM, Charleston, North Carolina, January 1993.

[9] M. Sharir. A strong-connectivity algorithm and its applications in data flow analysis. *Computers and mathematics with applications*, 7(1), 1981.

[10] Robert E. Tarjan. Depth-first search and linear graph algorithms. *SIAM Journal of Computing*, 1(2):146–160, June 1972.

[11] Philip Wadler. The essence of functional programming (invited talk). In *19'th Symposium on Principles of Programming Languages*, ACM, Santa Fe, New Mexico, January 1992.

DISTRIBUTED GARBAGE COLLECTION OF CYCLIC STRUCTURES

DAVID LESTER

DEPARTMENT OF COMPUTER SCIENCE, VICTORIA UNIVERSITY
OF MANCHESTER, OXFORD ROAD, MANCHESTER M13 9PL, UK

Abstract

One of the key features of modern high level programming languages is the automatic allocation and reclamation of space for data structures. This paper concentrates on the problem of providing these facilities, for a functional language, satisfying the following constraints:

- the programming language permits cyclic data structures;
- the architecture is a distributed multi-processor; and
- global synchronization is not required.

The algorithm has been specified and implemented in Haskell, a lazy functional language. The collector avoids the loss of "communications laziness" that occurs in previously published collectors. We have, as yet, no experience of the algorithm's performance on a distributed system.

1. Introduction

This paper describes a novel distributed garbage collector suitable for a distibuted graph reduction machine, such as the HDG-Machine [?]. The novelty lies in the ability of the collector to reclaim cyclic structures that become garbage, and to work in an environment where there is no sequentiality required of the message passing medium. This new scheme may be thought of as a synthesis of two previous schemes that each address one of the above areas and ignore the other.

The garbage collector has been prototyped in Haskell [?], giving some limited assurance that the algorithm is correct. A full proof of correctness is still awaited.

In Section 2, two previous proposals for distributed garbage collectors are reviewed. The fields required of nodes in the graph are described in Section 3. The new garbage collector is presented in Sections 4, 5 and 6. These deal respectively with creating or extending cycles; copying pointers; and deleting pointers. Finally, I conclude with a few thoughts on improvements in Section 7.

2. Two proposed Garbage Collectors

We begin by reviewing two previously proposed schemes for garbage collection on distributed machines. We begin by considering weighted reference counting garbage collection, and then consider Hughes' Algorithm [?].

2.1. Weighted Reference Counting

The weighted reference counting garbage collector – invented independently by Bevan [?] and Watson and Watson [?] – can be conveniently used in a distributed machine. Conceptually, the system provides three operations: creating a new node (with an associated pointer to the node); deleting a pointer; and copying a pointer. To perform these operations, each pointer has an associated weight, and each node has a reference count.

> **Creating a new node:** The node is given a maximum reference count (say 2^{32}) and the pointer to this node has a weight which is the same as the node's reference count.
>
> **Deleting a pointer:** To do this we subtract the pointers weight from the reference count of the node it points to. If this means that the node has a reference count of zero, then the node is garbage, and its pointers can be deleted.
>
> **Copying a pointer:** Provided the original pointer has a weight greater than 1, we can half the weight on the original pointer and giving the new copy a weight of half the original weight as well.
> If the original pointer has a weight of 1, it is not possible to divide the weight into two. We instead interpose an indirection node between the original pointer and its target node. This will have a maximum reference count (of, say 2^{32}), and is therefore divisible.

The nice feature of this collector is that it requires no ordering on the arrival of messages. That is, the existence of delete pointer messages in transit causes no problems, unlike naïve reference counting schemes. The reason? A reference count is only decremented; this contrasts with the naïve scheme, where there may be increment reference count messages that are still in transit.

The efficiency of this form of collector can be significantly improved by combining it with a copying collector for local garbage collections [?]. The use of this composite collector in a distributed graph reduction system is described in [?].

The only problem with the weighted reference count collector is that it is not possible to detect and reclaim cyclic data structures.

2.2. Cyclic Reference Counting

In his DPhil thesis, Hughes [?] discusses an extension to the straightforward reference counting technique, which enables the collector to detect and reclaim cyclic structures that become garbage. Conceptually the algorithm works by dividing the graph up into *maximal strongly connected components*. The nodes A and B are in the component if, and only, if A is reachable from B and *vice versa*. By treating each of these components as a node we obtain an acyclic graph. The acyclic graph can be handled by the usual reference counting techniques.

Instead of the general operations provided by the Bevan/Watson/Watson Collector, the Hughes' Algorithm provides operations for implementing graph reduction. In a graph reduction machine, one step involves replacing a piece of graph by another piece. It is relatively easy to work out how this replacement operation affects the components it deals with; see [?, Chapter 8] for details.

The algorithm – although complex – works very well for pure functional languages, because we know when we are creating or adding to a component. There are also relatively few places where we might break one of the components.

The only problem with Hughes' Algorithm is that it requires the decrement reference count messages to arrive in a particular order, *and this is often hard or inconvenient to arrange in a distributed system.*

3. A Composite Collector

Arranged as it is above, one possible line of attack is to see if there is any possibility to synthesize a new collector from the two we have presented.

3.1. Three types of node

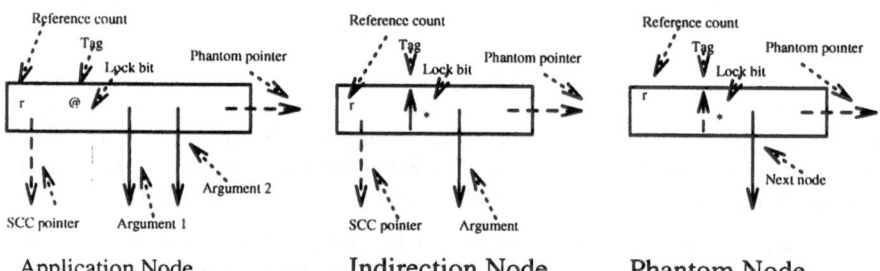

| Application Node | Indirection Node | Phantom Node |

FIGURE 1. Node Structures

In a real machine we would need a range of constant nodes (numbers, functions, and so forth) as well as constructors, and the following three types of special nodes, which are illustrated in Figure 1.

> **Applications:** The application node is the first node shown in Figure 1. Besides the usual information – the tag and two pointers (both weighted) – there are the following extra fields:
>> **Reference Count:** This is the nodes reference count and is used as in the Bevan/Watson/Watson schemes.

SCC Pointer: This is similar to Hughes cyclic reference count, in that all of the nodes in a strongly connected component point have this field set to point to the same real node, which is itself a member of the component. This pointer is *not* a weighted pointer.

Phantom Pointer: This is used to point to a node that will deal with incoming pointers from outside of the strongly connected component. It *is* a weighted pointer. It may be nil, in which case there are no external references to the node, or it is a singleton node.

Indirections: Ordinary indirection nodes – as shown in the second diagram in Figure 1 – have the same extra fields as application nodes.

Phantoms: Finally, in the last diagram of Figure 1 we have *phantom indirection nodes*, that are used to insulate strongly connected components from each other. The idea is that when we need to find a way to divide the weight of indivisible pointers into a strongly connected component, these phantoms provide us with way to do this. Both the next node and the phantom pointer are weighted pointers.

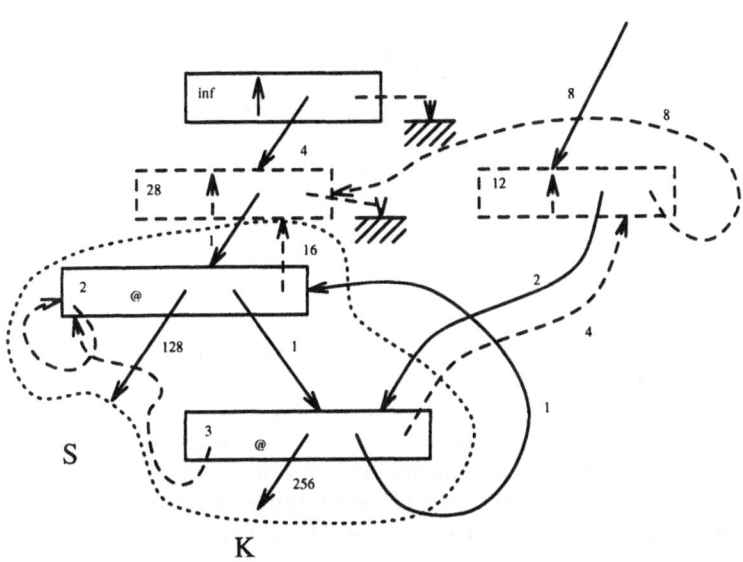

FIGURE 2. Example of a graph

In Figure 2 we have an example of the graph that might be produced by the following program:

```
letrec x = S (K x) in x
```

In this diagram we can see an incoming pointer of weight 8 which is the pointer we have just created. In the dotted strongly connected component, we can see the two application nodes. These have to be in the same component because they each point to one another. Each of these application nodes is accessible from outside the strongly connected component, so they each have a phantom node. Notice that each pointer has a weight, and that each node has a reference count.

We now consider each of the operations of Hughes' Algorithm in turn, beginning with the creation new cycles and the extension of pre-existent cycles.

4. Creating and Extending Cycles

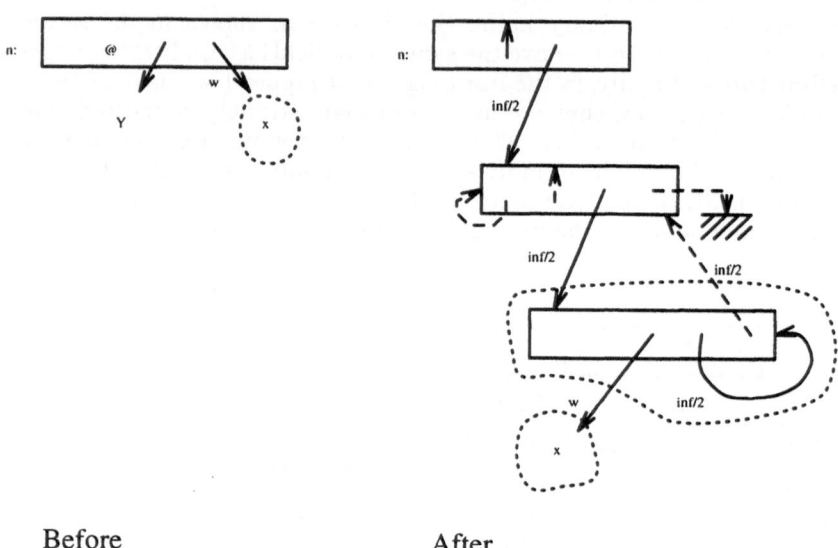

Before   After

FIGURE 3. Creating a new cycle with the Y combinator

Because we wish to show that the collector can deal with cycles, we had better provide a way to create cycles. The general way to do this is to equip the language with a **letrec** construct. As Turner has shown [?, ?], we can turn this construct into the reduction of a number of "knot-tying" Y combinators [?, Page 103]. As Y combinators are simpler than general **letrec**'s, we investigate their properties.

Let us first consider the case where the root of the expression Y x and x are in different strongly connected components. Recall that we can detect this by seeing whether the node x and n share the same SCC pointer. This is the situation depicted at the top of Figure 3.

Given that n (the address of the node that is the root of the redex) and x aren't in the same component, we are about to create a new cycle. This requires us to insert a phantom node between the two original components. This is shown in the lower part of Figure 3. The phantom node has an initial reference count of infinity (really 2^{32}), and its phantom pointer is nil.

To this phantom node we link the application node which represents the cycle. The application node is (initially) the only node in the cycle, so its SCC pointer

points to itself. The application node's phantom pointer points at the newly
created phantom node.

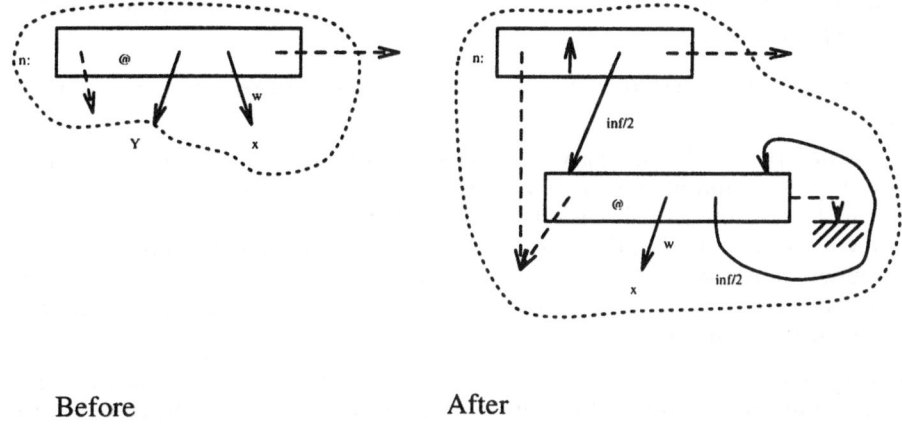

Before   After

FIGURE 4. Y: extending a cycle

The other case to consider is where the original root of the expression (n) and
the argument x are in the *same* strongly connected component. This situation
is shown at the top of Figure 4.

Because we can't easily deal with the pointer to the root of the redex, we
turn the original node into an ordinary indirection node, and create a new
application node for the sub-cycle created by the Y combinator. The new node
shares the SCC pointer of the node n and is given the nil phantom pointer.
Having seen how to create cycles, we now consider ways to copy pre-existent
pointers in Section 5.

5. Making copies of pointers

In this section we describe the different cases that arise when we wish to copy a
pointer. Again we assume that we are implementing a functional language using
graph reduction. Since the graphical behaviour of any combinator's reduction
can be modelled with a combination of S, K, and Y combinators, that is all that
I intend to exhibit. Although it is easier to think about the collector if we just
deal with these combinators, *this does not mean that the collector only works
for Turner's combinators [?, ?]*. The collector will work in the general case as
well.

In case the aforementioned combinators are unfamiliar, they are defined as:

```
> S f g x = (f x) (g x)
> K x y   = x
> Y f     = letrec a = f a in a
```

We will merely consider the rewriting of the S and K combinators. Rewriting
the S combinator (in the general case) involves:

(1) creating copies of the pointers to the three arguments;

(2) creating two application nodes;

(3) rewriting the root application node and deleting the first pointer in the spine.

The K combinator is simpler, in that no new nodes are required to build the body.

We can determine the strongly connected components of the newly created nodes of an S combinator rewrite, by looking at the strongly connected components of the arguments. If these differ from that of the root of the redex, then the new nodes are singleton nodes, *i.e.* each of them is in a strongly connected component of its own. In this case the pointers from the application node are *external pointers*, because they are external from the strongly connected component of the argument.

The alternative is that the argument and the root of the redex *are* in the same strongly connected component. This implies that the new application is also within the same component, and therefore its pointers are said to be *internal* to the strongly connected component. (See the discussion in [?, Page 109]).

This ability to determine to which strongly connected component to assign the new application nodes is a property of functional languages, and it appears that it is unlikely to be present in general for arbitrary programmin languages.

5.1. Creating external pointers

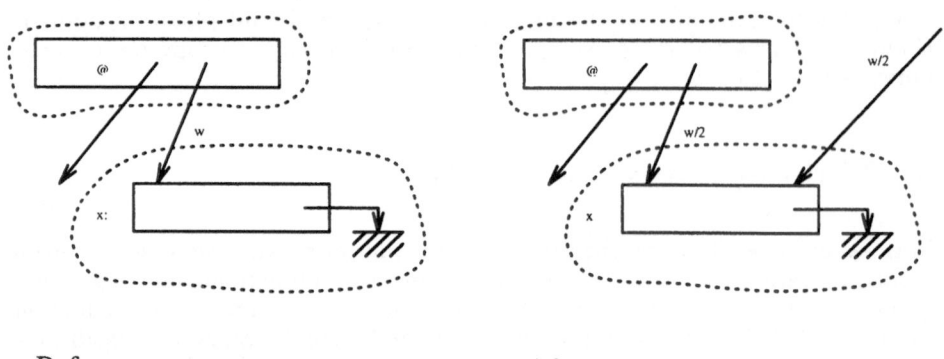

Before   After

FIGURE 5. Copying a pointer: the usual case

In Figure 5 we see the usual situation: we must copy a pointer whose source and target are in different strongly connected components of the graph. If the weight w is divisible then we divide the weight by two and the original pointer and the copy share the weight. This is exactly as it would occur in the Bevan/Watson/Watson Collector.

Sometimes this will not be possible, because the weight of the pointer is minimal *i.e.* it is 1. In this case we insert an ordinary indirection node between the original pointer and its target. We can now make the copy of the original pointer

point at the indirection node, giving it a weight of inf/2. Once more the transformed graph is exactly as it would have been in the Bevan/Watson/Watson
Collector.

We now consider the case of creating an *internal pointer*.

5.2. Creating internal pointers

Making a copy of a pointer (lying entirely within a strongly connected component) for use inside the same strongly connected component is straightforward.
We simply half the weight of the original pointer and assign the same weight
to the copy pointer. In the event that the pointer weight is already 1, then
we create a new ordinary indirection node between the two points copying the
dotted pointer to the root node of the cycle. It should be noted that the new
indirection node's SCC pointer is the same as that of the other nodes in the
cycle.

There would be another problem for us to consider if we are not implementing
a functional language: we may need to make a copy of an external pointer for
use as an internal pointer. This may then be used to extend or create cycles in
completely arbitrary ways, so we don't permit this.

We finally consider the most complicated case, where the spine application
node is in the same strongly connected component as the argument, but this
differs from the component in which the root of the current redex lies. We are
therefore creating an external pointer to a node that might have no previous
external references.

5.3. Creating external pointers for nodes with phantoms

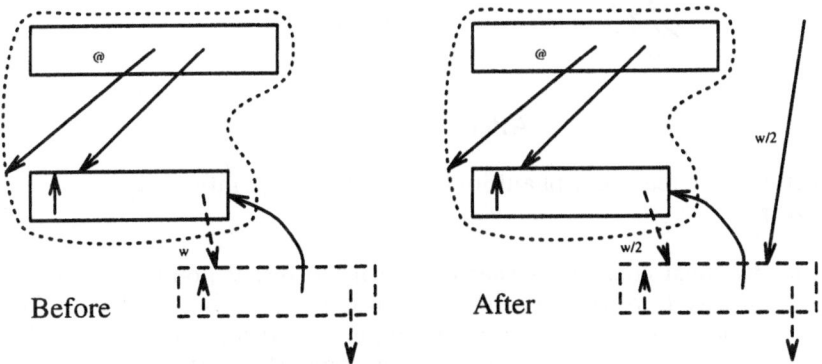

FIGURE 6. External pointer for a node with a phantom

Now suppose that we wish to create a pointer to a node **x**, to be used outside the
strongly connected component, and that the spine application node is within
the same component as **x**. There are two cases to consider: when the node **x**
already has a phantom node; and when a phantom node will need to be created.

164

In Figure 6 we see the situation where the node **x** already has a phantom node associated with itself. We can tell that this is the case because the node **x** has a non-nil phantom pointer. This phantom node is pointed to with a weight of **w**. Provided **w** is not 1 the transformation of the graph is shown as shown in Figure 6.

Of course we must have a way to deal with the case where this weight is 1. In this case a new phantom node has to be created which replaces the node originally used as a phantom by **x**. This new node will have a divisible weight, and so the new external pointer can be given the weight: one quarter infinity.

5.4. Creating external pointers for nodes without phantoms

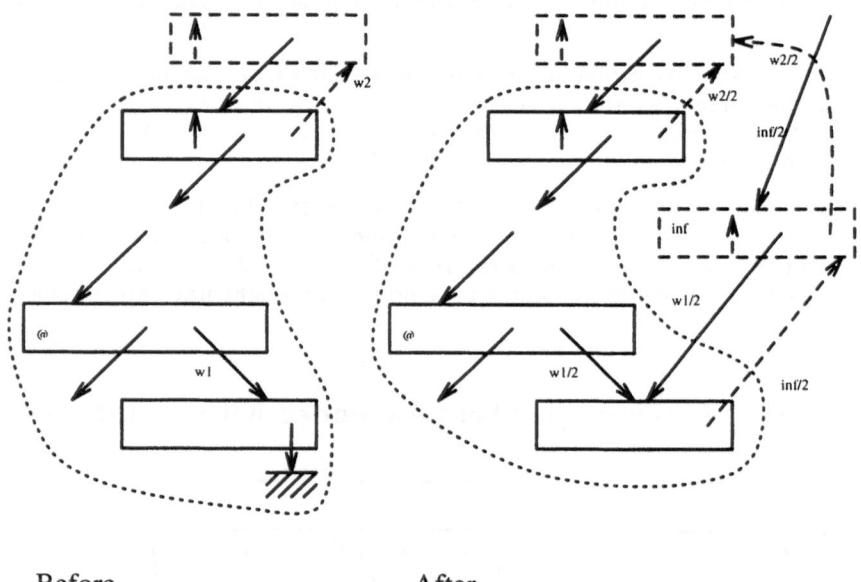

Before   After

FIGURE 7. Creating a phantom for an external pointer: **w1** ≠ 1, **w2** ≠ 1

The final case we must consider is that of creating external pointers to nodes which do not already have phantom indirection nodes pointing at them. The first observation is that – in a functional language setting – there must be a phantom node between the root of the redex and the strongly connected component that contains **x**. As the initial state of the graph, on the left of Figure 7 shows, there are two critical weights: **w1** and **w2**. We will need to consider what happens if either of both of them are 1.

The simple situation, in which both the weights **w1** and **w2** are divisible, is shown on the right of Figure 7. We have created a new phantom indirection node, which is the target of the external pointer we are creating. Notice that the new phantom is linked into the tree of phantom nodes that surround the strongly connected component.

We next need to consider the cases when w1 and w2 are independently 1. If the weight w1 is 1 we get a case which is analogous to the simpler case in which we insert a simple indirection node. We have created an (ordinary) indirection to the node x and then performed the operations shown in Figure 7.

Of course it may be that the weight w2 is indivisible, in which case we have to create a new phantom indirection to provide a node that can have its weight divided.

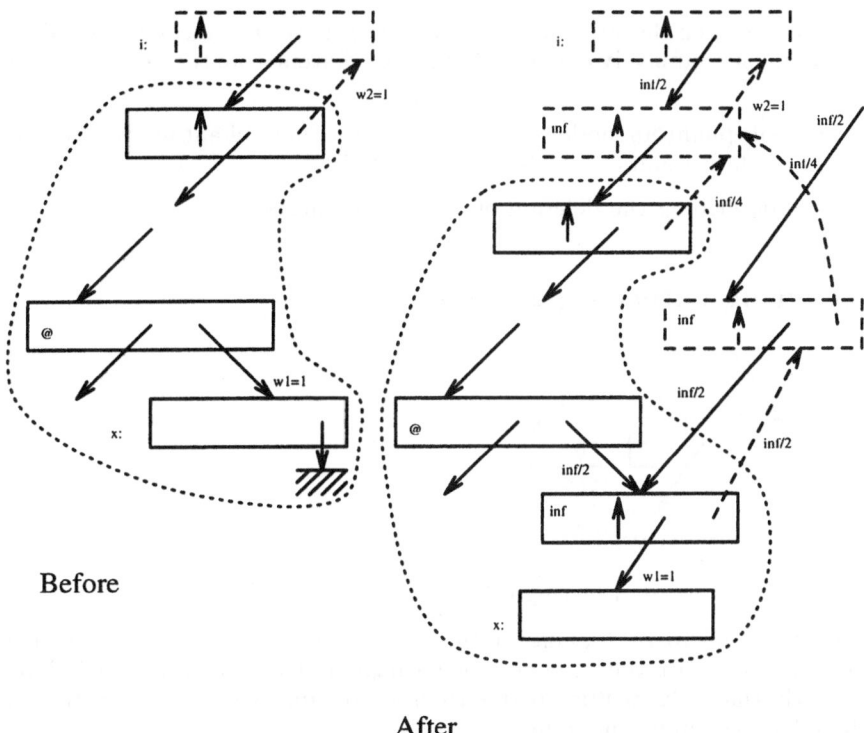

FIGURE 8. Creating a phantom for an external pointer: w1 = 1, w2 = 1

Finally, for those who like complexity, Figure 8 shows what happens when both w1 and w2 are indivisible. To obtain the transfomations when w1 or w2 are independently 1, we merely select which indirection nodes to include.

This concludes the various ways to copy a pointer that we will be needing to implement a functional language. We now discuss the problems involved in deleting pointers within the graph.

166

6. Deleting Graph Nodes

In this section we shall see how to delete pointers and graph nodes. The most important criteria for graph nodes is as follows: A 'real' graph node, *i.e.* a non-phantom node, is garbage whenever:

- it has a null phantom pointer and a reference count of 0.

A phantom node is garbage whenever:

- the weight of the pointer from the node pointed to by the phantom node equals the phantom's reference count.

Once a node has been declared garbage – because its reference count has fallen to zero – we must recursively delete all outgoing pointers from the newly deleted node.

When the root phantom node (the one with the null phantom pointer) is deleted, the cycle it points to is also to be deleted.

We begin by describing the deletion of external pointers.

6.1. Deleting external pointers

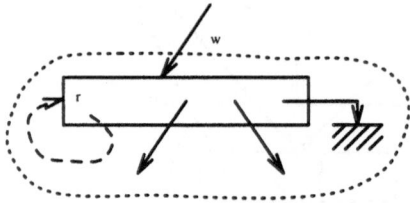

FIGURE 9. Deleting external pointer to real node

In Figure 9, we begin by looking at the case of deleting a pointer to a real node. If w is equal to r then the node is garbage and we recursively delete its pointers. Alternatively, if r is greater than w, we simply subtract the weight from the reference count and stop.

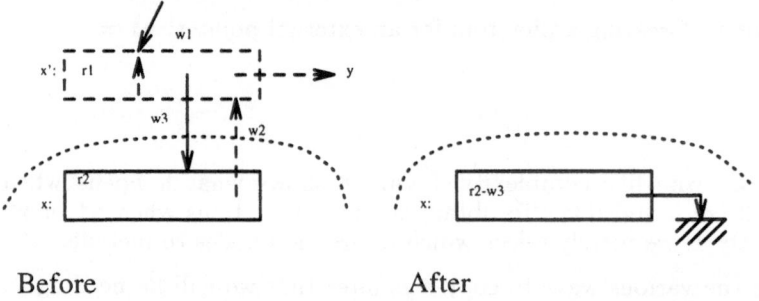

Before   After

FIGURE 10. Deleting external pointer to phantom

The next case to consider is the deletion of a pointer to a phantom node that is not the root phantom node. This situation is illustrated in the top part of Figure 10. the phantom node **x'** becomes garbage when **r1** is equal to **w1 + w2**. As this phantom node isn't the last one, we simply replace the phantom pointer of **x** by nil, subtracting **w3** from **x**'s reference count. The pointer to the phantom node **y'** is also deleted. This is shown in the lower part of Figure 10.

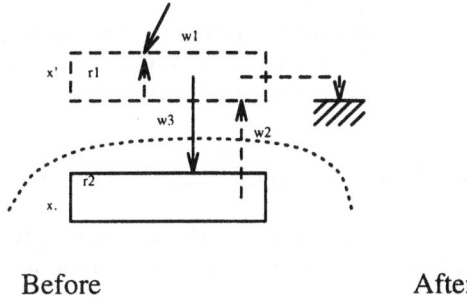

Before   After

FIGURE 11. Deleting external pointer to the last phantom

Another case is where the pointer *is* pointing at the last phantom node (the phantom node that has a null phantom pointer). This is shown in Figure 11. If the phantom node's reference count equals **w1 + w2**, the whole of the strongly connected component is deleted along with the phantom node **x'**.

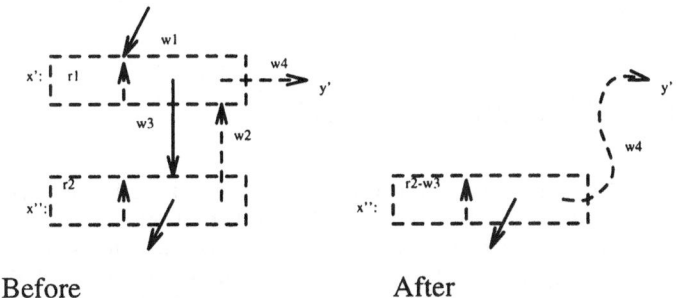

Before   After

FIGURE 12. Deleting external pointer between two phantoms

Suppose that the phantom node to be deleted doesn't have an associated 'real' node. Figure 12 shows what happens when the node **x'** is deleted. We adjust the weights of the incoming pointer and the phantom pointer to reflect the deletion of the node **x'**.

6.2. Deleting Internal Pointers

The final case to consider is deleting an internal pointer, *i.e.* one that lies between two nodes in the same strongly connected component. We need to check whether this causes the strongly connected component to be split into smaller components. Here is the sequence of operations that must be performed.

168

(1) Set the to-be-deleted pointer's weight to zero.
(2) Using the SCC pointer lock the root node of the strongly connected component.
(3) If the current task finds the root node already locked then another task is attempting to split the cycle. This means that the deletion may be assumed to have taken place and any needed rearrangement of the strongly connected component to be taking place.
(4) Otherwise, we are responsible for attempting to split the component. The task traverses the strongly connected component and its associated phantom nodes locking them, to prevent other tasks adjusting the nodes' reference counts.
(5) Using Targan's Algorithm [?] we analyse the nodes of the strongly connected component to discover the new strongly connected component(s).
(6) If the new set of components is not the same as the old strongly connected component then we must create a new set of phantom nodes for each new component.
(7) The old phantom nodes are turned into ordinary indirection nodes which point to the newly created phantoms.
(8) Finally, we unlock all of the previously locked nodes.

One optimization to the above scheme, is to turn singleton nodes that have been identified as new strongly connected components, but which in fact are not cyclic into the ordinary non-cyclic graphs, thereby eliminating the phantom node.

7. Conclusions and Further Work

Although I have no practical experience of the costs associated with this approach to garbage collecting, it should be observed that in the absence of cyclic graph the collector is almost as time-efficient as the Bevan/Watson/Watson collector. The nodes in the heap are slightly larger as we must store an SCC field and a phantom pointer field on each; this makes the space-efficiency worse.

It is also possible that the time-efficiency of the collector could be improved by using a similar technique to the one that is used in [?]. The idea is to use a compacting collector locally, and reserve the complexity of weighted reference counting for those places where the pointers really are pointing across processor boundaries. The problem I foresee with this collector is that we must mark all cycles when they are created, and treat them specially when they become distributed across the machine. This means that much of the complexity of the collector outlined in this paper must be retained.

Interestingly – as Partridge [?] has observed – we have a problem in distributed architecture implementations of lazy functional languages with what he terms loss of "communications laziness". This occurs where a node from a cyclic graph is copied from processor A to processor B, and it subsequently transpires that this same node is again required. The obvious situation in which this occurs is when a cyclic list (such as the infinite list of ones) is copied from one processor to another. A naïve copying process results in the copied list no longer being cyclic. If the copied version (on B) is unable to detect that it is already present on B, then yet another copy will be exported from processor A. The garbage collector I have outlined provides sufficient information about each cycle, to detect cyclic occurrences of a reference to a node.

It could be that it is cheaper to ignore cyclic structures until they have built up to a sufficient extent that we stop the whole machine to garbage collect them.

Update Avoidance Analysis by Abstract Interpretation

Simon Marlow

Department of Computer Science

University of Glasgow

Glasgow, U.K.

email: simonm@dcs.glasgow.ac.uk

Abstract

A requirement of lazy evaluation is that the value of any subexpression in the program is calculated no more than once. This is achieved by updating an expression with its value, once computed. The problem is that updating is a costly operation, and experimentation has shown that it is only necessary in about 30% of cases (that is, 70% of expressions represent values that are only ever required once during execution). The aim of the analysis presented in this paper is to discover expressions that do not need to be updated, and thus reduce the execution time of the program. The analysis has been implemented in the Glasgow Haskell Compiler, and results are given.

1 Introduction

Lazy evaluation of functional programs specifies a number of criteria to be adhered to during execution. One of these is that all sub-expressions in the program are evaluated at most once, and, if possible, not at all. The technique commonly used to implement this aspect of lazy evaluation imposes a run-time cost. This paper presents a method that can eliminate the overhead in cases where it is not required.

Functional programs are normally executed lazily using *graph reduction*. The program is represented as an object in memory which is gradually reduced as evaluation progresses; as each sub-expression in the program is evaluated it is overwritten, or *updated*, with its value. Thus, when the value of the expression is required again, it can be used directly without needing to be re-calculated. However, blindly updating every expression with its value is over-cautious; what if the value is never required again? Then the time spent performing the update is wasted. There is obviously an opportunity for optimisation based on analysis here, and that is the subject of this paper.

We cannot hope to decide in general whether a specific expression should be updated or not. It may depend on the input to the program at run-time, for instance[1]. The analysis will therefore be an approximation; for some expressions the analysis may show that an update is not required, but for others it will be impossible to tell. The notion of approximate analysis is a familiar one in the field of program optimisation, but it is useful to know exactly where the

---

[1]the problem would in fact be undecidable even if the input to the program were known.

approximation takes place and which classes of expression cause the analysis to generate cautious results. These questions will be answered for the analysis presented later.

To give some idea of the scope of the optimisation, we collected some statistics concerning updates during the running of some example programs compiled with the Glasgow Haskell Compiler. The results showed that on average, only 30% of all updates performed were necessary. This suggests that in the best case, 70% of updates could be avoided, and further experimentation shows that this can result in roughly a 20% performance increase. The gains arise from several areas (some of the details here are specific to the Spineless Tagless G-Machine, but the gains should be roughly the same in most execution models):

- Performing an update requires pushing an "update frame" on the machine stack. This can cause argument satisfaction checks to fail (an argument satisfaction check ensures that a function is called with all its arguments), and in any case will interrupt the normal execution of the program in order to perform the update.

- The code required to push an update frame can clearly be omitted if the update is not required—this is significant on architectures that rely on an instruction cache with a limited size.

- Performing the update requires overwriting the original closure with either an indirection to the value object, or, if the closure is large enough, with the value itself. In the Glasgow Haskell Compiler, the second option is used as often as possible to reduce heap usage.

- If the value of an expression is returned in registers (a common case in the Glasgow Haskell Compiler) and an update is not required, the value may never exist in the heap at all. In the case where the update would have been by indirection, we are actually saving heap space by not performing the update.

- Updates are the bane of generational garbage collectors [SP93], since an update may create a pointer from an old generation to a newer one. The garbage collector must keep track of pointers created in this way to avoid having to traverse all the old generations whenever collection of a new generation occurs. Therefore, the fewer updates there are, the greater the efficiency of the garbage collector.

So, an attractive property of update avoidance is that there are no tradeoffs involved; the optimisation reduces execution time, code size, and heap usage. The only loss is the time required to perform the analysis at compile time.

The analysis technique described in the rest of this paper is based on abstract interpretation. It is formulated in such a way that higher-order, polymorphic programs do not present a problem, although the analysis does make some approximation with regard to recursion.

Our main aim in formulating the analysis was to obtain results using a simple and general technique. In fact, the technique presented here has other applications aside from update avoidance analysis. Our secondary aim was to be able to implement the technique in a real compiler, imposing some efficiency

$f, g, h, u, v, w, x, y, z$				variable
p, q	$::=$	x		variable
	$\mid$	i		literal
e	$::=$	p		variable or literal
	$\mid$	$\lambda x.\, e$		lambda expression
	$\mid$	$e\, p$		application
	$\mid$	$p \oplus p$		primitive operation
	$\mid$	**let** $x = e_1$ **in** e_2		let expression

Figure 1: The Language

constraints on the analysis itself. Where there was a choice between an efficient analysis and a more powerful one, we opted for the former.

No apology is made for the fact that we do not as yet have a formal basis for the analysis, and that confidence in its correctness is gained from informal examination and experimentation with the implementation. A more formal treatment is, however, in the works.

A previous approach to the problem of update avoidance analysis involved using a type system to obtain information about updatability [LGH+92], but this has not been implemented successfully.

The rest of this paper is structured as follows: Section 2 describes the extended form of lambda calculus used to specify the analysis, but omitting recursion and algebraic data types. Section 3 outlines the subject of update avoidance analysis. Section 4 describes a first attempt at solving the problem using abstract interpretation. Section 5 shows how this initial analysis can be refined to give better results, and also shows how the new formulation allows a language involving recursion and algebraic data types to be analysed. Section 6 gives some concrete results generated from the prototype implementation of update avoidance analysis in the Glasgow Haskell Compiler.

2   The Language

In order to present the update avoidance analysis, a representation of the program is required that includes an explicit closure-building operation (a closure is the internal representation of an expression at run-time, and it is the object that may later be replaced by a value when the expression has been evaluated). The language chosen (Figure 1) is a stylised form of lambda calculus in which closure-building is represented by a **let** construct, and application is restricted such that the right hand side may only be a variable or literal. The reader may recognise this as being similar to the language used by Launchbury to describe the semantics of lazy evaluation [Lau93] in turn is similar to the intermediate language used in the Spineless Tagless G-Machine [Pey92].

With this representation, there is only *one* way in which a closure can be created, and this provides a way to tag every closure as to whether an update is necessary or not. There are three different tags that can be assigned to a closure: 0, 1, and ∞. The tag represents an upper bound on the number of times a closure will be *entered* at run-time (a closure is entered when its value is required). All tags greater than 2 are mapped to infinity. The tag has the following meaning when generating code: if the tag for a closure is 0 or 1, then an update would be redundant in this case since the closure will only be entered at most once. Closures with a tag of 0 are special in that the closure need never be created at all! Closures with a tag of ∞ must be made updatable.

3   The Problem

The way in which we decide if a closure should be made updatable or not is closely intertwined with the lazy reduction semantics of the language itself. Some examples will help to demonstrate why the problem is not as straightforward as it may appear.

Consider the following expression, in which we are interested in the updatability of u:

> **let** $u = \dots$ **in**
>   **let** $v = u + 3$ **in**
> $v + v$

Evaluation of this program fragment proceeds as follows

1. Closures are built for both u and v.
2. The + primitive is called with two arguments, both v.
3. + demands the value of its first argument, v.
4. + is called again, with arguments u and 3.
5. The value of u is demanded. Assume it returns the value 2.
6. u is updated with its value.
7. v is updated with its value, 5.
8. v is demanded again, but this time it has been updated with the value 5, so this is returned immediately.
9. The expression as a whole returns the value 10.

As can be seen from this breakdown of the execution, the value of the closure u is only required once, and the update operation on it could safely be omitted. This happens even though the value of v, which is required twice, depends on u.

The next example demonstrates that non-transitivity (a rule that could conceivably be concluded from the first example) can not be relied on:

> **let** $u = \dots$ **in**
>   **let** $f = \lambda x. u + x$ **in**
>   **let** $v = f\ 3$ **in**
>   **let** $w = f\ 4$ **in**
> $v + w$

The evaluation proceeds as follows:

1. Closures are built for u, f, v, and w.

2. The value of v is demanded,

3. The value of f is demanded (f is already in head normal form, so no evaluation is performed).

4. f is applied to the number 3.

5. The value of u is demanded (assume it returns 2, and is updated).

6. The application of f to 3 returns 5.

7. v is updated with 5.

8. The value of w is required.

9. The value of f is demanded.

10. f is applied to 4.

11. The value of u is demanded. It has been updated with 2, so this is returned immediately.

12. The application of f to 4 returns 6.

13. The expression as a whole returns the value 11.

In this case, the value of the closure u is required twice, once each time the function f is applied. So this time, the update operation on u is not redundant.

The analyser must also be able to cope with functions that use their arguments several times, for instance:

```
let u = ... in
  let f = λx. x + x in
    f u
```

The closure u must again be made updatable, because it is passed to the function f which enters its single argument twice before returning a result.

The functional programs we will be analysing will include polymorphic, higher order functions. The simplest of these is the function *apply* (the \$ function in Haskell):

```
let u = ... in
  let apply = λf. λx. f x in
    let id = λx. x in
      apply id u
```

The closure for u could safely be made non-updatable in this example. Our analyser presented in the next section will be able to derive the correct results for all of the above examples without loss of accuracy.

4   A First Attempt

The aim of the abstract interpretation described here is to discover updatability information by interpreting the program over an abstract domain of values.

4.1   Abstract Values

Abstract interpretation assigns values to program objects based on an abstract semantics, just as running the program assigns values to program objects based on an operational semantics. The aim of abstract interpretation, however, is to discover additional information about the program that will be useful in optimising it. For instance, in strictness analysis information is sought about the termination of the program. The abstract values are thus binary values representing termination/possible non-termination. In update avoidance analysis, the emphasis is on how many times a particular closure instance will be entered at run-time, and this is reflected in the representation of abstract values we have chosen.

There are in fact two useful pieces of information associated with each expression in the program that we require for update avoidance analysis. The first is the behaviour of the expression when it is evaluated, in terms of which closures (represented by its free variables) will be entered, and how many times. It is not necessary to determine exactly how many times a closure will be entered, only whether it is entered more than once or not.

The second piece of information required relates to the fact that we are working in a higher order language, and arbitrary program objects may have function type. Thus, we need to know how an expression behaves when it is applied to a closure (remember: the argument of an application may only be a literal or a single variable representing a closure). In our abstract values, this information will be represented as a function from abstract values to abstract values.

So, here is the type of our abstract values:

$$
\begin{array}{lll}
\text{type} & AbVal = & (Var, AbFun) \\
\text{data} & AbFun = & Fun\ (AbVal \to AbVal) \\
& \mid & K
\end{array}
$$

$$
\begin{array}{lll}
\mathcal{U}\,[\![x]\!]\,\rho & = & \rho\,x \\
\mathcal{U}\,[\![\lambda x.\,e]\!]\,\rho & = & (\{\,\}, Fun\ \lambda x'.\mathcal{U}\,[\![e]\!]\,(\rho + [x \to x'])) \\
\mathcal{U}\,[\![e\ x]\!]\,\rho & = & (b +\!\!+ b', f') \\
& & \text{where}\ (b, Fun\ f) = \mathcal{U}\,[\![e]\!]\,\rho \\
& & \qquad\quad (b', f') = f\,(\rho\,x) \\
\mathcal{U}\,[\![\textbf{let }x = e\textbf{ in }e']\!]\,\rho & = & (b +\!\!+ b', f') \\
& & \text{where}\ (b, f) = \mathcal{U}\,[\![e]\!]\,\rho \\
& & \qquad\quad (b', f') = \mathcal{U}\,[\![e']\!]\,(\rho + [x \to (\{x\}, f)])
\end{array}
$$

Figure 2: Abstract Interpretation

---

all literals		:	$(\{\}, K)$
	$(+)$	:	$(\{\}, Fun\ (\lambda(x, K).$
			$\qquad(\{\}, Fun\ (\lambda(y, K).\,(x \mathbin{+\!\!+} y, K)))))$
dont_know		:	$(\{\}, h)$
			where h = Fun $(\lambda(x, xf).\,(\{x, x\}, h))$
id	$\lambda x.\,x$	:	$(\{\}, Fun\ (\lambda x.\,x))$
double	$\lambda x.\,x + x$	:	$(\{\}, Fun\ (\lambda(x, K).\,(x \mathbin{+\!\!+} x, K)))$
apply	$\lambda f.\,\lambda x.\,f\ x$	:	$(\{\}, Fun\ (\lambda(b, Fun\ f).$
			$\qquad(\{\}, Fun\ (\lambda x.$
			$\qquad\qquad$ let $(b', f') =$ f x in
			$\qquad\qquad(b \mathbin{+\!\!+} b', f')))))$

Figure 3: Examples of abstract values

where braces are used to denote a *bag* of values, in which a particular value can occur any number of times. The type *Var* is the type of variables in the source program. Variables are assumed to be named uniquely, and support comparison operations (on their names).

The above definition of abstract values results in an infinite abstract domain. An unfortunate consequence of this is that finding the fixed point of a recursive function over this abstract domain is impossible. This problem is discussed in Section 5.2.

The relationship between a concrete value[2] and an abstract value (essentially defined by the abstract interpretation presented later), can be given informally as follows: if a concrete value e maps to an abstract value (b, a) then, for each closure that would be entered when e is reduced to head normal form, there is at least one reference in b to that closure. For instance, if a variable v is bound to a closure that will be entered once during evaluation of the expression e, then the bag b will contain at least one reference to v.

The second part of the abstract value, the *AbFun*, describes how a function behaves when applied to another value. Essentially, a concrete function $\lambda x.\,e$ will map to an abstract value $(b, Fun\ (\lambda x.\,a))$ and an object of base type will map to abstract values whose second component is K. The reason for representing base types explicitly will become clear when the results of the abstract interpretation are used.

4.2   Examples of Abstract Values

An abstract value for an arbitrary expression will be calculated by the abstract interpreter presented in the next section. There are, however, a few basic abstract values needed by the system. These are shown in Figure 3. Firstly, all literals are assigned the value $(\{\}, K)$. The + oeprator, and indeed most other primitive integer operators, is assigned a rather large looking structure as given in the figure. This value embodies the behaviour of + as follows: it is a function of two arguments, and will not evaluate either argument until it

---

[2]the term "concrete value" in this context includes all terms in the language defined in Figure 1.

is fully applied. At that point, both arguments are evalutated, once, and the result is of base type. The third example is a value we have called *dont_know*; this serves as a safe approximation to any value (the reason for this will become clear when the analysis is presented in the next section). The value *dont_know* can be used for any function or object that is not known to the analyser, for instance external functions.

Three examples of the abstract values for real functions are also given, to show how the analyser maps real functions to abstract values. The most interesting case here is the value for the function *apply*, which illustrates how the analyser deals with higher order functions without loss of accuracy. Obviously, the number of times the argument x to *apply* is evaluated in any given call will depend directly on the value of its first argument, f. This behaviour is encoded in the value derived.

4.3 Abstract Interpretation

The abstract interpretation function, $\mathcal{U}$, is given in Figure 2. The interpretation uses an environment, ρ, which maps variable names to abstract values. Thus, the interpretation of a variable is simply its mapping in the environment. The interpretation of a lambda expression is an abstract object in which the first component is an empty bag; this is consistent with the semantics of evaluating such an expression to head normal form—no further evaluation takes place. The second component is a straightforward mapping from a concrete function to an abstract function.

Interpretation of an application proceeds in two stages: firstly, the left hand side is interpreted to yield an abstract value in which the second component must be a function (in a type correct expression). This function is applied to the abstract value of the right hand side, and the abstract value of the whole expression is constructed by concatenating together the two bags, and using the abstract function value returned by the application as the second component.

The interpretation of a *let*-expression is where the lazy semantics come into play. Any closures that are entered as a result of entering the closure declared with a *let* can only ever be entered *once*; this is because after the first evaluation the closure will be updated with its value. So, the interpretation of a *let*-expression is performed by interpreting its two subexpressions. Interpretation of the body of the *let* proceeds in an environment extended with a mapping from the *let*-bound variable to an abstract value consisting of a singleton bag of the variable itself, and the abstract function value returned by interpreting the closure expression.

4.4 Tagging let expressions

Performing the abstract interpretation is only stage one of the analysis; to complete the optimisation we must tag each closure in the program, saying whether it will be updatable or not. For now, we will assign tags on the following basis: given an expression let $x = e$ in e' we interpret it using the abstract interpretation function $\mathcal{U}$ given in Figure 2. Examining the abstract function value f' returned by the interpretation of e', we can tell if the expression is of base type or not. If it is, then we can be sure that no references to the closure x remain, and it is simply a matter of counting the occurrences of x in the bag

$$\mathcal{U} \llbracket x \rrbracket \rho \quad = \quad \rho\, x$$

$$\mathcal{U} \llbracket \lambda x.\, e \rrbracket \rho \quad = \quad (\{\,\},\, b + \!\!+ \, r,\, Fun\; \lambda x'.\mathcal{U} \llbracket e \rrbracket\, (\rho + [x \to x']))$$
$$\text{where} \quad (b, r, f) \;=\; \mathcal{U} \llbracket e \rrbracket\, \rho$$

$$\mathcal{U} \llbracket e\; x \rrbracket \rho \quad = \quad (b + \!\!+ \, b',\, r',\, f')$$
$$\text{where} \quad (b, r, Fun\, f) \;=\; \mathcal{U} \llbracket e \rrbracket\, \rho$$
$$\qquad\qquad (b', r', f') \;=\; f(\rho\, x)$$

$$\mathcal{U} \llbracket \mathbf{let}\; x = e\; \mathbf{in}\; e' \rrbracket \rho \;=\; (b + \!\!+ \, b',\, r',\, f')$$
$$\text{where} \quad (b, r, f) \;=\; \mathcal{U} \llbracket e \rrbracket\, \rho$$
$$\qquad\qquad (b', r', f') \;=\; \mathcal{U} \llbracket e' \rrbracket\, (\rho + [x \to (\{x\}, r, f)])$$

Figure 4: Extended Interpretation Function

b' to assign a tag to this closure. If x occurs more than once in b', then the closure must be made updatable, otherwise we can safely omit the update on this closure at run-time.

If the expression is of function type, then assigning the tag is more difficult. We cannot decide by examining this expression alone how many times the closure will be entered. For example, consider the following term:

$$\mathbf{let}\; f = (\mathbf{let}\; y = 2 + 2\; \mathbf{in}\; \lambda z.\, z + y)\; \mathbf{in}\; f\, 1 + f\, 2$$

the closure y will be entered twice, but this cannot be determined by examination of the expression $\mathbf{let}\; y = 2 + 2\; \mathbf{in}\; \lambda z.\, z + y$ alone. It is advantageous to be able to assign the tag at the same time as performing the abstract interpretation, since this makes for a more efficient, one-pass algorithm. So in this case, the analysis would have to make a safe approximation and assume that the closure may be entered many times. The next section will show how the analysis can be extended, still allowing for a one-pass algorithm but giving better results for expressions such as this.

5 Refining the Analysis

In practice, expressions where the body of a *let* expression is of function type are fairly common, so a more accurate method for dealing with these is required. Furthermore, in order to use the analysis on real programs with user-defined algebraic data types and recursion we need to extend the analysis to cope with these new constructs. Rather than extend our notion of abstract values to cope with arbitrary data types, we chose to modify it slightly such that all of the above extensions can be accomodated within the same framework.

The idea is this: rather than keep track of whether a particular abstract value represents a concrete value with base or function type, we will record a list of all the closures possibly referenced from the object. Thus, an object of base type will have no references, but one of function type or algebraic type may have many references within it. By examining the list of references associated with an abstract value, we can determine whether a particular closure can be

$$\mathcal{U}\,[\![C\ x_1\dots x_n]\!]\,\rho \;=\; (\{\,\},r,\mathit{dontknow}\ r)$$

$$\text{where}\quad (b_1,r_1,f_1) \;=\; \rho\ x_1$$

$$\vdots$$

$$(b_n,r_n,f_n) \;=\; \rho\ x_n$$

$$r \;=\; b_1 +\!\!+ r_1 +\!\!+ \dots +\!\!+ b_n +\!\!+ r_n$$

$$\mathcal{U}\,[\![\mathbf{case}\ e'\ \mathbf{of}\ \{p_1 \to e_1\,;\dots;\,p_n \to e_n\}]\!]\,\rho$$
$$=\; (b',r',\mathit{dontknow}\ r')$$

$$\text{where}\quad (b,r,f) \;=\; \mathcal{U}\,[\![e']\!]\,\rho$$

$$(b_1,r_1,f_1) \;=\; \mathcal{U}\,[\![e_1]\!]\,\rho$$

$$\vdots$$

$$(b_n,r_n,f_n) \;=\; \mathcal{U}\,[\![e_n]\!]\,\rho$$

$$b' \;=\; b +\!\!+ \mathit{merge}\ c_1\dots c_n$$

$$r' \;=\; r +\!\!+ r_1 +\!\!+ \dots +\!\!+ r_n$$

Figure 5: Algebraic Data Types

entered as a result of applying the function (if it is a function) or deconstructing the object (if it is a constructor application).

The type of abstract values is now a 3-tuple:

$$AbVal ::= (\{Var\}, \{Var\}, Fun\ (AbVal \to AbVal))$$

We now have two bags in the abstract value; the first is as before, the second is a list of possible closure references from this object. The *AbFun* part has been incorporated into *AbVal* since it is always a *Fun*. For reasons mentioned above, we no longer need to keep track of whether an object is of base type or not. It may seem unnecessary to have to construct function values for every object in the program, even the non-functions, but this value can safely be $\bot$ when its value will never be required (i.e. it isn't a function). Note also that the bag of closure references in each value could be represented as a set, since the number of times a value occurs is immaterial. To avoid complicated notation, however, we have used a bag.

The revised form of the abstract interpretation is given in Figure 4. It is a straightforward extension to the original, the only difference being that we now keep track of the references buried within each object. Tagging let expressions is now performed on the basis of the reference list; if the closure name occurs in the list of references returned from the body, then it must be made updatable. Otherwise we can count the occurrences of the variable in the first bag as before.

5.1 Algebraic Data Types

The extension to the analysis dealing with references provides a way to analyse expressions using arbitrary algebraic data types. Rather than attempt to keep track of the exact value of an object built with a data constructor, we can simply keep a record of which closures are referenced from within the structure. Obviously this provides no way to deconstruct the object again and obtain

$$\mathcal{U}\,[\![\mathbf{letrec}\ \{z_1 = e_1\ ;\dots;\ z_n = e_n\}\ \mathbf{in}\ e'\,]\!]\,\rho$$
$$= \quad (c \mathrel{+\!\!+} c_1 \mathrel{+\!\!+} \dots \mathrel{+\!\!+} c_n, r', f)$$

$$\text{where}\quad
\begin{aligned}
\rho' &= \rho + [z_i \rightarrow (\{x_i\}, r'', dontknow\ r'')] \\
(b, r', f) &= \mathcal{U}\,[\![e']\!]\,\rho'' \\
\rho'' &= \rho + [z_i \rightarrow (\{x_i\}, r_i, f_i)] \\
(b_1, r_1, f_1) &= \mathcal{U}\,[\![e_1]\!]\rho' \\
&\ \ \vdots \\
(b_n, r_n, f_n) &= \mathcal{U}\,[\![e_n]\!]\rho' \\
r'' &= freevars\ e_1 \dots e_n
\end{aligned}$$

Figure 6: Recursion

accurate values for the usage of the closures referenced from a structure, but experimentation has showed that a large and complicated extension to the analysis to gain this information would be unproductive. It would only be of use where the actual data constructor used to construct the object is known, and since the vast majority of structures are built by recursive functions and are types with more than one constructor, such an extension would gain little.

Shown in Figure 5 is the small extension to the analysis that we have used to successfully analyse expressions involving algebraic data types. It uses the revised version of the *dont_know* function, defined as follows:

$$
\begin{aligned}
dont\_know\ r &= (\{\}, r, dont\_know'\ r) \\
dont\_know'\ r &= Fun(\lambda(b, r', f).\,\{\}, b \mathrel{+\!\!+} r' \mathrel{+\!\!+} r, dont\_know'(b \mathrel{+\!\!+} r' \mathrel{+\!\!+} r))
\end{aligned}
$$

The definition of *dont_know* is a 'black hole': it is a function that takes an infinite amount of arguments but keeps a track of all references passed to it. It never evaluates anything.

The rule for *case* also makes use of a function called *merge*. This function is similar to $\mathrel{+\!\!+}$. Its operation is defined as follows: in an application of *merge* to n bags $b_1, \dots, b_n$ if a variable v occurs a number of times in each bag $m_1, \dots, m_n$, then it occurs $max\ m_1\ \dots\ m_n$ times in the result.

5.2 Recursion

Another aspect to consider in building an analysis that is to be used on real programs is recursion. The usual way of dealing with recursion in the context of abstract interpretation is to repeatedly apply the interpreter until a fixed-point is reached; that is, the abstract value that represents the recursive function is identical to the previous iteration. The difficulty here is that to find the fixed-point one must be able to compare abstract values for equality, which is inherently difficult given that the size of the abstract domain is unbounded. Also, the natural implementation of the algorithm uses real functions to represent the abstract values, which are of course impossible to compare.

There are two approaches to finding the fixed-point of a function. The first is to start from the bottom of the domain, in effect an abstract function that provides the *most* information, and iterate towards the least fixed-point.

Program	Actual	Required	Omitted	%
compress	56622	18533	5233	12.08%
fluid	320314	71515	73152	22.72%
gamteb	3206077	1340111	800247	30.01%
gg	318479	58310	138290	34.71%
lift	19606	4190	1233	7.41%
maillist	155789	49538	67632	38.90%
parser	1027030	102227	119854	11.47%
pic	353078	105120	33605	11.94%
prolog	33291	6980	10301	28.14%
reptile	415879	32310	28863	7.00%
primetest	997665	566285	1138850	72.53%
hsc	5639770		7608022	60%

Figure 7: Results

This approach produces the best results. The second approach is to find a safe approximation and iterate towards the greatest fixed-point. All solutions generated using this method are guaranteed also to be safe approximations to the least fixed point, although they may contain more information than the first estimate.

The approach we use is the second method, with a fixed number of iterations. In addition, we conjecture that a single iteration yields the greatest information to effort ratio, for most functions found in real programs.

The rule used to analyse (mutually) recursive functions is given in Figure 6. There are two stages to the analysis of a set of mutually recursive functions. Firstly, the initial environment p' is constructed in which each variable is mapped to an approximate abstract value. This environment is used in analysing the definition of each function, yielding a more accurate abstract value for each of the variables involved. The results are used in constructing a new environment in which to analyse the expression e'.

6 Implementation and Results

Figure 7 shows some results from the prototype implementation of update avoidance analysis in the Glasgow Haskell Compiler. Instead of giving results as execution times, we have elected to use the more accurate method of showing the actual number of updates performed by a program after being compiled with the update avoidance analyser. These figures are constant from run to run, and are not subject to the wild fluctuations often seen when run-times are measured.

To collect these results, we used the "ticky-ticky" profiling feature of the Glasgow Haskell Compiler. Ticky-ticky profiling is a built-in profiling feature that collects statistics on a wide variety of aspects of the execution model during the running of the program. The output generated by a profiling run includes three figures that we are interested in (these correspond to the columns in the table): the number of updates performed, the number of updated closures that were subsequently demanded (a subset of the total updates), and the number of 'single entry' closures that were entered (those that had been detected as non-updatable by the analyser). The second figure here corresponds to the number of updates that were *necessary*.

Using these statistics, a figure can be calculated for the overall efficiency of the analyser as a percentage of the unnecessary updates that were avoided. This figure is calculated using the following formula, using the identifiers *total*, *required*, and *omitted* to refer to the three values obtained from profiling:

$$\frac{omitted}{total - required + omitted} \times 100\%$$

6.1 Discussion

The test programs are all large Haskell programs, and are taken from the "real" subset of the nofib benchmark suite [Par92]. The word real in this sense means that the programs were written to perform some useful task, rather than to be used solely as benchmarks. The last benchmark on the table is not from the nofib suite; it is in fact the Glasgow Haskell Compiler itself (reputedly the largest Haskell program in existence!), compiling one of its own modules. The results for this test are unfortunately incomplete, and the efficiency figure given is a low estimate.

As can be seen from the figures, the effect of update avoidance analysis is heavily dependant on the actual program, as results vary from about 7%–72%. The style of code in the program affects the ability of the analyser to detect unnecessary updates: for instance, the Glasgow Haskell Compiler makes heavy use of monads, and we believe this is partially responsible for the good result here.

The increase in efficiency of the analysed programs was generally proportional to the ratio of avoided updates to total updates. By informal experimentation we have determined that if all the unnecessary updates are removed then the on average the program displays a 20–25% improvement in speed (and also a small improvement in space behaviour). The prototype update analyser removed an average of 25% of the unnecessary updates, giving a speedup of about 5%. The actual results vary wildly from program to program for several reasons: the number of updates performed bares little relation to the amount of computation done by the program, and the number of updates that are required (those that cannot be removed by the update analyser) also varies considerably.

6.2 Effect of other optimisations

Another interesting phenomenon that we noticed while measuring results was the effect that some of the other optimisations in the Glasgow Haskell Compiler had on the effectiveness of our analysis. The two most notable ones are strictness analysis [PJ93] and let-floating [San93]. Strictness analysis is primarily concerned with the removal of closures altogether (obviously a better option than just saving the update), and as a large proportion of the closures detected as non-updatable are also strict this affected the results. For instance, the analysis performed particularly well on the `compress` program with the strictness analyser turned off: an efficiency of 75% was recorded, together with a significant reduction in space usage. This is because the program makes heavy use of a particular data type with a single constructor, that is too large to support update in place. The strictness analyser in Glasgow Haskell does a particularly good job on data types with a single constructor when they are used strictly, and it just so happens that this is the major operation performed by the `compress` program. In general, we noticed that better results were generated by update avoidance analysis with the strictness analyser turned off, but in the interests of showing more realistic results, we turned it on to take our measurements.

The optimisation of let-floating attempts to increase sharing by floating expressions towards the top-level of the program. In some cases this can remove computation from inside a loop and dramatically increase the efficiency of the program. It also tends to make closures that would previously have been non-updatable into updatable ones (since they are now shared). This can increase the number of updates performed, but it also increases the number of updates *required*, and therefore does not affect the percentage figures given in the table above.

It is worth noting here that, although we have no formal treatment for the analysis presented here, the implementation has provided confidence in its correctness. The Glasgow Haskell Compiler is able to detect when a single-entry closure is re-entered, which would happen if the update analyser made a mistake. This feature is a side effect of a technique called *black-holing*, and was extremely useful while debugging the update analyser. Also note that while we can detect when the update analyser errs on the aggressive side, it is much harder to identify the opposite, that is when it is too cautious. One way to do this is to examine the intermediate code from the compiler, and attempt to identify closures that should be non-updatable. Another solution would be to examine ticky profiles from real runs and identify which closures actually were entered once or not at all.

6.3   Separate compilation

The update avoidance analyser attempts to overcome the problem of separate compilation by placing update information in Haskell interface files as *pragmas* (annotations placed in comments which have a special meaning to the compiler). The information takes the form of a list of digits for each function, and is an approximation to the actual abstract value of the function derived by the analyser. Each digit represents a single argument position and gives the number of times the function will evaluate that argument. The digits are generated by examining the abstract value of each exported function during compilation, and abstract values for imported functions are generated automatically by the analyser. This technique improved the number of non-updatable closures detected for not only multi-module programs, but all programs that made use of the standard prelude.

184

7 Conclusion

We have developed an analysis technique that can detect non-updatable expressions in a lazy, higher-order, polymorphic language with algebraic data types. The technique has been implemented in the Glasgow Haskell Compiler and shown to give good results for real test programs.

References

[Lau93]   J. Launchbury. A natural semantics for lazy evaluation. In *Symposium on Principles of Programming Languages*. Springer-Verlag, 1993.

[LGH+92] J. Launchbury, A. Gill, J. Hughes, S. Marlow, S. Peyton Jones, and P. Wadler. Avoiding unnecessary updates. In Launchbury and Sansom [Par92].

[Par92]   Will Partain. The nofib benchmark suite of Haskell programs. In J. Launchbury and P. M. Sansom, editors, *Functional Proramming, Glasgow 1992*, Ayr, Scotland, 1992. Springer Verlag, Workshops in Computing.

[Pey92]   S. L. Peyton Jones. Implementing lazy functional languages on stock hardware: The Spineless Tagless G-machine. *Journal of Functional Programming*, 2(2):127–202, April 1992.

[PJ93]   Will Partain and Simon Peyton Jones. On the effectiveness of a simple strictness analyser. In *Functional Proramming, Glasgow 1993*, Ayr, Scotland, 1993.

[San93]   Andre Santos. Tuning a compiler's allocation policy. In *Functional Proramming, Glasgow 1993*, Ayr, Scotland, 1993.

[SP93]   P. Sansom and S. L. Peyton Jones. Generational garbage collection for Haskell. In *Functional Programming Languages and Computer Architecture*, pages 106–116, Copenhagen, Denmark, 1993.

Local Speculative Evaluation for Distributed Graph Reduction

James S. Mattson Jr.
Department of Computing Science
Glasgow University
Glasgow, Scotland
`mattson@dcs.glasgow.ac.uk`

William G. Griswold
Department of Computer Science and Engineering
University of California, San Diego
La Jolla, USA
`wgg@cs.ucsd.edu`

Abstract

In a parallel graph reduction system, speculative evaluation can increase parallelism by performing potentially useful computations before they are known to be necessary. Speculative computations may be coded explicitly in a program, or they may be scheduled implicitly by the reduction system as idle processors become available. A general approach to both kinds of speculation incurs a great deal of overhead that may outweigh the benefits of speculative evaluation for fine-grain speculative tasks.

The basic principle of local speculation is to permanently bind all implicit speculative computations to the sparking processor. Should all local mandatory tasks become blocked, local speculation offers a low-cost alternative to task migration. Restricting speculation to the local processor simplifies the problems of speculative task management, and opens the door for fine-grain speculative tasks.

Though there are fewer opportunities for local speculation than for more general speculation, local speculation can often make use of the same idle processor time that would normally trigger task migration. For distributed graph reduction systems, local speculation may prove to be a worthwhile, low-cost alternative to potentially expensive task migration.

1 Introduction

While a few programs achieve near-perfect speedups under a conservative reduction system, most programs are not so well-suited to parallel evaluation. Typical applications contain bottlenecks in which the parallelism is limited by data dependencies, control dependencies, or both. Data dependencies present a formidable barrier to parallelism, but control dependencies can usually be circumvented—for a price. At the risk of performing unnecessary work, a speculative reduction system tries to increase a program's parallelism by disregarding some of the constraints imposed by control dependencies and speculating on computations that may become necessary later on.

A speculative reduction system has imperfect knowledge of the future, and as this knowledge improves, it must recalculate the predicted usefulness of speculative tasks. Speculative task management is therefore complicated by the following scheduling issues [1]:

- Speculative tasks compete with mandatory tasks for processors. Ensuring that unnecessary tasks do not delay the execution of a mandatory computation requires a preemptive scheduling strategy that gives preference to mandatory tasks.

- A speculative task may be recognized as necessary, in which case it must be upgraded to mandatory.

- A speculative task may be recognized as unnecessary, in which case it must be terminated prematurely.

- Speculative tasks and mandatory tasks may share subgraphs. If a speculative task begins to evaluate a shared expression, the system must guarantee that another task can still evaluate the expression, even if the speculative task is terminated early.

Restricting speculative tasks to execution on the sparking processor will reduce the overhead required for making the above scheduling decisions, but it will also reduce the potential for increased parallelism. A local speculative task can only be executed when all local mandatory tasks are blocked and no other mandatory tasks are available from elsewhere in the system. However, in a distributed graph reduction system, the availability of remote mandatory tasks may be restricted by communications overhead. Once a task begins execution on a remote processor, its associated state may become so large that migration to another processor becomes prohibitively expensive. In this case, there will be more opportunities for local speculation. Because of its low overhead, local speculation may prove to be a more worthwhile use of idle processor time than the migration of large mandatory tasks.

We focus our attention on speculative evaluation for distributed graph reduction on GRIP [5]; however, we expect that the mechanisms described here are also appropriate for other distributed memory architectures. The details of the implementation are derived from a prototype developed for unrestricted speculative graph reduction on a shared memory machine [2].

2 Terminology

The program graph is represented by *closures* in the heap. A closure consists of a code pointer and a (possibly empty) set of arguments. A *spark* is a request for the concurrent reduction of a subgraph rooted at a particular closure. A spark is either *mandatory* or *speculative*, depending on whether or not its parent requires the value of the sparked closure. When a processor accepts a spark, it creates a new *thread* to evaluate the sparked subgraph. We adopt the STG-machine model of graph reduction, so each thread corresponds to a virtual STG-machine, with all of the state normally associated with a sequential STG-machine [4]. A thread is either *necessary* or *unnecessary*, depending on whether or not it

Program	5 PEs			10 PEs			15 PEs		
	Redn	Free	Idle	Redn	Free	Idle	Redn	Free	Idle
Boyer	12.2	21.8	34.6	6.47	9.28	67.2	4.34	6.19	78.2
Modeler	49.7	5.38	7.22	37.5	16.5	17.1	28.8	26.4	23.0
RSA	63.5	0.00	25.0	63.5	0.00	25.0	63.5	0.00	25.0
Ray	32.6	3.41	5.46	30.2	5.46	6.66	27.9	10.0	8.01
Soda	67.2	.826	11.8	56.4	.708	18.7	40.3	1.45	33.4
Taut	87.7	.860	.298	89.0	.974	1.16	89.1	1.44	1.66

Table 1: GRIP Activity Profiles

will be required to complete the execution of the program. In many cases, the necessity of a thread cannot be determined until its results are required by another thread that is known to be necessary. A thread that is known to be necessary is a *mandatory* thread, and a thread that is known to be unnecessary is an *irrelevant* thread. A thread whose necessity cannot be determined is a *speculative* thread.

3   Opportunities for Local Speculation

Before embarking on an implementation of local speculative evaluation, it is reasonable to ask whether or not there are ample opportunities to take advantage of such a mechanism. To answer this question, we have instrumented several benchmarks using the current (conservative) GRIP system to obtain activity profiles that indicate the amount of time spent performing various activities associated with graph reduction. Table 1 shows the resulting activity profiles for each benchmark on three different GRIP configurations. The activity profiles indicate the percentage of the overall runtime during which a processor was (a) actually performing graph reduction ("Redn"), (b) idle with blocked local threads ("Free"), and (c) idle with no local threads ("Idle"). Time spent in communication and garbage collection is not reported.

Speculative evaluation can occur whenever conservative evaluation would leave the processor idle. However, for local speculative evaluation, the parent of a potentially useful speculative task must be a blocked task on the local processor. Consequently, for local speculative evaluation, the most interesting figure is the "free" time (idle with locally blocked threads). At best, local speculative evaluation can turn some fraction of this time into useful reduction time.

The raw figures do not appear to be particularly promising. Although the time spent idle with locally blocked threads ranges from 0.00% to 26.5%, most of the numbers are at the low end of this range. However, in a few cases, the time spent idle with locally blocked threads comes close to or even exceeds the time spent performing conservative graph reduction. While the opportunities for local speculative evaluation vary considerably among different programs, these timings indicate that some programs do provide ample opportunities for taking advantage of local speculative evaluation.

4 Speculative Annotations

Eventually, the compiler is expected to identify potentially useful speculative computations, but initially we will provide programmer annotations to do the work. In the prototype system, we introduced new sparks with annotations of the form:

```
{-# PCT nn #-}
```

where nn was meant to represent the likelihood that the annotated expression would become necessary, expressed as a percentage. At runtime, this percentage was multiplied by the current likelihood of the parent to determine the base priority of the new speculative spark. To avoid cluttering the system with low probability sparks, speculative sparks that were less than 10% likely to become necessary were discarded. (This cutoff point was selected arbitrarily.) However, our experience was that the annotations were not particularly useful for assigning meaningful potentials. Instead, we found that they were most useful in controlling the *depth* of speculation to avoid contention for memory and other resources.

For local speculative evaluation, we intend to focus on fine-grain speculative threads that do not spark any children of their own (speculative or otherwise). Since the maximum depth of speculation is therefore fixed at one, it suffices to indicate potentially useful expressions with a simpler annotation, such as:

```
{-# LIKELY #-}
```

For every expression that is thus annotated as "likely to become necessary," a closure is built early and a pointer to the closure is deposited in a speculative spark pool. All sparks in the local speculative spark pool will therefore be the immediate children of mandatory threads. We leave the problems of deeper speculation for a future implementation of coarse-grain speculation.

5 Black and Grey Holes

When a mandatory thread enters an unevaluated shared closure, the standard entry code locks the closure by overwriting it with a *black hole*. If a mandatory thread tries to enter one of its own black holes, the program contains a cyclic data dependency and is therefore non-terminating. However, if a thread tries to enter another thread's black hole, it blocks until the other thread updates the black hole with the shared result.[1]

On GRIP, a black hole closure initially consists of a code pointer and a global address. Later, if another thread blocks on it, the black hole becomes a *black hole with blocking queue*, and it acquires a pointer to a list of blocked threads as well.

When a speculative thread enters an unevaluated shared closure, the locking mechanism must preserve the original closure, because speculative threads can be terminated prematurely, and any partially evaluated shared closures must

---

[1] Deadlock is possible if a cycle arises among the threads waiting on each other's black holes, but only if the program contains a cyclic data dependency. Deadlock cannot arise as an artifact of the scheduling policy.

be restored to their original form so that they can be re-entered by another thread later on. Unfortunately, once a closure has been overwritten with a black hole, the original code pointer is lost. When another task blocks on a black hole, another word of the original closure is lost. Therefore, speculative threads cannot use the standard black hole locking mechanism. Instead, they lock an unevaluated shared closure by overwriting it with a revertible black hole, or a *grey hole*.

A grey hole consists of a code pointer, a pointer to an auxiliary structure in the heap, and the remainder of the original closure. The auxiliary structure contains the original closure's code pointer and first word, a pointer to a list of blocked threads (initially empty), a pointer to the speculative thread's control block, and a record of the stack depth at which the speculative thread entered the original closure.

The last two items are used for updating the priority of the speculative thread if a higher priority thread blocks on the grey hole. Whenever a mandatory thread blocks on a grey hole, the speculative thread responsible for the hole is upgraded to mandatory. If the shared closure is also the root closure for the speculative thread, the thread stays upgraded for the rest of its life. However, if the shared closure is buried down inside the speculative computation, the speculative thread is only upgraded temporarily. Once it updates the shared closure, it reverts back to speculative. If several mandatory threads block on different grey holes that are under evaluation by same speculative thread, the speculative thread remains upgraded until the last of the shared closures is updated.

Note that the last of the shared closures to be updated happens to be the one that the speculative thread entered first (i.e. the one whose update frame is lowest on the thread's stack.) A "reversion depth" (initialized to a high value) is stored in the thread control block for each speculative thread. When a mandatory thread blocks on a grey hole, it updates the reversion depth of the associated speculative thread with the minimum of the grey hole's entry depth and the speculative thread's current reversion depth. Each time that the upgraded thread updates a grey hole closure, it checks its stack depth, and when it reaches the depth of the lowest shared closure, it reverts back to speculative.

6 Deferred Updates

Normally, when a shared closure is evaluated to WHNF, the result is written back into the program graph, overwriting the graph for the original expression. However, for speculative graph reduction, the standard update mechanism can lead to unbounded growth of the program graph. For example, consider any program graph that contains an infinite data structure. If the program terminates under conservative reduction, it will only require a finite portion of the data structure and a bounded amount of memory to store the required elements. In the course of speculative evaluation, however, speculative threads can exhaust the available memory with unnecessary elements of the data structure. With the standard update mechanism, the unnecessary elements will be written into the program graph like any other evaluated results. Once the unnecessary results are written into the program graph, it is impossible for the garbage collector to reclaim the space allocated to them until they are no longer reachable.

One solution to this problem is to modify the speculative update mechanism to provide hooks for *update reversion*: the ability to revert speculatively evaluated parts of the program graph to their unevaluated form if they are not yet necessary and if they occupy less space as unevaluated expressions [3]. We provide support for update reversion through a deferred update mechanism. When a speculative thread updates a closure in the program graph, it doesn't immediately overwrite the closure's grey hole with the evaluated result. Instead, it overwrites the grey hole with a "deferred update" closure.

The deferred update closure maintains the auxiliary structure from the grey hole so that it can recreate the original closure if need be, but instead of a pointer to a list of blocked threads, the deferred update closure keeps a pointer to the evaluated result. If another speculative thread enters a deferred update, it uses the pointer to the evaluated result and leaves the deferred update untouched. However, if a mandatory thread enters a deferred update, it immediately performs the update (overwriting the deferred update with an indirection) and then follows the pointer to the evaluated result.

Keeping both the unevaluated and the evaluated graphs obviously increases the program's memory requirements. If memory becomes scarce, it suffices for the garbage collector to revert some or all of the deferred updates back to their unevaluated form. Note that this approach does not attempt to minimize heap usage, but it does preserve the behavior of the program under conservative reduction. Any program that still exhausts the available memory after reversion would have done so in the absence of speculative evaluation.

7 Scheduling Speculative Threads

On GRIP, when a processor has no local runnable mandatory threads, it submits a request for a new thread to the IMUs and waits for a response. While the processor is waiting for a new thread to arrive, resumption messages for its blocked threads may also arrive. In this case, the processor reschedules the resumable thread immediately and asynchronously processes the arrival of the new thread later. Either way, the processor currently spins in an idle loop until work arrives in the form of a message from one of the intelligent memory units (IMUs).

With a local pool of fine-grain speculative sparks, the processor can now begin to speculate instead of spinning. We need only ensure that the processor can quickly put its speculative work aside and begin any mandatory work that arrives while it's speculating. Once a processor runs out of mandatory work and begins to speculate, the IMUs are the only source of new mandatory work. (The processor may receive either a resumption message for a blocked thread or a response to its pending request for a new thread).

The current load-balancing mechanism for mandatory sparks requires that the active processors respond quickly to "system hungry" messages from the IMUs, so that they can export their own local sparks to the global spark pool before the system runs short of distributable work. To this end, each time the processors check for heap overflow, they also process all pending messages from the IMUs. Because this spark processing can lead to garbage collection, the thread is guaranteed to be in a state where it can be temporarily suspended and later rescheduled. Consequently, when the processor is engaged in speculative evaluation, this heap check message processing is perfectly situated to handle the preemption of the speculative thread. Moreover, a thread is only preempted when a message arrives from the IMUs to resume a blocked mandatory thread. Since the thread already has to process incoming IMU messages, the preemption check comes for free. In practice, heap checks occur quite often, so the speculative thread is not likely to run for very long while there are pending messages from the IMUs.

When the root closure of a speculative thread is no longer reachable from any of the mandatory threads, the speculative thread becomes irrelevant, and must be terminated. However, reachability is difficult to determine on-the-fly, so termination is deferred until the next garbage collection cycle. After garbage collection, any speculative threads whose roots were not evacuated are terminated, and any grey holes created by irrelevant threads are reverted to their original form. By deferring the termination of irrelevant threads, the processor may continue to waste time on their evaluation, but the only time wasted will be speculative time, when there is no mandatory work available anyway.

8 Conclusions

Previously, we argued that speculative threads should be at least as large as conservative threads, because they would suffer the same communication costs as equivalent conservative threads and higher costs for the overhead of speculative thread management [2]. While this is true for speculative threads that will be executed on remote processors, it does not apply to fine-grain (childless) speculative threads that are permanently bound to the local processor. Local speculation actually encourages fine-grain threads. For distributed graph reduction, local speculation offers a low-cost alternative to heavyweight task migration, and may prove to be a worthwhile investment of idle processor time whenever all local mandatory threads are blocked on remote results.

The preemption and early termination mechanisms described here are also suitable for explicit speculative evaluation. However, some additional support is necessary to disseminate coarse-grain speculative threads to idle processors and to propagate management information for these threads among the processors involved. Because of the difficulties in performing speculative evaluation in a distributed environment, distributed speculation is perhaps best provided by explicit language constructs for expressing specific kinds of speculative computations.

References

[1] Paul Hudak. Distributed task and memory management. **Second Annual ACM Symposium on Principles of Distributed Computing**, pages 277–289, Montreal, Quebec, Canada, 17–19 August 1983. Association for Computing Machinery.

[2] James S. Mattson Jr. **An Effective Speculative Evaluation Technique for Parallel Supercombinator Graph Reduction**. PhD thesis, Department of Computer Science and Engineering, University of California, San Diego, Mail Code 0114, 9500 Gilman Drive, La Jolla, CA, USA, February 1993. Technical Report CS93-282.

[3] Andrew S. Partridge. **Speculative Evaluation in Parallel Implementations of Lazy Functional Languages**. PhD thesis, Department of Computer Science, University of Tasmania, GPO Box 252C, Hobart, Tasmania, 7001, Australia, October 1991.

[4] Simon L. Peyton Jones. Implementing lazy functional languages on stock hardware: the Spineless Tagless G-machine. **Journal of Functional Programming**, 2(2):127–202, April 1992.

[5] Simon L. Peyton Jones, Chris Clack, John Salkild, and Mark Hardie. GRIP–a high-performance architecture for parallel graph reduction. **Functional Programming Languages and Computer Architecture**, pages 98–112, Portland, OR, USA, 14–16 September 1987. Springer-Verlag.

Bidirectional Fold and Scan

John T. O'Donnell

Computing Science Department, University of Glasgow
Glasgow, Scotland
jtod@dcs.glasgow.ac.uk

Abstract

Bidirectional fold generalises `foldl` and `foldr` to allow simultaneous communication in both directions across a list. Bidirectional scan calculates the list of partial results of a bidirectional fold, just as `scanl` and `scanr` calculate the partial results of a `foldl` or `foldr`. Mapping scans combine a map with a scan, and often simplify programs using scans. This family of functions is significant because it expresses important patterns of computation that arise repeatedly in circuit design and data parallel programming.

1. Introduction

The `foldl` and `foldr` functions can be used to express communication among the elements of a list. The 'fold from the left' function `foldl` corresponds to communication across a list from left to right, while the 'fold from the right' function `foldr` communicates from right to left. This method for modeling communication is quite general:

- Parallel functional programs can use fold functions to transmit messages among processors.

- Functional specifications of digital circuits use fold functions to model physical wiring patterns.

- Sometimes the choice between `foldl` and `foldr` is determined by data dependencies, efficiency or laziness. In effect, fold is communicating demand across the list.

When a program uses fold to express communication, each element of the list can be thought of as a logical processor. The processor associated with the ith element of the list receives as input a partial fold over the list elements up to but not including the ith element. The partial fold starts at the beginning of the list for `foldl`, and at the end of the list for `foldr`.

Often it is important to specify the input to each logical processor in the list. That requires defining a list of partial fold results, and is called *scanning* the list. The `scanl` function computes the partial results of a `foldl`, while `scanr` computes the partial results of a `foldr`.

A more general pattern of computation sends communications across a list in both directions, from left to right and from right to left. This paper introduces bidirectional fold and scan functions that express bidirectional communication, presents a few of their basic properties, and shows some brief examples. It also defines the family of mapping scans, which combine a scan with a map. These have been used before individually (e.g. [3]) but not gathered together systematically.

When the auxiliary functions are associative, the fold and scan functions can be implemented in parallel. However, they are also useful for expressing sequential algorithms and for cases where the auxiliary functions are not associative.

Section 2 introduces bidirectional fold and shows how it generalises `foldl` and `foldr`. Sections 3 and 4 do the same for bidirectional scan, while Section 5 defines the important family of mapping scans.

2. Bidirectional Fold

Fold functions use an auxiliary function that takes a 'message' of type a and a list element of type b, returning a new message of type a. An auxiliary function can be pictured several ways, including

The `foldl` and `foldr` functions use such an auxiliary function to reduce the elements of a list, producing a singleton.

```
foldl :: (a->b->a) -> a -> [b] -> a
foldl f a [] = a
foldl f a (x:xs) = foldl f (f a x) xs

foldr :: (a->b->b) -> b -> [a] -> b
foldr f a [] = a
foldr f a (x:xs) = f x (foldr f a xs)
```

Both functions start at one end of the list, folding the elements until they reach the other end: `foldl` folds starting from the left and `foldr` folds starting from the right:

A natural generalisation is the bidirectional `fold`, based on an auxiliary function that receives two messages and computes two output messages. The messages moving left to right have type a, while the right to left messages have type b.

Bidirectional fold uses a bidirectional auxiliary function to reduce a list of type [c], with left input a and right input b. The result is a pair of messages:

```
fold
  :: (a->b->c->(b,a))   -- auxiliary function
  -> a                  -- left input
  -> b                  -- right input
  -> [c]                -- list input
  -> (b,a)              -- (left,right) output
```

We can define `fold` in a natural accumulator style, producing a clear and efficient function definition.

```
fold f a b [] = (b,a)
fold f a b (x:xs) = (b'',a'')
  where (b'',a') = f a b' x
        (b',a'') = fold f a' b xs
```

The definition's base case is trivial, while the inductive case splits the fold into two pieces (corresponding the two **where**-clause two equations) and connects the outputs together:

The `fold` function generalises `foldl` and `foldr`. The following lemma shows how both of the unidirectional folds can be defined in terms of the bidirectional fold.

Lemma.

```
(a) foldl f z = snd . fold g z ()
        where g a b x = ((), f a x)

(b) foldr f z = fst . fold g () z
        where g a b x = (f x b, ())
```

Proof (a) by structural induction over `xs`.

Case [].

```
foldl f z []
  = (snd . fold g z ()) []
  = snd (fold g z () [])
  = snd ((),z)
  = z
```

Case x:xs.

```
foldl f z (x:xs)
  = (snd . fold g z ()) (x:xs)
      where g a b x = ((), f a x)
  = snd (fold g z () (x:xs))
  = snd (b'',a'')
      where (b'',a') = g z b' x
            (b',a'') = fold g a' () xs
```

Now (b'',a') = g z b' x = ((), f z x), so b'' = () and a' = f z x.
Continuing,

```
foldl f z (x:xs)
  = snd (b'',a'')
  = a''
  = snd (fold g a' () xs)
  = snd (fold g (f z x) () xs)
  = (snd . fold g (f z x) ()) xs
  = foldl f (f z x) xs
```

The proof of part (b) is similar.

3. Unidirectional Scan

Fold functions compute a sequence of partial results while reducing a list, but they return only the final result, throwing away the partial results. Scan functions, in contrast, return the list of partial results.

```
scanl, scanr
  :: (a->b->a)
  -> a
  -> [b]
  -> [a]
```

The scans can be specified naturally using list comprehensions:

```
scanl f a xs =
  [foldl f a (take i xs)
    | i <- [0 .. length xs -1 ]]
```

```
scanr f a xs =
  [foldr f a (drop (i+1) xs)
   | i <- [1 .. length xs]]
```

The result of a scan is the list of horizontal messages that are input to each processor:

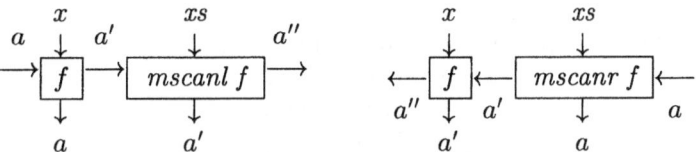

The scan functions defined above differ slightly from the usual ones that appear in textbooks [1] and Haskell [2]. The textbook definition attaches the complete fold result to the end of the list of partial results, while the definitions here do not. For some of the most important applications of scan (especially data parallel programming), length preservation is essential and the definitions here are more suitable.

The list comprehension definitions are clear but inefficient: if the auxiliary function always takes time $\Theta(1)$ then scanning a function over a list of length n takes time $\Theta(n^2)$. Fortunately, it is possible to derive efficient accumulator-style definitions from the list comprehension specifications; these require only time $\Theta(n)$.

4. Bidirectional Scan

Just as scanl and scanr compute the list of partial results obtained while folding a function over a list with foldl or foldr, the bidirectional scan computes the list of partial results obtained during an application of bidirectional fold.

```
scan
  :: (a->b->c->(b,a))   -- fold function
  -> a                  -- left input
  -> b                  -- right input
  -> [c]                -- list input
  -> [(b,a)]            -- partial results
```

Again, it's natural to define the bidirectional scan with a list comprehension, leading to a clear but inefficient specification:

```
scan f a b xs =
  [let
    (b'',a') = fold f a b' (take i xs)
    (b',a'') = fold f a' b (drop (i+1) xs)
   in
```

```
   (b',a')
   | i <- [0 .. length xs - 1]
   ]
```

A more efficient version called `ascan` uses an accumulator to propagate messages both directions at once. It returns the final `fold` result as well as the partial results.

```
ascan
  :: (a->b->c->(b,a))    -- fold function
  -> a                   -- left input
  -> b                   -- right input
  -> [c]                 -- list input
  -> (b,a,[(a,b)])       -- result

ascan f a b [] = (b,a,[])
ascan f a b (x:xs) =
  let (b'',a') = f a b' x
      (b',a'',ys) = ascan f a' b xs
  in (b'',a'', (a,b'):ys)
```

5. Mapping Scans

Many algorithms map a function over the result of a scan. A simple example is the specification of a digital circuit to perform binary addition. Let the type B represent a bit value, and let `carry` and `sum` be functions that add three bits:

```
carry, sum :: B -> (B,B) -> B
```

A full adder is a circuit that combines `carry` and `sum`:

```
fullAdd :: B -> (B,B) -> (B,B)
fullAdd c (x,y) =
  (carry c (x,y), sum c (x,y))
```

Now it is straightforward to specify a word adder:

```
adder c xs ys = (c',ss)
  where c' = foldr carry c (zip xs ys)
        cs = scanr carry c (zip xs ys)
        ss = map sum (zip3 xs ys cs)
```

However, this definition isn't very elegant, because of the excessive zipping and the separate specification of c' and cs.

A cleaner specification would combine a map with a scan. Such *mapping scans* are ubiquitous. For example, the specification of a right shifter circuit requires `mscanl`, while an ALU specification requires a bidirectional mapping scan.

There are three mapping scans, corresponding to the left, right and bidirectional scans. The unidirectional mapping scans have the same type:

```
mscanl, mscanr
   :: (a->b->(a,c))      -- fold & map
   -> a                  -- side input
   -> [b]                -- list input
   -> (a,[c])            -- result
```

Each of the mapping scans can be defined efficiently using an accumulator. The definitions of `mscanl` and `mscanr` differ only in the direction that information flows.

The 'from left' mapping scan sends information from left to right, computes intermediate fold results a' and a final fold result a'', and produces a mapped list y:ys:

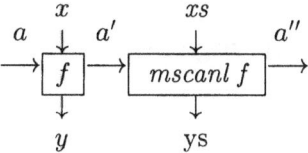

The function definition corresponds directly to the figure.

```
mscanl f a [] = (a,[])
mscanl f a (x:xs) = (a'',y:ys)
   where (a',y) = f a x
         (a'',ys) = mscanl f a' xs
```

The 'from right' mapping scan is similar, but it sends information in the opposite direction.

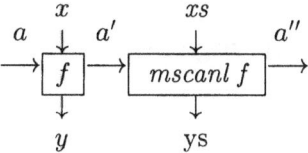

```
mscanr f a [] = (a,[])
mscanr f a (x:xs) = (a'',y:ys)
   where (a'',y) = f a' x
         (a',ys) = mscan f a xs
```

The bidirectional mapping scan requires both a left and right input, and its result includes a left and right output. By convention, the left port value always appears in a tuple before the right port value.

```
mscan
   :: (a->b->c->(b,a,d)) -- fold & map
   -> a                  -- left input
   -> b                  -- right input
   -> [c]                -- list input
   -> (b,a,[d])          -- result
```

The following figure illustrates the bidirectional flow of information.

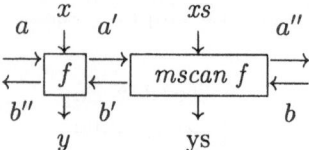

Again, the function definition corresponds directly to the figure.

```
mscan f a b [] = (b,a,[])
mscan f a b (x:xs) = (b'',a'',y:ys)
  where (b'',a',y) = f a b' x
        (b',a'',ys) = mscan f a' b xs
```

Now we can use mapping scans to improve the specification of the adder.

```
adder c xs ys =
  mscanr fulladd c (zip xs ys)
```

6. Conclusion

Bidirectional fold and scan capture important general patterns of computation, just as the unidirectional versions do. They play a central role in at least two application areas: circuit specification and data parallel algorithms.

The adder circuit given above transmits information across a word in one direction, from right to left. However, an arithmetic/logic unit also requires a comparator, which transmits from left to right, and shifters, which transmit information both directions. Thus an ALU specification requires bidirectional scan.

Data parallel architectures such as the Connection Machine use parallel scans to perform efficient parallel communications. The bidirectional scan fully exploits the parallel network's capabilities (unlike unidirectional scan), and some algorithms—such as VLSI circuit simulation—require bidirectional message passing.

References

1. R. Bird and P. Wadler, *Introduction to Functional Programming*, New York: Prentice Hall (1988).

2. P. Hudak, S. Peyton Jones and P. L. Wadler, et. al., "Report on the programming language Haskell: a nonstrict, purely functional language," *SIGPLAN NOTICES* (1992).

3. J. T. O'Donnell, "Hardware description with recursion equations," *Proc. 8th Symp. on Computer Hardware Description Languages and their Applications*, North-Holland (1987) 363–382.

Measuring the effectiveness of a simple strictness analyser

Simon Peyton Jones

Department of Computing Science, University of Glasgow

simonpj@dcs.glasgow.ac.uk

Will Partain

Department of Computing Science, University of Glasgow

partain@dcs.glasgow.ac.uk

Abstract

We describe a simple strictness analyser for purely-functional programs, show how its results are used to improve programs, and provide measurements of the effects of these improvements. These measurements are given both in terms of overall run-time, and in terms of internal operations such as allocations, updates, etc.

Despite its simplicity, the analyser handles higher-order functions, and non-flat domains provided they are non-recursive.

1   Introduction

A lot has been written about strictness analysis for non-strict functional programs, usually in the hope that the results of the analysis can be used to reduce run-time. On the other hand, few papers present measurements of how well it works in practice. Usually, all that is presented are the run-times of a variety of (usually small) programs, with and without strictness analysis enabled (eg Smetsers et al. [1991]). The goal of this paper is to provide detailed quantitative insight about the effectiveness of a simple strictness analyser, in the context of a state-of-the art compiler, running serious application programs.

2   What might we hope to gain

Before going further, we need a clear model of what one might hope to gain from strictness analysis. The discussion of this section is intended to be generic, applying equally to any implementation technology. Accordingly, we refrain from introducing details about *how* we implement anything; instead we concentrate on *what* gains are possible.

2.1   The classic case: integers

Let's start with the standard example, a strict function with an Int argument. Suppose f is strict, and has type

```
f :: Int -> Int
```

Consider what happens for the call (f (x+1)). Without the knowledge that f is strict, we would have to build in the heap a thunk[1] for (x+1) and pass it to f.

If f is known to be strict, we can instead evaluate (x+1) before the call. Better still, *we can pass the argument unboxed*, since it is by now certainly an evaluated Int. We need a different version of f, which we call fw to abbreviate "f's worker", with type

```
fw :: Int# -> Int
```

where Int# is the type of unboxed integers. Operationally, an Int is represented by a pointer to a heap object, which contains either evaluated integer, or possibly an unevaluated thunk. An Int# is represented by the integer itself, not a pointer at all.

The big gain is that no thunk for (x+1) is ever created, which means that:

- We may save a heap-overflow check.

- We save the costs of writing the thunk into the heap memory.

- We save the costs of reading it back in again when it is evaluated in f.

- We save the costs of updating the thunk with its final value, and of the stack manipulations associated with updates[2].

- We save the amortised garbage collection costs of the thunk.

To give an idea of scale, these additional costs amount to around 25 instructions per argument, most of which are memory references. It is clearly a big win to replace these instructions with a single instruction to place the argument in a suitable register! The gains are compounded if f is recursive, because we save all these costs every time around the loop.

Is there *always* a gain, though? Suppose the argument to f is itself just an argument to the enclosing function. For example:

```
foo False x = 0
foo True  x = f x + 1
```

(Here, foo isn't strict in x, so x has to be passed boxed to foo.) In this case there is actually no gain from evaluating x before calling f, but there is no harm either. Even in cases like this we may still gain by avoiding redundant evaluations. Suppose instead that the second equation for foo was:

```
foo True x = f x + f x
```

Now, it is possible to evaluate x *just once*, and pass the unboxed value to each of the two calls to f. Exactly the same number of thunks are built, but there is one fewer evaluation: we say that we have "eliminated a redundant EVAL".

To summarise, we may exploit strictness analysis in three ways:

---

[1] We use the term "thunk" for an as-yet unevaluated closure; when evaluated it will usually be overwritten by its (weak) head normal form.

[2] A separate analysis might be able to discover that f would evaluate its argument at most once. In this case, the caller can mark the thunk as non-updatable, thus saving the cost of performing the update. But that's another story, and the costs of writing the thunk into the heap, and reading it back out, are unchanged.

1. by avoiding the creation and updating of thunks;

2. by manipulating unboxed values, instead of heap-allocated boxed values;

3. by eliminating redundant evaluations.

2.2 Other single-constructor types

The same idea extends to unboxing any algebraic data type with just one constructor[3]. A particularly common family of such data types is the tuple types. For example, if g is strict, and has type

```
g :: (a,a) -> a
```

then g's worker, gw will take the *components* of the constructor:

```
gw :: a -> a -> a
```

As before, the pair is passed unboxed, as its two separate components. In a call (g <arg>), where <arg> is an arbitrary expression, we can evaluate <arg> before the call, and pass the components to gw rather than building a thunk for <arg> which is later evaluated by g.

If we find a call with an explicit tuple argument, eg (g (<arg1>,<arg2>)), then we are laughing: we can just transform the call to (gw <arg1> <arg2>).

Our implementation of Haskell adds extra *dictionary arguments* to overloaded functions. A dictionary is just a tuple of values, so many more functions end up with tuple arguments than those written explicitly by the programmer. (A separate pass, which specialises overloaded functions, may eliminate these dictionaries, however.)

2.3 Unboxing multi-constructor types

With multi-constructor types, such as lists, matters are rather murkier. Suppose we know that a function h is strict in its list argument, where h has type:

```
h :: [Int] -> Bool
```

How could we use this information? One possibility would be to have *two* workers for h, with types:

```
hwNil  :: Bool             -- The Nil case
hwCons :: Int -> [Int] -> Bool  -- The Cons case
```

Given a call (h e) we can evaluate e and call hwNil or hwCons depending on what it turns out to be. Unfortunately this scheme turns sour on us if the function has several arguments with multi-constructor types, because there's an exponential blowup in the number of versions of h required. We have not tried this option at all.

Another possibility would be to have some way of passing a variable-sized argument, along with a tag to say which constructor is meant. This is tricky territory for the code generator, and again we have not tried it.

---

[3]As we'll see later, Int is an example of such a type.

In any case, it is far from clear what gains might be expected from either approach. If the data type is recursive, and h is recursive, then all we are doing is moving the *topmost* evaluation of the argument from h to the call site.

In short, unboxing strict arguments of multi-constructor type seems complex and the returns are debatable. There is one obvious exception to this pessimistic conclusion: enumeration types, such as `Bool`, have several constructors but all of them are nullary. Enumeration types have an obvious unboxed representation as a small integer tag. We plan to exploit this, but have not yet done so.

2.4   Early evaluation of multi-constructor types

Even if we have to pass a multi-constructor typed argument in boxed form, there might still be gains from evaluating it early. In particular, consider the call (h <arg>) where <arg> is not a variable or literal. Without strictness analysis, we have to build a thunk for <arg> and pass it to h. Knowing that h is strict, we could evaluate <arg> in-line, allocate a suitable list cell (*cons* or *nil*), and pass that to h. The saving here is that we don't need to write the thunk into the heap, read it back and then perform the update; instead we simply write the final value into the heap. Howe's paper in this proceedings concentrates on precisely this point (Howe & Burn [1993]).

If the argument of a call is a variable, eg (h x), it depends on fine details of the implementation whether it is worth evaluating x before the call. Recall that in the case of single-constructor types the benefit was that the evaluation might be shared across two calls. In the multi-constructor case this benefit might also accrue *if evaluation and unpacking are two separate operations*, as they are in the G-machine. Then evaluation can be moved to the call site, while unpacking remains in the called function. In the STG-machine, evaluation and unpacking are performed simultaneously, so there is no benefit.

2.5   Improving `let` bindings

Consider the expression

```
let x = <x-rhs> in <body>
```

and suppose that strictness analysis tells us that <body> is sure to evaluate x. Can we make use of this information? Yes, of course. Just as in the case of a strict function, we evaluate x immediately instead of building a thunk for it, and waiting for <body> to evaluate it. For reasons which will become apparent, we call this the `let`-to-`case` transformation.

2.6   Non-flat domains

So far we have concentrated exclusively on "flat" strictness, which answers the question as to whether a function is strict in a particular argument position or not. Much work has been done on non-flat domains: can we take advantage of it? This question splits into three:

1. For *non-recursive types with just one constructor*, such as tuples, we should certainly be able to "see" inside the constructor to the strictness of its components. For example, we can do more with the function

```
f (x,y) = x+1
```

than to say that it is strict in its argument; it is obviously strict in the first component of the tuple.

2. For *non-recursive types with more than one constructor* it might be possible to do something similar, but it seems quite a bit more complicated. In our analyser we make no attempt to discover strictness in the components of multi-constructor types.

3. For *recursive types*, much theoretical work has been done relating the degree of evaluation performed on the result of a function to the degree of evaluation of its arguments (Burn [1990]; Wadler & Hughes [1987]). For example, the append function is strict in the spine of its arguments if it is called in a context which requires the spine of its result. We make no attempt to compute or exploit such information, for two reasons. First, it is a lot more work to compute the information. Second, the results of exploiting it are not always beneficial. For example, the version of the append function suitable for a spine-strict context will compute the whole of the result before returning any of it, which might have a terrible effect on the peak space requirement of the program.

There is very little published work which attempts to measure the effects of exploiting strictness in recursive data types. Finne & Burn [1993] use "evaluation transformers" to evaluate lists more strictly (in the same spirit as the work described here), but for sequential implementations they find few performance benefits, and occasional large costs. In contrast, Hall [1993] uses strictness information over list types to guide a new transformation which uses a more efficient list representation where possible. The transformation gives substantial performance benefits where it is applicable.

3   A simple strictness analyser

Now that we know how we can exploit strictness analysis, we will describe our simple strictness analyser itself. Our general approach has been *to try to gain a large fraction of the possible winnings with a small fraction of the effort*. To this end, our strictness analyser is simple, but apparently quite effective. (It is of course hard to be quantitative about such a claim, since we have not implemented a more sophisticated one with which to compare it.)

The process of detecting and exploiting strictness is split into three stages:

1. First, a simple abstract interpretation is used to annotate the binding occurrence of each variable with (a) an indication of whether or not it is sure to be evaluated, and (b) in the case of let(rec) bound variables, an indication of its strictness properties.

2. Next, a simple pass uses these annotations to make local transformations of the program.

3. Finally, a general program-transformation system is applied to the resulting program, to propagate the effects globally.

$$S\,[\![x]\!]\,\rho \;=\; \begin{cases} \rho\,x, & x \in dom(\rho) \\ \top & otherwise \end{cases}$$

$$S\,[\![e_1\ e_2]\!]\,\rho \;=\; (S\,[\![e_1]\!]\,\rho)(S\,[\![e_2]\!]\,\rho)$$

$$S\,[\![\backslash x.e]\!]\,\rho \;=\; \lambda y.S\,[\![e]\!]\,\rho[x \mapsto y]$$

$$S\,[\![\text{let } x{=}e \text{ in } b]\!]\,\rho \;=\; S\,[\![b]\!]\,\rho[x \mapsto S\,[\![e]\!]\,\rho]$$

$$S\left[\!\!\!\begin{array}{l} \text{letrec} \\ \quad x_1{=}e_1 \\ \quad \dots \\ \quad x_n{=}e_n \\ \text{in } b \end{array}\!\!\!\right]\rho \;=\; S\,[\![b]\!]\,\rho'$$

$$\text{where}$$
$$\rho' = \mathit{fix}(\lambda\rho'.\rho[\dots, x_i \mapsto \nabla(S\,[\![e_i]\!]\,\rho'), \dots])$$

$$S\,[\![C\ e_1 \dots e_n]\!]\,\rho \;=\; \begin{cases} (S\,[\![e_1]\!]\,\rho, \dots, S\,[\![e_n]\!]\,\rho), & C \text{ is mono} \\ \top, & otherwise \end{cases}$$

$$S\left[\!\!\!\begin{array}{l} \text{case } e \text{ of} \\ \quad \dots \\ \quad C_i\ x_1..x_n \;\text{->}\; r_i \\ \quad \dots \end{array}\!\!\!\right]\rho \;=\; \begin{cases} \bot, & v = \bot \\ S\,[\![r_1]\!]\,\rho\left[\begin{array}{l} x_1 \mapsto v_1, \\ \dots, \\ x_n \mapsto v_n \end{array}\right], & v = (v_1,..,v_n) \\ \bigsqcup S\,[\![r_i]\!]\,\rho, & otherwise \end{cases}$$

$$\text{where}$$
$$v = S\,[\![e]\!]\,\rho$$

Figure 1: The abstract interpretation

The first stage is described in the rest of this section, while the second two stages are described subsequently, in Section 4.

3.1 The abstract interpretation

Our strictness analyser uses abstract interpretation. The abstract domain contains top, bottom, functions, and finite products:

$$D = \mathbf{1} + (D \to D) + \sum_i D^i$$

(Here, $\mathbf{1}$ is the one-point domain, $+$ is lifted sum, and D^i is ordinary (non-lifted) product.) The abstract interpretation itself is given in Figure 1. The syntax of the language is conventional: lambda calculus together with let, letrec, case, and constructors from algebraic data types. We assume that the source program is well typed by the time it reaches the strictness analyser.

There are several features worthy of note:

- The abstract interpretation is higher order, along the lines of Burn, Hankin & Abramsky [1986].

- The product space in the abstract domain is used only for constructors from data types with just one constructor (Figure 1 calls such constructors "mono"). For constructors from multi-constructor types we use the simple two point domain only.

- The interpretation of `case` expressions takes advantage of a product-space value. (In this case there can be only one alternative, of course.)

- `let` expressions are handled with no approximation at all, including the case where the variable has a functional type.

- The interpretation of `letrec` uses the fixpoint operator, of course, but it also uses a *widening operator*, w, which is the subject of the next section.

Using this abstract interpretation it is straightforward to annotate each `let`-bound or lambda-bound variable with its strictness properties.

3.2 Finding fixpoints

Our analyser uses a crude but fast approximation technique for finding fixpoints. The main payoff is that it converges in worst case time $O(N^2)$, where N is the number of arguments to the function being fixpointed. The square law comes from the fact that at most N iterations are required, each of which requires N evaluations to compute.

Suppose we want to find the fixpoint of a functional F. The usual idea is to compute the chain of approximations $\bot, F(\bot), F^2(\bot), \ldots$, and stop when $F^k(\bot) = F^{k+1}(\bot)$, at which point $F^k(\bot)$ is the least fixpoint of F. The trouble is that computing equality between successive approximations is horribly expensive; a variety of solutions have been proposed, for example Hughes [1992], Peyton Jones & Clack [1986].

Our approach is simple. Instead of finding the fixpoint of F, we will find the fixpoint of ∇F, where $\nabla F(x) = \nabla(F(x))$, and ∇ is a *widening operator*. A widening operator makes things bigger[4]; formally, ∇ is a widening operator iff

$$\forall x.\ x \sqsubseteq \nabla(x)$$

The key idea is this: *we choose ∇ so that it is easy to compare successive iterations, $(\nabla F)^k(\bot)$ and $(\nabla F)^{k+1}(\bot)$ for equality.* Why does this do us any good? Because of this theorem:

Theorem 1: *fix* $F \sqsubseteq$ *fix* ∇F

That is, *the fixpoint of ∇F is a safe approximation (from the point of view of strictness analysis) to the fixpoint of F.* The proof is in the Appendix.

---

[4]The cognoscenti will know that widening operators have a slightly tighter definition than this, but this one is sufficient for our purposes.

3.2.1 Choosing a widening operator

Now, how do we choose the widening operator ∇? There are a variety of choices, but the one we use is to characterise a widened function by giving a "demand" for each argument, saying how much evaluation the function guarantees to perform on that argument. A "demand" is one of the following:

L   Lazy; no evaluation of this argument is guaranteed.

S   Strict; the function is strict in this argument, but its type is a multi-constructor type, function, or type variable.

$U(d_1 \ldots d_n)$ Unpack; a strict argument of a single-constructor type, to be passed unboxed. The demands which can be guaranteed for the components are given by $d_1 \ldots d_n$.

For example, if f is defined like this:

```
f x y z = if z then x else y
```

then f's "strictness signature", which gives s safe demand for each argument, is "LLS". We think of f's strictness signature as specifying $\nabla(\text{f})$, a very crude uppper (and hence safe) approximation to the true abstract value of f:

$$
\begin{aligned}
\nabla(\text{f}) \ x \ y \ \bot &= \bot \\
\nabla(\text{f}) \ x \ y \ z &= \top, \text{ if } z \neq \bot
\end{aligned}
$$

Notice that the "joint strictness" between x and y is lost by the widening process.

In general, suppose f is a function of n arguments. A *safe demand*, d_i, for argument i has the property that:

$$
\forall x \in \theta(d_i).f \ \top_1 \ \top_2 \ \ldots \ x \ \ldots \ \top_{n-1} \ \top_n = \bot
$$

where $\theta(d_i)$ is defined as follows:

$$
\begin{aligned}
\theta(L) &= \emptyset \\
\theta(S) &= \{\bot\} \\
\theta(U(d_1, \ldots, d_n)) &= \{\bot\} \cup \{(t_1, \ldots, t_n) \mid t_1 \in \theta(d_1) \vee \ldots \vee t_n \in \theta(d_n)\}
\end{aligned}
$$

Informally, if d_i is a safe demand for argument i, then $\theta(d_i)$ is a set of values of argument i which are certain to make the function diverge.

A strictness signature for f is a sequence of safe demands $d_1 d_2 \ldots d_n$. Then $\nabla(\text{f})$ is easy to define:

$$
\nabla(\text{f}) = \lambda x_1 \ldots x_n.if \ (x_1 \in \theta(d_1)) \ \vee \ \ldots \ \vee \ (x_n \in \theta(d_n)) \ then \ \bot \ else \ \top
$$

It is an easy theorem that ∇ is indeed a widening operator.

Given the abstract version of a function, it is easy to find a safe demand for each argument, by "probing". First, evaluate the function with that argument bound to $\bot$ and all the others bound to $\top$; if it returns $\bot$ then S is a safe demand, otherwise U is. If S is a safe demand and the argument is of a single-contructor type we can try probing with $(\bot, \top, \ldots, \top)$, $(\top, \bot, \top, \ldots, \top)$, and so on, to find a safe demand for each component. The strictness analyser can then widen a function by (a) probing it to compute its strictness signature and then (b) using the strictness signature to define the widened function.

So, finally, to find the fixpoint of a function, compute a chain of widened approximations, and stop when two iterations have the same strictness signature.

Working through this theory, which was done subsequent to the implementation, actually revealed several bugs in the implementation, one of which was in the widening process. Theory actually helps!

4 Exploiting the results of strictness analysis

The results of strictness analysis are often exploited by deeply mysterious processes within the code generator of the compiler. Our approach is instead:

- to express the results of strictness analysis by means of simple, local program transformations, and

- to propagate the effects of these transformations using the compiler's general program-transformation system which is required in any case.

To do this requires a language in which the evaluation of (for example) integers is explicit. We do this by making use of *unboxed types*; the ideas are sketched below, but full details can be found in Peyton Jones & Launchbury [1991].

4.1 Unboxed types

In Glasgow Haskell, unboxed types like Int# are (nearly) first-class citizens[5]. Indeed, the Int type is built from Int#, using an ordinary data type declaration:

```
data Int = I# Int#
```

Consider again the call f (x+1). The idea of evaluating the (x+1) before the call, and passing it unboxed, can now be expressed like this:

```
case x of
I# x# -> case x# +# 1# of
           a# -> fw a#
```

The outer case evaluates x, and extracts its unboxed component x#. The inner case is the STG language's way of saying[6] "add x# to 1# and call the result a#". Then a# is passed to fw.

---

[5]The only respect in which they are not first-class is that unboxed types cannot instantiate polymorphic type variables (Peyton Jones & Launchbury [1991]).

[6]We use 1# rather than just 1, and +# rather than + because the values and operations involved are the unboxed ones.

4.2 Workers and wrappers

Suppose that the strictness analyser found that f is strict in its Int argument x, where f is defined like this:

```
f x = <rhs-of-f>
```

To express this fact, a local program transformation is made which splits f into two functions: a *wrapper* and a *worker*, thus:

```
f x   = case x of
          I# x# -> fw x#
fw x# = let x = I# x#
        in <rhs-of-f>
```

Now, the global program-transformation phase can unfold all calls to f, but not fw, which has precisely the effect of moving the argument evaluation to the call site.

Notice the somewhat curious re-construction of x from x# in the body of fw. Does this mean that the argument is taken apart by the wrapper only to be reconstructed by the worker? The answer is that such reconstruction does not usually take place. To see the common case, suppose <rhs-of-f> was x+x. Substituting this into fw, and unfolding the definition of +, gives

```
fw x# = let x = I# x#
        in case x of
             I# x1# -> case x of
                         I# x2# -> case x1# +# x2# of
                                     a# -> I# a#
```

Now, both case expressions are scrutinising a variable which is directly bound to a I# constructor, so they can be eliminated in favour of binding x1# and x2# to x#. Now x is not mentioned at all, so it can be dropped, giving the satisfactory result:

```
fw x# =  case x# +# x# of
           a# -> I# a#
```

4.3 The let to case transformation

As remarked in Section 2.5 it should be possible to generate better code for a let binding which binds a variable which is sure to be evaluated in the body of the let. To express this, we can make the transformation:

```
let x = <rhs-of-x>        ===>        case <rhs-of-x> of
in <body>                             x -> <body>
```

This is called the let-to-case transformation. In our implementation, the original let would build a thunk for <rhs-of-x> while the case will instead evaluate it in-line[7]. A heap allocation does still take place: if <rhs-of-x> was

---

[7]In Haskell, case e of x -> b is the same as let x = e in b, but not in our compiler's internal language, in which case is always strict.

a pair, for example, the pair would be allocated in the heap, and bound to x[8].
The gain is that the thunk does not need to be written out, read back in later,
and updated.

The let-to-case transformation implements the optimisation discussed in
Section 2.4. Given a function application (h <arg>), for some non-atomic
expression <arg>, we first transform to

```
let a = <arg> in h a
```

and then use let-to-case to obtain

```
case <arg> of
a -> h a
```

However, in the case of single-constructor types we can do better. For example,
if x is a pair we can transform like this:

```
let x = <rhs-of-x>  ===>   case <rhs-of-x> of
in <body>                  (p,q) -> let x = (p,q) in <body>
```

Why is this better? Because the construction of x as a pair is then visible
in <body> which often results in the elimination of one or more case expressions. A particularly important example of this case-elimination concerns lazy
pattern matching. Suppose we start with the Haskell definition

```
f x y = if x then p else q
        where
        (p,q) = h y
```

This translates naively to:

```
f x y = let t = h y
            p = case t of (p,q) -> p
            q = case t of (p,q) -> q
        in if x then p else q
```

The pattern binding for (p,q) gives rise to three thunks, one for each of t, p
and q, which is horribly inefficient. Now, the strictness analyser will discover
that t is sure to be evaluated, even though neither of p and q are. Using the
let-to-case transformation gives:

```
f x y = case (h y) of
          (p1,q1) -> let p = case t of (p,q) -> p
                         q = case t of (p,q) -> q
                     in if x then p else q
```

Very simple automatic transformations can now eliminate the inner case expressions to give:

```
f x y = case (h y) of
          (p1,q1) ->  if x then p1 else q1
```

---

[8]Incidentally, precisely because it needs to heap-allocate the value returned by <rhs-of-x>,
our implementation will only handle a case with a single-variable alternative if the type of x
is a statically determinable data type.

In effect, this composition of simple transformations implements the more complex rule "if any variable in a pattern binding is sure to be evaluated, then the pattern binding can be taken apart using `case` rather than the full lazy-pattern-binding mechanism". Using a `case` expression allocates no thunks, and (in our implementation) does not even build the pair `(p1,q1)` in the heap — the two components are simply returned in registers.

4.4 Floating `case` out of `let`

There is yet another way in which we can exploit strictness information to reduce the construction of thunks and remove repeated evaluation. Consider the expression

```
let x = case y of
          <pat> -> <rhs>
in <body>
```

Furthermore, suppose that `x` is used strictly by `<body>`; that is, if `x` is bottom then so is `<body>`. Then `x` is sure to be evaluated, and hence so is `y`. This means that it is safe to transform to:

```
case y of
<pat> -> let x = <rhs>
            in <body>
```

Notice that the transformation works *regardless of the type of* `x` — for example, it does not have to be a single-constructor type, or even a data type. (If `x` were a single-constructor type, then the `let` to `case` transformation would be used.) Floating the `case` out of the `let` is a Good Thing to do for two reasons:

- It widens the scope of the `case`. For example, it may be that `y` is evaluated somewhere else in `<body>` (that is, there is a `case y of ...` in `<body>`). Now that `<body>` appears inside the `case y`, the second `case y` can be eliminated, saving an evaluation.

- It may be that `<rhs>` is a simple variable, in which case the `let` expression can now be eliminated entirely. Alternatively, `<rhs>` might be a constructor application, so now the `let` expression would allocate an immutable constructor, rather than a thunk which later has to be updated.

4.5 Absence

Consider this definition:

```
f t = case t of (a,b,c,d) -> b
```

The strictness of `f` is U(LLSL), which leads to the following worker/wrapper split (after some simplification):

```
f t = case t of (a,b,c,d) -> fw a b c d
fw a b c d = b
```

This is a bit silly, because the components of the tuple are passed to `fw` even though only one is used. It would be better if we could figure out when an argument is guaranteed *not* to be evaluated, so that we needn't pass it to the worker at all! Using "A" (absent) to indicate this, we would like f's strictness to be U(AASA). In the absence of product types absence is rare, because programmers seldom write functions which ignore one of their arguments, but once products are added absence becomes quite common (notably in the form of selector functions).

The property of "guaranteed not to be evaluated" (that is, absence) is dual to that of "guaranteed to be evaluated" (that is, strictness), and a second abstract interpretation is needed to gather absence information. Why is a full abstract interpretation needed? Can we not simply use a syntactic criterion? Consider:

```
g x = fst (fst x)
```

We would like to get the strictness property U(U(SA)A) for g, even though the absence of the arguments is not syntactically apparent.

We have implemented absence analysis, using the same infrastructure as for the strictness analysis (abstract interpreter, fixpointing, etc), but the details are beyond the scope of this paper.

4.6 Modules

It is absolutely essential to convey strictness information across module boundaries. Like most compilers, we do this by adding strictness annotations to the module's interface file, which is imported by other modules using this one's resources. For example, the following might appear in an interface file:

```
f :: Int -> [Int] -> Bool -> Bool
{-# GHC_PRAGMA ... _S_ "U(LL)SL" ... #-}
```

In order to keep the strictness annotations small, they only encode widened functions, using the demand notation described in Section 3.2.1. The strictness of non-recursive functions is expressed in this way, as well as recursive ones; some details of their full abstract value is therefore lost across module boundaries.

5 Results

We exercised our strictness analyser on each of 17 programs, from the "Real" part of the (still-unreleased) nofib suite of Haskell programs. They cover a broad spread of application domains, including theorem proving, RSA encoding, geometric modelling, type inference, and data compression. They vary from 70 to 11,000 lines of Haskell source, with 500 lines being typical.

Each program was compiled with and without strictness analysis enabled, using a development version of GHC from November, 1993. All the other transformations used were identical, and in each case, the programs were linked with a standard Prelude which was compiled in the same way as they were.

	None		Strictly	
	R	U+S	R	U+S
anna	8.4	8.2	−3.6%	−3.8%
veritas	4.4	0.6	+18.2%	−16.7%
gg	7.3	4.3	−2.7%	−7.0%
hidden	412.0	395.1	−31.3%	−32.1%
maillist	94.2	15.2	+7.3%	+5.9%
bspt	6.1	3.6	−13.1%	−19.4%
compress	83.1	81.1	−21.7%	−21.7%
infer	18.8	16.7	−9.6%	−9.6%
lift	2.2	0.3	+13.6%	—
parser	15.2	12.0	−13.8%	−14.2%
prolog	2.3	0.7	−8.7%	—
reptile	5.9	3.7	+23.7%	−2.7%
rsa	27.3	25.6	−9.2%	−9.0%
fluid	7.5	3.5	−1.3%	−22.9%
gamteb	64.2	61.1	−33.0%	−33.7%
pic	13.0	9.6	−37.7%	−44.8%
fulsom	129.7	126.0	−10.3%	−10.6%

Table 1: Run times (in seconds [real; user+system])

All programs were compiled with "ticky-ticky" profiling: when run, they collect many dynamic counts, e.g., the number of three-word closures allocated, the number of updates, etc.

All the figures presented in the next section refer to *dynamic* counts. For example, the number of function calls which managed to call the worker of a strict function is the dynamic count, not the static number of such calls in the program text. The dynamic counts are what affects run-time.

There is one main caveat: too many programs have input data which leads to a runtime which is too small to measure reliably. This is partly a problem of success (the compiler has improved) and partly that they are run on a fast machine.

5.1 Run times

In a sense the runtime is the result that "really matters", although it doesn't give much insight in itself. Table 1 shows the change in runtime for each of the programs without strictness analysis ("None" column) and the percentage change when strictness analysis is enabled ("Strictly" column). "R" is real, wall-clock time, presented for completeness; "U+S" is user+system time, which is more informative. A dash (—) means "no discernible change". Each was run on a Sun SparcStation 10 with 48Mbytes of memory.

The performance gains are modest but consistent, ranging from near-zero to an improvement of 30% or more. maillist, whose execution time actually increases, is an unusual program, being totally dominated by input/output. We believe it is amplifying a small infelicity in the transformation system.

	None			Strictly		
	Thunks	Others	Total	Thunks	Others	Total
anna	622,624	175,511	798,135	−15.9%	+25.6%	−6.8%
veritas	29,101	3,635	32,736	−4.8%	+4.1%	−3.8%
gg	335,104	151,972	487,076	−14.9%	+18.8%	−4.4%
hidden	61,178,224	6,449,232	67,627,456	−46.4%	+13.1%	−40.7%
maillist	144,555	313,380	457,935	−19.0%	+69.9%	+41.8%
bspt	390,280	48,979	439,259	−26.9%	+246.3%	+3.6%
compress	1,623,431	8,209,918	9,833,349	−5.8%	—	−1.0%
infer	619,273	274,155	893,428	−5.7%	+7.9%	−1.5%
lift	20,099	9,646	29,745	−9.1%	+15.1%	−1.2%
parser	1,276,925	614,789	1,891,714	−34.8%	+26.4%	−14.9%
prolog	44,189	22,426	66,615	−30.4%	+43.0%	−5.7%
reptile	474,845	82,681	557,526	−22.2%	+29.7%	−14.5%
rsa	553,934	414,186	968,120	−91.6%	−47.7%	−72.8%
fluid	268,514	83,288	351,802	−30.3%	+58.6%	−9.2%
gamteb	4,333,275	2,015,412	6,348,687	−49.8%	+74.1%	−10.4%
pic	599,024	369,784	968,808	−72.9%	+139.6%	+8.2%
fulsom	16,305,421	7,937,428	24,242,849	−6.0%	−28.1%	−13.2%

Table 2: Thunks (and other objects) allocated

5.2 Allocations saved

In Section 2 we identified the main saving from strictness analysis as the reduction in the number of thunks allocated. Table 2 quantifies this by counting how many thunks are allocated in a run of each program under each build. Just to reassure ourselves that we aren't making savings in one place only to incur costs in another, the "Others" column counts all allocation *other* than thunks; mostly allocation of head normal forms, such as data constructors and partial function applications. As before, the "Strictly" columns are given as percentage changes from the corresponding "None" column.

The number of thunks allocated always decreases, sometimes dramatically so (eg hidden). There are, unsurprisingly, more non-thunks allocated, but the total allocation is usually reduced. We would expect the total allocation to *always* be reduced; the cases where it is not (maillist, bspt, pic) show a rather large increase in non-thunk allocation). This deserves further investigation.

5.3 Updates saved

As well as reducing the number of thunks, we hope also to reduce the number of updates. Indeed, since every one of the thunks we do not allocate is one which would be entered, one might expect approximately one update to be saved for every thunk saved. This is confirmed by comparing the first two columns in Table 3. The figures are not exactly the same because other transformations are enabled or disabled by the effects of strictness analysis.

The picture is complicated slightly by *update analysis*, which tries to infer when a thunk can only be entered at most once, and hence does not need to be

	Thunks	Updates	None		Strictly	
	eliminated by		without	with	without	with
	strictness analysis		update analysis		update analysis	
anna	99,010	90,096	535,148	−11.5%	445,052	−5.5%
veritas	1,397	1,366	28,466	−3.2%	27,100	−0.4%
gg	49,858	49,566	330,051	−3.8%	280,485	−0.5%
hidden	28,362,677	14,034,948	39,774,327	−6.9%	25,739,379	−5.2%
maillist	27,509	27,509	104,139	−8.7%	76,630	—
bspt	104,889	102,461	382,558	−9.4%	280,097	−1.5%
compress	94,872	94,872	1,623,318	—	1,528,446	—
infer	35,389	35,370	443,570	−9.0%	408,200	−1.5%
lift	1,821	1,871	19,228	−7.6%	17,357	−1.8%
parser	443,965	290,793	720,170	−1.5%	429,377	−1.9%
prolog	13,448	13,423	36,908	−32.4%	23,485	−1.3%
reptile	105,313	105,900	474,142	−16.9%	368,242	−2.1%
rsa	507,463	455,299	501,469	−38.5%	46,170	—
fluid	81,310	78,438	238,861	−6.2%	160,423	−0.7%
gamteb	2,156,738	2,053,226	4,175,334	−2.3%	2,122,108	−0.9%
pic	436,633	427,670	578,972	−0.2%	151,302	—
fulsom	970,177	859,845	12,191,166	−7.1%	11,331,321	−6.6%

Table 3: Updates

updated (Marlow [1993]). An interesting question is: *does strictness analysis eliminate exactly those thunks which update analysis identifies as single-entry, or does update analysis find some more beside?* The "with" columns on the right side of Table 3 quantify the answer. It says how many updates happened even with the update analyser. On some numerically-intensive programs (rsa, compress) the update analyser can't find much to do after the strictness analyser has done its stuff. However, there are often handy winnings still to be had (eg anna, hidden).

5.4 Evaluations saved

A side benefit of strictness analysis is that sometimes a thunk may be evaluated just once instead of twice (cf Section 2.1). The second enter will encounter an evaluated data value, so with strictness analysis one would expect the number of data-value enters to drop. And so it does (Table 4). The reduction in the number of data-value enters is often modest (veritas, infer) but sometimes very substantial (reptile, gamteb) — the numerical programs seem to be the ones which work well, unsurprisingly.

The number of thunks entered also drops, which is unsurprising since fewer thunks are allocated.

5.5 Function calls

How many function calls are able to exploit strictness at all? Table 5 gives the answers. It splits all function calls into three groups: the "non-wrapperised"

	None			Strictly		
	data-vals	thunks	others	data-vals	thunks	others
anna	1,875,349	522k	2,187k	−5.1%	−16.9%	−20.8%
veritas	11,293	27k	37k	−6.2%	−3.7%	−8.1%
gg	657,597	322k	1,144k	−33.3%	−15.2%	−23.8%
hidden	79,661,596	38,842k	104,354k	−21.3%	−35.3%	−37.1%
maillist	1,072,984	101k	1,077k	−26.6%	−26.7%	−41.3%
bspt	475,832	373k	799k	−20.5%	−26.8%	−32.5%
compress	36,689,810	1,585k	24,311k	−5.7%	−5.9%	−64.3%
infer	7,177,846	433k	6,339k	—	−8.1%	−38.1%
lift	22,368	18k	37k	−2.7%	−11.1%	−10.8%
parser	2,041,658	703k	3,347k	−4.0%	−40.4%	−14.6%
prolog	98,091	36k	157k	−6.6%	−38.9%	−29.9%
reptile	449,386	463k	929k	−50.3%	−22.5%	−33.2%
rsa	1,032,357	489k	1,678k	−63.6%	−90.8%	−40.9%
fluid	589,827	233k	864k	−42.9%	−33.0%	−49.8%
gamteb	11,096,188	4,077k	15,683k	−59.1%	−49.2%	−54.6%
pic	2,281,123	565k	2,915k	−50.1%	−74.0%	−65.4%
fulsom	13,816,368	11,905k	26,017k	−24.6%	−7.1%	−32.3%

Table 4: Number of enters

	Non-wrapperised	Workers	Wrappers
anna	1,309,080	76,303	7,964
veritas	31,292	1,394	128
gg	472,077	158,189	67,687
hidden	47,582,515	11,840,378	3,796,296
maillist	452,020	150,096	12,129
bspt	322,805	143,250	19,290
compress	8,535,426	126,507	8
infer	2,963,582	12,763	2,630
lift	23,875	3,455	1,902
parser	2,398,474	100,531	28,363
prolog	98,359	6,253	191
reptile	518,598	96,612	12,454
rsa	67,227	729,738	18,882
fluid	279,668	83,186	22,691
gamteb	2,350,999	2,977,282	805,196
pic	267,546	442,348	167,144
fulsom	11,054,384	2,308,330	318,209

Table 5: Number of function calls to... ("Strictly" build)

	c	i	j	f	d	t	s	U
anna	17.39	32.73				6.38	28.85	9.35
veritas	1.39	7.37				73.35	4.03	8.38
gg	6.60	16.62	38.37	0.01	0.18	7.54	0.27	29.99
hidden	0.33	1.27	1.98	0.01	0.00	1.44	71.68	23.29
maillist		41.59				41.08	6.54	6.54
bspt		36.61				5.94	44.31	11.69
compress		99.98				0.01	0.00	0.00
infer	24.13	43.34				0.18	17.29	15.00
lift	21.47	19.05	2.14			9.37	13.11	34.77
parser	60.38	7.86				4.99	0.20	20.51
prolog	76.49	14.75				1.16	0.54	2.96
reptile	1.46	90.11				0.03	0.00	8.33
rsa		0.22	96.90			0.47	0.00	2.40
fluid	8.61	33.01	25.06	5.07	0.14	4.20	0.01	18.85
gamteb	0.00	35.67	33.04		0.87	8.39	0.24	21.79
pic	0.00	40.70	1.69		1.65	27.67	0.00	28.29
fulsom	0.00	28.06	1.34		28.03	24.86	0.37	14.77

Table 6: Wrappers' strict arguments were...

ones, which have no exploitable strict arguments; the "workers" which are the function calls to a strict function where the worker was called directly; and the "wrappers" which are the calls to strict functions where the wrapper was called. Why are there any calls in the last category? Because data abstraction means that (currently) we may not be able to unpack the argument(s) at the call site even though they are known to be strict.

5.6   Argument distribution

In the discussion of Section 2 we distinguished between various argument types: Int, single-constructor, tuples, multi-constructor, and so on. Table 6 tells the distribution of these argument types over all calls. The proportions are given as percentages of all strict argument positions, so that non-strict arguments don't appear at all.

The first group of columns are all single-constructor types that could "unpack" effectively: c=Char, i=Int, j=Integer, f=Float, d=Double, t=tuple, s=other single-constructor type. Column U gives the percentage of single-constructor arguments that we *failed* to unpack, because of data abstraction.

The most unexpected measurement is the prevalence of the "s" column, indicating that generalising the unboxery to types other than numeric ones and tuples is quite worth while.

Lastly, Table 7 addresses the question of the number of arguments which are passed to workers. In principle, a worker might take very many more arguments than its wrapper, since several arguments may be unpacked. In extreme cases this might be quite counter-productive. Table 7 is reassuring: a worker seldom takes many more arguments than its wrapper.

	−3	−2	−1	0	+1	+2	+3	+4	+5
anna		0.00	0.30	86.78	8.29	4.32	0.00	0.31	
veritas	0.14	1.43	2.08	25.90	42.97	25.61	0.36		1.51
gg				41.72	0.31	19.72	0.26	37.86	0.14
hidden			0.02	93.97	1.42	2.35	0.02	2.22	0.00
maillist				7.18	88.78		4.03		
bspt				48.60	8.91	39.06	1.14		2.29
compress				99.99	0.01				
infer			0.01	99.74	0.23	0.02			
lift				81.22	16.12	0.61		2.00	0.06
parser			0.10	92.77	0.04	0.28	6.82		
prolog				98.74	1.23		0.03		
reptile			0.10	99.85	0.02	0.03			
rsa				1.25	0.00	22.86		75.89	0.00
fluid		1.15		63.88	7.01	3.92	0.40	23.62	0.01
gamteb			0.00	46.72	14.24	4.94	0.17	33.40	0.52
pic			0.00	26.31	70.95	1.05	0.01	1.67	0.00
fulsom		0.00	0.00	55.88	0.00	0.98	41.69	1.45	0.00

Table 7: Worker functions' # of arguments vs. their wrappers' # (percentages)

6   Conclusion

Our main conclusion is this: strictness analysis on large, realistic programs leads to solid but modest improvements in execution speed. The best speedup we observed was about 30% (ie the runtime dropped to about 70% of its previous value), but 10–20% is more typical. This contrasts with other papers which describe dramatic speedups, but these are usually measured on small programs which spend a lot of time in an optimisable loop.

A second general conclusion is that program behaviours really do vary widely, even in large programs — see, for example, the distribution of strict argument types in Table 6. There is no "silver bullet" — a good compiler has to be more like a shotgun, with many transformations targetted at many situations.

A third conclusion is that making detailed quantitative measurements of the internal behaviour of programs, as we have done, often shows up compiler "performance bugs"; that is, places where the compiler generates significantly (but not drastically) less good code than it could. These can lie (and in our experience have lain) undiscovered for a very long time, since they do not cause programs to fail, until uncovered by making measurements.

There is plenty of scope for refining our measurements. In particular, each outcome (eg number of thunks allocated) is the effect of a combination of causes (eg let-to-case, unboxing, etc); it would be nice to isolate the effect of each of these causes.

Acknowledgements

Many thanks to John Launchbury for keeping us honest with the maths; to André Santos whose transformation system exploits and propagates the results of strictness analysis; and to Andy Gill, who wrote the first version of this strictness analyser.

Appendix: proofs

Our theorem was:

Theorem 1: If w is a widening operator, then $fix\ F \sqsubseteq fix\ wF$

That is, the fixpoint of wF is a safe approximation (from the point of view of strictness analysis) to the fixpoint of F. The proof is in two steps.

$$\begin{aligned} F(fix\ wF) &\sqsubseteq\ wF(fix\ wF) &&\text{Since } w \text{ is a widening operator} \\ &=\ fix\ wF &&\text{By definition of } fix \end{aligned}$$

In the jargon, $fix\ wF$ is a *post-fixpoint* of F. In general, z is a post-fixpoint of F if $F(z) \sqsubseteq z$. The following theorem holds for post-fixpoints:

Theorem 2: a post-fixpoint of F is greater than $F^n(\bot)$ for all n. More precisely, if z is a post-fixpoint of F, then $F^n(\bot) \sqsubseteq z$.

The proof is a simple induction on n. Certainly $\bot \sqsubseteq z$, which is the base case. Assuming $F^n(\bot) \sqsubseteq z$, applying F to both sides gives $F^{n+1}(\bot) \sqsubseteq F(z)$; but since z is a post-fixpoint of F, $F(z) \sqsubseteq z$, and hence $F^{n+1}(\bot) \sqsubseteq z.\square$

Corollary 3: if z is a post-fixpoint of F, then $fix\ F \sqsubseteq z$. This follows immediately from Theorem 2.$\square$

Corollary 4: since $F(fix\ wF) \sqsubseteq fix\ wF$, once we have found $fix\ wF$ we can get a better (or at least no worse) approximation to $fix\ F$ by computing $F^n(fix\ wF)$, for some arbitrarily chosen n. No tests for equality are required here, because $fix\ F \sqsubseteq F^n(fix\ wF)$ for any n.

References

GL Burn [April 1990], "The evaluation transformer model of reduction and its correctness," in *TAPSOFT 91, Brighton*.

GL Burn, CL Hankin & S Abramsky [Nov 1986], "Strictness analysis for higher order functions," *Science of Computer Programming* 7, 249–278.

S Finne & G Burn [June 1993], "Assessing the evaluation transformer model of reduction on the spineless G-machine," in *Proc Functional Programming Languages and Computer Architecture, Copenhagen*, ACM, 331–340.

CV Hall [July 1993], "A framework for optimising abstract data types," in *Glasgow Functional Programming Workshop, Ayr*.

DB Howe & GL Burn [July 1993], "Using strictness in the STG machine," in *Glasgow Functional Programming Workshop, Ayr*.

RJM Hughes [Sept 1992], "A loop-detecting interpreter for lazy higher-order programs," Department of Computer Science, Chalmers University.

S Marlow [July 1993], "Update avoidance analysis using abstract interpretation," in *Glasgow Functional Programming Workshop, Ayr*.

SL Peyton Jones & CD Clack [1986], "Finding fixpoints in abstract interpretation," in *Abstract Interpretation of Declarative Languages*, C Hankin & S Abramsky, eds., Ellis Horwood, Chichester, 246–265.

SL Peyton Jones & J Launchbury [Sept 1991], "Unboxed values as first class citizens," in *Functional Programming Languages and Computer Architecture, Boston*, Hughes, ed., LNCS 523, Springer Verlag, 636–666.

S Smetsers, E Nocker, J van Groningen & R Plasmeijer [Sept 1991], "Generating efficient code for lazy functional languages," in *Functional Programming Languages and Computer Architecture, Boston*, Hughes, ed., LNCS 523, Springer Verlag.

PL Wadler & John Hughes [Sept 1987], "Projections for strictness analysis," in *Functional Programming Languages and Computer Architecture*, G Kahn, ed., Springer Verlag LNCS 274.

Implementing Fudgets with Standard Widget Sets

Alastair Reid & Satnam Singh*
Computing Science Department
University of Glasgow

January 18, 1994

Abstract

Carlsson and Hallgren [1] describe the implementation of a set
of "functional widgets" (Fudgets): components for programming
graphical user interfaces under the X window system using the
non-strict functional programming language Haskell. We describe
an alternative implementation based on existing widget sets (currently Openlook and Motif). Our purpose is twofold: to show that
the Fudgets approach can be applied to existing widget sets; and
to discuss problems experienced with Fudgets during an industrial
case study.

1   Introduction

Imperative language programmers enjoy relatively easy access to the graphics resources of workstations. The graphics hardware is manipulated by side-
effecting procedure calls. Even if the library of graphics procedures is written
in one imperative language (e.g 'C'), programs written in another imperative
language can usually make calls to foreign procedures. For example, Ada allows
foreign procedures to be called by giving a standard pragma. Ada compilers
also allow Ada routines to by called by alien procedures.

This report describes a library for building high quality user-interfaces for
the purely functional lazy programming language Haskell. Graphics operations
are produced by making alien procedure calls to C language routines. Communicating data between Haskell and C programs is not trivial because Haskell is
a lazy language, has a garbage collector and uses a very different representation
for data (even for simple types like integers). We outline how to write Haskell
programs that communicate data with C routines in an orderly fashion using
the Glasgow IO monad.

The style of our interface is deliberately similar to the idiomatic style used
in C for writing X Windows graphics software. This invites comparison with
equivalent C programs and makes it easier to use the extensive body of X11
programming manuals.

---

*Email: {areid,satnam}@@dcs.glasgow.ac.uk

The structuring technique employed is based on the excellent Fudgets systems which uses higher-order combinators to glue together collections of user interface components. We describe some of the problems that arise from the static nature of the user interfaces generated by the Fudgets system. The Fudgets system defines its own user interface components. We also show how the Fudgets approach can be modified to use existing user interface components. In particular, we have adapted Fudgets to use OpenLook and Motif for building commercial quality and standardised user interfaces.

2   C Programmer's view of X widgets

The target graphics system for our graphics library is the X Window System. This system runs on a large variety of graphics workstations and affords us some degree of device independence.

The X Window System is based around a server-client model. A client program (e.g. a drawing program) need not run on the machine that actually supports the display (a graphics workstation). Indeed, the client machine may have no display at all because the client and server are connected over a network. A client program sends requests to the server to draw lines, points etc. The client program is also notified about events on the server's display.

At the lowest level, the X Window System is a network protocol which provides a network transparent interface for servers and clients. A C program language interface to this protocol is called Xlib. This provides data types and procedures for performing very basic graphics operations. Xlib is usually the lowest level at which X11 applications are written. However, little support is provided for building user interfaces comprising of components like buttons, menus and scrollbars.

The X Intrinsics Toolkit (Xt) is a collection of C types and procedures that describe the infrastructure need to build graphical user interfaces. A mechanism is provided for creating user interface components called *widgets*. Composite widgets may contain other widgets, allowing user interfaces to be constructed in a modular fashion as a widget tree. Widgets contain local state and are often implemented as finite state machines. The system we describe uses Xlib and Xt.

Xt does not define the behaviour or appearance of any particular widget. It only provides a 'backplane' into which specific *widget sets* can be plugged into. Widget sets include Athena (distributed with Xt), OpenLook Intrinsic Toolkit (OLIT) and Motif. Though broadly similar, different widget sets have different resources and callbacks, so it is hard to modify a program written with one widget set to work with another widget set.

The Xt system for managing events like button clicks and menu selection is based around *callbacks*. Callbacks are similar to interrupts. A widget can have several kinds of events. For each widget and each kind of event, a callback routine can be specified. (For example, a button would have a handler that is called whenever it is clicked. The callback routine is like a closure (it is basically a code-environment pair). Unlike an interrupt, the client program is not immediately interrupted and control transfered to the handler. Instead, this event is queued. The top level of an Xt program contains a loop that waits for an event and then dispatches the event by calling the appropriate callback.

Thus, only one callback can occur at any time. The rest of the program is held up until the callback routine has finished.

The execution of Xt programs takes place in three distinct phases. First a connection to the X server is created. Once the connection is formed, a widget that corresponds to the root window of the server display is returned. A client has as its top level a *shell* widget whose parent is the root window. The widgets of the client program are realised and the client program enters its event loop.

Each widget has associated with it a set of *resources*. Resources allow certain aspects about the behaviour or appearance of a widget to be determined either when it is initialised or during execution. Resources are also useful for describing the positioning of widgets on the screen, colouration or internationalisation. Both X11 and Xt are equipped with sophisticated resource database managers.

To illustrate the idiomatic C style for writing X11 software, we show below a (slightly simplified) program that changes the label text of a user interface component (taken from [1]):

```
static int count = 0;

static void setDisplay(Widget display, int i)
{
  char s[10];
  Arg wargs[1];

  sprintf(s, "%d", i);
  XtSetArg(wargs[0],XmNlabelString, s);
  XtSetValues(display, wargs, 1);
}

static void increment(Widget display)
{
  count++;
  setDisplay(display, count);
}

void main()
{
  Widget top, row, button, counter;

  top = XtInitialise();
  row = XmCreateRowColumn("row", top);
  display = XmCreateLabel("display",row);
  button = XmCreatePushButton("button",row);
  setDisplay( display, count );
  XtAddCallback(button, increment, display);
  XtRealizeWidget();
  XtMainLoop();
}
```

The main procedure sets up a connection to the X11 server and creates a hierarchy of widgets. A callback routine is declared for the button, namely increment. Whenever the button is clicked, an event is registered. The XtMainLoop procedure processes this event by looking up and then executing the callback declared for the button (i.e. increment). The increment routine simply updates a global counter variable and then makes the label display the decimal representation of this count as its label text. The label text is modified by updating the label resource (XmNlabelString) for the button widget.

3   Accessing widgets from Haskell

Our method of accessing the various X and widget libraries might be regarded as the most straightforward approach: for every library function that we want to access, we define a Haskell function that calls that function.

Since the X-library functions have various side-effects (the most obvious of which is drawing an image on the screen) it is necessary to ensure that the operations occur in the correct sequence. Previous approaches [8, 7] have guaranteed that actions occur in a strict sequence by sending a list of commands to an interpreter (written in an imperative language) which executes the commands in the order they are received.

A more recent approach (supported by the Glasgow compiler) is to use a *monad* [4] to execute a series of side-effecting actions in a strict sequence. Briefly, the *Glasgow IO monad* provides:

- A data type IO α which is the type of a (possibly side-effecting) action which, when executed, returns a value of type α.

- A mechanism that allows arbitrary code written in an imperative language to be used as an action of type IO α.

- A function returnIO :: $\alpha \to$ IO α which, when executed returns its argument.

- The combinator thenIO :: IO α -> (α -> IO β) -> IO β which combines two actions into one action. When executed, a1 'thenIO' a2 first executes a1 obtaining a result r and then executes the action a2 r.

We refer the reader to [4] for further details.

Using the monadic approach, the main task of providing access to a set of imperative library functions is to define a set of Haskell functions which call the corresponding imperative function. The major difficulty here is in passing values from Haskell into the imperative functions and from imperative functions into Haskell. For simple values such as integers and strings, we were able to use the method of "unboxing" described by Peyton Jones and Launchbury [3]; to allow us to pass more complex values such as callbacks, we made a small, general-purpose extension to the Glasgow compiler.[1]

---

[1] Our initial implementation used a different approach based on the fact that callbacks are only called by the event loop and it is possible to write your own eventloop for X. All we had to do was write callback routines which insert "callback events" into an event queue and replace the event loop with a Haskell loop which repeatedly calls the normal event-handling routines (which might cause callbacks to happen) and then dispatches any callbacks found in the event queue. Since the event loop is written in Haskell, there is no difficulty in calling callback routines written in Haskell.

This basic approach can also be used to translate programs which use the X and widget libraries into Haskell. One further difficulty lies in the implementation of global variables. We use the following solution described by Launchbury in [5].

- The type Var α is an abstract data type of mutable variables of type α.

- Given an initial value x say, executing the operation newVar x allocates a variable with initial value x, and returns a reference to the variable.

- Given a variable v::Var α, executing readVar v reads the current value of the variable v. Similarily, executing writeVar updates the value of the variable.

For example, the program at the end of section 2 may be "translated" into the following Haskell program.

```
>  increment :: Label d => Var Int -> d -> IO ()
>  increment var display =
>    readVar var                              'thenIO' \ count ->
>    writeVar var (count + 1)                 'thenIO' \ _ ->
>    setDisplay display (count + 1)
>
>  setDisplay :: Label d => d -> Int -> IO ()
>  setDisplay display count =
>    setLabel display (LabelString (show count))
>
>  mainIO :: IO ()
>  mainIO =
>    initialise "Xtest"                       'thenIO' \ top ->
>    createRowColumn "row" top                'thenIO' \ row ->
>    createLabel "label" row                  'thenIO' \ display ->
>    createButton "Press Me!" row             'thenIO' \ button ->
>    newVar 0                                 'thenIO' \ countVar ->
>    setDisplay display 0                     'thenIO' \ _ ->
>    addButtonCallback button
>           (increment countVar display) 'thenIO' \ _ ->
>    realizeWidget top                        'thenIO' \ _ ->
>    mainloop
```

The above example illustrates how one might (naively) write GUI's in Haskell: first write the program in C and then translate it into Haskell. However, even if with practice we learn to avoid writing the program in C first, this kind of approach cannot be expected to lead to functional GUIs which are any simpler than their imperative counterparts. The next section discusses an approach which is dramatically simpler than the above.

This approach could be used quite effectively (and efficiently!) by those wishing to apply our overall approach under other compilers.

4 Fudgets

In [1] Carlsson and Hallgren argue that functional languages are better for implementing GUIs because they offer better abstraction facilities. In particular, their approach makes extensive use of higher-order functions to capture common patterns of coding within GUI programs.

The essence of Carlsson and Hallgren's approach is to treat each component of the user-interface as a "black box" (a *Fudget*) receiving input on a single "input pin" and sending output on a single "output pin."

In Carlsson and Hallgren's implementation (see figure 1a), each (primitive) fudget is responsible for (at most) one window whose appearance it controls by sending X-protocol requests to the X-server and which communicates with the fudget by sending X-events to the fudget.

In our implementation (see figure 1b), each (primitive) fudget is responsible for (at most) one widget whose appearance and behaviour is controlled by calling resource setting routines (such as setLabel) and which communicates with the fudget by executing callbacks.

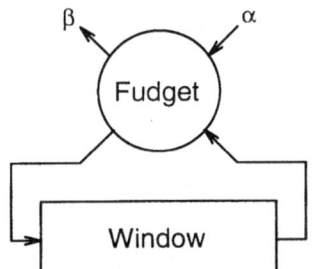

Figure 1a. A Swedish Fudget

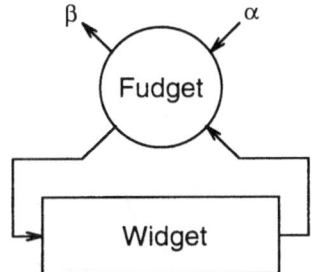

Figure 1b. A Glasgow Fudget

From the programmer's point of view, there is little difference between the two approaches.

Some examples of simple fudgets are:

- button :: String -> F α Click encapsulates the pushButton widget. The String is used as the label displayed on the button. When the user clicks on the button, a value Click[2] is sent to the output pin. (All input is ignored.)

- label :: Text α => F α β encapsulates the label widget used for outputting (small) pieces of text. When a value is received on its input pin, its textual representation is displayed on the label widget. (No output is produced.)

- textField :: F α String encapsulates the text field widget used for inputting (small) pieces of text. When a value is received on its input pin, the current text entered by the user is sent to the output.

It is also useful to create fudgets which are not associated with any widgets at all. Two such fudgets are:

---

[2]In Haskell, the type Click is defined by **data** Click = Click.

- ioToFudget :: $(\alpha \to IO\ \beta) \to (F\ \alpha\ \beta)$ encapsulates an IO operation. When a value is received on its input pin, the IO operation is applied to that value (and executed) and the result is sent to the output pin.

  A typical use of this function is to write the input text to a file or to perform a database transaction on receiving data on the input pin.

- stateMachine :: $((s,\ \alpha) \to (s,\beta)) \to s \to F\ \alpha\ \beta$ encapsulates a piece of local state. When a value is received on its input pin, the input and current state are used to calculate an output and a successor state and the output is sent to the output pin.

The strength of Carlsson and Hallgren's approach lies in the provision of fudget combinators which allow simple fudgets to be combined into more powerful combinators. For example fudget composition is achieved with the combinator <==< :: $F\ \beta\ \gamma \to F\ \alpha\ \beta \to F\ \alpha\ \gamma$ which connects the output of the second fudget to the input of the first fudget (see figure 2). Like function composition, fudget composition is associative.

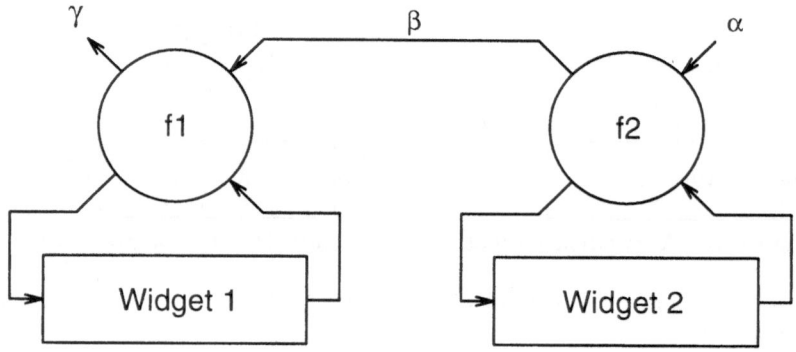

Figure 2. The fudget f1 <==< f2

For example, the example discussed in the previous sections can be implemented as follows (see figure 3):[3]

```
> mainIO :: IO ()
> mainIO = doFudget counter
>
> counter = label 0                       <==<
>           stateMachine count 0          <==<
>           button "Press Me!"
> where
>   count (c, Click) = let c' = c+1 in (c',c')
```

---

[3]The function doFudget :: $F\ \alpha\ \beta \to IO\ ()$ initialises the widgets contained within a fudget and enters the event loop.

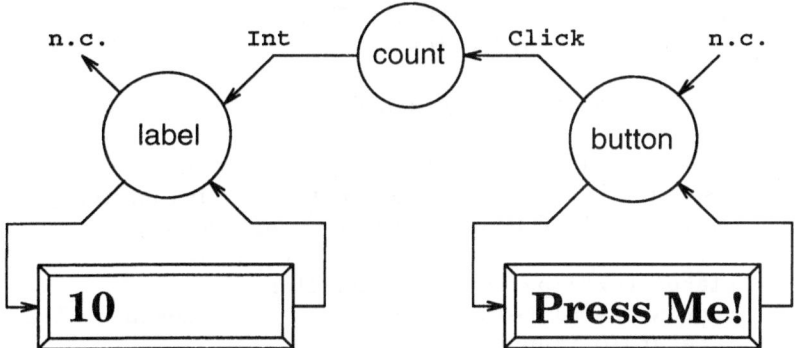

Figure 3. The Counter Fudget

5 Implementation of Fudgets

It is straightforward to implement fudgets using the library discussed in section 3. Our implementation of fudgets is based on the following observations:

- When a fudget is created, we must call the creation function to create the corresponding widget. All creation functions have a **parent** parameter which is used by X-toolkit to create the widget hierarchy. Therefore a fudget must be a function taking (at least) a parent widget as a parameter.

- Since widgets communicate with fudgets by executing callbacks, the simplest way for fudgets to communicate with each other is by executing functions of the same type as callbacks. We call such functions "handlers."

  type Handler α = α → IO ()

  That is, when a fudget is created, it is passed an output handler (which it will call when it wants to send output) and returns an input handler (which is called when it is being sent input).

For these reasons, the type F α β is defined by:

type F α β = Widget → Handler β → IO (Handler α)

The definition of the four fudgets and combinators used in the above example is straightforward:

- The **button** fudget creates a pushbutton widget; adds a callback; and returns an input handler. When the button is pressed, the callback applies the button's output handler to a Click (thus "sending" a Click to the button's output); the button's input handler ignores all input.

```
>   (button text) parent outputHandler =
>     createButton text parent              'thenIO' \ but ->
>     addButtonCallback but
```

```
>                    (outputHandler Click)    'thenIO' \ _ ->
>    returnIO inputHandler
>    where
>    inputHandler a = returnIO ()
```

- The `label` fudget creates a label widget and returns an input handler which sets the label string to the input value's textual representation. The output handler is ignored since labels have no output.

```
>  (label text) parent outputHandler =
>    createLabel text parent               'thenIO' \ lab ->
>    returnIO (inputHandler lab)
>    where
>    (inputHandler lab) a =
>                setLabel lab (LabelString (show a))
```

- The `stateMachine` fudget creates a variable in which to store the state. The input handler returned applies the transition function `f` to the current state and the input value and then updates the state and applies the output handler to the output value.

```
>  (stateMachine f init) parent outputHandler =
>    newVar init                           'thenIO' \ stateVar ->
>    returnIO (inputHandler stateVar)
>    where
>    (inputHandler stateVar) a =
>      readVar stateVar                    'thenIO' \ s ->
>      let (s', b) = f (s, a)
>      in  writeVar stateVar s'            'thenIO' \ _ ->
>          outputHandler b
```

- The fudget composition operation `<==<` creates two fudgets in order.

```
>  (f1 <==< f2) parent outputHandler =
>    f1 parent outputHandler  'thenIO' \ handler ->
>    f2 parent handler        'thenIO' \ inputHandler ->
>    returnIO inputHandler
```

The combinators described so far are, at most concerned with the *local* appearance of the interface: none are concerned with the overall layout of the widgets on the screen. This issue can be tackled in several ways.

1. The default layout of widgets on the screen is determined by the order in which the widgets are created: the first widgets created will be nearer the top or the left-hand side of their parent than the last widgets. Therefore, in a fudget of the form `f1 <==< f2`, (where data flows from right to left) `f1` will appear above or to the left of `f2`.

   A simple way of changing the layout of widgets is to change the order in which they are created. For example, using an alternative fudget combinator $\texttt{>==>} :: \text{F } \alpha \ \beta \rightarrow \text{F } \beta \ \gamma \rightarrow \text{F } \alpha \ \gamma$ (in which data flows from left to right) it is possible to swap the order in which a fudget (or group of fudgets) is created.

This combinator is a little tricky to implement because it is necessary to create the first fudget before its output handler is known. One way to implement this is to use a mutable variable as a "place-holder" until the second fudget is created (when the output handler for the first fudget will be known).[4]

2. Most widget sets provide an extensive range of layout modifiers which allow non-default layouts to be created. For example, the children of a Motif `RowColumn` widget will either be arranged in a row or in a column depending on the current value of the `XmNorientation` resource.

   At present, we provide three such "fudget modifiers": `row`, `column`, `grid` (all of type $F \ \alpha \ \beta \rightarrow F \ \alpha \ \beta$) which arrange the widgets in the fudgets they are applied to in a horizontal row, a vertical column or in a rectangular grid.

6 Problems with Fudgets

We have applied a set of Fudgets based on the above implementation technique to a large industrial project. Overall, our experience of using Fudgets is that they allow one to generate sophisticated interfaces quickly and easily. However, in some circumstances, we found the structured approach required when using Fudgets overly restrictive.

During the summer of 1993, the first author carried out a case study for BT — investigating the suitability of Functional Programming Languages for industrial use [6] — during which we implemented a front end for a small part of BT's database. A (simplified) version of a single screen had the following characteristics:

- When a button is pressed, a query (consisting of a name and an address) is to be sent to the database and the result displayed in an output field.

- Queries are to be "validated" before being sent to the database. (For example, one might check that the name is a non-empty sequence of letters.)

- In the event of an error (whether caused by failing the validation check or an unsuccessful query), an error shell must "popup" and display the error message.

Figure 4 shows the dataflow within this application.

There are three major problems in turning this diagram into a valid fudget:

1. The two search strings must be received simultaneously by the validation section. With the above definition of Fudgets, we must send messages to the two input fudgets requesting them to output their current contents;

---

[4]Peyton-Jones has shown us a simpler solution based on the fixpoint monad operator `fixIO :: ` $(\alpha \rightarrow IO \ \alpha) \rightarrow IO \ \alpha$.

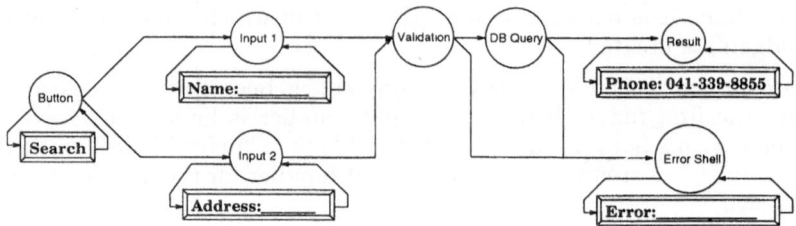

Figure 4. A Database Frontend

there is no possibility of sending these messages "simultaneously" and so no possibility of receiving the responses "simultaneously."

Our solution is to define a second kind of Fudget consisting of those widgets which cannot generate callbacks. Fudgets of this kind can be represented by the type

$$\text{type F2 } \alpha \ \beta = \text{Widget} \rightarrow \text{IO } (\alpha \rightarrow \text{IO } \beta)$$

and combined with the combinator $>|<$ :: F2 $\alpha 1 \ \beta 1 \rightarrow$ F2 $\alpha 2 \ \beta 2 \rightarrow$ F2 $(\alpha 1, \ \alpha 2) \ (\beta 1, \ \beta 2)$ which, on receiving a pair of values, sends the first value to the first fudget and the second value to the second fudget and returns the two replies received.

```
>   (f1 >|< f2) parent =
>     f1 parent                              'thenIO' \ h1 ->
>     f2 parent                              'thenIO' \ h2 ->
>     returnIO (h1 'combine' h2)
>   where
>     (h1 'combine' h2) (a1, a2) =
>       h1 a1                                'thenIO' \ b1 ->
>       h2 a2                                'thenIO' \ b2 ->
>       returnIO (b1, b2)
```

This second kind of fudget is readily converted to the first kind. It is neither possible nor sensible to convert the first kind to the second kind.

Carlsson and Hallgren have confirmed [2] that their implementation of Fudgets suffers from a similar problem though they solve it in a different manner.

2. Both the validation section and the database lookup section have two outputs; with both Carlsson and Hallgren's Fudgets and our own, Fudgets are only allowed to have a single output.

There are two solutions to this problem:

- We might design the validation and database lookup fudgets so that they "tag" their output according to whether it is an error message or a valid result. Special "routing combinators" could use these tags to decide where to send the result.

Problems with this solution are that they tend to introduce a lot of tagging and untagging functions into the program and also, because the dataflow is no longer explicit in the structure of the program, much of the benefit of the Fudget approach is lost.

- An alternative solution is to provide a third kind of Fudget (and associated combinators) with a single input but two outputs. This is perfectly possible but we see no reason to suppose that we won't also find a need for still more kinds of Fudget with two inputs and two outputs, one input and three output, etc.

  The tension here is between providing a small but restrictive library of well-understood components or a larger library of less general, less well-understood components. We favour the former.

3. One aspect of the way the X window system organises windows in hierarchies is that popup shells must be children of the top-level shell to work correctly. On the other hand, we would probably want to use a fudget modifier such as row to control the layout of the other fudgets and so the other fudgets will not be parents of the top-level shell. With the widget combinators and modifiers discussed above, it is not possible for the input widgets and the error widget to have different parents.

   This is just a single instance of a basic problem: in widget-based programs, the overall structure of the visual layout of the interface is determined by the widget hierarchy; in fudget-based programs, the widget hierarchy is determined by the dataflow within the application. That is, the dataflow within the application will determine the overall structure of the visual layout of the interface. It follows that it may be hard or even impossible to obtain a particular visual layout without significantly sacrificing the clarity of the program.

It is worth noting that the last two problems are caused by the structured approach imposed by the use of combinators. In the first case, the problem is that a highly structured approach doesn't seem to be appropriate; while in the second case, there is a clash between the structure imposed by the dataflow and the structure imposed by the visual appearance required of the interface.

7 Conclusions

Till recently, there has been no easy way to create graphical user interfaces in lazy functional languages. Carlsson and Hallgren have implemented a complete widget (or, rather, fudget) set and combinators for combining simple fudgets to create complete applications. Though not without problems, their system is very impressive: it provides a fast and effective way of generating graphical user-interfaces.

The alternative fudget implementation described here suffers from many of the same problems as Carlsson and Hallgren's implementation but differs in one important respect: our implementation approach can be applied to standard widget sets. This has two advantages:

- Applications developed with our fudgets will be consistent with other applications developed with the same widget set (irrespective of which

234

language they are implemented in). In particular, they will have the same "look and feel" and the same resource databases can be used to control their overall colouration, etc.

- It takes a substantial effort to create a widget set. By using pre-existing widget sets, we avoid the need to recreate that effort.

We see two ways of developing this work further:

- Many imperative programmers do not directly write programs like that shown at the end of section 2. Instead, they use a "GUI builder" which allows them to place widgets directly on the screen. The GUI builder automatically generates a program to which the programmer need only add the callback routines.

  We see this approach as a useful way of overcoming one of Fudgets main problems: obtaining the correct layout. We imagine that one would first write the application and then use the GUI builder to rearrange the widgets on screen.

  (We understand that there is a GUI builder for Carlsson and Hallgren's Fudget system though we have not been able to see this builder in operation.)

- Ideally, one would like to model each user interface component as a concurrent function (widget). User interface components then communicate with each other and the client program via streams of messages. This removes the need for callback functions, which are only needed in languages like C because they have no support for concurrency.

  Currently, the Glasgow Haskell compiler does not generate code which can be executed concurrently. However, this facility might be available in a future version. The authors have already built a concurrent X11 interface for Ada which results in much simpler software. An interface in a concurrent Haskell should benefit similarly.

Acknowledgements

The work reported here is based on an Openlook version developed while at Glasgow University's Computing Science Department. The Motif version and (a *considerably extended* variant of) the database example were developed by the first author while working at BT Research Labs on the FLARE project whose support we gratefully acknowledge. Thanks too to Will Partain and Simon Peyton-Jones for their patience in explaining how to extend the Glasgow Haskell Compiler.

References

[1] M. Carlsson and T. Hallgren. Fudgets: A Graphical User Interface in a Lazy Functional Language. In *Proceedings of the Conference on Functional Programming and Computer Architecture*, 1993.

[2] M. Carlsson and T. Hallgren. Private communication. 14 October, 1993.

[3] S.L. Peyton Jones and J. Launchbury. Unboxed values as first class citizens in a non-strict functional languages. In J. Hughes, editor, *Proceedings of the Conference on Functional Programming and Computer Architecture,* pp. 636–666, Cambridge, Massachussets, USA, 26–28 August 1991.

[4] S.L. Peyton-Jones and P. Wadler. Imperative Functional Programming. In *Proceedings of the 1993 Conference on Principles of Programming Languages,* Charleston, ACM, 1993.

[5] J. Launchbury. Lazy Imperative Programming. In *Proceedings of the Workshop on State in Programming Languages,* pp. 46–56, Copenhagen, 1993. (Available as YALEU/DCS/RR-968, Yale University.)

[6] A. Reid. A Window-based Application Front-End in Haskell BT Research Labs, Martlesham Heath. September 1993.

[7] D. Sinclair. Lazy Wafe — Graphical Interfaces for Functional Languages. In Heldal et al., editor, *Glasgow Workshop on Functional Programming,* 1992.

[8] S. Singh. Using XView/X11 from Miranda. In Heldal et al., editor, *Glasgow Workshop on Functional Programming,* 1992.

Profiling Parallel Functional Computations (Without Parallel Machines)

Colin Runciman and David Wakeling
University of York

1. Introduction

Pick up a textbook on functional programming. Somewhere amidst the introductory remarks the author will almost certainly claim that functional languages are well suited for programming parallel computers. But are they? Not, it would seem, without the use of *annotations* to indicate where parallel evaluation should be performed. Such annotations have at least two advantages over a *laissez-faire* approach to parallelism. Firstly, they make it easier to reason about the program's behaviour when it is run on a parallel machine. The annotated program describes both *what* is to be computed and *how* it is to be done, while maintaining a clean separation between the two aspects. Secondly, annotations mean that the compiler does not have to tackle the difficult problem of determining a suitable parallel evaluation strategy for the program. That remains the programmer's responsibility.

Many authors have described annotation schemes for parallel functional programming. Hudak's Para-functional programming [6] allows the programmer to describe the mapping of parallel tasks onto the processor configuration of the machine at hand. Kelly's Caliban [8] requires the program to be transformed so that it corresponds to a process network; annotations are then added to identify the tasks which should be allocated to neighbouring processors. Variants of the *spark model* [3] proposed by Clack and Peyton Jones are widely used: when the program is run, annotated expressions are evaluated in parallel if there is a processor available.

But regardless of the annotation scheme adopted, the central question remains the same: *where should the annotations be placed so as to achieve maximum performance?* Our experience with the spark model has taught us that placing annotations effectively is not always straightforward. They can be as as delicate as jackstraws, and adding or removing one may disturb the balance of others. As a result, developing parallel functional programs can be an uncertain and frustrating business. The crux of the problem is that there are no decent tools to analyse the effect of a particular annotation. It may produce tasks which

---

Authors' address: Department of Computer Science, University of York, Heslington, York YO1 5DD, United Kingdom. Electronic mail: colin@minster.york.ac.uk, dw@minster.york.ac.uk

always perform just a few reductions, or which always collide with other tasks and then have to wait. However, the programmer may only be able to tell that something is amiss from a low-level trace of hardware activity, or from the "processor busy" lights on the front of the machine.

This paper describes the design and use of a new tool for profiling the parallelism present in annotated functional programs. One component of the tool is a compiler modified to produce programs that run in *quasi-parallel* on an ordinary workstation. A quasi-parallel implementation has several advantages for profiling parallelism. Firstly, it allows the programmer to concentrate solely on the details of parallel program design by abstracting away from the details of parallel machine design. No attempt is made to *simulate* the organisation or workings of any particular parallel computer. Secondly, a parallel program's behaviour is *reproducible* at different times and on different computers — a very important property when investigating the causes of poor performance. Finally, it is comparatively easy to experiment with different parallel primitives and evaluation strategies, and to generate different kinds of profiling information. The other component of the tool aids understanding of profiling information by converting it to various different graphical forms.

We are specifically interested in *lazy* parallel functional programs. It can be hard to write an efficient lazy sequential program, and it is at least as hard to write a lazy parallel program as it is to write a lazy sequential one. So, by using a quasi-parallel implementation and ignoring the extra constraints imposed by a parallel computer, we are by no means avoiding "all the hard problems".

2. Profiling Parallelism

Our parallel functional programs are written in Haskell [7] using two extra *combinators*, seq and par. Semantically, the behaviour of these combinators is described by the equations:

$$\text{seq} \perp \text{y} = \perp$$
$$\text{seq x y} = \text{y}$$

$$\text{par x y} = \text{y}$$

Pragmatically, seq arranges for its arguments to be evaluated in *sequence*, x then y, and par arranges for its arguments to be evaluated in *parallel*, x on another processor (if possible) and y on the current processor. As we shall see later, these two combinators are important because together they can be used to control the temporal order of expression evaluation.

During execution of a parallel program, all kinds of activity could be monitored. In this paper, however, we choose to monitor only the *transitions* that tasks make between different states. At any instant, each task is considered to be in one of three states:

- *running*;
- *runnable* (awaiting a processor);
- *blocked* (awaiting another task).

As the program runs, tasks make transitions between these states. For example, when a task is created, its initial state is *running* if there is a processor available, and *runnable* otherwise. Should two tasks collide by evaluating a shared expression, the first task to reach the expression remains *running* and the second task moves from *running* to *blocked*. At the same time, another task can move from *runnable* to *running*. And so on.

The first component of our parallelism profiling tool is an implementation which assigns a unique *tag* to every task. A tag has two parts: the name of the function containing the annotation that created the task, and a global task counter. These are separated by a ".". So, for example, f.372 is one possible tag. Multiple annotations within a single function can be distinguished by numbering them, giving rise to tags such as f/1.372. Sometimes it is useful to be able replace the standard task tags with more informative ones. The first part of the task tag created by a *tracing annotation* is obtained by evaluating a string-valued expression supplied by the programmer.

When the programmer requests a parallelism profile, the program is run as usual, but at each task transition information is written to a log file (see Figure 1). Each line of the log file consists of a reduction number, the abbreviated

```
JOB "queens -n 4"
DATE "Wed Sep 15 09:58:57 1993"
0          *G    MAIN.1
34         *G    pcm/1.2
35         *G    pcm/2.3
36         GR    MAIN.1 (pcm/1.2)
37         G*    pcm/2.3
42         RG    MAIN.1
           G*    pcm/1.2
44         *G    pcm/1.4
45         *G    pcm/2.5
46         GR    MAIN.1 (pcm/1.4)
55         *G    pcm/1.6
56         *G    pcm/2.7
57         GR    pcm/2.5 (pcm/1.6)
65         *G    pcm/1.8
           *A    pcm/1.9
              ...
149375     G*    MAIN.1
```

FIGURE 1.   An extract from the text of a typical log file

names of two task states, and a task tag. In the case of a task collision, the tags of both tasks are recorded. For historical reasons, the running, runnable and blocked task states are abbreviated to 'G' (for *green*), 'A' (for *amber*) and

'R' (for *red*). The void state '*' is used to indicate the creation or destruction of a task.

3. Data Graphics

It is usually hard to discover anything useful about a parallel program by simply inspecting the textual form of a log file — there is just too much data. The second component of our parallelism profiling tool is a program that generates a *parallelism profile graph* from a log file (see Figure 2). A parallelism profile shows how the number of running, runnable and blocked tasks varies over the time that the program takes to run (measured in reductions).

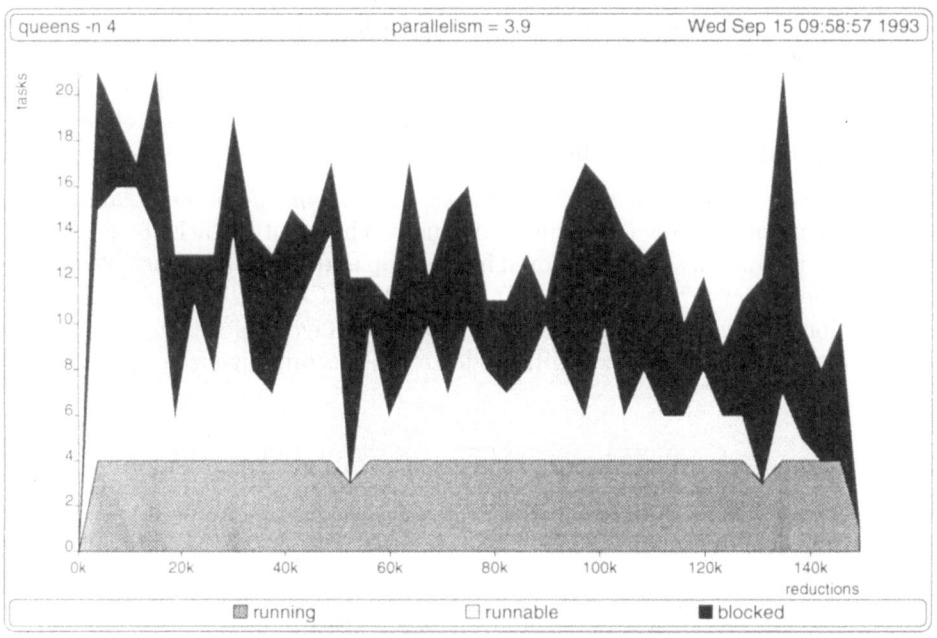

FIGURE 2. An example parallelism profile

The title of the graph gives three pieces of information: the name of the program together with the number of processors available, a figure describing its parallelism, and the date on which it was run. The program in Figure 2 was called "queens", and it was run on a four processor machine. If the number of processors is not specified, then an unlimited number were available. The parallelism figure is calculated as the area of the band representing running tasks divided by the time that the program takes to run. When the number of processors is unlimited, this is the *average parallelism* as defined by Eager [4].

4. Implementation

Our implementation centres on a version of the standard Chalmers HBC compiler modified to produce programs that run in *quasi-parallel* on an ordinary workstation. Below, we shall assume some familiarity with both the Chalmers compiler and the basics of parallel graph reduction; for those without such familiarity, we strongly recommend Augustsson and Johnsson's overview paper [2] and Peyton Jones' textbook [9].

The easiest way to make a quasi-parallel HBC compiler is to extend the standard G-machine to allow multiple threads of control, each represented by a different task. The processor switches between these tasks giving each a small "slice" of its time. This immediately raises the question of how large a slice should be. A balance must be struck between efficiency and accuracy. If the slice is too small, then the overhead of switching will be too great. If it is too large, then significant interactions between tasks will be lost because they do not all progress simultaneously. From the profiling perspective, interactions between tasks are of considerable importance. So, in our implementation, running tasks are scheduled round-robin, with a processor slice of just one (lambda-lifted) function application.

For us, it is essential that tasks incur a *very low memory overhead*, allowing a very large number to be active simultaneously. The pointer stack of each task is broken up into small segments stored in the heap and linked together. When the G-machine makes a "subroutine call" via an EVAL, CALLFUN or CALLGLOBAL instruction, a new *stack frame* is allocated whose layout is shown in Figure 3. Three registers are associated with each frame: the *frame pointer* fp, the *stack*

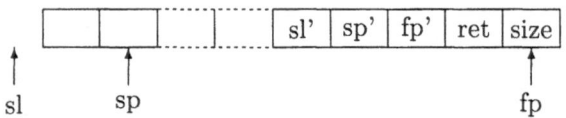

FIGURE 3.   Layout of a stack frame

pointer sp, and the *stack limit* sl. When a new frame is created, the previous values of these registers are saved in the topmost locations along with a return address. The RET instruction restores the saved registers before jumping to the return address. An EVAL instruction allocates a frame of just 12 words, while the two CALL instructions allocate a frame whose size is calculated by rounding the number of arguments supplied up to the next multiple of 8, and then adding 4. Of course, such small stack frames could easily overflow, and so a test for stack overflow must be made at the start of the code for each function and in the code for the UNWIND instruction. When an overflow is about to occur a new stack frame with sufficient extra space is allocated in the heap and the contents of the old frame are copied to the new one.

In [1], Augustsson and Johnsson observed that about 70% of EVAL instructions immediately encounter a node in normal form. When this happens, the stack frame set aside for the EVAL is not used. Our implementation avoids this waste by using a *testing* EVAL instruction which allocates a new stack frame only when it encounters a node that is *not* in normal form. Augustsson and Johnsson originally proposed the testing EVAL to avoid breaking the processor's pipeline unnecessarily, whereas here we use it to avoid allocating storage unnecessarily.

As the reader may have already summised, the result of our modifications is not the world's most efficient implementation of graph reduction! Quasi-parallel evaluation adds a lot of interpretive machinery to the run-time system, and it all costs. But, so far, performance has not been a real problem — even using quite modest hardware. Compared with code produced by the standard HBC compiler, our sequential code runs 3–6 times as slowly, and our parallel code (on a machine with unlimited processors) runs 4–9 times as slowly.

5. The Aim of the Game

When developing a parallel program, our aim is to replace a long computation performed by a single task with a short computation performed by many tasks in parallel. That is, we aim to turn "short wide" profiles into "tall narrow" ones. In doing so, we try to attain a perfect trade-off between the number of processors (the height of the profile) and the number of reduction steps (the width of the profile). Ideally, the product of the two remains constant; in practice, we try to minimise its increase. It follows that we prefer smooth profiles to those showing eratic spikes of parallel activity. Also, task-blocking is something to be avoided so far as possible. As the size of input data rises, these properties should continue to hold. Just as we prefer sequential programs whose costs rise only linearly with data size, so-called "optimal parallel" algorithms have the property [5]:

$$\text{no. of processors} \times \text{computation time} = O(n)$$

We deliberately ignore (in this paper) the cost of communication between tasks, excepting only the cost of keeping a task that is blocked waiting for another to reduce something. We also ignore the cost of scheduling, so that granularity of tasks is not an issue.

6. An Example

In May 1984, the Yorkshire Evening Press ran a word search competition, the prize for which was a soda siphon for making fizzy drinks from tubes of concentrated ingredients. The idea of a word search is as follows: certain words are hidden horizontally, vertically and diagonally in a grid of letters. The hidden words may be written both forwards and backwards. Given the list of hidden words and the grid of letters, the aim is to locate the words within the grid.

Below, we give the core of **soda**, a Haskell program which performs the word search for the original competition (the rest of the program can be found in Appendix A). We shall take this program as our example.

```
main = appendChan stdout (concat (map find hidden)) abort done
    where
    find word = word ++ " " ++ concat dirs ++ "\n"
        where
        dirs = map snd (
            filter (any (contains word) . fst)
                [(r,"right "), (d,"down "),
                 (dl,"downleft "), (ul,"upleft ")]
            ++
            filter (any (contains drow) . fst)
                [(r,"left "), (d,"up "),
                 (dl,"upright "), (ul,"downright ")] )
        drow = reverse word
    r  = grid
    d  = transpose grid
    dl = diagonals grid
    ul = diagonals (reverse grid)
```

The **soda** program works by applying a **find** function to each of the hidden words in turn. This function looks for a word written forwards or backwards in the rows of four different grids: the original grid, and three derived grids representing its columns and diagonals. An application of **find** returns all the directions in which the word was found.

Version 0. When the **soda** program is run sequentially, a single task takes a little over 91k reductions to find the 12 hidden words (see Figure 4).

Version 1. It is natural to search for all the hidden words in parallel. In the **soda** program, the search is expressed as (**map find hidden**). So our first idea is to replace the sequential **map** with a parallel **parmap**, performing each **find** application in parallel.

There are various possible definitions of the **parmap** function. The one that we shall use is

```
        parmap f [] = []
        parmap f (x:xs) = par fx (seq fxs (fx :  fxs))
               where
               fx = f x
               fxs = parmap f xs
```

An alternative definition uses a second **par** in place of **seq**, but this runs counter

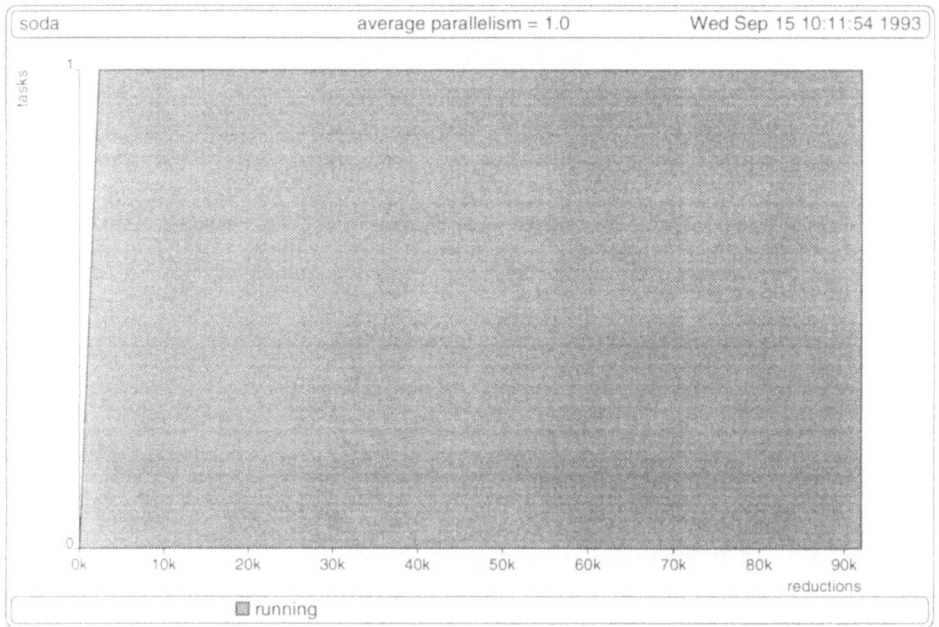

FIGURE 4. Parallelism profile for version 0

to the intuition that `parmap` creates one task for each list item*.

Unfortunately, (`parmap find hidden`) results in a profile which is almost indistinguishable from that of version 0!

Version 2. Our use of `parmap` fails because all the tasks it creates terminate almost immediately. The problem is with the intuition that `parmap` "evaluates every item of its result list in parallel". This is a half-truth. It actually evaluates every item of its result list to *normal form* in parallel. In `soda`, the items of `parmap`'s result list are applications of `find` to the various hidden words. Each of these applications requires just *one reduction* to reach normal form! This (`++`) reduction produces the first character of the one-line report. The search itself is not even begun.

Clearly, we must complete searching for a result before reporting one. The search is only complete when we have the full list of directions in which the word was found. In the definition of `find` below, the `seq` combinator and the function `unilist` are used to ensure that the search is complete before the result is reported.

---

* Little parallelism is lost by adopting the single `par` version, unless the cost of traversing the list spine exceeds that of computing a result of `f`.

```
find word = seq (unilist dirs)
(word ++ " " ++ concat dirs ++ "\n")
```

The function `unilist` is defined in terms of `unimap` by the equation:

```
unilist = unimap id
```

An application `unimap` `f` to a list has a void result, but the process of evaluating it ensures that the list has a fully evaluated spine, and that each item in it is evaluated as far as the strictness of `f` requires.

```
unimap f [] = ()
unimap f (x:xs) = seq (f x) (unimap f xs)
```

Figure 5 shows the effect of these modifications.

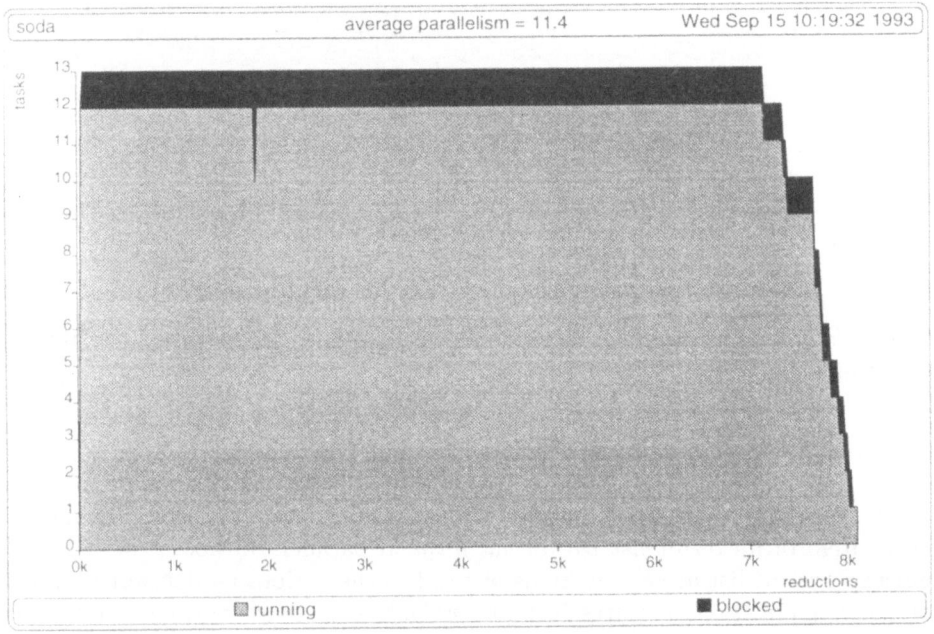

FIGURE 5. Parallelism profile for version 2

Version 3. Things are now much better. As Figure 5 shows, there are 12 tasks searching for the 12 hidden words, while the main task blocks waiting for their results. The program exhibits an average parallelism of 11.4. However, the sharp downward spike indicates that the searching tasks do block. Examining the log file, we can see that this is because the transposed and/or diagonalised versions of the original word grid are not yet fully evaluated when the searching tasks come to need them. To avoid this blocking, we can evaluate the transposed and diagonalised grids in parallel with the search of the plain grid. As with `dirs` above, we ensure a sufficient degree of evaluation in the derived grids by applying `unigrid` (defined as `unimap unilist`) to them. The soda program now begins

```
main = par (unigrid d)
(par (unigrid dl) (par (unigrid ul) (...
```

Figure 6 shows the result of this modification.

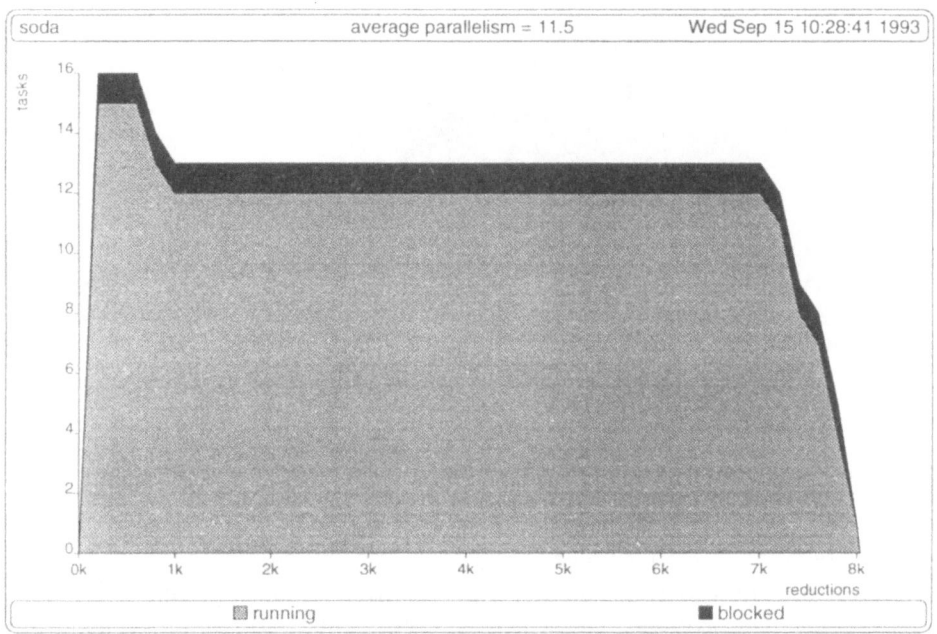

FIGURE 6. Parallelism profile for version 3

Version 4. Although the searching tasks no longer block and there is a slight increase in the maximum number of active tasks, the average parallelism is almost unchanged at 11.5. We want more parallelism than this, to make use of more processors. It seems that the two filters which look for a word written forwards and written backwards could proceed in parallel. So we name the two `filter` applications and redefine `dirs` as

```
dirs = par forw (seq back (map snd (forw ++ back)))
forw = filter (any (contains word) .  fst)
       [(r,"right "), (d,"down "),
       (dl,"downleft "), (ul,"upleft ")]
back = filter (any (contains drow) .  fst)
       [(r,"left "), (d,"up "),
       (dl,"upright "), (ul,"downright ")]
```

Figure 7 shows the resulting profile of parallel activity.

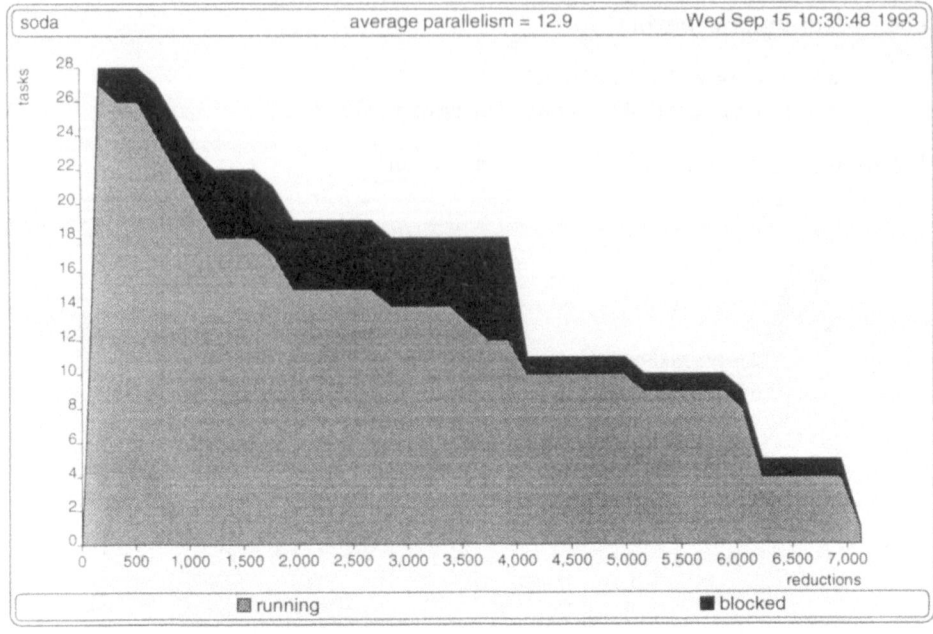

FIGURE 7. Parallelism profile for version 4

Version 5. The program now takes a little over 7k quasi-parallel reductions to run, and the average parallelism is 12.9. This is an improvement, but nothing like the factor of two that we might have hoped for. About half way through the computation there is a sharp drop in the number of searching tasks. Prior to that point several of the searching tasks are blocked. With the aid of tracing annotations, we can obtain enough information to explain this behaviour. Consider the `dirs` task searching for some particular `word`. Its action depends on whether it is `back` (computed by the task itself) or `forw` (computed by a parallel auxiliary) that reaches normal form first, on finding an instance of the word. If it is `back`, the `dirs` task blocks waiting for `forw` before starting to reduce `forw ++ back`. If it is `forw`, the `dirs` task continues alone, computing `back` before proceeding to the `++` application. But *in either case* the `dirs` task must later complete the evaluation of either `back` or `forw` previously reduced only as far as its first item. This is because `find` demands the whole of the `dirs` list — that is, *all* directions in which the word can be found.

We must ensure that the `forw` and `back` filter tasks complete only when they have looked for the word in all four directions. Since the evaluation of `dirs` is forced by the `unilist` application in `find`, the evaluation of `forw` is also forced. To force evaluation of `back`, we make use of `unilist` again.

```
dirs = par (unilist back) (map snd (forw ++ back))
```

The effect of forcing **forw** and **back** is shown in Figure 8.

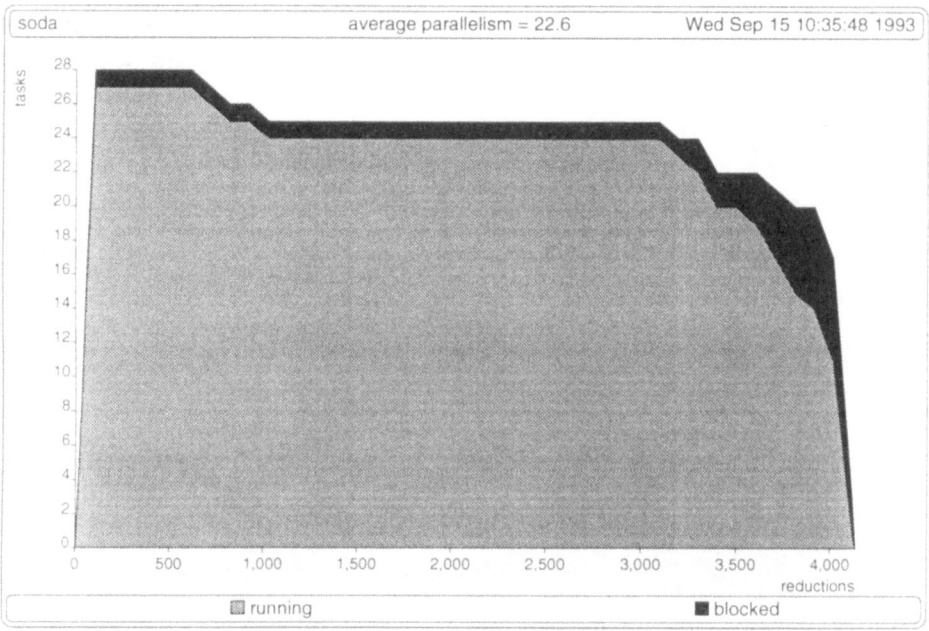

FIGURE 8. Parallelism profile for version 5

Version 6. As Figure 8 shows, the improvement is now close to the factor of two that we originally hoped for: the program now takes a little over 4k quasi-parallel reductions to run, and the average parallelism is 22.6.

What if we take a more aggressive approach to parallel search by putting parallelism into the "inner loop"? Searching each parallel line of letters in parallel introduces speculation — since a result can be returned from the first such line to contain the word — so is it worth it? Assuming that word occurrences are rare, very little such speculation would venture uselessly beyond the point where the sequential computation yields a result. So we define **parany = or . parmap** and replace **any** by **parany** in each of **forw** and **back**.

```
forw = filter (parany (contains word) .  fst)
       [(r,"right "), (d,"down "),
       (dl,"downleft "), (ul,"upleft ")]
```

```
back = filter (parany (contains drow) .  fst)
       [(r,"left "), (d,"up "),
        (dl,"upright "), (ul,"downright ")]
```

Figure 9 shows that the result of this modification is a large increase in the amount of parallel activity. The program now takes about 800 quasi-parallel

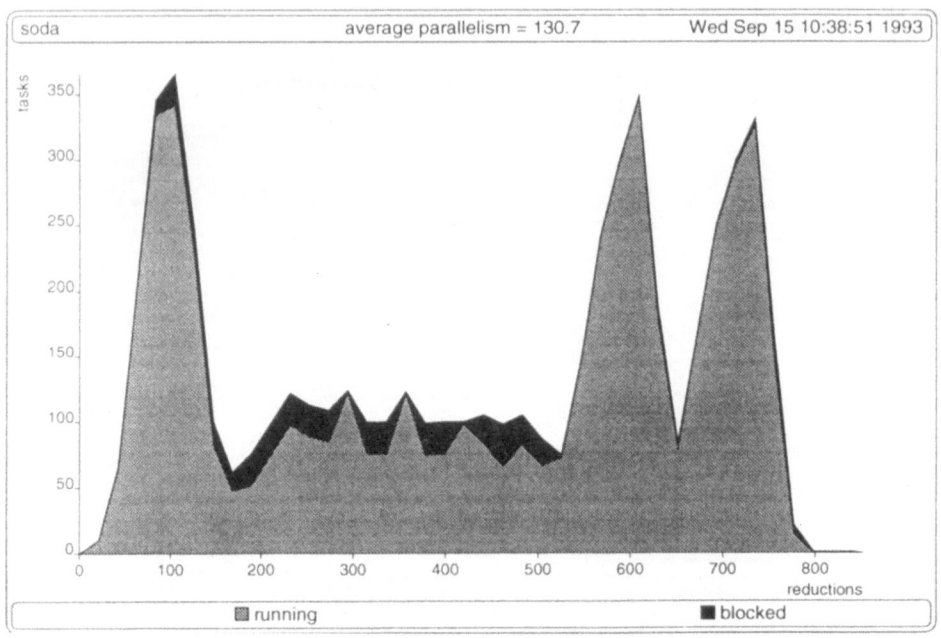

FIGURE 9. Parallelism profile for version 6

reductions to run, and the average parallelism is 130.7.

Experiment shows that a single sequentially computed grid-extraction takes around 800 reductions. We have reached the stage where grid-extraction dominates and determines the limit of parallel speed-up. Assuming the list representation, grid-extraction does not seem amenable to parallel evaluation. So we shall "declare" at this point, to consider the relationship between the results obtained using our quasi-parallel evaluator and those obtained using a real parallel evaluator.

7. Quasi-parallel and Parallel Evaluation

Figure 10 plots the speedup of the quasi-parallel evaluator *vs* the speedup of the Glasgow GRIP machine for 5 versions of the soda program. There are 14 data points for each program version, recording the results for 1–14 processors.

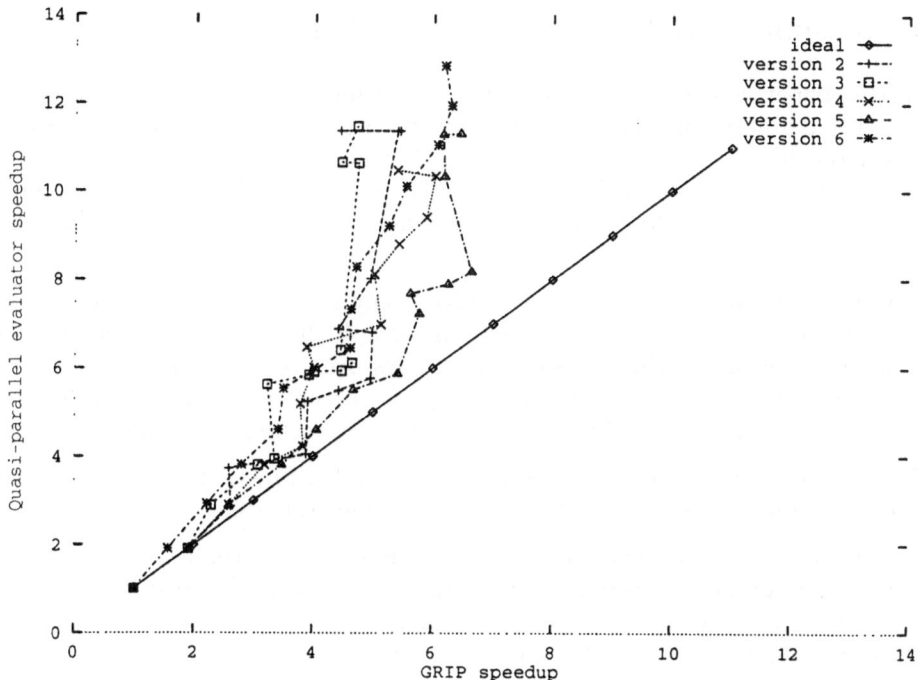

FIGURE 10. Speedup of quasi-parallel evaluator *vs* speedup of GRIP

For small numbers of processors, there is good agreement between the two implementations. A speedup of around 4 is recorded by both using 5 processors. Thereafter, the speedups diverge — presumably as costs ignored by the quasi-parallel evaluator, such as interprocessor communication and garbage collection, become significant for GRIP.

Our hypothesis is that good quasi-parallel performance is necessary, but not sufficient, for good parallel performance. This hypothesis forms the basis of an experimental parallel program development method. Briefly, the method involves profiling a program and improving its quasi-parallel performance until it is satisfactory. Thereafter, the program is transferred to the GRIP machine (say) where the remining problems of locality and communication are resolved.

In practice, of course, things are never this clinical. The definition of satisfactory quasi-parallel performance is strongly influenced by the capabilities of the parallel machine at hand. For some machines, a large number of tasks with small granularity may be appropriate; for others, the reverse may be true. Figure 8 and Figure 10, for example, suggest that version 5 of the soda program may be best for the GRIP machine with 14 processors.

8. Summary, Related and Future Work

In this paper we have described a tool for profiling the parallelism present in annotated functional programs. The tool allows the programmer to concentrate solely on the details of parallel program design by abstracting away from the details of parallel machine design. For small programs, and for a modest number of processors, its results are in close agreement with those from a real parallel machine.

The tool described is quite basic. It uses only a fraction of the information available in a log file to produce a simple graph showing how the number of tasks in each of the three basic states varies over time. Nonetheless, it has already proved useful as a second system for users of the GRIP machine to compare the quasi-parallel and parallel behaviour of their programs.

Others have investigated the behaviour of parallel functional programs with the aid of different quasi-parallel implementations [11, 10].

We are currently working on increasing the amount of information recorded in a log file, and on new ways of presenting this information. For example, we have started recording which functions are applied by each task and how frequently, drawing graphs which highlight task collisions and processor utilisation, and designing a simple query language for examining log files.

Acknowledgements

Our thanks as always to Lennart Augustsson and Thomas Johnsson, whose work on the HBC compiler forms the basis of our own. Thanks also to Jim Mattson who ran the soda program on the GRIP machine for us on several occasions, always at short notice and with great care.

This work was funded by the Science and Engineering Research Council.

Appendix A. The Soda Program Auxiliaries

This appendix contains the auxiliary definitions of the soda program — the definition of the main function was given in Section 6.

```
diagonals [r] = map (:[]) r
diagonals (r:rs) = zipinit r ([]:diagonals rs)

zipinit [] ys = ys
zipinit (x:xs) (y:ys) = (x : y) : zipinit xs ys

contains xs ys = any (prefix xs) (suffixes ys)

suffixes [] = []
suffixes xs = xs : suffixes (tail xs)

prefix [] ys = True
```

```
prefix xs [] = False
prefix (x:xs) (y:ys) = x == y && prefix xs ys

grid =
  [['Y', 'I', 'O', 'M', 'R', 'E', 'S', 'K', 'S', 'T'],
   ['A', 'E', 'H', 'Y', 'G', 'E', 'H', 'E', 'D', 'W'],
   ['Z', 'F', 'I', 'A', 'C', 'N', 'I', 'T', 'I', 'A'],
   ['N', 'T', 'O', 'C', 'O', 'M', 'V', 'O', 'O', 'R'],
   ['E', 'R', 'D', 'L', 'O', 'C', 'E', 'N', 'S', 'M'],
   ['Z', 'O', 'U', 'R', 'P', 'S', 'R', 'N', 'D', 'A'],
   ['O', 'Y', 'A', 'S', 'M', 'O', 'Y', 'E', 'D', 'L'],
   ['R', 'N', 'D', 'E', 'N', 'L', 'O', 'A', 'I', 'T'],
   ['F', 'I', 'W', 'I', 'N', 'T', 'E', 'R', 'R', 'C'],
   ['F', 'E', 'Z', 'E', 'E', 'R', 'F', 'T', 'F', 'I'],
   ['I', 'I', 'D', 'T', 'P', 'H', 'U', 'B', 'R', 'L'],
   ['C', 'N', 'O', 'H', 'S', 'G', 'E', 'I', 'O', 'N'],
   ['E', 'G', 'M', 'O', 'P', 'S', 'T', 'A', 'S', 'O'],
   ['T', 'G', 'F', 'F', 'C', 'I', 'S', 'H', 'T', 'H'],
   ['O', 'T', 'B', 'C', 'S', 'S', 'N', 'O', 'W', 'I']]

hidden =
  ["COSY", "SOFT", "WINTER", "SHIVER", "FROZEN", "SNOW",
   "WARM", "HEAT", "COLD",  "FREEZE", "FROST",  "ICE" ]
```

References

1. L. Augustsson and T. Johnsson. Parallel Graph Reduction with the ⟨ν,G⟩-machine. In *Proceedings of the 1989 Conference on Functional Programming Languages and Computer Architecture*, pages 202–213. ACM Press, September 1989.
2. L. Augustsson and T. Johnsson. The Chalmers Lazy-ML Compiler. *Computer Journal*, 32(2):127–141, April 1989.
3. C. Clack and S. L. Peyton Jones. The Four-Stroke Reduction Engine. In *Proceedings of the 1986 ACM Symposium on LISP and Functional Programming*, pages 220–232. ACM Press, August 1986.
4. D. L. Eager, J. Zahorjan, and E. D. Lazowska. Speedup Versus Efficiency in Parallel Systems. Technical Report 86-12, Department of Computational Science, University of Saskatchewan, August 1986.
5. A. Gibson and W. Rytter. *Efficient Parallel algorithms*. Cambridge University Press, 1988.
6. P. Hudak. Para-functional Programming in Haskell. In B. K. Szymanski, editor, *Parallel Functional Languages and Compilers*, chapter 5, pages 159–196. Addison-Wesley (Reading), 1991.
7. P. Hudak, S. L. Peyton Jones, Arvind, B. Boutel, J. Fairbairn, J. Fasel, M. Guzman, K. Hammond, J. Hughes, T. Johnsson, R. Kieburtz, R. S. Nikhil, W. Partain, and J. Peterson. Report on the Functional Programming Language Haskell, Version 1.2. *SIGPLAN Notices*, 27(5), May 1992.
8. P. H. J. Kelly. *Functional Programming for Loosely-Coupled Multiprocessors*. MIT Press, 1989.
9. S. L. Peyton Jones. *The Implementation of Functional Programming Languages*. Prentice-Hall, 1987.
10. R. Plasmeijer and M. van Eekelen. *Functional Programming and Parallel Graph Rewriting*. Addison Wesley, 1993.
11. P. Roe. *Parallel Programming Using Functional Languages*. PhD thesis, University of Glasgow, April 1991.

Time Profiling a Lazy Functional Compiler

Patrick M. Sansom*
University of Glasgow
Glasgow G12 8QQ
Scotland
sansom@dcs.glasgow.ac.uk

Abstract

Recent years has seen the development of profiling tools for lazy functional language implementations. This paper presents the results of using a time profiler to profile the Glasgow Haskell compiler. So far as we know ghc is the only lazy functional language compiler to support source-level time profiling. The benefits of having such a tool can be spectacular, as this paper demonstrates.

1 Introduction

As the use of lazy functional languages for applications programming has grown there has been a strong call for source-level profiling tools to aid the applications programmer in the identification of execution hot-spots and inefficiencies. Recent years has seen a significant response to this need with a number of profiling tools being proposed and developed [1,6,7,9].

The Glasgow Haskell compiler, ghc, incorporates a profiling technique based on *cost centres*. These enable both the execution *time* and *space* consumption of the program to be profiled. The ideas were first presented in [9], but have undergone significant changes since then. We have now implemented a profiling semantics similar to that described in [1].

A paper by Runciman and Wakeling presents the results of heap-profiling the Chalmers hbc/lml compiler [8]. This paper continues in the same vein, profiling the Glasgow Haskell compiler, with the emphasis on the results of the *time profiler*.

2 Profiling with Cost Centres

The ghc profiler is based on "cost centres". Source expressions of interest are annotated with cost centre labels. This can be done explicitly by the programmer using an scc ("set cost centre") expression annotation or, alternatively, the compiler can be instructed to annotate the top level expressions within a module. For example, the annotation

---
*The author gratefully acknowledges the support of the Commonwealth Scholarship Commission.

```
scc "sorting" (sort xs)
```

attributes the costs of executing (`sort xs`) to the cost centre `"sorting"`. Only the costs of doing the sorting are so attributed; the costs of evaluating `xs` are not, *even though its evaluation may occur interleaved with the sorting process.* These costs are attributed to the code which constructed `xs`.

Furthermore, *all* the costs of evaluating `sort` are attributed to `"sorting"`, including the costs of executing any functions called by `sort`. This applies even if those functions are also called from elsewhere, which is especially common in a polymorphic functional language.

Finally we note that *costs are only attributed to the immediately enclosing (or calling) cost centre.* The costs of evaluating any `scc` annotated sub-expressions, within sort or any functions called by sort, will be attributed to the sub-cost-centre, not `"sorting"`. We provide an indication of these sub-costs, which are not attributed to the cost centre, by reporting the number of `scc` sub-expressions evaluated.

The main contributions made by the Glasgow Haskell profiler are:

- Time profiling which is related back to the original source[1]. The transformations within the compiler preserve the attribution of costs.

- The subsuming of costs up the call graph. This provides a logical aggregation of costs:

  - The costs of functions called from many places are attributes separately to their call sites.

  - The costs of a large nest of function calls can be aggregated together.

This is especially important when profiling large programs.

2.1 Implementation

We have implemented the profiling scheme within the Glasgow Haskell compiler [5] which is based on the STG-machine technology [4].

Every heap-allocated closure has an extra field which identifies the cost centre for the lexical scope which encloses the expression. The cost centre for the currently-executing computation is identified by a global register. This *current cost centre* is stored in each closure when it is constructed. Whenever a closure is entered the register is set from the cost centre stored in the closure. Normally a closure is entered as a tail call, so the cost centre of the entering expression can be safely overwritten as it has just completed. Evaluation of a **case** is the only situation where the evaluation sequence enters a closure and subsequently returns to the scope of the entering expression. The cost centre of the entering expression is saved before evaluating the **case** scrutinee and restored when the evaluation has completed.

---

[1]Profiling tools, such as UNIX `prof`, have been used to profile the code generated by functional compilers. However they relate the profiling data back to the code generated by the compiler, not to the original source. Though this may be of some use to the compiler writer, who has a notion of the relationship between the code generated by the compiler and the original source, it is not suitable for an applications programmer.

Any costs of unprofiled top-level functions are subsumed by the caller, as if the function was unfolded at the call site. This is achieved by leaving the caller's cost centre in the cost centre register on entry; i.e. the cost centre register is not set when an inherited function is entered. This mechanism provides dynamic inheritance of costs to the logically enclosing cost centre.

2.2 Profiling Output

The main outputs of the profiling tool are an aggregate time profile and a serial heap profile.

The **aggregate time profile** presents the proportion of execution time and heap allocation attributed to each cost centre. An example profile is depicted in Figure 1. For each scc-annotated expression the time profile reports:

- The number of times the scc annotated expression was evaluated. If the entire body of a function is annotated with an scc expression the scc entry count is the number of function calls.

- The number of scc annotated sub-expressions evaluated. The costs of these sub-expressions are not attributed to the cost centre.

- The proportion of CPU time spent executing this expression. (The *current cost centre* is sampled every 20ms.)

- The proportion of the total heap allocation which was allocated by the execution of this expression. (The space allocation for each closure is attributed to the cost centre stored in the closure.)

The **serial heap profile** shows the closures occupying the heap over the execution of the program (Figure 2). It is constructed by scanning the entire live heap at regular intervals during execution. During each scan information about the closures currently occupying the heap is gathered and stored in a file. The heap profile can be limited to a particular subset of closures by instructing the profiler to gather only information about closures with a particular cost centre and/or of a particular *type* etc. This is very similar to the heap profiler provided by the Chalmers hbc/lml compiler [6,8]. Indeed the same post processor (hp2ps) is used to provide the graphical visualisation.

There is one important difference: our heap profile uses logical cost centre aggregation rather than the static module / group aggregations provided by the hbc/lml profiler. For example, Figure 2 of Runciman & Wakeling's paper [8] has a large "band" attributed to lib (the standard prelude) rather than to the user's program source. The ghc profiler attributes the closures constructed by the standard prelude to the cost centre responsible for calling the standard prelude function.

We are also beginning to experiment with a **serial time profile** which reports the execution time attributed to each cost centre for each time interval.

3 Profiling our Compiler

To evaluate the effectiveness of our compiler, we undertook the (somewhat incestuous) task of profiling the Glasgow Haskell compiler, with the aim of

```
        Sat Jun 26 11:52 1993 Time and Allocation Profiling Report

        hsc-0.13   +RTS -H25M -p -RTS   -C -hi ...

        total time  =        240.48 secs   (12024 ticks @ 20 ms)
        total alloc = 619,779,088 bytes   (51846277 closures)


    COST CENTRE      MODULE       GROUP        scc subcc  %time %alloc
    TypeChecker      Main         main          1     0   45.4   44.6
    Renamer          Main         main          1     0   25.0   27.0
    builtinEnv       Main         main          1     0    7.6   14.4
    PrintRealC       Main         main          1     0    4.5    4.3
    Core2Core        Main         main          1     0    3.9    2.5
    MAIN             MAIN         MAIN          1     1    2.7    2.7
    CodeGen          Main         main          1     0    1.5    1.1
    rdImports        ReadPrefix   reader        1     0    1.4    1.1
    Stg2Stg          Main         main          1     0    1.1    0.5
    FlattenAbsC      Main         main          1     0    0.7    0.5
    cvModule         Main         main          1     1    0.6    0.5
    Core2Stg         Main         main          1     0    0.6    0.3
    rdModule         Main         main          1     1    0.4    0.1
     ...
```

Figure 1: Time Profile for the GHC compiler (compiling `TcExpr.lhs`)

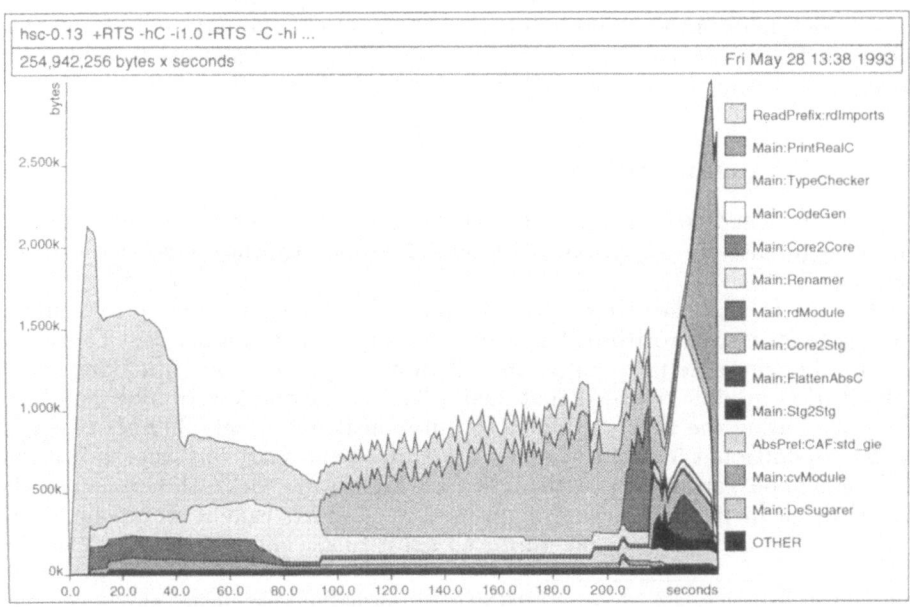

Figure 2: Heap Profile by Cost Centre (compiling `TcExpr.lhs`)

identifying its inefficiencies and improving them. First the compiler was annotated with `scc` expression around the major passes, providing logical groupings of the execution required by each pass. Figure 1 shows the time profile of the compiler compiling one of its own modules (`TcExpr.lhs`). Each cost centre (except `MAIN`) corresponds to a particular pass of the compiler. `MAIN` is the initial cost centre — it is not introduced by an annotation. It is attributed with the costs of processing the request dialogue, as this is outside the scope of the source program. For the `ghc` compiler this consists of the actual character I/O.

The compilation required 240 seconds of profiled execution time on our SS10-41. 45% of that time is spent in the typechecker and 25% in the renamer with a further 7% spent in the built-in name environments (`builtinEnv`) by the renamer. As these passes take up a large proportion of the execution time they are the obvious places to focus on when optimising the compiler.

The profile also reveals that the rate of allocation is not constant across the different passes in the compiler — the %time and %alloc figures often differ (e.g. `lookupSubst` in Figure 3). This raises a question about the validity of using allocation to compare the effectiveness of different compiler optimisations.

A heap profile of the same compilation is shown in Figure 2. It reveals a space leak late in the compiler, which turns out to be in the code generator. Our focus in this paper is on reducing compilation *time*, rather than *space* so we do not investigate the code-generator space leak here. Of course, space usage does have an indirect time cost, because it increases garbage-collection overheads. Unprofiled compilation of `TcExpr.lhs` with a 10Mb heap imposes a generational GC overhead of about 10%[2]. Reducing the space requirements can only improve compilation time by a fraction of this amount.

These initial profiles were produced after a lazy pattern matching space leak, which held onto *all* the input until the name of the output filename was demanded, was identified and removed. This bug was identical to a bug discovered in the `hbc/lml` compiler a year earlier [8,11]!

3.1 Execution Hot Spots

Figure 1 revealed two execution hot spots: the type checker and the renamer. However further investigation was required to identify the cause of the inefficiencies.

For the typechecker we suspected that the inefficiencies were due to inefficient substitution algorithms based on a simple association list, but had never previously been able to quantify this. Annotating each of the functions in the substitution module revealed that nearly 36% of the entire compilation time is spent extending the substitution (a routine consisting of only 30 lines of code), with an additional 5% of the execution time spent searching the association list for a type variable's substitution (see Figure 3). Once the extent of the substitution inefficiencies were quantified we decided that it would be worth investing the time to develop improved substitution algorithms which used a

---

[2]This 10% garbage-collection overhead assumes the machine has enough physical memory to avoid paging. If paging overheads are significant, reducing the space requirements to enable efficient execution with a smaller heap can result in substantial reductions in elapsed execution time.

```
      Sun Jun 27 21:46 1993 Time and Allocation Profiling Report

      hsc-0.13  +RTS -H25M -p -RTS   -C -hi ...

      total time  =      230.20 secs   (11510 ticks @ 20 ms)
      total alloc = 619,779,216 bytes  (51846289 closures)

  COST CENTRE        MODULE      GROUP         scc  subcc  %time %alloc
  extendSubst        Subst       basicTypes   1304  28768   35.5   43.6
  buildLookupFn      NameEnv     envs         2617      0   28.3   38.0
  PrintRealC         Main        main            1      0    4.9    4.3
  lookupSubst        Subst       basicTypes  30678      0    4.8    0.0
  Rename             Main        main            1   2617    3.9    3.4
  CoreSimplify       SimplCore   simplCore       2   9542    3.9    2.0
  TypeChecker        Main        main            1   4035    3.5    0.8
  ...
```

Figure 3: Further Time Profile Breakdown (compiling TcExpr.lhs)

mutable array data structure. This is described in Section 3.3. First, though we address the inefficiencies in the renamer.

3.2 The Renamer

The job of the renamer is to resolve the scoping of source identifiers, replacing them with unique integers. We suspected that string-based lookups in name environments were consuming a lot of the time. Annotating the function which constructed and returned a function to look up names in an environment revealed that a total of 28% of the entire compilation time was spent building environments and looking up strings within them (see Figure 3). More significantly, the function buildLookupFn was called a total of 2617 times, resulting in the construction of 2617 environment lookup functions! This was very suspicious, as there are only 47 environments required (7 explicit environments plus 2 for each of 20 modules imported). This certainly does not account for the construction of 2617 environment lookup functions!

The current name environment implementation uses different algorithms depending on the number of elements in the environment.

- A simple unordered list search is used for small (less than 8 element) environments.

- If the environment is already sorted a binary tree is constructed.

- If not sorted a hash table (with 17 buckets) is constructed.

Using cost centres to provide a breakdown of the costs associated with the different environment implementations produced the (partial) profile

COST CENTRE	MODULE	GROUP	scc	subcc	%time	%alloc
mkHash	NameEnv	envs	2977	0	13.9	26.9
mkTree	NameEnv	envs	3983	0	13.1	11.0
lookupHash	NameEnv	envs	2977	0	0.3	0.1
lookupTree	NameEnv	envs	3983	0	0.2	0.0
lookupList	NameEnv	envs	58	0	0.0	0.0
mkList	NameEnv	envs	58	0	0.0	0.0

These reveal that the environment lookup functions (`lookupHash`, `lookupTree` and `lookupList`) are called the same number of times as the corresponding functions which build the lookup data structures (`mkHash`, `mkTree`, and `mkList`)! One would have expected many lookups to be performed on each structure. Examining the STG-machine code (dumped by the compiler) we saw that

```
mkGenericLookupFun_hash_tbl eq_k lt_k hash_k stuff
  = lookup_Hash eq_k lt_k hash_k (mk_Hash eq_k lt_k hash_k stuff)
```

was translated to

```
mkGenericLookupFun_hash_tbl eq_k lt_k hash_k stuff sat.T1
  = let hash_tbl = mk_Hash.wrk hash_k stuff
    in lookup_Hash.wrk eq_k hash_k hash_tbl sat.T1
```

This reveals an error in the argument saturation pass of the compiler — the hash_tbl is built only after, and every time, the lookup argument is supplied! Fixing this optimisation bug did not completely fix the problem — the compiler still built 295 environments. Continued investigation revealed a second similar optimisation bug which duplicated work by substituting bindings inside anonymous lambda expressions.

After fixing these compiler bugs the total execution time dropped from 240 seconds to 158 seconds, an improvement of 82 seconds (34%). Most of this improvement was in the renamer and builtin environments where the lookup tables were no longer being rebuilt on every lookup. The combined renamed and builtin environment costs dropped by 74 seconds, from 78 seconds to just 4 seconds — only 2.7% of the total execution. Compilation was now dominated by typechecking, with the substitution algorithms now consuming 62% of the total execution time.

3.3 The Substitution

The substitution implementation was inefficient for two reasons:

- The lookup structure was based on a simple association list which had to be searched every time a type variable's substitution was required.

- The type being substituted for each type variable was stored idempotently — the type to be substituted for a type variable is applied to all the existing types in the substitution whenever the substitution is extended.

We decided to make use monadic mutable array technology [3,12] to implement a graph-rewriting version of the substitution algorithm. This idea was proposed by Hammond in [2], in response to an intuition that the substitution

Algorithm	Substitution	Total
Idempotent association list	98s	150s
Non-idempotent association list	18s	68s
Non-idempotent mutable array	1.8s	50s

Figure 4: Performance of monadised substitution algorithms (`TcExpr.lhs`)

was a bottleneck within the compiler. (Our profiling results have confirmed and quantified Hammond's intuition.) At that time, an implementation was not practical since efficient array implementations were not available. Since then, support for mutable arrays was added to `ghc`.

The typechecker already had a customised monad threaded through it. It was responsible for:

- Carrying the current substitution, a unique name supply, and the current source location.

- Catching, reporting and recovering from any typechecking errors.

This monad had to be extended to enable the implementation to be modified to use a mutable array. The following modifications were required:

- The monad was threaded through the unifier (previously the substitution was passed explicitly through the unifier).

- The monad interface was extended to provide the required substitution functions.

- A special unique supply used only by the type variables was added. This was used to directly index the substitution array. The array is dynamically resized if it overflows.

These modifications were not trivial and took a significant amount of time to implement. However once they were in it was a simple matter to change the implementation of the monad and experiment with different substitution algorithms.

We compared three different substitution implementations:

- An idempotent association list (the original implementation).

- A non-idempotent association list. This algorithm has to apply the substitution to the type being substituted before returning it.

- A non-idempotent representation stored in a mutable array. This provides constant-time lookup and modification.

The results in Figure 4 show quite spectacular speedups. Making the substitution representation non-idempotent improved the performance of the substitution algorithm by a factor of 5. This could have been undertaken without all the mutable-array modifications described above. However the modifications proved worthwhile as the introduction of a mutable array as the underlying data structure provided a further 10 times speedup. Overall the performance of the substitution algorithm was improved by a factor of more than 50!

```
        Tue Aug 17 14:13 1993 Time and Allocation Profiling Report

            hsc-0.13 +RTS -p -hC -i0.5 -RTS  -C -hi ...

    total time  =      50.46 secs   (2523 ticks @ 20 ms)
    total alloc = 97,950,284 bytes  (8076271 closures)

COST CENTRE       MODULE      GROUP        scc subcc  %time %alloc
PrintRealC        Main        main          1    0    21.4   26.5
CoreSimplify      SimplCore   simplCore     2    0    13.9   13.0
MAIN              MAIN        MAIN          1    1    11.4   17.4
TypeChecker       Main        main          1    0    10.2   11.3
Renamer           Main        main          1    0     7.0    3.9
rdImports         ReadPrefix  reader        1    0     6.5    6.9
CodeGen           Main        main          1    0     5.6    6.3
FlattenAbsC       Main        main          1    0     3.0    3.2
cvModule          Main        main          1    1     2.7    3.5
Core2Stg          Main        main          1    0     1.7    1.3
StgFloat          SimplStg    simplStg      1    0     1.3    1.1
CoreStranal       SimplCore   simplCore     1    0     0.9    0.7
DeSugarer         Main        main          1    0     0.8    0.7
StgUpdAnal        SimplStg    simplStg      1    0     0.7    0.6
builtinEnv        Main        main          1    0     0.6    0.1
rdModule          Main        main          1    1     0.4    0.3
   ...
```

Figure 5: Final Time Profile (compiling **TcExpr.lhs**)

4 Overall Improvement

The final time profile is shown in Figure 5. Comparison to Figure 1 shows an overall reduction in execution time of over 75%, with total execution time dropping from 240 seconds to 50 seconds. Figure 5 reveals a much more balanced time profile with no unexpected inefficiencies — though **PrintRealC** and **CoreSimplify** still look like good candidates for optimisation. The dominant compilation tasks are now I/O related as the following summary reveals.

Task	Time	Components
Input/Output	39%	PrintRealC rdImports rdModule
		MAIN (actual character I/O)
Optimisation	17%	CoreSimplify CoreStranal
and Analysis		StgFloat StgUpdAnal
Typechecking	10%	TypeChecker (including the substitution)
Code Generation	8%	CodeGen FlattenAbsC
Renaming	8%	Renamer builtinEnv
Translation	5%	cvModule DeSugarer Core2Stg

Module		Initial	Improved	Reduction
`TcExpr.lhs`	(best)	240s	50s	79%
`AbsPrel.lhs`		1499s	1015s	32%
`PrefixSyn.lhs`	(worst)	19s	16s	16%
TOTAL (211 modules)		15612s	7604s	51%

Figure 6: Performance Improvements Compiling the Whole Compiler (`-O`)

The particular module we were profiling had a particularly "hard" type checking problem. This resulted in spectacular overall performance improvements when the substitution algorithm was improved. Figure 6 gives a summary of the performance improvements for the compilation of all 211 modules which make up the compiler. The reduction in execution time for the compilation of all modules was 51%. However, the compilation of some modules is dominated by inefficiencies that were not revealed by the profiling of `TcExpr.lhs`. For example the compilation of one module, `AbsPrel.lhs`, accounts for over 10% of the total compilation time! This is due to inefficiencies in the optimisation and analysis phases of the compiler when presented with a very large static data object. Further investigation is required — at least we now have the tools to undertake this.

5 Profiling Overheads

One important consideration of any profiling system is the overheads it imposes on execution time and space requirements. If the profiling overheads are too high the tool may become unusable. Our profiling system imposes a number of overheads:

- The manipulation of cost centres and time sampling interrupts (every 20ms) reduce execution speed somewhat.

- Heap profiling increases the garbage collection pause times as the entire heap must be collected to determine what heap is actually live. Our generational garbage collection scheme cannot be used [10], though it could be if only time profiling was required. The particular heap-profiling sample interval specified by the user may also require more frequent garbage collections. (Profiling and garbage collection pauses are not included in the times reported in the profiling output.)

- The heap space occupied and allocated is increased as every closure has two extra words storing the cost centre and creation interval. (This space overhead is discounted in the allocation/live heap data reported in the profiling output.)

- Executable size increases, due to cost centre manipulation code and static profiling data structures and strings.

	Optimised C Execution			Portable C
	Normal	Profiled	Overhead	Profiled
Useful Reduction Time	2,709s	3,437s	64%	8,576s
GC and Profiling Pauses	258s	2,478s	n.a.	5,214s
Total Execution Time	2,967s	6,915s	133%	13,790s
Total Heap Allocation (Mb)	12,119	19,873	64%	19,873
Executable Size (Mb)	6.7	9.7	44%	14.1

Figure 7: Profiling Overheads Compiling the Whole Compiler

- The current profiling implementation requires the use of the two-space copying collector which imposes an additional 100% heap space overhead. We are currently working on an implementation of the profiling runtime system which uses our one-space compacting collector — thus avoiding this additional overhead.

Figure 7 provides a summary of the optimised profiling overheads measured over the compilation of the whole compiler. The profiled execution times were for runs generating both a time and a heap profile with a heap sampling interval of one second and time sample of 20ms. Profiled execution imposes a basic 64% time overhead. Additional pauses to profile the heap (every second) brought the total execution overhead to 130%. The heap space overhead is about 64%[3] (excluding the current requirement to use the two-space copying collector). We consider these overheads to be acceptable.

The profiling experiments, reported in this paper, were conducted when profiled programs were still being compiled using portable C compilation. Using a more sophisticated code generation route improves performance by a factor of more than 2, for both profiled and unprofiled programs.

It is intriguing to note that slower execution is not necessarily bad, as it results in an increased number of timer samples improving the accuracy of the resulting profile; i.e. if your profile does not contain enough timer samples run it on a slower machine!

6   Conclusions

The ghc profiler measures the distribution of execution time within a lazy functional program. By integrating the profiler with the compiler the profiling data can be related back to the original source in a way which has meaning to the application programmer. This enables:

- The identification any execution hot-spots.

- Optimisation efforts to be focus where they will be of most benefit.

- The evaluation and comparison of alternative implementations.

---

[3] It is possible to build a version of the profiler which does not store the creation interval in each closure. This would halve the 64% space overhead reported here.

We used our tool to focus our efforts to optimise a particularly large lazy functional program, the ghc compiler. We identified two execution hot-spots. Investigation revealed a compiler transformation bug and an inefficient substitution algorithm within the typechecker. Fixing the compiler bug (once and for all), and developing a graph-rewriting substitution algorithm (which was 50 times faster), improved the performance of the compiler by over 50%.

6.1 Time Profiling is Not Enough

It is not enough to simply profile and identify the execution hot-spots. The cause of the inefficiencies must also be identified before they can be addressed. This may require specific information about the dynamic behaviour of the algorithm being executed which is not provided by the profiler, which requires additional tools.

One such tool is the heap profile which can be used to investigate the dynamic space behaviour of the executing program. Another tool which the ghc compiler provides is a side-effecting trace "function". When entered, trace evaluates and prints its first argument on stderr and returns the value of its second argument. It is a useful debugging tool as it can be used to reveal specific information about the dynamic execution. Unfortunately trace affects the evaluation order — forcing the evaluation of its first argument. More work needs to be done developing suitable diagnostic tools.

6.2 Future Work

The profiler is still in the early stages of development. There is much which could be done to improve and extend it. Possibilities include:

- Alternative schemes for annotating source expressions.

- Runtime selection of "active" cost centres to allow different costs to be subsumed without requiring re-compilation.

- Additional profiling data and improved data presentation e.g. the serial time profile.

- An integrated development environment.

These extensions are not really research issues, but more product development.

Bibliography

1. C Clack, S Clayman & D Parrott, "Lexical Profiling: Theory and Practice," Dept of Computer Science, University College London, April 1993, Submitted to Journal of Functional Programming.
2. K Hammond, "Efficient type inference using monads," in *Functional Programming, Glasgow 1991*, R Heldal, CK Holst & P Wadler, eds., Springer-Verlag, Workshops in Computing, Portree, Scotland, Aug 1991.

264

3. J Launchbury, "Lazy imperative programming," in *Proceedings of ACM Sigplan Workshop on State in Programming Languages, Copenhagen (available as YALEU/DCS/RR-968, Yale University)*, June 1993, 46–56.

4. SL Peyton Jones, "Implementing lazy functional languages on stock hardware: the Spineless Tagless G-machine," *Journal of Functional Programming* 2 (Apr 1992), 127–202.

5. SL Peyton Jones, CV Hall, K Hammond, WD Partain & PL Wadler, "The Glasgow Haskell compiler: a technical overview," in *Joint Framework for Information Technology Technical Conference, Keele*, March 1993.

6. C Runciman & D Wakeling, "Heap profiling of lazy functional programs," *Journal of Functional Programming* 3 (April 1993).

7. C Runciman & D Wakeling, "Problems and proposals for time and space profiling of functional programs," in *Functional Programming, Glasgow 1990*, SL Peyton Jones, G Hutton & CK Holst, eds., Springer-Verlag, Workshops in Computing, Ullapool, Scotland, Aug 1990.

8. C Runciman & D Wakeling, "Heap profiling of a lazy functional compiler," in *Functional Programming, Glasgow 1992*, J Launchbury & PM Sansom, eds., Springer-Verlag, Workshops in Computing, Ayr, Scotland, July 1992.

9. PM Sansom & SL Peyton Jones, "Profiling lazy functional programs," in *Functional Programming, Glasgow 1992*, J Launchbury & PM Sansom, eds., Springer-Verlag, Workshops in Computing, Ayr, Scotland, July 1992.

10. PM Sansom & SL Peyton Jones, "Generational garbage collection for Haskell," in *Functional Programming Languages and Computer Architecture, Copenhagen*, ACM, June 1993.

11. J Sparud, "Fixing some space leaks without a garbage collector," in *Functional Programming Languages and Computer Architecture, Copenhagen*, ACM, June 1993.

12. PL Wadler, "Comprehending Monads," in *1990 ACM Conference on Lisp and Functional Programming*, Nice, France, June 1990.

Solving recursive domain equations by term rewriting

Julian Seward

Department of Computer Science, University of Manchester

sewardj@cs.man.ac.uk

Abstract

Despite intense theoretical work on broad range of advanced abstract interpretation techniques, such technology has not seen wide integration into functional language compilers. One stumbling block often turns out to be how to solve the recursive domain equations produced by abstract interpretation.

In this paper, we return to an old idea: using a term rewriter to solve such equations. By careful design of the terms and their reduction system, various nice properties are obtained: cheap polymorphic analysis, and a way to avoid excessive work. A prototype projection analyser has been completed, and shows promising performance on realistic Haskell programs.

1 Introduction

Many semantic analysis systems divide neatly into two parts: an abstract interpreter, which takes the source program and turns it into recursive domain equations, and a fixpointer, which solves those equations. Intense work on strictness, projection and binding-time analyses has yielded an embarrassment of abstract interpretations to choose from. Curiously, though, the problem of solving equations has not received nearly as much attention.

Such an anomaly is alarming because the performance and hence usefulness of semantic analysis systems depends crucially on their ability to solve recursive domain equations efficiently. This paper shows how established term rewriting techniques can be applied to solving first order recursive domain equations. Using an such a solver, augmented to partially deal with higher orderness, a strictness analyser for Haskell that runs fast enough to be useful has been built.

This paper is not about and assumes no knowledge of strictness analysis. For those interested in the analyser proper, a companion paper [Sew93b] is available. Certain seemingly arbitrary design decisions can only be justified by reference to the abstract interpreter. Since that falls beyond the scope of this paper, we refer, when necessary, to the relevant section of the companion paper. Nevertheless, this presentation is self contained.

First, we define an *abstract lambda calculus* as a convenient vehicle for expressing recursive domain equations. The calculus is strongly typed: typing rules and a denotational semantics are given. Later, a term rewriting system which can be used to solve equations in a first order subset of the calculus is outlined. The last part of this paper sketches how such a system has been integrated into a strictness analyser for Haskell, and shows some performance figures.

266

Notation	Lattice denoted
data Lattice = Lift [D1 ... Dn]	$(D_1 \times \ldots \times D_n)_\perp$
| Lift2 [D1 ... Dn]	$((D_1 \times \ldots \times D_n)_\perp)_\perp$
| Func Ds Dt	$[D_s \to D_t]$

Figure 1: Lattices for the abstract lambda calculus

2 The Abstract Lambda Calculus

As far as possible, the notation used below follows a Haskell-like syntax. We define two kinds of entities: lattices and terms, and assume the existence of some type Id denoting identifier names. In what follows, variable declarations are:

```
D, D1 ... Dn   :: Lattice
e, e1 ... en   :: Term
x              :: Id
n, m           :: Int
```

2.1 Domains

Different kinds of semantic analysis entail different kinds of domain. The domains here are a family $\mathcal{L}$ of finite, complete, distributive lattices. One way to build these is using products, liftings and monotonic function spaces:

$$(D_1 \times \ldots \times D_n) \in \mathcal{L} \quad \text{if} \quad D_1 \in \mathcal{L} \quad \text{and} \ldots \text{and} \quad D_n \in \mathcal{L} \quad (n \geq 0)$$
$$D_\perp \in \mathcal{L} \quad \text{if} \quad D \in \mathcal{L}$$
$$[D_1 \to D_2] \in \mathcal{L} \quad \text{if} \quad D_1 \in \mathcal{L} \quad \text{and} \quad D_2 \in \mathcal{L}$$

This is a good start, but too general. Because of the way the abstract interpreter works, certain domains are guaranteed never to appear (see [Sew93b]). Specifically, we never generate any term whose value is a member of a product domain. Instead, products are only ever used together with liftings: each product is lifted either once or twice. So the new $\mathcal{L}$ is:

$$(D_1 \times \ldots \times D_n)_\perp \in \mathcal{L} \quad \text{if} \quad D_1 \in \mathcal{L} \quad \text{and} \ldots \text{and} \quad D_n \in \mathcal{L} \quad (n \geq 0)$$
$$(D_1 \times \ldots \times D_n)_{\perp\perp} \in \mathcal{L} \quad \text{if} \quad D_1 \in \mathcal{L} \quad \text{and} \ldots \text{and} \quad D_n \in \mathcal{L} \quad (n \geq 0)$$
$$[D_1 \to D_2] \in \mathcal{L} \quad \text{if} \quad D_1 \in \mathcal{L} \quad \text{and} \quad D_2 \in \mathcal{L}$$

For example, since an empty product () is a one point domain, the familiar two point domain is modelled by $()_\perp$. A four point chain could be written

```
data Term = Stop1
          | Up1      [e1 ... en]
          | Stop2
          | Up2
          | UpUp2    [e1 ... en]
          | Join     [e1 ... en]
          | Meet     [e1 ... en]
          | Var      x
          | Lam      x e
          | App      e1 e2
          | SelU     n e
          | SelUU    n e
          | CaseU    e e1 e2
          | CaseUU   e e1 e2 e3
          | DefU     e
          | DefUU    e
```

Figure 2: Terms in the abstract lambda calculus

$(()_\perp)_{\perp\perp}$, although that's not the only way. A domain suitable for modelling pairs of integers in Haskell is $(()_\perp, ()_\perp)_\perp$. Figure 1 shows the final domains, along with the Haskell syntax used henceforth.

2.2 Terms

Figures 2, 3 and 4 show, respectively, all the possible terms, the associated type rules and the denotational semantics. The semantics, expressed in lattice-theoretic terms, are intended to:

- Provide a formal basis against which to verify the semantic invariance of each rewrite rule.

- Ensure the type rules are observed.

- Ensure that all terms denote a monotonic mapping from the values of their free variables to the value of the term.

The monotonicity requirement together with the semantics imply certain "well-formedness" constraints. Terms fall into four groups:

- Stop1, Up1, Stop2, Up2 and UpUp2 are for constructing "literal" values in non-function-space domains, a notion refined below.

- Meet and Join are neither constructive nor destructive, denoting respectively the greatest lower and least upper bound of the listed subterms.

- Lam, Var and App are used to introduce and refer to variables, and to apply one expression to another. A Var can be used to refer to the equation's formal parameters, or to other equations.

```
                                          e1 :: D1 ... en :: Dn
    ─────────────────────────     ────────────────────────────────────
    Stop1 :: Lift [D1 ... Dn]     Up1 [e1 ... en] :: Lift [D1 ... Dn]


        Stop2 :: Lift2 [D1 ... Dn]       Up2 :: Lift2 [D1 ... Dn]
        ───────────────────────────   e1 :: D1 ... en :: Dn
                            ───────────────────────────────────
                            UpUp2 [e1 ... en] :: Lift2 [D1 ... Dn]


        e1 :: D ... en :: D          e1 :: D ... en :: D
        ─────────────────────        ─────────────────────
        Join [e1 ... en] :: D        Meet [e1 ... en] :: D


        e :: Lift1 [D1 ... Dn]           e :: Lift2 [D1 ... Dn]
    ──────────────────────────────   ──────────────────────────────
    SelU m e :: Dm,    1 ≤ m ≤ n     SelUU m e :: Dm,    1 ≤ m ≤ n


        e :: Lift1 [D1 ... Dn]   e1 :: D   e2 :: D
        ──────────────────────────────────────────
                    CaseU e e1 e2 :: D
    e :: Lift2 [D1 ... Dn]   e1 :: D   e2 :: D   e3 :: D
    ───────────────────────────────────────────────────
                    CaseUU e e1 e2 e3 :: D


        e :: Lift [D1 ... Dn]            e :: Lift2 [D1 ... Dn]
    ──────────────────────────────   ────────────────────────────────
    DefU e :: Lift [D1 ... Dn]       DefUU e :: Lift2 [D1 ... Dn]


                Var x :: D1   e :: D2      e1 :: Func D1 D2   e2 :: D1
    ──────────     ──────────────────────     ──────────────────────────
    Var x :: D     Lam x e :: Func D1 D2          App e1 e2 :: D2
```

Figure 3: Type rules for the abstract lambda calculus

- SelU, SelUU, CaseU, CaseUU, DefU and DefUU comprise the most inter-esting group. They are used for the disassembly and inspection of values. Their description is deferred to section 2.4.

2.3 The notion of "literal values"

Any non-function term not containing variables can be described purely with the five constructors Stop1, Up1, Stop2, Up2 and UpUp2. Such terms can be regarded as literal values. When defining the Term type, it is tempting to partition the literals to their own type, and refer to it indirectly via a Lit constructor in the Term type:

```
data Literal
    = Stop1
    | Up1 [Literal]
    | Stop2
    | Up2
    | UpUp2 [Literal]
```

$$
\begin{aligned}
E\ [\texttt{Stop1}] &= \bot \\
E\ [\texttt{Up1 [e1 ... en]}] &= \mathrm{lift}(E\ [\texttt{e1}],\ \ldots,\ E\ [\texttt{en}]) \\
E\ [\texttt{Stop2}] &= \bot \\
E\ [\texttt{Up2}] &= \mathrm{lift}(\bot) \\
E\ [\texttt{UpUp2 [e1 ... en]}] &= \mathrm{lift}(\mathrm{lift}(E\ [\texttt{e1}],\ \ldots,\ E\ [\texttt{en}])) \\
E\ [\texttt{Join [e1 ... en]}] &= (E\ [\texttt{e1}])\ \sqcup\ \ldots\ \sqcup\ (E\ [\texttt{en}]) \\
E\ [\texttt{Meet [e1 ... en]}] &= (E\ [\texttt{e1}])\ \sqcap\ \ldots\ \sqcap\ (E\ [\texttt{en}]) \\
E\ [\texttt{SelU m e}] &= v_m \quad \text{where } \mathrm{lift}(v_1,\ldots,v_m,\ldots,v_n) = E\ [\texttt{e}] \\
E\ [\texttt{SelUU m e}] &= v_m \quad \text{where } \mathrm{lift}(\mathrm{lift}(v_1,\ldots,v_m,\ldots,v_n)) = E\ [\texttt{e}]
\end{aligned}
$$

$$
\begin{aligned}
E\ [\texttt{CaseU e e1 e2}] &= E\ [\texttt{e1}] \quad \text{if } E\ [\texttt{e}] = \bot \\
&= E\ [\texttt{e2}] \quad \text{otherwise}
\end{aligned}
$$

$$
\begin{aligned}
E\ [\texttt{CaseUU e e1 e2 e3}] &= E\ [\texttt{e1}] \quad \text{if } E\ [\texttt{e}] = \bot \\
&= E\ [\texttt{e2}] \quad \text{if } E\ [\texttt{e}] = \mathrm{lift}(\bot) \\
&= E\ [\texttt{e3}] \quad \text{otherwise}
\end{aligned}
$$

$$
\begin{aligned}
E\ [\texttt{DefU e}] &= E\ [\texttt{e}] \\
E\ [\texttt{DefUU e}] &= E\ [\texttt{e}] \\
E\ [\texttt{Var x}] &= x \\
E\ [\texttt{Lam x e}] &= \lambda x.\ E\ [\texttt{e}] \\
E\ [\texttt{App e1 e2}] &= (E\ [\texttt{e1}])\ (E\ [\texttt{e2}])
\end{aligned}
$$

Figure 4: Semantics of the abstract lambda calculus

```
data Term
   = Lit Literal    -- replaces Stop1, Up1, Stop2, Up2 and UpUp2
   | Join [Term]
   | ...            -- all other cases unchanged
   | DefUU Term
```

Unfortunately, this is not practical. We need to be able to have arbitrary expressions as the subterms of Up1 and UpUp2 values. Nevertheless it is still useful to retain the notion of a literal value, and to have a separate notation for them:

- Stop1 and Stop2 are written as an underscore, _.

- Up2 is written as U_.

- Up1 [e1 ... en] and UpUp2 [e1 ... en] are written as U[e1 ... en] and UU[e1 ... en] respectively.

From this and the semantics defined in Figure 4, it should be clear that ⊥ is denoted by the underscore, liftings by U, and products by [...]. As an example, the five points in Lift [Lift [], Lift []] are written { _, U[_,_], U[_,U[]], U[U[],_] and U[U[],U[]] }.

A final word on notation. In what follows, (Lam v e) is written as (\v -> e), (App e1 e2) as (e1 e2), and (Var v) as v. This gives a reasonably natural notation for domain equations.

2.4 Destructive terms

CaseU and CaseUU are branching terms, which partially disassemble their first argument to decide which of the other arguments to return. In this sense they denote a mapping from the switch expression to one of the alternatives. Given some terms

```
CaseU   v v1 v2
CaseUU  v v1 v2 v3
```

the need to maintain monotonicity, together with the semantic rules for CaseU and CaseUU, imply the semantic constraint that v1 ⊑ v2 ⊑ v3, for any binding of free variables in v1, v2 and v3.

SelU and SelUU select components from lifted products. As is evident from Figure 4, it is illegal to apply SelU or SelUU to a value unless that value is provably equivalent, in the framework presented here, to an Up1 [...] or UpUp2 [...] value respectively. This means, for some arbitrary value e, the following expressions are likely to be ill formed:

```
SelU   n e
SelUU  n e
```

One way to make them well-formed is to wrap the appropriate species of Case term around them, leaving the Sel in the greatest-value arm:

```
CaseU   e (...whatever...) (SelU n e)
CaseUU  e (...whatever...) (...whatever...) (SelUU n e)
```

In both cases, the term (Sel n e) may not appear in any place marked "...whatever...". Note that the Sel term may appear anywhere within within the greatest-value arm, and is not restricted to the top level, as this example seems to suggest.

The third pair of terms, DefU and DefUU, are a little strange in that they denote the same value as their subterm. DefU and DefUU are provided purely to make engineering the term rewriter a little easier, as described in Section 3.2. They provide an assertion that the value they contain will always eventually simplify to an Up1 [...] or UpUp2 [...] respectively. The Def prefix is intended to be read "is definitely", so that, for example, DefUU e intuitively means "e is definitely (semantically equivalent to) a UU[...] value."

2.5 Discussion

These semantic constraints invoke many subtle issues pertaining to the existence of normal forms. The most tricky part is the design of the destructive

Case and Sel terms. SelU and SelUU extract components from lifted products, while CaseU and CaseUU provide a way to avoid nonsensical applications of SelU and SelUU. Doing a CaseU or CaseUU on a value exposes partial information about that value, and the DefU and DefUU assertions supply a clean mechanism for using such information.

One might ask why the Case expressions are so restricted to this curious two or three way partial disassembly. For example, we could define a generalised Case which takes a switch value, and an association list to look up the switch expression in. This would also avoid the need to have SelU and SelUU:

```
data Term = ...
        | Case Term [(Term, Term)]
        | ...
```

Although initially attractive, such an approach is fraught with problems. We have to ensure that the key values in the association list cover all possible values of the switch expression, for the expression would otherwise be only a partial mapping. What if two key values which are syntactically different rewrite to the same thing: which alternative do we then choose? This last problem is avoided if key values are restricted to being literals, but there is still the hassle of maintaining the association list sorted by key values, with duplicates removed, so a sensible normal form for Case terms can be defined.

Using a generalised Case may cause terms to be larger than they need be, because it means listing out all the possible values of the switch expression, even if many of the alternatives are the same: a common occurrence. For example, to use a generalised Case term to extract the first product component from a value e in domain Lift [Lift [], Lift []], all five cases must be listed:

```
Case e [ ( Stop1,                   non_product_alternative ),
         ( Up1 [Stop1, Stop1],      Stop1 ),
         ( Up1 [Stop1, Up1 []],     Stop1 ),
         ( Up1 [Up1 [], Stop1],     Up1 [] ),
         ( Up1 [Up1 [], Up1 []],    Up1 [] )
       ]
```

Using CaseU and SelU, this can be written:

```
CaseU e non_product_alternative (SelU 1 e)
```

The generalised formulation gets into real difficulties if we extract the first product component from a domain Lift [D1, D2] where D1 and D2 are much more complicated than merely Lift []. The number of alternatives, and hence the size of the term, blows up enormously. But the CaseU and SelU version, by contrast, stays the same size regardless of what D1 and D2 are.

The final nail in the coffin of the generalised Case expression appears when the solver is extended to deal with higher order equations, a topic not treated in this paper. If we now wish to examine a value from domain Lift2 [..., D1 -> D2, ...], the generalised scheme brings the unedifying prospect of having to enumerate, and hence implement equality on, function valued keys, even if we are not really interested in their values. Using a CaseUU, the value can be partially disassembled in a useful way, without having to enumerate the function space itself. In fact, it is impossible to use a CaseU or

`CaseUU` to disassemble a function space directly. To establish some property of a function extracted from a larger domain, it is first necessary to apply that function to something, to get a non-functional result that can be disassembled further. In this our scheme bears similarities to the CDSs of Hughes and Ferguson [FH93].

What this boils down to saying is that the `Case` constructs, and their associated `Sel` and `Def` appendages exhibit a very useful form of parametric polymorphism with respect to the lattice constructions in use. Section 2.6 discusses this a little further.

Another implied "well-formedness" constraint is that it is impossible to examine a term without first examining its parent term, if one exists. For example, given a value e in `Lift2 [D1, D2]`, the `D1` component cannot be directly disassembled merely by use of, say, `CaseU`. It is not sensible to do so because e could be `Stop2` or `Up2` and thus no product components exist. The individual semantic constraints on our terms accordingly disallow this. At first, it looks as if

```
CaseU (SelUU 1 e) e1 e2
```

will do the trick. However, we cannot legitimately write (`SelUU 1 e`), because there is no way to guarantee the semantic requirement for `SelUU` terms that e is or will reduce to the form `UpUp2 [...]`. Instead, e must be disassembled first:

```
CaseUU e e3 e4 (CaseU (SelUU 1 e) e1 e2)
```

Notice how the `SelUU` has been "made legitimate" by being placed in the greatest value arm of a `CaseUU` examining the same object. Once again, an analogy can be drawn with the CDS principle that "no node may be examined before its parent". Later on, we introduce machinery which imposes yet another CDS-like constraint: that no term may be `CaseU` or `CaseUU`'d on more than once.

2.6 Exploiting polymorphism

The polymorphic nature of the terms brings a huge potential benefit. If the abstract interpreter used to generate terms maps polymorphism in the original program into polymorphism in our terms, a pleasing property accrues: first-order polymorphic analysis for free. In truth, a few small refinements to the terms are needed, but the principle stands. The strictness analyser discussed below almost has this property, and work is well advanced on a fully polymorphic first-order projection analyser for Haskell which relies explicitly on such properties.

As an example, Figure 3.3 shows a set of equations and their maximal solution for the Haskell append function (`++`)[1]. What is significant is that this solution describes the behaviour of (`++`) at *any* instance, because the abstract interpretation which generated it mapped polymorphism of (`++`) onto polymorphism of the corresponding equations.

---

[1] Without knowing what the abstract interpretation is, these equations mean nothing. Nevertheless, for the record they say roughly that (`++`) maps demand on its result directly to the first argument. Demand on the second argument is the same, except when the result is required only to WHNF, in which case no demand is propagated.

The lattice points here can be regarded as corresponding to Geoffrey Burn's Evaluation Transformers: `_` is E_0, `U_` is E_1 and `UU[x]` is $E_{(n+2)}$ if x corresponds to an E_n evaluator.

3   The term rewriting system

Although the basic construction of the term rewriter is unremarkable, quite a lot of sophistication is needed to get reasonable time and space behaviour. No such system can guarantee to solve higher order equations: the discussion below pertains to first order equations, which are sufficient, for example, to implement projection analysis.

The rewriter consists of a collection of semantically invariant rewrite rules, not discussed further, and a mechanism for selecting suitable redexes and applying an appropriate rule. Many rules have complex side conditions. Much of the difficulty of programming the rewriter arises because, having decided on the normal form required, it is necessary to fiddle with both the rewrite rules *and* the redex-selection mechanism to get a system which normalises quickly and without building huge intermediate terms. In truth the system as implemented is only seminormalizing. For reasons which space precludes elaborating, it is possible and very convenient to get away with seminormalisation: construction is much easier, and first order fixpointing is still guaranteed to work.

3.1   Outermost or innermost first?

There is a possibly unresolvable conflict between these two redex-selection strategies. Initial experimentation showed an innermost-first strategy is generally faster, because rewrite rules seem to apply more often to terms whose immediate subterms are normalised. This implementation primarily uses innermost-first reduction. Yet by itself this is in practice unworkable: a certain degree of outermost-first reduction is essential, partly because the abstract interpreter emits enormous terms largely composed of literals, for example CaseUU x a b c where x is a literal but a, b and c are large. In this case it is obviously best apply the fundamental CaseUU rule (that is, select a, b or c) and *then* reduce the resultant. Similar care must be taken with rules which float material from Case switch expressions into the alternatives, such as: CaseU (CaseU a b c) x y ==> CaseU a (CaseU b x y) (CaseU c x y).

Unfortunately, much of this fine tuning is rather empirical and involves tradeoffs between different costs. It is difficult indeed to arrive at a setup which gives suitable normal forms and *always* does so in reasonable time. The safest approach is feed the biggest possible test programs though the analyser to do fine tuning. This at least avoids falling into the pit of adjusting the dynamics using trivial test inputs and then finding the thing goes to pieces on realistic workloads.

Lambda terms and applications are dealt with in the usual way, by carrying inwards an environment binding variables to terms. As before, the details of how this is done influences the overall reduction strategy, as well as the precautions needed to avoid name-capture problems.

3.2   Using partial information about values

Examining a term using CaseU or CaseUU exposes partial information on the value of that term, and this information *must* be used to achieve normal forms. For example, clearly

```
CaseU e (CaseU e w x) (CaseU e y z)   ==   CaseU e w z
```

and this is not a contrived example: fixpointing invariably creates nested `Cases` on the same term. The information is partial in the sense that, here, we know e is ⊥ in the (`CaseU e w x`) branch, and not-⊥ in the other one, but not its precise value. Such information is also useful for simplifying other kinds of terms, particularly `Meet` and `Join`.

The solution adopted is to carry inwards a second environment binding terms to partial values. The environment is augmented every time a new `Case` scrutinee is discovered. Every new term is looked up in the environment. For most terms this yields nothing, but for a lucky few we discover some information. When the term is ⊥ it is simply replaced by an appropriate literal, and when non-⊥ we wrap the term in a `DefU` to advertise this fact[2] to any interested rewrite rules. Those rules which can use such properties are then modified to see and act appropriately on `DefU` and `DefUU` markings.

3.3 Approximation

Delivering a robust strictness analyser which runs in reasonable times even faced with unreasonable inputs is difficult, partly because the analysis time depends crucially on the complexity of types in the source program, not just its length. For a function with a complex type, the abstract domains can have thousands of points, causing the associated equations to be enormous. The framework presented here lends itself to an approximation technique which can be used to set a threshold on the amount of work done. Basically, the idea is to prune a term so that only a specified number of levels of detail remain. A domain is considered to have n levels of detail if a literal value from it could have at most n nested `Up1` or `UpUp2` constructors in it. For example,

```
UU[   U[U[], _], _]
```

has at least three levels of detail. Pruning it to level i removes `Up1` and `UpUp2` terms with a nesting depth greater than i, replacing them with an approximation which is safe with respect to the abstract interpretation in use. Pruning the above term, approximating unknown values to ⊥, gives:

```
Original:  UU[   U[U[], _], _]
Level 2:   UU[   U[_,   _], _]
Level 1:   UU[   _,         _]
Level 0:   _
```

Initial experiments show pruning like this is very effective in evening out analysis times, whilst not losing information useful to a compiler. There are some subtleties involved in maintaining monotonicity in the pruned trees, but no serious difficulties.

---

[2]For `CaseUU` terms there will be three rather than two possibilities, but the mechanism is otherwise identical.

```
++1 = \c -> (CaseUU c _
              (Meet [ UU[_], Join [ U_, (++1 _)              ] ])
              (Meet [ DefUU c, Join [ U_, (++1 (DefUU c)) ] ]))
     = \c -> c

++2 = \c -> (CaseUU c _
              (Meet [ U_,           (++2 _)            ])
              (Meet [ DefUU c, (++2 (DefUU c)) ]))
     = \c -> (CaseUU c _ _ (DefUU c))
```

Figure 5: Possible equations and corresponding maximal solutions for
(++) :: [Int] -> [Int] -> [Int]

4 Putting it into practice

4.1 Using the solver in a strictness analyser

A projection analyser, called **Anna**, for a large subset of Haskell has been built around a term rewrite based solver [Sew93b]. In practice, the system employed is considerably more complicated than that presented here, because of the need to deal with higher orderness.

The mixed forward and backward analysis presented by Hughes in Section 6 of [Hug87] was modified to deal with data structures in the manner of Burn's Evaluation Transformers [Bur87]. This produces terms in which model both forward and backward flows of information. Despite the larger number of terms and significantly different approach to currying, the fundamentals of the term rewriter are unchanged. Note that the techniques of sections 2.6 and 3.3 were not used in this implementation.

It is worth pointing out that higher order equations render the fixpointing process undecidable. Such problems are dealt with using a two-pronged approach:

1. Before analysis, we try and transform as much of the source program as possible to first order, using the techniques of Nelan [Nel92]. This tends to catch all consistent recursion over a data structure, as exemplified by foldr and map. Such transformations are beginning to be used in sophisticated compilers as a matter of course.

2. The residual higher order equations may well fixpoint anyway, in particular those whose fixpoints don't depend on the fixpoints of their functional parameters (eg map, filter). For those that don't seem to stabilise within some predefined iteration limit, a safe approximation is inserted instead. Such problem cases are probably rare. In analysing over two thousand lines of Haskell (three non-trivial programs), no approximations were needed.

Polymorphism was dealt with by the crude mechanism of monomorphisation. Recent measurements by Mark Jones seem to suggest this doesn't give

Program	Lines	Overall		Analysis	Using ghc-0.10	
		Time seconds	Resid kbytes	Time seconds	Time seconds	analysis as %age
concat	< 10	0.42	47	0.18	0.92	19
zip3	< 10	0.52	56	0.17	1.00	17
wang	385	23.62	908	9.15	43.61	21
wave4main	619	43.40	2897	21.62	199.29	11
ag2hs	1047	208.95	9653	126.42	100.68	126

Table 1: Some performance figures for **Anna**. **Overall** is for a complete run of the analyser. **Analysis** pertains to analysis-only costs. **Using** ghc-0.10 is the cost for compiling with Glasgow Haskell 0.10.

nearly as much of a code explosion as had previously been thought. Monomorphic analysis is problematic in the presence of modules, and a polymorphic variant is under construction.

4.2 Absolute performance results

Five test programs were used, giving results shown in Table 1. The first two, concat and zip3, are utterly trivial and were included as comparison against figures presented in [Sew93a]. wang and wave4main are taken from Pieter Hartel's benchmark suite [HL92]. The biggest one, ag2hs, is preprocessor for a dialect of Haskell augmented with attribute grammar [Joh87] facilities, written by David Rushall. The analyser was compiled with Chalmers Haskell-B 0.999.4, and tests were run on a quiet Sun Sparc 10/31, using a generational collector.

The analysis phase proper is considered to begin at the point where the desugarer produces a type annotated Core tree. As a more accurate measure of analysis costs, we also present "analysis phase only" figures.

To assess whether or not analysis times were beginning to look plausible, we timed Glasgow Haskell 0.10 compiling the programs into C, using options -C -O2, and compared those times with the analysis phase time of Anna.

For the big three, times are, roughly, divided equally between the front end and analysis phases. ag2hs has a relatively large analysis time in comparison to its size. This may be because it makes considerable use of lazy pattern matching, which translates to a large quantity of complex Core expressions. These in turn generate some large, complex sets of equations for the fixpointer to solve. Additionally, those equations have complex types, and this seems to slow down the fixpointer (see section 3.3). Much, if not the majority, of the space used is related to front-end processing, and it seems likely that the analysis itself is relatively cheap on space. Further investigation with a heap profiler is necessary.

Space limitations preclude further detailed discussion of these results, although one can be found in [Sew93b]. Suffice it to say that such numbers should be treated with extreme caution because of the very large number of complicating factors involved. Nevertheless, one can perhaps arrive at the heartening conclusion that we are indeed approaching the right ballpark for analyser performance.

5 Related work

Clack and Peyton Jones introduced Frontiers as a way of solving fixpoint equations [PC87]. Implementors made much of the Frontiers algorithm, massaging it extensively to deal with higher order functions [HH91], sum-of-products types [Sew91] and polymorphism [Sew93a]. Despite this and other trickery [HH92] [Sew92], frontiers failed to deliver usable performance for high-definition strictness analysis for anything other than trivial inputs, and there are good theoretical reasons for believing the situation cannot be improved.

More recently, people have been looking at other ways of solving recursive domain equations. There has been a discernible shift towards term oriented approaches. Ferguson and Hughes developed "concrete data structures" (CDSs) [FH93] based on Curien's work on sequential algorithms [Cur86]. CDSs deal with higher-orderness by regarding a higher order function as containing a CDS interpreter for each functional parameter. This is really a disguised way of substituting in functional parameters before fixpointing. Whether or not CDSs can deliver a viable fixpointing mechanism remains to be seen. Early implementations hinted at space problems, but these may now have been solved [Hug93]. CDSs can also be viewed as a higher-order generalisation of the minimal function graph scheme originally described by Neil Jones [JM86]. Minimal function graphs are used in the Semantique analyser [KHL91] built into Glasgow Haskell. Eric Nocker's work on abstract reduction [Noc93] seems to be of similar ilk to CDSs, but with the notion of approximation built-in.

The term rewriting based fixpointer described here was, in part, inspired by Charles Consel's strictness analyser in the Yale Haskell compiler. Consel's paper [Con91], which seems to have passed by almost unnoticed, described a successful, if simple, strictness analyser solving fixpoint equations by term rewriting. In view of how well this and Consel's system work, it is perhaps a pity that Clack and Peyton Jones made disparaging remarks about term-based fixpointing in their seminal frontiers paper [PC87].

6 Conclusions and further work

Implementation seems to show this fixpointing scheme works well, even for large sets of equations over complex lattices, because the `Case` and `Sel` constructs provide a concise way of selecting the lattice subparts which matter whilst ignoring irrelevant subparts. The current implementation moves fast enough to be useful, but could do with further tuning. Even so, performances are hundreds of times faster than the best frontier based schemes, and the approximation technique mentioned offers the prospect of making run-times more consistent.

Higher order functions are, as ever, problematic. The higher order removal transformation helps a lot, but not everything can be translated to first order. This doesn't always matter, but there are still (rare) examples where fixpoints cannot be obtained, necessitating the use of a safe approximation. The compiler community do not much like higher order functions for other reasons – they defeat advanced code generation techniques like argument-check avoidance and calls-in-registers – and make some effort to transform them out. Certainly it appears safe to say that overloading induced higher orderness (dictionary applications) will probably disappear shortly, as automatic overloading specialisation techniques [Aug93] have already appeared in Haskell compilers from Chalmers (`hbc-0.999.5`) and Glasgow (`ghc-0.19`).

The link between term rewriting and the lazy fixpointing exemplified by Ferguson and Hughes' CDSs [FH93] and by Eric Nocker's "Abstract Reduction" [Noc93] should be investigated. It may be possible to define a different reduction mechanism, along with a way of noting self-dependencies. This would provide the basis for a bridge between the three techniques.

One problem bedevilling many analyses and optimisations is how to deal with modules. Further work developing this and other fixpointing mechanisms should be conducted with the modules issue always in mind: doing otherwise risks severely curtailing the real world usefulness of such work.

References

[Aug93]   Lennart Augustsson. Implementing haskell overloading. In *Proceedings of the Functional Programming Languages and Computer Architecture Conference, Copenhagen, Denmark*, June 1993.

[Bur87]   G.L. Burn. *Abstract Interpretation and the Parallel Evaluation of Functional Languages*. PhD thesis, Imperial College, University of London, March 1987.

[Con91]   Charles Consel. Fast strictness analysis via symbolic fixpoint iteration. Unpublished. Yale University, Department of Computer Science, September 1991.

[Cur86]   P.-L. Curien. *Categorical Combinators, Sequential Algorithms And Functional Programming*. Research Notes in Theoretical Computer Science series. Pitman Publishing Limited, London, 1986.

[FH93]   Alex Ferguson and John Hughes. Abstract interpretation of higher-order functions using concrete data structures. 1993.

[HH91]   Sebastian Hunt and Chris Hankin. Fixed points and frontiers: a new perspective. *Journal of Functional Programming*, 1(1):91 – 120, January 1991.

[HH92]   Sebastian Hunt and Chris Hankin. Approximate fixed points in abstract interpretation. In *Fourth European Symposium on Programming, Rennes, France*, 1992. LNCS 582.

[HL92]   Pieter H. Hartel and Koen G. Langendoen. Benchmarking implementations of lazy functional languages. Technical report, Department of Computer Systems, Faculty of Mathematics and Computer Science, University of Amsterdam, December 1992.

[Hug87] John Hughes. Backwards analysis of functional programs. Technical Report CSC/87/R3, University of Glasgow, Department of Computing Science, March 1987.

[Hug93] John Hughes. Private communication regarding cdss, 1993.

[JM86] Neil D. Jones and Alan Mycroft. Data flow analysis of applicative programs using minimal function graphs: Abridged version. In *Unknown, but definitely in an ACM proceedings*, 1986.

[Joh87] T. Johnsson. Attribute grammars as a functional programming paradigm. In G. Kahn, editor, *Proceedings of the Functional Programming Languages and Computer Architecture Conference*, pages 154–173. Springer-Verlag LNCS 274, September 1987.

[KHL91] R. Kubiak, J. Hughes, and J. Launchbury. A prototype implementation of projection-based first-order polymorphic strictness analysis. In R. Heldal, editor, *Draft Proceedings of Fourth Annual Glasgow Workshop on Functional Programming*, pages 322–343, Skye, August 13–15 1991.

[Nel92] George C. Nelan. Firstification. Date unknown, but must be 1992 or after. Based on Nelan's PhD thesis. Arizona State University, 1992.

[Noc93] Eric Nocker. Strictness analysis using abstract reduction. In *Proceedings of FPCA93, Copenhagen, Denmark*, June 1993.

[PC87] Simon Peyton Jones and Chris Clack. Finding fixpoints in abstract interpretation. In S. Abramsky and C.L. Hankin, editors, *Abstract Interpretation of Declarative Languages*, Computers and Their Applications, chapter 11, pages 246–265. Ellis Horwood, 1987.

[Sew91] Julian Seward. Towards a strictness analyser for haskell: Putting theory into practice. Master's thesis, University of Manchester, Department of Computer Science, 1991. Available as University of Manchester Technical Report UMCS-92-2-2.

[Sew92] Julian Seward. Polymorphic, higher order strictness analysis using frontiers. Unpublished paper, 1992.

[Sew93a] Julian Seward. Polymorphic strictness analysis using frontiers. In *Proceedings of the Symposium on Partial Evaluation and Semantics based Program Manipulation, PEPM93, Copenhagen, Denmark*, June 1993.

[Sew93b] Julian Seward. Strictness analysis à grande vitesse: Rewriting the rules of the evaluation transformers game. Unpublished manuscript, June 1993.

Separating Interaction

Duncan C. Sinclair*

Department of Information Science, University of Strathclyde,
Glasgow, G1 1XQ, UK.

December 1993

Abstract

We examine the monadic I/O system, and put forward some ideas on
how functional programmers should use it to build programs that inter-
act with the "Real World", advocating separation of functionality from
communication with external systems.

1 Overview

So we all know why functional languages are so good [3]. They are particularly
good in applications which involve some linear process of transformation of
input data into output data [8]. Compilers are an obvious and well exercised
example of this [1].

It is also clear that there are problems when functional programs are asked
to talk to the "Real World". This is the world of window systems and operating
systems usually written in an imperative language, and using side effects.

In this paper we shall be mainly looking at interaction with window systems,
but shall sometimes refer to "external systems" to include other systems which
exist outside of the realm of functional languages.

There are some functional languages, e.g. Scheme and SML, for which this
is not a problem. This is because they use side effects, typically within a strict
evaluation framework, which seems to make most of the difficulties go away at
the expense of referential transparency. In this paper we restrict our attention
to the pure, non-strict functional language Haskell.

We will look at a currently popular way of doing I/O in Haskell, the Glasgow monadic system. With a discussion of the benefits of this system, we will
also examine some problems that arise from its use. We will then present an
approach to interaction that acknowledges the respective strengths and weak-
nesses in imperative and functional languages.

The ideas explored in this brief paper are covered in greater detail in my
forthcoming Master's thesis [6].

2 Monadic I/O

Communication with external systems in a functional language is typically
encapsulated within its I/O system so that information can be passed between

---

*E-mail: `sinclair@dis.strath.ac.uk` -or- `sinclair@dcs.gla.ac.uk` the two separate worlds without referential transparency being compromised within the pure functional framework.

There are a number of ways of achieving this [2], but we shall restrict ourselves to the new monadic system used in the Glasgow implementation of Haskell [5].

The idea behind monads is that of a token representing the state of the real world. This token is incrementally modified by primitive monadic functions in a strictly sequential manner.

The primitive monadic functions provide sequencing operations and the ability to call C functions, the later understandably requiring impure extensions to the functional language. Thus we have access to the imperative world. Changes of state are controlled by the fact that each monadic function has a different monadic token to use which is never shared in computations.

2.1 Benefits

There are a number of direct benefits to be gained from the monadic system.

For the implementor of the functional language, the ability to call C functions means that it is possible to create the whole I/O system from within the functional language. If it is easier to write parts of it directly in C, then they can still be called from the functional language.

For the programmer, a highly imperative style can be used within a functional framework. This means that translating from C into the monadic style is fairly straightforward, and perhaps could be done automatically.

2.2 Limitations

The monadic system is by no means perfect, and there is is much research to be done on problems such as the difficulty in handling more than one monadic token in a program. If you have a single-threaded line of interaction, and a single-threaded line of state-transforming functions, you may wish these threads of operation to work together. Currently, this is not possible.

Even with the ability to call C functions through monads, there are times when it is necessary to subvert the monadic control and use a lower level interface. For example, in order to implement lazy I/O, as defined in the standard Haskell I/O system, the Glasgow Haskell implementors had to do this to avoid a heavy efficiency penalty.

The need for this subversion arises because we are trying to build a representation of the world within our single thread of monadic functions, whereas other I/O systems that are implemented outside the language can better reflect the non-sequential nature of interaction.

2.3 Dangers of C-calls

The monadic I/O system allows programmers to write in a very imperative style, which is deceptively attractive, but can lead to some ghastly programs. A common result is a functional program which is mostly imperative code. Even worse, out of the programmer's frustration with the non-global state of functional programming the imperative code will be written to do its own

```
mainIO =
    malloc 4                    'bindIO' ( \ state ->
    malloc 4                    'bindIO' ( \ flag  ->
    assign state normal         'seqIO'
    assign flag  false          'seqIO'

<<application code deleted>>

    free state                  'seqIO'
    free flag                                  ))
```

Figure 1: Example of embedded C in a functional language

global memory management, rather than passing small amounts of data back and forward with a state monad, with its high overhead.

Figure 1 contains a section of code from an application written as a student project showing heavy use of monadic I/O with C function calls, and is an example of how badly the C function calling system can be abused when writing "imperative" code.

This code does explicit memory allocation and assignment for two variables so that they may be used efficiently in other parts of the application. This approach is even more error-prone than the equivalent in C, for which automatic allocation and initialisation of variables would be provided.

This code is not using any of the features of functional languages; instead it is using the functional language as a meta-language, holding sections of imperative code together. Its programmer is battling against the clean semantics of the functional language to generate state transforming semantics.

2.4   Two way communication

Monadic I/O provides a convenient way for a functional program to call out to external systems, but for these systems to call parts of the functional program is more difficult. For example to allow an external system to map user events into actions, or to handle exceptional conditions occurring during the execution of the program.

A common paradigm in window system toolkits is to map user actions into function calls which then act on the global state to achieve the user's desired result. When this paper was first written direct calling of functional code from C code was not possible. Since then a couple of schemes have been proposed, although not yet fully evaluated in practice. Asynchronous calls to user written code is still without a good solution, meaning that exceptional conditions arising during on-going functional computation cannot receive proper attention.

External systems commonly wish to call user code to handle exceptional conditions and user input, but there is no easy way to make this work in functional programs without compromising referential transparency, or extending the language in some manner.

2.5 State in functional languages

As noted in the introduction, there are some non-pure functional languages for which interaction with external system is not a problem. Could it be that there is some inherent property of pure functional languages which means that this will always be a problem? I believe so. Unless the language is tolerant of side-effects in some way, then state changes as a result of external systems will always be hard to control. Perhaps some radical change to functional languages could bring about better handling of state and interaction. In current systems, the ease of programming is certainly difficult, and program readability can be compromised.

The management of state cleanly in functional languages is difficult, while in imperative languages it is simple. The imperative language's semantics are concerned with a global environment with some scoping rules, and as such directly addresses side effects. The functional language's semantics are based more on manipulating values, and so do not address global state well at all.

2.6 Modularity

An important concept in software engineering is separation of low-level code, dealing with operating systems, etc, from the higher-level "application" code, which is more concerned with functionality. This allows the low level code to be ported between systems, or rearranged, without any modification of the main application code.

There is little that the monadic I/O scheme gives the programmer which would encourage modular programming. The fact that a monadic token has to be threaded around a program makes it hard to structure code without dependences between high-level and low-level code.

Furthermore, if you wish to have any sort of global state in your program, perhaps encapsulated in a data-type, then this type must be declared in one place, making it difficult to create truly modular programs.

2.7 Summary

The monadic style of I/O has little over other systems. Its major contribution is that of providing a controlling mechanism to allow C function calls, enforcing a sequence on them, and thus ensuring that referential transparency is not compromised.

Programming using C functions and monadic I/O using an imperative style is hazardous. It can lead to a poor coding style, unless carefully controlled. Further, it only provides a means of communication from the functional program to the outside world, but not in the reverse direction.

3 Separation of Interaction

Here is a proposed practical solution, workable without any changes to the design of functional languages. By moving interaction with external systems into a separate process, which communicates with the functional program at a higher level, you can improve modularity, portability and coherence of design.

3.1 A separate interface

Currently the functional program has to communicate with external systems at their low level of abstraction, directly using whatever I/O system the language provides. Instead we want to have the functional program communicate with a separate interface body of code, which has been specially written for the particular application and which can do the low-level interaction separately from the functional program, communicating with it in a higher-level dialogue.

This interface would probably be be written in an imperative language, such as Tcl[4,7], or C. Choosing an imperative language allows the programmer to negotiate the problems of managing side-effects inherent in interaction, which is the main stumbling block for interfaces done in functional languages.

The interface and the application would communicate using the I/O system of the functional language, and whatever I/O system is available in the interface's coding language. The two parts of the program do not have to be separate processes in operating systems terms, they can exist as cooperating threads of execution as most I/O systems currently do, or perhaps as true concurrent threads in the same process. The simplest, and most powerful way is for the two entities to be separate processes, with at least two communication channels open between them.

3.2 Addressing modularity

If you have the interface of a program as a separate, or logically separate, process then it is easy to maintain the modularity of the code; as separate entities, intermixing of interface code and application code cannot happen.

An especially useful consequence of this separation is that it should become much easier to modify the interface without requiring much, if any, restructuring of the rest of the program.

3.3 High level interaction

Naturally, the functional program will still have to communicate with the outside world, but via our separated interface. This will have to managed using the traditional I/O system of the language. The difference is that the interaction that the functional program will now take part in is at a much higher level, and so more information can be communicated, thus increasing the bandwidth. Instead of negotiating the complete dialogue needed to, e.g. save a file, the functional program would only have to communicate the intention, with any necessary data, and the interface would then look after all the details.

Equally, the information returned from the interface to the program could be at a much higher level than that in typical I/O systems. For example, user input can be processed within the interface and translated to higher-level events, some of which the functional program would never need see.

3.4 Systems interaction

As the interface would be written in imperative languages such as C, all the usual interaction with external systems not possible in a functional language can now be managed.

Callbacks from window systems and signals from operating systems can be programmed in standard ways. These would be handled within the interface without affecting the operation of the functional program. If a callback or signal requires some action on the part of the functional program, then they can be turned into high-level events and handled in the normal manner.

By programming only the application code in a functional language, the functional programmer is saved from having to worry about low-level details of interaction with external systems, where functional languages have always performed poorly.

3.5 Coherence

The monadic system of embedding C code inside the functional language, as shown, can lead to ugly code. By having a separate interface which would contain the previously embedded imperative code, the "purity" and coherence of the functional code can be improved. It certainly makes more sense to write imperative code in an imperative language, and functional code in a functional language.

3.6 Summary

By separating the interface code and application code into two cooperating programs, some problems found in writing functional programs that need to communicate with the outside world can be reduced or solved.

4 Conclusions

New solutions to the problems of I/O in functional languages are now emerging. These solutions are good at hiding the problems of the side-effecting nature of interaction with the outside world. However, they don't solve all the problems. The programs written in the monadic style can lose coherence and can lack modularity. Solutions for full, flexible two-way communication between functional programs and external systems are still to be found.

By separating the interaction with window and operating systems into a separate interface, written in an imperative language, all these problems can be overcome.

The ideas presented in this paper have been implemented, as covered in full in my forthcoming thesis [6].

Acknowledgements

My thanks go to the people who led me to believe that there had to be a better way to program interaction in functional languages. Also to the supplier of the example code. Special thanks to Aran Lunzer and my referees for comments on drafts of this paper.

Bibliography

1. C Hall, K Hammond, W Partain, SL Peyton Jones & PL Wadler, "The Glasgow Haskell Compiler: A Retrospective," in *Functional Programming, Glasgow 1992*, J Launchbury & PM Sansom, eds., Springer-Verlag, Workshops in Computing, Ayr, Scotland, 1992.

2. P Hudak & RS Sundaresh, "On the expressiveness of purely-functional I/O systems," YALEU/DCS/RR-665, Department of Computing Science, Yale University, March 1989.

3. John Hughes, "Why functional programming matters," PMG-40, Programming Methodology Group, Chalmers Inst, Sweden, Oct 1984.

4. John K. Ousterhout, "Tcl: An Embeddable Command Language," in *Proc. USENIX Winter Conference 1990*.

5. SL Peyton Jones & PL Wadler, "Imperative functional programming," in *20th ACM Symposium on Principles of Programming Languages*, ACM, Jan 1993.

6. Duncan Sinclair, "Interacting with Functional Languages," Master's Thesis (*In preparation*), University of Glasgow, 1994.

7. Duncan C. Sinclair, "Graphical User Interfaces for Haskell," in *Functional Programming, Glasgow 1992*, J Launchbury & PM Sansom, eds., Springer-Verlag, Workshops in Computing, Ayr, Scotland, 1992.

8. Duncan C. Sinclair, "Solid Modelling in Haskell," in *Functional Programming, Glasgow 1990*, Workshops in Computing, Springer-Verlag, Aug 1990, pp. 246–263.

Author Index

Published in 1990–92

AI and Cognitive Science '89, Dublin City University, Eire, 14–15 September 1989
Alan F. Smeaton and Gabriel McDermott (Eds.)

Specification and Verification of Concurrent Systems, University of Stirling, Scotland, 6–8 July 1988
C. Rattray (Ed.)

Semantics for Concurrency, Proceedings of the International BCS-FACS Workshop, Sponsored by Logic for IT (S.E.R.C.), University of Leicester, UK, 23–25 July 1990
M. Z. Kwiatkowska, M. W. Shields and R. M. Thomas (Eds.)

Functional Programming, Glasgow 1989 Proceedings of the 1989 Glasgow Workshop, Fraserburgh, Scotland, 21–23 August 1989
Kei Davis and John Hughes (Eds.)

Persistent Object Systems, Proceedings of the Third International Workshop, Newcastle, Australia, 10–13 January 1989
John Rosenberg and David Koch (Eds.)

Z User Workshop, Oxford 1989, Proceedings of the Fourth Annual Z User Meeting, Oxford, 15 December 1989
J. E. Nicholls (Ed.)

Formal Methods for Trustworthy Computer Systems (FM89), Halifax, Canada, 23–27 July 1989
Dan Craigen (Editor) and Karen Summerskill (Assistant Editor)

Security and Persistence, Proceedings of the International Workshop on Computer Architectures to Support Security and Persistence of Information, Bremen, West Germany, 8–11 May 1990
John Rosenberg and J. Leslie Keedy (Eds.)

Women into Computing: Selected Papers 1988–1990
Gillian Lovegrove and Barbara Segal (Eds.)

3rd Refinement Workshop (organised by BCS-FACS, and sponsored by IBM UK Laboratories, Hursley Park and the Programming Research Group, University of Oxford), Hursley Park, 9–11 January 1990
Carroll Morgan and J. C. P. Woodcock (Eds.)

Designing Correct Circuits, Workshop jointly organised by the Universities of Oxford and Glasgow, Oxford, 26–28 September 1990
Geraint Jones and Mary Sheeran (Eds.)

Functional Programming, Glasgow 1990 Proceedings of the 1990 Glasgow Workshop on Functional Programming, Ullapool, Scotland, 13–15 August 1990
Simon L. Peyton Jones, Graham Hutton and Carsten Kehler Holst (Eds.)

4th Refinement Workshop, Proceedings of the 4th Refinement Workshop, organised by BCS-FACS, Cambridge, 9–11 January 1991
Joseph M. Morris and Roger C. Shaw (Eds.)

AI and Cognitive Science '90, University of Ulster at Jordanstown, 20–21 September 1990
Michael F. McTear and Norman Creaney (Eds.)

Software Re-use, Utrecht 1989, Proceedings of the Software Re-use Workshop, Utrecht, The Netherlands, 23–24 November 1989
Liesbeth Dusink and Patrick Hall (Eds.)

Z User Workshop, 1990, Proceedings of the Fifth Annual Z User Meeting, Oxford, 17–18 December 1990
J.E. Nicholls (Ed.)

IV Higher Order Workshop, Banff 1990 Proceedings of the IV Higher Order Workshop, Banff, Alberta, Canada, 10–14 September 1990
Graham Birtwistle (Ed.)

ALPUK91, Proceedings of the 3rd UK Annual Conference on Logic Programming, Edinburgh, 10–12 April 1991
Geraint A.Wiggins, Chris Mellish and Tim Duncan (Eds.)

Specifications of Database Systems International Workshop on Specifications of Database Systems, Glasgow, 3–5 July 1991
David J. Harper and Moira C. Norrie (Eds.)

7th UK Computer and Telecommunications Performance Engineering Workshop
Edinburgh, 22–23 July 1991
J. Hillston, P.J.B. King and R.J. Pooley (Eds.)

Logic Program Synthesis and Transformation Proceedings of LOPSTR 91, International Workshop on Logic Program Synthesis and Transformation, University of Manchester, 4–5 July 1991
T.P. Clement and K.-K. Lau (Eds.)

Declarative Programming, Sasbachwalden 1991 PHOENIX Seminar and Workshop on Declarative Programming, Sasbachwalden, Black Forest, Germany, 18–22 November 1991
John Darlington and Roland Dietrich (Eds.)

Building Interactive Systems:
Architectures and Tools
Philip Gray and Roger Took (Eds.)

Functional Programming, Glasgow 1991
Proceedings of the 1991 Glasgow Workshop on
Functional Programming, Portree, Isle of Skye,
12–14 August 1991
Rogardt Heldal, Carsten Kehler Holst and
Philip Wadler (Eds.)

Object Orientation in Z
Susan Stepney, Rosalind Barden and
David Cooper (Eds.)

Code Generation – Concepts, Tools, Techniques
Proceedings of the International Workshop on Code
Generation, Dagstuhl, Germany, 20–24 May 1991
Robert Giegerich and Susan L. Graham (Eds.)

Z User Workshop, York 1991, Proceedings of the
Sixth Annual Z User Meeting, York,
16–17 December 1991
J.E. Nicholls (Ed.)

Formal Aspects of Measurement
Proceedings of the BCS-FACS Workshop on
Formal Aspects of Measurement, South Bank
University, London, 5 May 1991
Tim Denvir, Ros Herman and R.W. Whitty (Eds.)

AI and Cognitive Science '91
University College, Cork, 19–20 September 1991
Humphrey Sorensen (Ed.)

5th Refinement Workshop, Proceedings of the 5th
Refinement Workshop, organised by BCS-FACS,
London, 8–10 January 1992
Cliff B. Jones, Roger C. Shaw and
Tim Denvir (Eds.)

Algebraic Methodology and Software
Technology (AMAST'91)
Proceedings of the Second International Conference
on Algebraic Methodology and Software
Technology, Iowa City, USA, 22–25 May 1991
M. Nivat, C. Rattray, T. Rus and G. Scollo (Eds.)

ALPUK92, Proceedings of the 4th UK
Conference on Logic Programming,
London, 30 March– 1 April 1992
Krysia Broda (Ed.)

Logic Program Synthesis and Transformation
Proceedings of LOPSTR 92, International
Workshop on Logic Program Synthesis and
Transformation, University of Manchester,
2–3 July 1992
Kung-Kiu Lau and Tim Clement (Eds.)

NAPAW 92, Proceedings of the First North
American Process Algebra Workshop, Stony Brook,
New York, USA, 28 August 1992
S. Purushothaman and Amy Zwarico (Eds.)

First International Workshop on Larch
Proceedings of the First International Workshop on
Larch, Dedham, Massachusetts, USA,
13–15 July1992
Ursula Martin and Jeannette M. Wing (Eds.)